1,00

The Other German
Willy Brandt's Life & Times

Other Books by David Binder

BERLIN—EAST AND WEST

The Other German
Willy Brandt's Life & Times
David Binder

THE NEW REPUBLIC BOOK COMPANY, INC.

Washington, D.C.

Published in the United States of America
in 1975
by The New Republic Book Company, Inc.
1220 Nineteenth St., N.W., Washington, D.C., 20036

© 1975 by The New Republic Book Company, Inc.

Library of Congress Cataloging in Publication Data

Binder, David.
    The other German.

    Includes bibliographical references and index.
    1. Brandt, Willy, 1913-   I. Title.
DD259.7.B7B5   943.087'094'4 [B]   75-29024
ISBN 0-915220-09-1

Printed in the United States of America

In memory of Carroll Binder
and
Lieutenant Ted Binder, USAF

Preface

Whadt follows is a kind of biography of Willy Brandt. But he is a living politician-statesman, and as such his story cannot be completely told. Rather, I have conceived this as a vehicle for describing his life and his setting in the divisions of the German Left and the divisions of the German nation—geographic and social. In the course of preparing this manuscript I discovered more than one parallel to my own life, and so it became a kind of self-education and revelation—occasionally with a highly personal view.

I am a newspaperman. While chapter notes provide sourcing for some of the more controversial aspects of Willy Brandt's career, this book is not intended as an academic work. Brandt was kind enough to answer a number of my questions about his life over a period of two years. He has read the first ten chapters and verified or corrected much of the data. But this is not an authorized work. Mistakes of fact or interpretation are entirely my own.

In 1946 Brandt published an account of the Nürnberg Trials entitled, *Criminals and Other Germans*. The phrase, "Other Germans" had been used since the 1930s, mostly by political exiles, to encompass those Germans who were opposed to Adolf Hitler. It was a title and a concept that caused Brandt a lot of difficulty throughout his postwar political career. But he was also one of those "Other Germans" who was eventually chosen by a German electoral majority to lead his nation. Hence the title.

This study was begun in the spring of 1973 with a series of interviews of Brandt and his associates and the gathering of printed source material. I returned to Germany in November 1973 and June and November 1974 for more research and interviewing. I have corresponded intermittently with the principals. The proposal for this book came from Lois O'Neill, then of Praeger Publishers, who also guided its development. The final editing was done by Joan Tapper of New Republic Books.

A number of men and women helped me here and in Europe:

In Bonn: H. Wehner, K. Wienand, R. Bartholomäi, H. Schneider, H. Ehmke, C. Ahlers, I. Krämer, S. Backlund, K. Kirchner, D. Cramer, F. Nowottny, E. Eppler, A. Renger, B. Schulien, W. Höfer, A. Reif, H. Schmidt, J. Weichert, E. Bahr, G. Börner, D. Polgar, R. Wechmar, G. Wehner, L. Wehner, A. Lais, D. Anderson, R. Brandt, K. Schiller, G. Scherhorn, D. Wolf, G. Heinemann, F. Darchinger, L. Bauer, J. Schulz, E. Selbmann, K. Rush.

In Berlin: K. Schütz, E. Lentz, D. Bartens, K. Korn, A. Broecker, H. Herz, R. Lowenthal, K. Mattick.

In Oslo: O. Aas, P. Monsen, I. Scheflo, E. Loe, A. Ording.

In Washington: H. Binder, R. Livingston, M. Mautner, E. Dulles, C. Sönksen, E. Daniel, J. Krag, B. Skou, H. Midttum, L. Wiesner.

In Cambridge, Mass.: L. Blaschke.

In New York: L. Fenton, A. Dolin.

I am grateful to them and to the people of West and East Germany who provided a reason for writing something about their nation.

Chevy Chase, Md.   DAVID BINDER
June 1975

Contents

A section of photographs follows page 22 and page 160

1:

Erfurt, 1970

They strode stiffly out of the yellow-brick railroad terminal on the red carpet that covered Erfurt's rough-hewn paving stones, their faces starchy masks of protocol, stateliness, dignity: Willy Brandt and Willi Stoph. The Federal Chancellor of the Federal Republic of Germany and the Prime Minister of the German Democratic Republic had met and shaken hands for the first time a few minutes before at 9:30 a.m. on the station platform. Two middle-aged Germans, well-dressed and fairly good-looking: Willy-West nearly a head taller, a natty tie peeking out of the vee of his dark blue topcoat; Willi-East, neck wrapped in a crimson muffler against the blustering March winds, carrying a felt hat in his left hand. They walked abreast, swiftly and in step, almost marching to their destination fifty yards across the Bahnhofsplatz, the Erfurter Hof Hotel. Looking on were 200 reporters and cameramen, most of them bunched on the steps of wooden bleachers freshly erected in the middle of the square on either side of the red carpet. There were perhaps forty husky plainclothesmen as well. But no public spectators were permitted to watch the first-ever mustering of the heads of government of the two states of divided Germany, the Germany split by the victorious allies a quarter of a century earlier at the end of World War II.

Units of East Germany's *Volkspolizei,* still in their bulky green winter uniforms and fur-lined caps, had cleared the large square hours before, ordering citizens to move beyond the portable steel barriers that had been set up to block off access to the Bahnhofsplatz from the Schmidtstedter Strasse, Juri Gagarin Ring, Bürgermeister Wagner Strasse, and the narrow Büssleber Gasse, which runs behind the hotel.

Commuters accustomed to disembarking at the main terminal were rerouted to the North Station, two miles distant in an outlying district. Many travelers headed for Erfurt were turned back. Factory foremen, office managers, and schoolteachers for miles around had been given strict orders to make certain that nobody played hooky to see the official guest from West Germany. Nonetheless, a large crowd of young and old Thuringers had assembled at the north end of the square along Bahnhof Strasse, the major north-south thoroughfare perpendicular to the railroad. The Communist authorities had kept this thoroughfare open presumably because the streetcar lines 2, 3, 4, and 5 run on it. Closing off Bahnhof Strasse would have prevented scores of thousands from reaching their jobs. The East German economy tolerates no margins, and plan fulfillment apparently had an even higher priority than state security in the city of Erfurt on March 19, 1970. Besides, there were 100 policemen manning the gap.

By the time Brandt and Stoph left the station more than 1000 East Germans had jammed into Bahnhof Strasse. They were so quiet that newsmen standing on the bleachers eighty feet away in the square could hear policemen telling them, "Keep back, keep back." The bleachers blocked the spectators' view of the arrival, but the crowd could sense the moment from the movement of the reporters better situated on the bleachers, and as Brandt and Stoph set foot on the steps of the Erfurter Hof a guttural roar rose from the throats of the people waiting for them.

"Aaaarrrroh!" It seemed to come from the very bowels, a deep, hoarse, angry bellow, the cry of an enormous wounded animal, the animal of the German nation in raging pain, a nation divided against its will, divided against itself, the bellow of Germans denied the chance to see the separate German leaders together for once. "Aaaarrrroh!" Frightening. It lasted four, maybe five seconds, and the crowd was pushing, pushing against the locked-arm line of *Volkspolizisten,* who had been joined by a score or more plainclothesmen of the *Stasi,* the State Security Police. Inside the lobby Willi Stoph's pale Prussian face drained of its last color. Beads of sweat formed on his brow. Brandt's expression was impassive. He went to his second-floor room with his aides and two of his bodyguards.

Outside, in the shoving of the tightly packed mass of East Germans a yellow-and-black striped glass pedestrian-crossing sign gave way and crashed, tinkling on the sidewalk. As if the sound were a signal, the crowd surged forward. The police line broke, and then the East Germans were moving, brushing past the policemen, breaking the grip of the *Stasi* men—an old man running, holding his hat on with his right hand, a housewife with her plastic market bag, trotting along smartly, a blond boy sprinting, an elderly man with a cane, limping slowly but purposefully, still others walking at an ordinary pace, singly and in knots. Three metal traffic signs fell in the crush.

The bulk of the people came as if by disciplined habit along the sidewalk, shunning the broader, empty square, heading past the corner confectionery-café, past the hotel restaurant where all the white-capped cooks and white-jacketed waiters stood at the broad first-floor windows gaping at the spectacle, aiming for the narrow passage beside the press bleachers. Another cry went

up from the crowd, but this time 2000 strong, "Willy!" and again, "Willy!"
Then, apparently realizing this could also be understood as "Willi" for Prime
Minister Stoph, the East Germans changed to "Willy Brandt, Willy Brandt,
Willy Brandt!" and, "Willy Brandt to the window!" They were smiling,
grinning, suddenly a happy crowd of East Germans, some of them almost
ecstatic. For six or more minutes, they kept up the chant. Euphoria.

One of Brandt's junior press aides appeared at a second-floor window and
played the fool, making cheerleader gestures and grimaces (he was demoted
the following week). "Willy Brandt to the window!" The police were
perplexed, helpless in the face of such spontaneity. They couldn't send in the
riot squad under the eyes of a hundred or more Western newsmen.

At 9:45 a.m. Brandt appeared at the second-floor bay window of the hotel's
luxuriously proportioned oriel, his features still stony, as always in moments
when he is tense. In the cold, sleet-tipped electric air the Erfurt crowd, now as
merry as could be, let out a long "Ahhhhh," and then switched back to
shouting, "Willy, Willy!" Plainly attuned to the charged atmosphere Brandt
nodded to the crowd and flashed a tiny, tight-lipped smile of acknowledgment. Raising his arms he delivered, palms down, a choir leader's pressing
gesture for softness: *pianissimo, per favore, pianissimo.* The East Germans
comprehended instantly and went silent. He turned lightly and vanished into
the darkness of his room.

The crowd hung on for a few minutes, mesmerized by what it had done and
seen. Then it quietly dispersed. Some of the demonstrators, perhaps two
score, were picked up by the *Stasi* as they reached the cordons, which had been
quickly reestablished, and held for interrogation—held until West German
authorities requested their release a week later. There was even a theory, born
at the moment of the demonstration, that it had been secretly arranged by
hard-line elements of the East German leadership as a means of showing
everyone, and especially their big Russian brothers, how dangerous it was to
have truck with West Germany. Three years later East German Communists
were still airing this theory among Western acquaintances. Yet anyone who
witnessed this moment in Erfurt found it hard to question its impulsiveness,
whether or not it had been triggered by *agents provacateurs.* For those who
were there, it was compelling, unforgettable, an awesome manifestation of
long-pent-up emotions, unleashed national feelings and, for most—observers
and participants—the surfacing of the genuine, deep-seated desire for
national unity.

For a fleeting instant the spell of carefully constructed and prudently
guarded separation of the country, the nation, into two mutually hostile social
systems and allegiances was broken. The almost savage hailing of Brandt
lifted him for that instant, less than five months after he had been elected

Federal Chancellor of West Germany, to the symbolic leadership of the split nation. It made him, for a long time thereafter, the embodiment of the aspirations of a majority of his countrymen for a lowering of the barriers and easing of the tensions characterizing the German division.

Erfurt, a strange venue for such a momentous meeting, far from the heavily trodden fields of German politics: Berlin, Leipzig, Frankfurt, Munich. Yet peculiarly appropriate. Erfurt was and is an eminently German city, one of the oldest, chosen as the sea of a bishopric by St. Boniface in 741. It lies in that hilly forested triangle that natives call "the green heart" of Germany, encompassing parts of Thuringia, Franconia, and Hesse. Karl der Grosse—Charlemagne—saw his most important colonization-Christianization mission among the doughty German heathens of this region, and Erfurt was one of the first towns he accorded market rights in 805. Hans Jakob Christoffel von Grimmelhausen, the seventeenth-century novelist, was born in nearby Gelnhausen and set his satiric masterpiece of the Thirty Years' War, *Simplicius Simplicissimus,* in the region. Luther was a friar in Erfurt. The Peasant War reached a fiery high point at neighboring Muhlhausen in September 1524. A contemporary, Tilman Riemenschneider, the greatest woodcarver of the epoch, sided with the downtrodden across the ridges in Franconia and was tortured for it. Bach grew up in nearby Eisenach. Goethe and his fellow poet Wieland met Napoleon here in 1808, when the Emperor was trying to forge an alliance with the Russian Tsar.

In 1850 Erfurt was briefly the scene of an abortive attempt at German political unity fostered by Baron Joseph Maria von Radowitz, conservative adviser of Prussia's King Friedrich Wilhelm IV. His union Reichstag, convened in a former Erfurt theater two years after a burgher uprising had swept the land, dissipated like the seeds of a ripe dandelion.

In his formal address to the East Germans, Chancellor Brandt recalled both Napoleon's stay and the 1850 convention, which he called "the last attempt at that time to unite Germany in a free and democratic fashion." The Stoph delegation passed over those allusions, dubious to a Marxist-Leninist understanding of German history. But the East German Premier and the West German Chancellor found common ground in their recollections of yet another Erfurt meeting, the merger convention of the radical Social Democratic Worker Party and the reformist Universal German Worker Association in 1891.

What came out of that historic conclave was the new name, Socialdemokratische Partei Deutschlands (Social Democratic Party of Germany or SPD), and the Erfurt Program, a document drawing more on the militant strains of the late Karl Marx in the German socialist movement than on the milder reformist ideas of one of the founders of the movement that became the Social

Democratic Party, Ferdinand Lassalle. The nineteenth-century Erfurt Program, firmly anticapitalist, firm also on the definition of international proletarian solidarity and worker class consciousness, was worth keeping in mind March 19, 1970, in Erfurt. For over 100 years before and after the 1891 convention, the twin strands of German socialism, radical and reformist, had intertwined and split repeatedly. Now they were personified across the green baize table top in the Erfurter Hof by the Marxist Stoph and the non-Marxist Socialist Brandt.

Stoph said, reading his opening address: "And by the way, Herr Bundeskanzler, you are the chairman of a Social Democratic Party, aren't you? Actually you must welcome it that in the DDR* the workers and farmers possess the political power, that all state organs have been purged of Fascists and that the major enterprises are the property of the people. With that the DDR accomplished what German Social Democracy unanimously resolved here in 1891 in the Erfurt Program."

Brandt retorted with *his* understanding of the meaning of Erfurt: "For a Social Democrat it is obvious to consider the role the Erfurt Program of 1891 played for the aspiring German workers movement. However you categorize this program in the history of ideas, what great misfortune would have been spared the German nation, Europe, and the whole world if the will to democracy, the will to greater social justice, and the will to peace had duly prevailed."

Devilish, the orthodox Communist wiggling the cloven hoof to the apostle of political temperance, inviting him to join the real gang, and the pragmatic Socialist turning it all around, shying away from ideological pigeonholes, reminding Lucifer's minion of the innocent virtues of democracy, justice, and peace.

For a Communist nothing could be more pernicious than a Social Democrat. Unlike the clear-as-a-mugshot foes of Communism among the Fascists and other branches of monopoly-capitalist imperialism, the Social Democrats, foster fathers and stepsons of the revolution, were an insidious threat. The 1969 election of Brandt, the Social Democrat Mayor of West Berlin, as Chancellor of West Germany meant profound changes in the policy set by the three double-dyed Conservatives, Konrad Adenauer, Ludwig Erhard, and Kurt Georg Kiesinger, who had preceded him. It also meant a change for East Germany. For the first time its leaders were confronted with a German politician willing to accept European Communists as negotiating

---

*The German abbreviation (for Deutsche Demokratische Republik) is used throughout this book instead of GDR.

partners, a competitor in the realm of social ideas and practice—in a sense, a ghostly challenge from a shared past.

From the time of their great split in 1919 German Socialists under the Social Democratic and Communist banners had vied with increasing ferocity for the allegiance of workers. Their rivalry created hostility scarcely fathomable for non-Europeans, to the point where, in the late 1920s, German Communists were denouncing German Social Democrats as *Sozialfaschisten,* and temporarily making common cause later against the Social Democrats with Hitler's Nationalist Socialists. The enmity of the two groupings—each calls the other a splinter—is unallayed to this day. Each has birth defects in the eyes of the other. The Social Democrats tended toward nationalism to the extent that they approved Kaiser Wilhelm's war credits in 1914 and supported the capitalist establishment four years later. The Communists allied themselves with a foreign power, Bolshevik Russia, in 1919 and served Moscow's interests with increasing dedication. Further, the West German Social Democrats cast off the shreds of their Marxist heritage in 1959. The Communists of East Germany had submerged the numerically predominant Social Democrats of their region in an unequal alliance under Soviet military authority in 1946. So the taints remained, for the one and for the other.

Odd, a German Communist head of government receiving a German Social Democratic head of government, and each, in effect, legitimizing the other, like two feuding stepsons acknowledging one another as joint heir to the true patrimony. Ironic, the meeting taking place in Erfurt, the city grown wealthy in the Middle Ages on the production of blue woad dye before indigo came along to take over, the city that had been called "Red Erfurt" in the 1920s.

An elderly German once resident in Erfurt and acutely tuned to what the Socialist-Communist reunion signified was sitting in East Berlin that chill March 19, waiting impatiently for the on-the-spot reports of his underlings in the Erfurter Hof: Walter Ulbricht, chairman of the DDR State Council (head of state), first secretary of the Socialist Unity Party of Germany (SED), chairman of the DRR Defense Council. Ulbricht had cut his Communist teeth in Erfurt forty-nine years before. Now he was undisputed boss of East Germany, the man who had done more than any other to create the separate German state. He, the wily backroom boy, was grimly suspicious of the Social Democratic designs. As the twenty-eight-year-old district secretary of the Communist Party of Germany in Erfurt he had learned, bitterly, what it meant to have the Social Democrats against you. He had been arrested on charges of sedition. They had caught him in 1921 in the tavern "At the Sign of the Trout" at No. 5-6 Grafen Strasse and jailed him for several days. Ever after that, the Social Democrats were the archenemies for Walter Ulbricht. "Traitors," he called them, and later, with Stalin's blessing, "Social Fascists"—people to be used but never trusted.

It was in Erfurt also that Ulbricht, then advertised as "The Red Soul of Thuringia," had developed his penchant for organization, grouping the faithful in tiny cells, earning the sardonic nickname, "Comrade Cell," among his peers. In 1970 there were no physical reminders of Comrade Cell except his old lieutenant and toady, Foreign Minister Otto Winzer, a narrow-minded loyalist who had stood the tests even in the 1920s and '30s against the Social Democratic foe and now had been sent as prefect to make sure nothing out of the party line occurred in Erfurt. The diminutive Winzer, nine years Ulbricht's junior, was hopping up every few minutes to telephone his superior in East Berlin, a participant reported later.

As Foreign Minister, Winzer was also there to personify Ulbricht's insistence that West Germany remained "foreign" to East Germany, a "foreign" state, a "foreign" government, no different than El Salvador or Burma. For a comparable reason, Willy Brandt had brought along his Minister for Inter-German Relations Egon Franke, personifying the Bonn Government's thesis that relations between the two German states had a "special" character.

Red Erfurt, Red Thuringia. The hosts had done what they could to ruddle the reception: red carpet in the station, red carnations on the negotiation tables, red towels in the washrooms, red flags in abundance. No need to remind the visitors that Thuringia, a depressed area before and after the Depression, had also been susceptible to the sirens of the radical Right, that the National Socialists had achieved representation in a state government for the first time in Thuringia in 1929. (Their stalwart, Wilhelm Frick, became Thuringian Interior Minister.)

It had been a long road to Erfurt, twenty-five years after the war: a western Germany occupied by armed forces of the United States, Britain, and France and driven increasingly toward military-economic integration with those powers; an eastern Germany occupied by the armed forces of the Soviet Union and compelled ever more effectively into integration with that power. There were Germans to enforce the separation on both sides: Adenauer in the West and Ulbricht in the East. Yet throughout the quarter century there were Germans and non-Germans toying with the other variant of a united neutral Germany: Stalin in 1952 and his police chief Lavrenti Beria in 1953, with experiment-minded Germans responding on both sides. Ulbricht himself dreamed to the end of a German "confederation" steered by the (true) Socialists. But no West German Government had dared take the bit in its teeth and engage directly with the East German Government until Willy Brandt came along. The East Germans, prodded by the Russians and their overriding interests, had to go along.

As Mayor of West Berlin Brandt for nine years had had thorough first-hand experience in the Cold War politics of confrontation between East and West. He had seen the creation of an ever deeper divison in his nation, his country, climaxing in the erection of the Berlin Wall in 1961 by the East German Communists and the toleration of the wall by the Western Allies. After a period of pondering, he and his idea man, Egon Bahr, had come to the conclusion that the only way to prevent a further widening of the split was to practice "a policy of small steps," with the aim of *Wandlung durch Annäherung* (change through rapproachment) in relations between West and East Germany. Bahr broached this policy in a 1963 speech in Tutzing, and Brandt tried gingerly to implement it with "small steps" in the following three years. Not until he was Chancellor, however, could Brandt take the necessary larger step of considering establishment of formal relations between Bonn and Berlin. It was the first thing he did, declaring in his maiden speech before the Bundestag on October 28, 1969, that he acknowledged "the existence of two states of the German nation."

That signal was picked up by Walter Ulbricht, who wrote a letter on December 17 to his Bonn counterpart, President Gustav Heinemann. Just for the spite of it Ulbricht sent along an "annex" containing a nine-article draft treaty saying this was how he expected relations between the two states to be established. It included that ancient DDR chestnut, the demand for full diplomatic recognition from West Germany. Heinemann politely told the DDR *Staatsratsvorsitzende* to try it at a lower level, and so the dialogue began.

Through January, February, and into March 1970 a lot of tortuous haggling went on between Bonn and East Berlin over the form and content of the first state-to-state meeting. The East Germans continued to flail away with the Ulbricht treaty draft, accompanied by sharp polemics in the East German party press against the Brandt government. On January 19 Ulbricht held an "international press conference," the East Berlin term for one in which representatives of the despised but sometimes useful "Western imperialist press" were also admitted. It was his first since the week before his Berlin Wall was started. He used it for the double purpose of saying he was "prepared" for Bonn-East Berlin negotiations "without preconditions," and that he was in no hurry. He made it evident that the Soviet leadership was twisting his arm to get him moving. The behind-the-scenes pressure moves between Moscow and East Berlin showed up again on January 25, when the Communist authorities ordered a temporary slowdown of traffic on West Berlin's lifeline highway ties with West Germany in protest against a flight by

Brandt to West Berlin that day. They said he didn't belong in the "separate entity" of West Berlin as Chancellor of West Germany.

For a time it seemed the East-West German heads of government meeting would take place in February in East Berlin, as Prime Minister Stoph proposed. But this idea had to be dropped, too, when the East Germans insisted that Brandt come directly to East Berlin by air instead of driving in from West Berlin. That was too much to ask of the man who had been the Mayor of West Berlin at some of its critical moments. So it was that Erfurt, equidistant from both German capitals and forty miles from the West German border, was chosen in a last-minute compromise. The remaining seven days hardly left the East Germans time to clean up the old railway station.

There was no fixed agenda. With "Willy" cheers still in their ears, Brandt and Stoph sat down in the Erfurter Hof to listen to each other's carefully prepared declamations, both 5000 words in length. In retrospect they seem to have been shrewd presentations, properly low-keyed but firm in commitment and keeping the stakes high in the German-German game. Together they made clear that neither side could win out. Speaking first, Stoph cataloged in detail the origin of the German division from the Communist point of view, blaming it entirely on the West. He said the Chancellor's call for "easing the human condition" in divided Germany caused him to perk up his ears with "bad memories" of the years before the Wall when West Germany had "eased the citizens of the DDR out of more than 100 billion marks." He was alluding to the 3 million East Germans who fled to the West before 1961 and other economic damage to the DDR. Stoph demanded that Bonn pay this "debt." Picking up another Brandt remark, he said perhaps the two of them should agree that there could be "no blending, no rotten compromise" between the social systems of East and West Germany. The logical consequence, said Stoph, was a "realistic policy" of establishing full diplomatic ties between the two. Not that he was denying the possibility of reunification *after* the "victory of Socialism" in the Federal Republic. But that, he coldly stated, was solely a matter for "the worker class and all other toiling elements in the Federal Republic." Then he reiterated Ulbricht's nine-point treaty draft and thanked Brandt for his attention.

Brandt was in his element now, the politics of Germany, the politics of being a German. He had been led by some advisers to expect Stoph to be "rigid" and was pleased to find him a modest, comfortable host. He was prepared to be showered with pointless polemics and the most stubborn arguments but found instead a flexible, agile conversation partner able to convey nuances. He was here to break the taboo of twenty-one years' standing on personal contacts between leaders of the two German states—a high point in a series of taboo-breaking developments in which he had participated and was still to participate. It was easier than he had expected, and the declaration he had drafted together with his aides was reassuringly suited to the occasion.

"No contest over history carries us forward now," he said at the outset. "That the path of the German nation divided, that it could not be trod as a unitary state after 1945 may be felt by the individual or by many as tragic—but we cannot unmake it.

"That the growing apart is viewed on the whole as evil becomes evident in that people saw it and see it as necessary to heap the blame or the responsibility on the other side."

Brandt dwelt at length on the meaning of the German nation, the "bonds of family, language, culture, and the immeasurable elements that allow us the feeling of belonging together." This was reason enough to protect what remained of national substance, however fragile it had become, he argued. He also insisted that in seeking a rapproachment between the two states the responsibility of the four victor powers of World War II for Germany as a whole remained in force, also for the whole of Berlin. Stoph, following the Ulbricht line, had dismissed this idea even though it was a residual interest of the Soviet Union, as well as of the United States, Britain, and France. Brandt outlined his ideas in the form of five basic principles—a counterpart to the nine-point Ulbricht treaty. Since both states must acknowledge the obligation to the unity of the nation, neither, in his view, could be a "foreign country" for the other. Beyond this, universal principles of international law should prevail between them. The two should promote mutual cooperation and respect the responsibilities of the four powers in Germany, he concluded.

The twelve-man delegations repaired for lunch and a bit of levity. The meal included trout from the Harz Mountains, veal cutlets, and one of the few choice wines from East Germany's slopes, Meissner Fürstenberg. Conrad Ahlers, Brandt's saucy press secretary, produced as a present for Stoph, who fancied himself a Goethe buff, a book of sayings of the master—one for each day of the year. He read out a sample: "Celebrate things that end happily—all ceremonies at the beginning diminish joy and strength."

Fifteen miles to the east of Erfurt is the Ettersberg, the plateau where the Nazis before World War II erected the concentration camp of Buchenwald, pride of Thuringia's Gauleiter Fritz Sauckel. Buchenwald was one of the earliest concentration camps in Germany, and it was here, among 56,000 inmates killed, that the bulk of the political prisoners of the Nazis were murdered. The victims included the prewar KPD chief, Ernst "Teddy" Thälmann, and the prewar SPD leader, Rudolf Breitscheid.

Otto Winzer drove Willy Brandt to Buchenwald the afternoon of March 19 for a wreath-laying at the Buchenwald memorial built by the Communists in 1958—in part, as the propaganda of that time made clear, to warn against "Neo-Nazism in West Germany." In an almost grotesque parody of the start-stop-start attempts of prewar German Communists and Social Democrats to establish a "united front" against the Nazis, Brandt was subjected to a solemn performance of the DDR national anthem played by a *Volksarmee* band in uniforms reminiscent of the Wehrmacht. He was silent.

The Nazi era was heavy on the minds of the two German leaders at Erfurt. It was an era that had caused the collapse of the Reich and the emergence of two German states. In his formal statement Brandt declared that the crushing of that terrible patrimony "binds us all, whatever else may divide us," and he added: "The world was filled with horror at the misdeeds practiced in the name of Germans, at the destruction wrought. We are all liable for what happened, regardless of where fate placed us." That fate had placed Willy Brandt in exile and Willi Stoph, formerly a Communist activist, in the Wehrmacht in Adolf Hitler's time. "This liability," Brandt continued, "for which the world holds us accountable, with good reason, is one of the causes for the present situation in Germany."

Stoph, too, spoke of the Nazi catastrophe, but in terms characteristic for the Soviet leadership—"the smashing of Hitler Fascism, the unconditional surrender of the generals of German imperialism, the collapse of the imperialist German Reich." He blamed both world wars entirely on "imperialist Germany," coupling this with the accusation that previous West German governments had vainly sought "to annul the results of World War II through quickened rearmament and undermining of the DDR."

That evening after Brandt returned from the Buchenwald memorial, he and Stoph sat down for two hours of private conversation. Brandt told Stoph to forget about the demand for repayment of "100 billion marks" or anything else resulting from the domestically repulsive policies of the Socialist Unity Party. Stoph appears to have taken him at his word, because the demand was never raised again afterward. The two also agreed to meet next in Kassel, a city not unlike Erfurt, just across the frontier in West Germany. They dined that night on Thuringer sausage and Russian salmon. Brandt's press spokesman and intimate of the moment, Conrad Ahlers, drove up the hill to an improvised news center in Erfurt's international garden show fairgrounds to read out the brief joint communiqué and tangle for a few minutes with his East German counterpart, Peter Lorf. Then Ahlers, who had helped Willy Brandt reach power, dashed back to catch the night train for Bonn with the Chancellor. On the way, Ahlers, a former newspaperman, wrote an article on the great German reunion for the archconservative tabloid *Bild,* a publication whose anti-DDR policy had caused its exclusion from the Erfurt events. (Ahlers, a wartime paratrooper, would jump into Brandt's life in other lighter and darker moments.)

Nothing substantive came out of the Erfurt meeting, although most of the themes that emerged in later German-German negotiations got an airing— including the eventual entry of the two states into the United Nations. Yet the outburst of national emotion at the Bahnhofsplatz alone served notice on all concerned that it was time to work out a new accommodation regulating ties between the two Germanys. To do otherwise in the face of onrushing détente between other Communist and capitalist nations would be to feed the frustrations and potentially volatile sentiments deriving from the German division. The enthusiasm for Brandt also had been enough to make the East Germans organize some half-hearted Willi Stoph demonstrations in front of the hotel in the latter part of the day.

Over the centuries the mainstream of German politics has been conservative. Even the Communists have been basically conservative where German traditions are concerned, and Brandt, for all his seemingly daring actions associated with *Ostpolitik* and his Socialist background at Erfurt showed himself fully compatible with this mainstream, upholding eternal German values of nationhood, determined to conserve what could and should be conserved through change.

Destruction of the German Reich had presented German politicians with the task of reassembling the pieces of defeated Germany into a state— states—that could function credibly and, in time, attract support from the citizenry. Adenauer had started this in the West, Ulbricht in the East. Until the late 1960s the task had been made brutally simple by the client relationships of the two to their respective guardian powers in the capitalist West and the Communist East. The Cold War reflections had been archconservative-Christian Democratic Union (CDU) rule in Bonn for two decades and archconservative-SED rule in East Berlin for as long. Brandt's Chancellorship had changed that constellation as far as West Germany was concerned, and his appearance in Erfurt demonstrated that it had implications for the East Germans as well. (One aftereffect of his visit to Erfurt was to be a year-long struggle by younger and more flexible men in the East German leadership to oust their stubborn old boss, Ulbricht. In Erich Honecker, a dedicated Communist, they found a man of Brandt's generation capable of handling their new problems and changing world relationships, and he became the new party chief.) Erfurt, all who were there sensed,* marked the beginning of a new phase in the history of the German nation. Seen in

---

*The author covered the Brandt-Stoph meeting for *The New York Times*.

retrospect, it also marked the point where everything Willy Brandt stood for and worked for came together.

Immediately after his dinner of sausage and salmon with his guest from the West, Willi Stoph took a train back to East Berlin. That same night on television he remarked, soberly and in character: "I consider the meeting to have been useful."

As his own special train rattled across the switchings at the heavily guarded German-German boundary at midnight, Brandt, sipping red wine in a salon car and using an uncharacteristic superlative, told his aides that he had been "overwhelmed" by his Erfurt reception.

"I am richer for the experience," he said, and it was plain to those with him that he meant it.

II:

Who Is Willy Brandt?

The man known to the world as Willy Brandt was born Herbert Ernst Karl Frahm on December 18, 1913, in Lübeck, the proud Hanseatic port at the continental gateway of the Baltic Sea. His birthplace was the room-and-a-kitchen apartment of his grandfather in the birch-lined Töpferweg—Potters Lane—a cobblestoned street of modest, low dwellings in a working-class borough of St. Lorenz. His mother, Martha Frahm, a diminutive brown-haired clerk in the neighborhood cooperative store, was just nineteen years old. His father? The name was not mentioned in the tiny Frahm household, though he heard it much later, and it sounded Scandinavian—"Swedish, Danish, or Norwegian," he recalled more than forty years afterward in his "as told to" autobiography, *My Road to Berlin*. A sailor? A salesman? Eight months after Frahm's birth World War I began, and it might have carried the father away with it. In fact, the father was a native of Hamburg who survived that war and World War II. The son never saw him.[1] Grandfather Frahm was drafted in 1914; Martha Frahm had to manage on her own.

One can imagine the situation: a maiden in the bloom of youth facing gravid responsibility, not much money in the kitty, girlfriends envious but disdainful, the wet cold of the Baltic winter riding into the front yard with the morning fog, her lover gone with the four winds, papa off to the war, and she, the breadwinner, laboring a six-day week at the Konsumverein. How many working girls faced a like lot in 1914 and later in literature and life? A St. Lorenz neighbor, Paula Bartels-Heine, took care of the infant during the week, from Sunday evening until Saturday noon, while Herbert Frahm's mother worked. The neighbor fed him, played with him, darned the holes in his clothes. On those short weekends his mother spoiled him with goodies from the cooperative—whatever there was in increasingly spare times. War hit workers hardest. But in 1917, when he was three, his mother managed to dress him up in a sailor suit, high-buttoned shoes, an oversized white belt and cap, and with a tiny cane to have him photographed in the role he cherished in his fantasy then and much much later: a man of the sea. A year before Martha Frahm had had him snapped in what was surely a borrowed uniform: high-collared tunic, toy rifle, leather message box, and on his head, the spiked *Pickelhaube.* The photographer stood him on a chair and obtained the same look of wonderment from him that he was to have toward the military as an adult.

To be born in Lübeck had been something special for over 700 years. The city had gotten its first charter from the Saxon duke, Henry the Lion, about 1157. At that time the Baltic coast was still pioneer country for the German tribes who had acquired a polity farther to the south and west and were colonizing, assimilating, or driving back the Danes and the Slavic Wends who had given place names to the region. Lübeck, with its natural moat formed by the Trave and Wakenitz rivers, got its second charter in 1181 from Emperor Frederick I. He made it a free imperial city. Within the next century *Lübisches Recht,* the laws of Lübeck, were adopted by practically every major town on the Baltic and well inland in what is now eastern Germany and western Poland, serving as the court of appeals even for the German settlement of Russian Novgorod, its easternmost trading partner. From the thirteenth century onward for close to 300 years Lübeck was synonymous with civilization as it was spread by the adventurous merchants of the Hanse across the northern reaches of Europe. Lübeckers regarded their city as the queen of the Hanseatic League that linked them with Bremen and Hamburg in the same latitude and with thirty other port cities. Then and later Germany was less a nation than a series of cities, high-walled and bristling with arms, defiant of strangers, each fearful for its own security and treasure. Lübeck, with its thick brick walls that made the city a water fortress, was a prime example. The Holsten Gate's massive twin cylinders of red brick topped with cones of gray slate joined by a stepped Gothic gatehouse proclaimed the city's might and solidity to all the lands westward.

Inside the gate were the famed seven towers of the medieval churches, the Gothic facades, the elegant Mengstrasse where Thomas Mann's family had its house and coddled its senator and mayor, Thomas's father. To live inside Lübeck's walls was to belong, as Thomas Mann related in 1901 throughout the more than 500 pages of *Buddenbrooks.* In his ironic novel Mann dwelt exhaustively on the meaning of a house in the Mengstrasse opposite the Rathaus and the meaning of a home outside the old wall. Decline, in Lübeck's scale of values, could be measured by the distance one was removed from the ennobling vicinity of the town hall. The chronicle ends with the male heir transplanted beyond the Castle Gate to the northeast and succumbing to typhoid fever in a home without an inscription on the lintel. The Mann family house at Number 4 Mengstrasse, with its beauteous Renaissance facade and the lasting, graven inscription, "God Will Provide," above the door, actually was the setting of *Buddenbrooks*. There was no motto above the Frahm door in the Töpferweg, a mile southwest of the double-towered Holsten Gate.

Herbert Frahm was born outside the ancient fraternity of contented burghers in every way: outside the city walls, outside wedlock in a society whose laws penalized the mothers of such children even into the 1970s, outside the small circle of families who dominated Lübeck affairs. The city state had begun life with three classes of inhabitants: full freemen, half freemen, and aliens. A caste system based on these ancient differences still prevailed. In Lübeck proper, proper Lübeck, one was not merely born but born *of,* as Mann recounted, introducing "Madame Antoinette Buddenbrook, born Duchamps" and her daughter-in-law, "Frau Consul Elizabeth Buddenbrook, born Kröger" in his very first chapter. Herbert Frahm was not only illegitimate—he was not born *of.* He came from that multitude of German plebs who had done the nation's work on the heavy sod, in the soggy swamps, along the wet streets, and across the bloody battlefields—far from the silver candlesticks and vintage wines and hearth comfort and splendid clothes of the rich and the aristocrats.

A healthy, husky boy, Herbert had, in the care of Frau Bartels-Heine, few playmates. This, too, must have contributed to the formation of the loner's streak that remained with him the rest of his life. "I had many friends," Brandt wrote in 1960, "but not one who was really close to me. I felt it difficult to confide in other people. From my early years, I maintained this reserve. Accustomed to live within myself, I found it not easy to share my sentiments and inner thoughts with others."

Herbert's grandfather, Ludwig Frahm, a broad-shouldered fellow with a strong nose and a wide, expressive mouth, had come over from the plains of Mecklenburg where more than 60 percent of the soil belonged to great property owners: 17,000 acres to one nobleman, 22,000 acres to another, 33,000 acres to Prince Schaumburg-Lippe. Like his father, Frahm too had been a farm laborer for an estate-owning family in the days when sparsely populated Mecklenburg was among the most backward of the German lands, only a breath removed from feudalism. Serfdom had been fixed in laws of 1645 and 1654 that not only required peasants to get permission of their lords to marry but made their offspring serfs, too—this on the eve of the Age of Enlightenment and only a few decades before serfdom was eliminated in other German duchies.

Mecklenburg officially abolished the laws of bondage in 1820, but the master-servant relationship lasted for many years afterward. Grandfather Frahm told young Herbert how his father had been held over a trestle and whipped repeatedly for disobedience, as if serfdom persisted. That had made a lasting imprint on Ludwig Frahm, and the recounting of it made an indelible impression on the grandson, who tells it as one of the core memories of his Lübeck childhood. (History, in its quirky way, made a princely palace in Bonn, the Schaumburg Palace, the seat of the West German Government in 1949 and twenty years later the Chancellery of Chancellor Willy Brandt. One of the Bundestag deputies of his Social Democratic Party in that first term was Lenalotte von Bothmer, whose family estate had held the Chancellor's great-great-grandfather as a serf.)

Ludwig Frahm provided a sequel for his grandson, relating that as a young man—it must have been about the turn of the century—he had been called to the house of the estate overseers on election day to cast his ballot along with the other farmhands. The ballot box was a soup tureen, making it easy for the landlord's men to see each vote and make sure it was for the Conservatives. Grandfather Frahm said he "outwitted" the landlord, overturning the tureen, as if by accident, making it impossible to see who had voted for whom. He had cast his ballot for August Bebel's Social Democratic Party of Germany, which in 1890 had 26,000 registered voters in Mecklenburg, almost as many members as the Conservatives. Ludwig Frahm came to Lübeck a Social Democrat, and he stayed one.

A touch of Mecklenburg remained in the family, at the very least in certain accents and intonations. To this day Willy Brandt pronounces the West Slavic suffix, "lin" with two syllables, "le-en"—as the Mecklenburgers do when speaking such names as Berlin (Ber-LEE-en) or the old Mecklenburg family, Zeppelin (Zep-pe-LEE-en). It is an unmistakable legacy. That and the memory in the marrow of the Frahm family that there had been such a thing as bondage in their past, a time when working men in Mecklenburg could be sold like slaves. Matthias Claudius, the poet born in 1740 near Lübeck, had written of those victims:

> And many walk bowed down and wilt
> In misery and pain,
> While others drag them every way
> And milk them just like cows.
> Yet of defense there can be none
> For such an evil use:
> Since peasants walk not on all fours
> But are men all the same.

A Mecklenburg poet whose father had been a serf, Johann Heinrich Voss, wrote of masters "who beat us like horses, though hardly feeding us as well."

Though freed from legal bondage, German workers were still economically downtrodden, and so the transition from serfs to Social Democrats, though long in the making, was a causal development. Even when they became politically organized, the workers remained the niggers of Germany, often despised and mocked by the well-to-do: poorly housed, inadequately schooled, skimpily paid.

Professor Arnold Brecht (born 1884) tells in his memoirs of walking with his father down Moislinger Allee, the street where Herbert Frahm lived for a time, and seeing a Lübeck worker demonstration. He wrote: "Social Democrats (a word spoken in Lübeck as 'Sozi-aldemokraten' with a strong and derisory separation between the 'i' and the 'a', as if they said 'Indi-ans,' and not Indians) were 'enemies of the state.'" Brecht, who fled the Nazis in 1933, a few months after Herbert Frahm went into exile, recalls asking his father about that Lübeck demonstration. The father explained that the workers wanted better wages and a better life, but that the main thing was that everybody had a job. In *Buddenbrooks* Thomas Mann also has a passage about the Social Democrats. He wrote of the art teacher, Herr Drägemüller: "He would lecture on the policy of Bismarck, accompanying himself with impressive spiral gestures from his nose to his shoulder. Social Democracy was his bugbear—he spoke of it with fear and loathing. 'We must keep together,' he used to say to refractory pupils, pinching them on the arm. 'Social Democracy is at the door.'"

Lübeck, as *Buddenbrooks* made clear, was declining well before Herbert Frahm's birth. The Hanseatic League that Lübeck had helped to found waned from the 1500s on, and in the nineteenth century, its shallow harbor hospitable mainly to wooden ships, the port faced growing competition from Hamburg, Bremen, Stettin, Rostock, and Danzig. Lübeck's transition to a manufacturing center and the influx of farm laborers to the regional metropolis made it susceptible to the new political movement of the proletariat. Lübeck sent its first Social Democratic deputy to the Reichstag in 1890. A secret police report to the Lübeck Senate, dated September 24, 1893, noted: "Workers, craft apprentices, small innkeepers, tradesmen, shopkeepers, and the lower civil servants, and no little proportion of subaltern officials in the state and community services, the menial railway workers, specifically the postal and telegraph employees, belong with few exceptions to the Social Democrats. They make no secret of their membership, rather they declare it sometimes very deliberately."

Seven years later, in 1901, the Social Democratic Party held its national convention in Lübeck, and in his opening address August Bebel said: "Class domination did not prevent our comrades here in Lübeck from working and agitating and carrying things to the point where the old free imperial city of Lübeck has become a citadel of Social Democracy."

World War I, that great leveler, broke the back of Lübeck's self-reflected patrician vanity; by 1920 Ludwig Frahm's party had 8000 card-carrying members in a population of 130,000. In his curious autobiography—curious for its ellipses and occasional lack of precision—Willy Brandt recalls a memorable event involving his grandfather, home from the war. Ludwig Frahm's first wife had died, and he remarried on the strength of a new job as a truck driver for the Dräger Works, a large factory on the Moislinger Allee and a stone's throw from the boy's birthplace. They took young Herbert in with them, into a comfortable house on the factory grounds with a garden and a white picket fence. One day there was a walkout; it was probably in the autumn of 1921, a year filled with strikes and political violence in Germany. A lockout followed. Brandt wrote, in the third person, about the eight-year-old Herbert Frahm: "He knew that he belonged to the poor, that there was much beyond his reach. But real misery he had not known. Now suddenly hunger was standing in the kitchen, like an evil landlord." The boy went down the street to the neighborhood bakery and became almost "dizzy" from the smell of fresh bread. A "gentleman" asked him if he were hungry.

"Herbert swallowed with difficulty. Then he nodded."

The "gentleman" was a director of the Dräger Works who took him into the bakery, bought two loaves, and pressed them into the boy's hands. Herbert ran home and "breathlessly" told Grandfather Frahm of "the unexpected luck."

"Take the bread back at once," he quoted Ludwig Frahm as saying and, answering Herbert's puzzled queries, he declared: "A striker accepts no gifts from his employer. We will not allow ourselves to be bribed by the enemy. We are no beggars, to whom one throws alms. We ask only for our rights, not for gifts. Take the bread back." Brandt writes that he "proudly" went back to the bakery "like a soldier who was sent with a message into the camp of the enemy." He plopped the loaves on the counter with the words "We don't want it."

Poor, but not wretchedly poor, as he and his childhood pictures make plain. There is a studio photograph of him at about age ten in a sailor suit with a lanyard, knee socks, and boxy shoes laced up through sixteen eyelets. His light brown hair falls over his right eye. He did not seem to want for proper clothes, then or later. Photographs of Martha Frahm about the same time show her pert and almost elegant, one with a huge flowered and fruited hat, a tasseled umbrella, and a sparkling necklace around her throat. Brandt has said that he was less deprived than some contemporaries, and his classmate, Rudolf Wilken, who occasionally visited Herbert Frahm at home, recollects: "I thought he was better off than me. He was the only child; there were four children in my family. He got gruel. We had diluted gruel—literally. He even had his own little room."

Herbert was an outstanding pupil, and at age thirteen he was put ahead into the *Realschule,* the central secondary school, far above his *Volksschule* classmates. His grandfather had pushed him along and, as the dominant influence at this stage of his life, had also introduced him to a different kind of German hero than the traditional ones of the Frederick the Great-Bismarck liturgy he was learning at school: Ludwig Frahm celebrated the memory of Bebel and told young Herbert stories of that great German and of the founder of the labor movement, Ferdinand Lassalle.

"To grandfather," Brandt wrote:

> socialism was more than a political program; it was a kind of religion. It would make all men brothers, eliminate all injustice from the world, even money would disappear. Herbert never tired of listening to these prophecies, and his heart beat faster when Grandfather started to sing the revolutionary songs of the workers."

When proto-Nazi radicals on June 24, 1922, had murdered Walther Rathenau, Foreign Minister of the Weimar Republic, and workers went into the streets all over the country, Ludwig Frahm had participated in the disarming of the Lübeck police and the formation of a workers' militia (Herbert, bringing lunch to his grandfather, had found him wearing the red armband of the Republican Guards).

That action had cost old Frahm his company house, although rent protection regulations and legal proceedings made it possible for him to stay another two years on the Moislinger Allee. Then the family moved a few blocks north of the railway yards to Trappenstrasse. Ludwig Frahm had a new job as a driver for the cooperative association that had employed his daughter; Herbert got his own room under the eaves of their three-story brick apartment house with white-silled windows and a Germanic god in stone above the door. Here the boy lived the rest of his Lübeck days.

His fourteenth year was full of change. Herbert's mother married Emil Kuhlmann, a Social Democrat like all the Frahms, and a Mecklenburger. He was a mason, and Herbert called him "Uncle," liking the "warmhearted" man a lot better than he did his grandfather's second wife. That year too, Herbert was sent up to the Johanneum, a full-fledged high school, rich in prestige. It was like being admitted to Harrow or to Boston Latin, and only a handful of boys from Lübeck's working class made it. Still, Lübeck, was less and less a patrician stronghold, having elected its first Social Democratic Mayor, Paul Löwigt, in 1926.

Spurred on by his grandfather, Herbert had enrolled in the children's section of the Workingmen's Sports Association when he was nine, moving on to the SPD Kinderfreunde. Now he was running distances for the Workers Gymnastic Association, once winning a 5000-meter race, "because no one else entered," and joined the Workers Mandolin Club. "Musical?" he was asked four decades later about his mandolin artistry. "It wasn't so much," he replied. "We just thrummed with our picks."[2]

The Social Democratic Party was becoming a home to a boy who had known several, and none. Klaus Schütz, long an aide of Brandt in Berlin, remarked: "In those days the SPD was the entire life of people like him. If you did gymnastics it was in the Workers Association. If you skated you skated in the SPD Skating Club. The party was the only home."[3] A home, a faith, and a place to have fun.

In his autobiography Brandt switches abruptly from the third person in which he had described his childhood to the first person in describing his life from age fourteen on. He concludes the period 1913-27 with the passage: "An opaque veil hangs over those years, gray as the fog over the port of Lübeck. Figures and faces are like shadows—they rise to the surface and disappear again, like flotsam on the waves of the northern sea. It is hard for me to believe that the boy Herbert Frahm was—I, myself."[4]

His treatment of what follows flows more easily as he recalls his four years at the Johanneum high school. It is worth noting that, in 1972, twelve years after the autobiography was completed, his memory of childhood was fresher, stronger in detail. Perhaps he became reconciled with what had been a lonely, painful, and uncertain time. Was he perhaps also finally reconciled to the Willy Brandt he had created out of Herbert Frahm?

At age fourteen Willy Brandt, still officially Herbert Frahm, began his conscious political life and the beginning, however modest and tentative, of his literary life—two central commitments of his career that he always found comfortable to discuss. It was at this age that people beyond his immediate circle began to take notice of him, providing that inspirational force so necessary for politicians, actors, writers, and others who seek the public eye. Frahm had caught the attention of two men who had a strong influence on him: his German and history teacher, Eilhard Erich Pauls, and the local Social Democratic leader, Julius Leber.

Pauls must have been an unusual teacher for his generation. Conservative in outlook and dress—he wore the old-fashioned pince-nez—he nevertheless had very liberal classroom habits, preferring discussion with his pupils in that big neo-Gothic pile of red bricks to lecturing from a podium. He had a custom of starting his German classes with the declamation of a poem by a pupil. To be called on for this was a torture for most of the growing boys. "But not for Herbert," his classmate, Friedrich Scharmer, remembered. "He had his big moment then. He would recite poems critical of social conditions and let his voice swell from *pianissimo* to *fortissimo* until the walls rattled. The amazing thing was, nobody laughed. We were just plain impressed. I think he was a better speaker then than he is today." Brandt in his autobiography says,

> I did not share the enthusiasm of my schoolmates for poetry. I was
> not carried away by the rhythm and the melody of the poems we had
> to learn by heart. I was interested in novels which had something
> to say, in biographies, such writers as the Danish Socialist novelist
> Martin Andersen Nexö, Erich Maria Remarque, and Thomas
> Mann.

But that he was superb at declaiming the poetry that interested him less than other writing, there is no doubt. Another Johanneum classmate, Hans Dreyer, recalls a morning when it was his turn to perform and he was unprepared. Frahm, who sat in the second row on the right, told him: "Let me do it this time."

"He had that waggish smile even then," says Dreyer, "and when Pauls came into the classroom he jumped up and thundered a poem of Richard Dehmel." That naturalist writer's poem was deceptively entitled "Harvest Song." In reality, it was a forecast of revolt, whose latter verses go:

> The wind dies down across the land
> On the rim of heaven many mills stand
> Grind, mill, grind
> The twilight skies grow darker red
> The masses of poor cry out for bread
> Grind, mill, grind
> The storm lies in the lap of night
> Tomorrow the cause begins aright
> Grind, mill, grind
> Through the fields the storm will sweep
> Then no man will from hunger weep
> Grind, mill, grind

It is hard to imagine many *Gymnasium* professors of that day tolerating such stuff. The majority had entered World War II singing exuberant Fatherland songs with all their hearts. They had come back forlorn and tattered to find their homeland prostrate in defeat, their Kaiser in exile, revolutionaries in full cry, inflation raging. They were bitter over what

Herbert Frahm, in one of the several studio photographs of his childhood.

Winter 1929: the high school student in his Sunday suit and school cap.

Herbert Frahm (sixth from right in back row) with his graduation class at the Johanneum.

The young socialist on a Lübeck park bench, about 1932, reading one of the SAP papers.

Willy Brandt in Oslo, 1934. "As a young man, I thought of myself as a Left socialist."

During a crisis in the Berlin *Senat* in April 1952, the SPD traditionalists tried to oust Mayor Ernst Reuter (right). Brandt, behind him, spoke of "long and bitter quarrels."

"You have infiltrated the American government by way of my sister," said Secretary of State John Foster Dulles (left) of Brandt the Mayor. Eleanor Dulles (center) was a dauntless friend of Berlin.

Erich Ollenhauer (right), chairman of the SPD went to see Nikita Khrushchev in East Berlin in 1959, but the Americans discouraged Mayor Brandt from doing the same.

Brandt respected Chancellor Adenauer's (left) political abilities, but he didn't like the man who called him "Herr Frahm" in an election campaign.

"Ich bin ein Berliner," U.S. President John F. Kennedy declared in front of the Schöneberg Rathaus and became Brandt's strongest ally. In the center is Otto Bach, president of the Berlin parliament.

"The sensible boy he always was," Martha Frahm-Kuhlmann remarked about her son.

doubtless seemed to them unfair peace terms dictated by the victors at Versailles. Those frustrations they could not vent in their classrooms, they aired in their circles of like-minded veterans. The hives where these drones swarmed were the *Stammtische* of a hundred thousand taverns across the Reich, the "regular tables" where regular guests appeared at regular times to drink regular amounts of beer in that ordered fashion so many Germans cherished—and woe to the stranger who sat down uninvited. After World War II it became something of a fashion to explain the rise of Hitler in terms of *Stammtisch* politics, drawing perhaps unconsciously on the memory of the Beer Hall *Putsch* of November 8, 1923. Albert Krebs, the first Gauleiter of Hamburg, recalled meeting Heinrich Himmler, the future SS leader, in 1929, and described him as a "remarkable mixture of martial boasting, petit bourgeois *Stammtisch* twaddle and the zealous prophecies of a sectarian preacher."[5] Friedrich Meinecke, the conservative historian who attempted in 1946 to explain how his nation arrived at "the German Catastrophe," quoted his archconservative friend, Siegfried von Kardorff, a Reichstag deputy, as saying, sometime before his own life and the worst of all wars ended: "The Weimar Constitution went to pieces at the *Stammtisch*. The schoolmasters and court clerks who sat there together made it (the Weimar Constitution) contemptible with their arrogant condemnation smacking of the stab-in-the-back legend. A drop of strong poison spread in this manner throughout public life after the war."[6]

Eilhard Erich Pauls was plainly not a carping German schoolmaster. An enthusiast, he encouraged Herbert's writing efforts and his reading and apparently allowed the boy rather free range with his political involvements. After he joined the Socialist Worker Youth in 1929, Frahm wore his blue uniform blouse and red party kerchief to school on occasions like Constitution Day and was sent home each time because uniforms were against school rules. "I remember him wearing that red neckerchief," a classmate said four decades later. Rudolf Wilken, who was with Frahm in the Red Falcons and later in the Socialist Worker Youth, remembered: "We never disavowed our commitment, neither as Social Democrats in the *Gymnasium* nor as *Gymnasium* pupils in the party." Pauls let Frahm write his final paper in history on the Socialist leader August Bebel, a figure who so attracted him for the rest of his life that he continued to entertain the dream of writing a book about him. "Politics was my favorite dish," he wrote in his autobiography. "Even in school I grasped at every opportunity to start a political discussion."

One of his professors was moved by such a discussion to call in Herbert's mother. He told her of an exchange in which he had described a rally of unemployed men clamoring for bread and had told the class, "What they really wanted was sausage for that bread." Frahm had spoken up: "And why not? Why should the unemployed be satisfied with a piece of dry bread." The professor remonstrated to Martha Frahm-Kuhlmann: "Keep your son away from politics. The boy is gifted—what a pity. Politics will ruin him."

But with continuing support and stimulation from Pauls, Frahm began submitting pieces to the local Social Democratic paper, the *Lübecker Volksbote*. His first piece, published when he was not yet fifteen, earned him five *Reichsmark;* another won him a prize, a copy of James Fenimore Cooper's *Leatherstocking Tales.* These successes were infectious and began an affair with journalism that lasts to the present. It also brought him into contact with the *Volksbote* editor, Julius Leber, who quickly became his political and journalistic mentor, and a bit more.

If Pauls was an unusual Weimar Republic schoolteacher, Julius Leber was equally an exception among the mass of Social Democratic officials. In 1972, nearly forty years after he had left Lübeck, Brandt spoke of the "lasting influence on him" of those two men—of Pauls as his "great" teacher and of Leber as "the fighting republican and Social Democrat."[7] Leber clearly had an electrifying effect on the boy, and, reading about that indomitable German democrat, it is understandable. There were certain parallels between the editor and the boy twenty-two years his junior. Both came from hardscrabble origins; both had obtained higher schooling through excellence in studies; both leaned to oratory.

Grandfather Frahm had put Herbert on the Social Democratic track, where he stayed except for a brief time when, Brandt himself acknowledges, he "played truant." While still in the *Realschule,* he demonstrated interest in the nationalist cause of the German minority in North Schleswig, the section of northern Germany that had been annexed by Denmark after a 1920 plebiscite in accordance with the Versailles Treaty. Social Democrats, including the prominent Carl Severing, also supported the Schleswig cause. Later, it was Leber, more than any other, who kept him on the track.

No wonder the boy looked up to him. Leber was a tough bird, a big man with a massive head, scarred, it appears, on the front lines of World War I. He was, in the memory of those who knew him, "forthright," "dynamic," "the strongest personality." (Roland Freisler, the fanatical Nazi judge who passed the death sentence on him in October 1944 in the *Volksgerichtshof* after Leber had been identified as one of the plotters against Hitler, called him admiringly, if inaccurately, "the German Lenin.")

Julius Leber was born in 1891 in the Rhenish village of Biesheim, Alsace, the son of a mason whose wife still worked the small family plot. A Catholic priest spotted his abilities and had him admitted to the nearby junior high school in Breisach. His performance there won him a scholarship across the river in Freiburg where he completed high school in 1912, earning his keep in part by selling wallpaper, tutoring, and writing pieces for local papers. He went on, with considerable sacrifice, to complete two years of studies at the universities of Freiburg and Strasbourg. Along the way he joined the SPD.

A classmate of Leber's recalled: "In the burgher world before 1914 to be a Socialist was somehow to be in the vicinity of a moral defect." Yet on August 3, 1914, two days after World War I became inevitable, he volunteered for the army. A year later he was commissioned a lieutenant. After being gassed and wounded, he finished the war on the Eastern Front. He was stationed in Belgard (now Bialogard), Pomerania, when, on March 13, 1920, a group of right-wing military men attempted to overthrow the virgin Weimar Republic Government in the Kapp *Putsch* (named for Wolfgang Kapp, spokesman of the surviving Junkers, briefly installed as Reichskanzler in Berlin). Unlike most of his Reichswehr peers, Leber, officer *and* Social Democrat, stood by the republic, occupying Belgard and protecting the elected officials. His fellow officers mutinied and arrested him; only the collapse of the *Putsch* rescued him from their vengeance. He quit the army and went to Freiburg to get his doctorate in political science. From there he moved to Lübeck, taking the job of managing editor of the *Volksbote*. The newcomer was, apparently, an immediate success with Lübeck's workers and with his fellow Social Democrats, who elected him a deputy to the Lübeck citizens council in 1921 and a Reichstag deputy in 1924. Meanwhile, Leber transformed the *Volksbote* into the voice of Lübeck's 30,000 workers, and more. He was, to reread his 1920s articles, a superb political journalist—clear and straight—a democrat for all seasons.

If Leber was an inspiration to Herbert Frahm, the young Frahm must have seemed a godsend to the editor who, toward the end of 1926, had written about "Rootless Youth." "The last war lasted about five years," Leber remarked. "In these years a younger generation grew up. Many of these youngsters were uprooted through the collapse of the war. . . ." He went on to note the many young Germans who were "marching through the streets with nationalist buttons," sometimes in uniform, and with their "great feelings of unsatisfied disappointment," calling this the "breeding ground for enemies of the state." Seven years later, in "investigatory arrest," Leber concluded that the bulk of Germany's younger generation had missed the political boat after World War I. "There was nothing like a young generation with conscious aims and common tasks," he wrote in solitary confinement and blamed that situation, with retrospective pessimism, on the older men of his own party. "Naturally there were some," he went on, "but they appeared as individuals." This came, he said, "in part from the splintering in different political directions."[8] Young Herbert Frahm was one of the exceptions.

At age fourteen Herbert had made his first trip abroad, to Denmark, in a school exchange program that put him briefly with a family in Vejle. He had traveled before to a Falcons' summer camp on a Rhine Island, opposite Namedy, north of Andernach, relishing, as he wrote much later, the "romanticism: it meant hiking and camping, close companionship, life in tents, songs at an open campfire." He loved the castles then and later, and the Rhine boasted plenty: the Andernach Archbishop's Castle, Hammerstein, Arenfels, Rheineck, Linz, Ockenfels, all within a few hours' walk from the shores opposite the island. The Denmark venture, however, was the first exposure to a foreign atmosphere for Frahm, who came from a part of Germany where it was popular to look down on neighbors.

Julius Leber had come from a mixed Franco-German society that put him very early on the path of tolerance. Unlike so many of his contemporaries, he never became a Francophobe, even though he fought against France. He recalled his French-inclined grandfather saying at the outbreak of war: "All that ranting about archenemies was cooked up by a couple of generals and schoolmasters. It's just a big fraud and humbug. The peoples aren't enemies— just the big shots because they want to make a profit."

Tolerance, a lively interest in the outside world, a sensitivity to what was new, a nose for politics, and, perhaps, a somber sense of social mission—these were the qualities the mentor, Leber, tried to strengthen and develop in his newfound Telemachus. Some of his lessons penetrated immediately; others took longer to implant themselves. "His activity and example had a strong impact on my thinking and on my work—and not only in those years," Willy Brandt wrote later.

> He exercised a lasting influence on my whole life. I had grown up without a father. There was an emptiness in my life—Leber filled it. . . . I would never have admitted that I lacked self-confidence, but secretly I had my doubts. Leber dispelled them by giving me recognition and encouragement.

Leber and his associates, Fritz Solmitz, the political editor, and Erich (later Jakob) Gottgetreu, the publisher—both of them Jews—spent considerable time teaching the young protégé the rudiments of journalism. Brandt still relates the incident in which he had written an article about the social significance of angling and was "rudely jolted" by a letter from the Workers Association of Fishermen protesting the "nonsense" he had published.[9] (Angling was later to become his favorite hobby.) Soon, however, the *Volksbote* was carrying his articles—written under the byline, in the Continental fashion, of his initials, H.F.—about SPD athletic competitions and, not so long afterward, about youth politics. On May 6, 1930, a *Volksbote* article by H.F. ran under the headline "We and the Parental Home" and advocated:

> Our parents shouldn't say now: "We weren't allowed to do that at
> your age." No, they should allow youngsters more liberty. For we
> need strength and freedom, friendship and trust, if we want to win
> a world, just the same, dear older comrades, along our own path.

At sixteen the author of that article drank beer and *schnapps* like a good North German and smoked cigarettes. Tall, slender, perhaps a bit awkward, he was a good-looking lad with a big, strong head. Soon he had a girlfriend, Gertrud Meyer, a tall, slender brunette with dimpled cheeks. An office worker and a Socialist, Trudel Meyer became the first of a number of women in Frahm-Brandt's life.

Leber had taken on Frahm, the leader of the Karl Marx Group of Lübeck's Socialist Working Youth, as a regular contributor to the *Volksbote* in 1929. A year later, though Herbert had not reached the mandatory minimum age of eighteen, Leber promoted the boy's membership in the SPD. But Frahm was not an uncritical protégé. He already had a modest political following in the youth organization, and he was beginning to develop ideas of his own in the confusing eddies of latterday Weimar politics. Some of his classmates were beginning to sport the emblems and ideas of the Hitlerites, while Frahm and his friends considered themselves "Leftists" within the SPD, placing themselves at a certain distance from the moderates like Julius Leber and his *Volksbote* editors. Their differences were to become accentuated, as a split developed in the SPD over defense policy, placing Leber on one side and Frahm on the other in the Lübeck party debates.

The issue was one that had tragically divided the SPD leadership once before, at the outset of World War I. At that time the question on the surface had been whether Socialists should adopt an "internationalist" stance toward military matters by pursuing a policy of "international proletarian solidarity," as Karl Liebknecht had defined it, or should rather choose the "nationalist" position justifying the right of "self-defense." In a deeper sense, the contest developed on the question of whether the SPD was to remain a party of revolution or to evolve into a party of reform.[10] The SPD's August 1914 approval of war credits to build up the German military machine was a decision cataclysmic in its repercussions, not only on the party's role as the major force in the Socialist International, but also on its future role in German politics. "The truth which no German Socialist cared to face," William H.

Maehl states in *German Militarism and Socialism,* "was that the SPD had been bitten by the bug of nationalism."[11] The party of the proletariat had rallied to the Kaiser.

In the next four years the split caused by World War I and the war-credits vote widened into a chasm, leaving the majority of reformist Social Democrats on the one side, building a fragile new German Government, and the minority radicals, calling themselves Spartacists, on the other, soon to form the revolution-minded German Communist Party (KPD). The chasm was never to be freely crossed in the next fifty-five years, and the hostility it created was to poison German political life through all those years. From a Nazi jail in Lübeck on July 26, 1933, Julius Leber, reflecting on the tragedy inherent in this, wrote: "August 1, 1914, was the great curse for my generation, from which it plainly won't be able to recover."[12]

Amidst the welter of interwar Germany's political parties—twelve of the twenty-four were represented in the Reichstag—few save the Social Democrats had any real commitment to the preservation of the democratic republic. Even the SPD, for all its republican pretensions, indulged itself in moves perilous to the tender institutions of the new state, voting with the German Nationalists to oust the Stresemann government in 1923, dividing itself over the issue of the defense budget, and breaking up the Cabinet coalition with Conservatives in 1930.

In 1929 the SPD's problem was with an embarrassing decision concerning armored cruisers and whether the coalition government, under its weak Chancellor, Hermann Müller, should authorize their construction. Leber, who had specialized in defense policy as a Reichstag deputy and was an impassioned advocate of a democratized German Army, couldn't have cared less about one or more armored cruisers. What he cared for, heart and soul, was the solidity of his party and of his republic.

In a letter from Berlin to Lübeck that year he wrote:

> By the way, we are sitting here in the middle of a very vehement debate concerning the thrice-cursed armored cruisers. . . . What kind of worries this party has at a time when everything is up for grabs. . . . When one day the hours of decision of the German republic stand under the spotlights of history they will raise only a sympathetic smile about how, in those hours, the largest republican party quarreled over whether construction of a substitute armored cruiser should begin in 1931 or 1932.[13]

About the same time he said: "I don't know how many armored cruisers I could be ready to vote for if I could save the republic and democracy in Germany with it."[14]

Herbert Frahm and other young Socialists saw such compromise and pragmatism differently. "Some of us youngsters came into contradiction with him," he recalled, "because we leaned to the left opposition out of deep dissatisfaction with an impotent coalition and the policy of tolerance (by the SPD)."[15] The Depression had begun: Unemployment reached 3 million at the end of 1929—20,000 persons out of work in Lübeck. More and more Germans were attending the exhortations of the National Socialists—young Germans, too. Frahm and his pals clashed frequently with the junior Nazi sympathizers, whose party had swiftly grown to be the second strongest in the old Hanse city. The young Socialists believed it was more important, at that moment, to think about providing food for hungry children of the unemployed than funding armored cruisers—and they said so.

Soon Frahm was speaking for the young hotspurs in party meetings and challenging his patron, first on the armored-cruiser issue, later on still deeper issues. Karl Albrecht, a *Volksbote* reporter and, after the war, a Lübeck senator, recalled one of those occasions—it must have been about 1930:

> Imagine a mass meeting of 2,000 people. Leber spoke stirringly, he had the crowd in the palm of his hand. And then, when he was finished, Frahm asked to speak and talked extemporaneously against the man whom we all respected. Sometimes people shouted him down. But he didn't lose his train of thought. If he had to, he pounded with his fist to make himself heard. He had enormous courage and colossal equilibrium. I was very impressed by him then although I wasn't on his side, but on Leber's.[16]

The conflict with the older Social Democrats—with Leber himself—broadened as a natural generation gap was forced ever wider. Passions were honed by the abrasives of an increasingly desperate situation: the country gripped in unemployment, the government machinery half-paralyzed and operating mainly under emergency powers, ruthless extremists of Left and Right gaining strength by the hour. Heinrich Bruhn, another contemporary of Herbert Frahm's, recalls a meeting where Leber was the main speaker and Frahm went to the rostrum "without any inhibitions." Older party officials stood up to complain, one of them saying, what do the kids know? They have no experience, and now they're trying to be snotty to the old man." Frahm replied: "I can't help it that I am young. But I can do something about knowing what is going on."[17]

The national elections of September 14, 1930, were streaks of lightning that zigzagged down to opposing rods of the Nazi and Communist parties and suddenly illuminated the jagged landscape of German politics. The National Socialists abruptly found themselves the second most powerful party in the land, with 107 parliamentary seats. The Communists, too, increased their strength, to seventy-seven seats. Both party's gains were at the expense of the Social Democrats.

The shift wasn't as bad in Lübeck, still a Socialist stronghold. But it was bad enough. In the face of the worst economic crisis Germans had known since the Thirty Years' War, the Nazis were jubilantly gathering new support with slogans like: "Rather an end with horror than horrors without an end!" In a postelection editorial Leber wrote: "Evil is among us, the first gusts of the growing tempest are blowing past us." And, "The question is whether the German nation wants to rescue its freedom or whether the black flag of Fascism shall be raised."[18]

Recollecting that grim election shock, Brandt noted:

> In the ranks of the Socialist Youth more and more voices were raised against the leadership of our party. It was accused of a large measure of responsibility for this disaster. The accusations became more and more violent, the criticism against the policy of retreat and compromise more and more bitter.[19]

While Leber stuck with his reformist vision of the German polity, Frahm was attracted more and more to the radical slogans of the New Left of the day, and he recited them: The republic "favors its sworn enemies and persecutes its followers." Reforms are "sedatives to paralyze the energy of the masses." Democracy is "an empty word." Unemployment compensation is "too little to live on and too much to die on."

"The crisis demanded revolutionary measures," he wrote.[20]

But whose revolution? Adolf Hitler was speculating on a Rightist revolution *after* he seized power. The Communist leadership imagined, following their textbooks, that the downfall of the republic, and of the capitalist system, would carry them to power. Both forces chopped at the Social Democratic middle, which was weak and disorganized.

Leber, setting down his thoughts in 1933 in his Nazi prison cell, in retrospect approved of the view adopted at the time by young Frahm and wrote:

> Depression and helplessness dominated the Social Democratic camp for days. . . Those very Social Democrats whose antimilitar- ism knew no bounds placed their last weak hopes in the Reichswehr now. They proved in this way again that they didn't have a clue about the essence and limitations of armed force in a modern national state.[21]

Leber despaired also of the SPD leadership, which had concluded that the lesson of the 1930 defeat at the polls was simply to reelect the same party executive, whose twenty members were all at least fifty years of age, and continued:

> There was really no younger generation. There was also no leadership that could have collected one around it. . . . After the election defeat of September 14, 1930, one detected for the first time a strong disaffection toward one's own leadership in the ranks of Social Democrats. For years Communist as well as National Socialist propagandists had been drumming away with all their might against the Social Democratic leaders. Without real success! Now, with one blow, it was different. A strong "boss-fatigue" overcame the Social Democratic organization. Even then the party was threatened with a catastrophe of the greatest proportions. The wearisome discussion about tolerance, democracy, the party apparatus wore down the party.[22]

Such weakness was catastrophic in a year in which the Storm Troops swelled to a strength of nearly 100,000—the strength of the Reichswehr—and the big bruisers of Heinrich Himmler's newly established SS, the Elite Guard of the Führer, neared the 3000 mark.[23] The Nazis were passing out millions of leaflets and beating up Germans who refused to take them. Walls were scrawled with ugly graffiti: "Death to Jews!" "Germany, Awake!" One evening Frahm's chums battled with a group from the Lübeck Storm Troopers on the outskirts of town, and as a result of that encounter a Nazi was gravely injured. Frahm, one of the trial defendants even though he was not in on the fight, was acquitted. The incident caused embarrassment for the respectable teachers at his high school.[24]

Another incident, this one in the spring of 1931, marked the widening chasm in the party between the militant young Left and the Conservative establishment. Frahm noticed an article by a leading Prussian Landtag deputy, Ernst Heilmann, in a SPD periodical, *Das Freie Wort,* suggesting that Adolf Hitler was as bad as Karl Liebknecht, the bold Socialist who had opposed war credits in 1914 and who led his radical splinter group into the Spartacist-Communist uprising of 1918. "I was enraged," Willy Brandt recalled in his autobiography.[25] His immediate response was a letter to the editor of the periodical slamming Heilmann. The day after it was published, Frahm was called into the Johannis Strasse headquarters and bawled out by an official for violating SPD discipline. Then Leber took him aside. "You know how to write," he said. "But why don't you let your articles lie on your desk at least one night before you send them off to the press. The next morning, look at your manuscript; you yourself will find that some rewrite might be called for. As a result your articles will improve, don't you think?"

The advice, though eventually put to good use later in his political career, went unheeded for the moment, and for some years thereafter Frahm continued to be impetuous. On May 1, 1931, he carried a banner in the annual Labor Day parade that read: *Republic das ist nicht viel/Sozialismus ist das Ziel!* ("Republic, that's too tame/Socialism is the aim!")

The model for disobedience and deviation existed at a much higher level in the SPD. Already on March 20, nine Social Democratic Reichstag deputies had broken ranks and voted against approving funds for armored cruisers despite a vote by the majority of the party deputies in favor of the funds to uphold the shaky Cabinet of Chancellor Heinrich Brüning of the Catholic Center Party. Five days later, in another vote on the same bill, the nine broke away again, effectively splitting the SPD for the first time since World War I.[26] Among the nine were two left-wing Socialists, Max Seydewitz, forty, and Kurt Rosenfeld, fifty-three, who were soon to carry their opposition to the SPD leadership an irrevocable step further. Even then they were vigorously defending their action in *Klassenkampf (Class Struggle)*, a bimonthly founded in October 1927 as the voice of the militant Left of the Party.

The spiritual father of the Left-leaning faction was Dr. Paul Levi, co-founder of the Spartacus League and the Communist Party of Germany, who had been cast out by the Communists in 1921. From then on Levi, Rosenfeld, Seydewitz, and other Leftists of varying ideological origins had formed a loose grouping in and around the SPD. Unlike most Social Democrats, they were against compromise coalitions with burgher parties, nor did they believe fatalistically in the eventual downfall of capitalism. Instead they advocated determined class struggle, with the goal of revolution being socialism. Yet these Leftists deplored the antidemocratic, mechanistic methods of the Communists, some of them out of bitter personal experience. The splinter group made its views known at the 1927 SPD convention in Kiel in a resolution that stated: "The battlefront in the German Repubic is no longer to be found under the slogan: Here republican—there monarchist, but rather, here socialist—there capitalist."[27] The resolution was voted down by a majority content to participate in a bourgeois government as coalition partners. But the Left opposition had begun to march, and it was finding such a strong echo among German Socialists that at the Kiel convention the party chairman felt compelled to inveigh against the pernicious influence of the far Left among the young.[28]

By spring 1931 the struggle between the SPD leadership and the numerically small but noisy and persuasive minority had grown intense and rancorous. Levi's death the previous year in an accident was a grave loss to the

Leftist cause, but Seydewitz and Rosenfeld pressed on, undeterred by the conservative mood of the SPD majority, which, at the Leipzig party convention at the beginning of June 1931, voted sharp disapproval of their March breach of discipline. The two Leftist leaders unsuccessfully pleaded for opposition to the Brüning government on the ground that the Chancellor's notorious emergency laws—the means by which he maintained his tenuous rule—were paving the way to Fascist dictatorship.

The other outstanding event of the Leipzig convention was the elimination of the Young Socialist organization of which Frahm had been such an enthusiastic leader. Their ouster was the culmination of a protracted struggle in which Erich Ollenhauer, the thirty-year-old SPD chief of the youth group, concluded that out of 80,000 young party members only 3000 were enrolled as *Jungsozialisten*—and that the majority of them, like Frahm, stood well to the left of the parent party. The SPD establishment, refusing to listen to any of the youth representatives at Leipzig, quietly dissolved the disagreeable junior branch. In what he called an epilogue, Professor Erik Nölting remarked:

> The Young Socialists died first because of their stubborn orthodoxy, because of an unyouthful cult of the past and the prehistoric, second because of a disdainful and highly unsympathetic arrogance. The Young Socialists died because they confused politics with a sociological study hour out of Karl Marx.[29]

(It was an establishment elegy that could have been spoken for the *Jusos* of the 1960s and 1970s by any right-of-center SPD establishment figure except Willy Brandt. Indeed, the excesses of the radical Left before and during his tenure as Chancellor drew many a similar rebuke from Brandt's SPD colleagues, not to mention the coalition partners or opponents of the SPD.)

The debate provoked by the Leftists in the SPD sharpened to the point where the party leadership was asking: What is the use of saving principles and losing unity? The Left retorted: What is the use of saving unity and losing principles?[30] Seydewitz, Rosenfeld, and their friends opted for the principles and they promoted their cause in *Klassenkampf* and other periodicals, demanding that the SPD oppose Chancellor Brüning's new Emergency Law of July 5. Their intransigence caused the party committee of the SPD to hold hearings on their expulsion.

These events apparently hardened Frahm's determination to side with the minority. He wrote in recollection: "The radicalization of the Left, furthered by the growing economic crisis, widened the gap between the youth and the party leadership."[31] His disgust with the paralysis of German politics was evidently strengthened by his exposure that summer to the freer and easier ways of Scandinavia.

The vacation trip that summer of 1931 was his second journey northward, and this time he and a friend took a freighter from Copenhagen to Bergen to hike along the Norwegian fjords. "Probably my strongest experience of that trip," he wrote:

> was the realization of the complete lack of pride of class or rank, which in the Weimar Republic was hardly less dominant than under the Kaiser, in spite of the (1918) revolution and the influence of the Democrats and the Socialists. I thought it natural that every Social Democrat regarded himself not only as a political opponent but also as a personal enemy of the Conservative.[32]

It was certainly natural back home in Germany, where personal enmity was the order of the political day and where Herbert Frahm had become militant enough to follow a group whose principal organ was called *Class Struggle*.

By the time Frahm had returned to Lübeck, the split in the SPD was virtually complete. Seydewitz, Rosenfeld, and their friends continued to defy party discipline and publish their rebel rhetoric, and, finally, on September 29, after some formalistic back-and-forth, the party executive expelled the two Reichstag deputies from the SPD. Three days later Leftist sympathizers, backed by a number of *Jungsozialisten,* founded a branch of what they called the Socialist Workers Party of Germany (SAP) in Breslau, after Rosa Luxemburg's proposed name for the German Communist Party in 1918. On October 4 a hastily improvised Reich convention of opposition Social Democrats—88 delegates from 25 of the SPD's 33 districts and 200 mostly young German guest delegates—established the national SAP. From a podium decorated with a banner proclaiming: "Karl Liebknecht Warns—The Enemy Is in Our Own Country![34] the new SAP leaders debated a "provisional action program" and proved themselves to be ideological waverers. On one hand, they condemned the German Communists as "dictatorial-centralist." On the other, they adopted a rather indulgent line toward the Soviet Communists—who were running the German Communists—on the grounds that the miseries of the Depression had changed the alternatives of democracy or dictatorship to the alternatives of socialism or capitalism. Those first debates, in which Seydewitz and Rosenfeld turned out to be "less the leaders than the pursued,"[35] forecast even deeper fractures. The SAP was doomed, like so many before and after it, to be a splinter party that splintered itself.

Nevertheless, the SAP, in its early weeks, won the enthusiastic and expectant approval of a variety of Germans and even some non-Germans. It seized the minds of young people with little or no political experience: Herbert Frahm, who was to return to the Social Democratic fold one day; Edith Baumann and Hans Seigewasser, who were to drift to the Communists after World War II. In its first days the SAP was also welcomed openly by popular author Lion Feuchtwanger, who wrote Rosenfeld congratulating him on founding a political organization to which he could say, "*Ja!*" Carl von Ossietzky, the Socialist-leaning publicist, was equally hopeful, wishing "all the best" to the SAP.[35]

By late October the SAP was claiming 57,000 members, more than double the actual number, plus 8000 to 10,000 youth cadres drawn in large part from the traditional Social Democratic and Communist youth associations. It was a serious threat to the larger parties—who evidently shared a fear of the splinter party's effectiveness in calling for a reunification of the Left, a "united front," against the growing menace from Hitler's brown and black columns— enough that a member of the Communist inner circle could write:

> The party leadership had every imaginable worry, among others that there was a new "centrist peril," which was why the attempts of leftist radical Social Democratic groups to create a new core within the workers' movement around the Socialist Workers Party (SAP) were hammered with the biggest guns. Each declaration of Social Democratic politicians calling for united action in the face of threatening Nazi danger was denounced as a dangerous sign that the Social Democrats strove for domination in the united front— and therefore vigilance and struggle were necessary against such attempts.[36]

The KPD attitude toward the SAP drew on an early formulation by Stalin that characterized the Social Democrats as providing "active support" for the bourgeoisie, whose battle organization was Fascism.[37] Thus, the German Communists immediately treated the SAP as "henchmen of Fascism" and "agents of Brüning." The SPD reacted with equal fervor against the "splitters," the "apostates" of their party.

The big parties were content to travel on their familiar, well-laid tracks, as Julius Leber had noted and as the satirist, Kurt Tucholsky, had revealed in his 1930 essay about the "elderly, but slightly drunk gentlemen" who visited various party branches in Berlin during an election campaign. Of a Social Democrat (it could as easily have been a Communist), Tucholsky wrote:

> I've been voting for this party for twenty-two years. But why I do it I don't know. Look. In my district I'm the second secretary. And

when we get together it's always so comfortable; we know the
joint, and the beer is always good, and on the First of May we make
an excursion with the kids and everybody, the whole gang. And in
the evening there is a torchlight parade. Everything is nice and neat.
Who needs principles when you've got an apparatus?[38]

A year later Tucholsky quoted a colleague's verse about the "domestic tyrant
Krause," who kept "two angels above the marriage bed" and next to all his
other souvernirs from the church and the army, a lone picture of Lenin:

Only when he's standing at the bar
Is Krause a Socialist:
There he sweats class struggle wide and far
And shows the burghers his fist.
Otherwise he fills his belly
As holy as the Eucharist.[39]

It was against such self-satisfied party routine that Herbert Frahm and his
Leftist contemporaries rebelled. That, together with an overwhelming
combination of political circumstances must have been infuriating to a
passionate and somewhat headstrong youth. There had been the relative
indifference of the SPD leadership toward the Brüning administration,
suppression and then expulsion of the Left opposition, Frahm's experience in
Scandinavia, and, by October 9, 1931, a further Conservative shift in the
construction of the second Brüning Cabinet. Three days later, at Bad
Harzburg, in a new lurch to the Right, Hitler succeeded in gathering with
representatives of the Conservative veterans organization, the Stahlhelm
(steel helmet), with Brigadier General von Seeckt, with Junker landowners,
and with financiers and industrialists like Hjalmar Schacht, Rudolf Blohm,
Max Schlenker, Emil von Strauss, Louis Ferdinand Ravené, and Ernst
Poensgen. Together they formed the Harzburg Front. It was more than
enough to make any young man of the Left turn to radicalism.

Before Frahm made a complete break, however, he had it out once more
with Julius Leber, who asked him if he was utterly mad. The new party was a
group of political cripples. Revolutionary? They were impotents aware of
their own weaknesses, escaping into radicalism. "In spite of your youth you
can appreciate a good book, a good drink, the favors of a beautiful girl," he
later quoted Leber as having told him. "You are quite normal. You don't
belong with that band of sectarians.[40]

He didn't. But then again, he did.

Heinrich Bruhn remembered the October evening in the Lübeck trade
unions building, where Leber was the main speaker at a huge meeting. Bruhn
and Frahm were there from the disbanded *Jungsozialisten:*

We made catcalls, Herbert, too. There was a tumult. We were bounced, beaten out by the goons. One block beyond, in a workers' gym, we founded the Lübeck branch of the SAP. Herbert became the agitation-propaganda leader, who drafted the speeches and leaflets and all those things. He succeeded in carrying all the young people into the SAP. There was practically no Social Democratic youth in Lübeck after Frahm joined the SAP.[41]

"I thought Leber unjust . . ." Brandt recalled. "We separated in bitterness." On October 23 Leber's *Volksbote* carried a page-one story under the headline: "Scandal Among Lübeck's Worker Youth."[42]   Frahm had broken with the party of his grandfather, his mother, and Leber to move closer to what he believed was needed, to what he believed in : Socialism. He gave up a great deal in addition to his party membership—his job on Leber's paper and the eventual prospect of university studies, which Leber had offered to help finance personally.[43] Graduation from the Johanneum was only six months away. He had completed his *Abitur* (university entrance examination) in the late spring with the overall grade of *gut*—roughly B—but instead of entering a university he took up an apprenticeship with a ship brokerage.

Although he had been active enough as a *Jungsozialist,* the SAP made new demands on the eighteen-year-old. "We were at it from dawn to dark," recalled Heinrich Bruhn. "We rode our bikes to Hamburg (a distance of forty miles) to talk to comrades there. We went to the factories and distributed leaflets to the workers. But we didn't get a political footing."[44] Frahm was chairman of the new party's youth association in Lübeck and simultaneously a member of the SAP branch executive. He was on his own, and, after the frustration of compromise in the petrified SPD, politics were fun again.

"I learned a lot," he asserted in a conversation nearly forty-two years later. "Those who go into splinters or to the fringe have to work harder than those in the big heaps. We accomplished a lot. In a big party you can't do much. In a small party you depend on the next guy. In retrospect it's silly to split a party. But against that it stands that it did me good, me more than others. I don't regret that I took that path. But there are different kinds of rightness. The SPD would not have become more potent if there had been no split. However, one shouldn't split, but try to renew, to activate from within."[45]

The roiling ideological struggles in which the SAP was entangled continued, not only with the half-dozen organized party formations of the Left, but also within its own ranks. Lev Trotsky, already in exile from the Soviet Union, polemicized against the splinter group, saying, A disappointed Social Democrat doesn't make a Communist by a long shot." Trotsky argued that true Communists were obliged to work for destruction of all forms of Social Democracy and for the reconstruction of the "decadent" Communist

Party organization.[46] The KPD, on the other hand, had the nerve to brand the SAP leaders as "Trotskyite agents" when they weren't indulging in other sloganeering somersaults, such as the accusation that the SAP represented "the Leftist branch of Social Fascism."[47]

Even the anticonstitutional coup managed by Chancellor Franz von Papen, who dismissed the duly elected Prussian Government on July 20, 1932, failed to bring the Left together. That night in Lübeck Herbert Frahm, hoping for a general strike, joined in trying to mobilize the city's workers—and Social Democrats—"to form a union with all parties and groups opposed to a Hitler regime."[48] But he and the other SAP leaders were let down by Prussia's spineless Interior Minister, Carl Severing, an SPD man who declined the offer of Magdeburg's Mayor Ernst Reuter to send his city's police to Berlin. The SPD executive warned against "rash actions" and argued that the unemployed—there were close to 5 million jobless—couldn't go on strike anyway.

Looking back in his autobiography, Brandt wrote:

> Active resistance, which the republican leaders regarded as senseless, would definitely have made sense. Even though the fight would have cost many lives, it would at least have proven to the world that a great part of the German people believed in democracy, it would have united the republican forces and banished the general feeling of defeatism and hopelessness which—later on, even more than at that moment—demoralized the democratic Left and facilitated the stabilization of Hitler's dictatorship. To be defeated in battle, heroically fought against tremendous odds, is tragic; to surrender without a fight makes the tragedy a farce. It robs the victim of his last most precious possession: his self-respect.[49]

Nine months after Frahm had broken with Leber, the two found themselves allies again in a common cause, the elimination of the Nazi menace. Following the Papen coup the SPD and the SAP organized a mass meeting of the Left in Lübeck, one of the few such to take place in all Germany in the desperate months before Hitler came to power. Leber spoke. "We are in the midst of a counterrevolution," he said. "But we declare: Our movement is stronger. History is on the side of freedom, and freedom will be with you as long as you fight for it. . . . Victory or no victory, if one fights for liberty one doesn't ask what tomorrow will bring."

The crowd rose from its seats cheering and raising their arms, fists clenched in the sign of workers' solidarity. "I wanted to jump on the platform to squeeze Leber's hand," Brandt wrote. "I had found him again, I had never lost him."[50]

Then the Storm Troopers burst into the hall and began clubbing their way toward the podium. "Leber stood alone on the stage," Brandt recalled. "The Nazis thought they could finish him. But they were wrong. Leber smashed a chair, took a chair leg in one hand and then one in the other hand and clubbed his way through the murder-thirsty mob to safety, more or less in one piece."[51] Leber's physical resistence had a precedent—he had personally thrown Joseph Goebbels, the Nazi propagandist, out of neighboring Eutin on one of those turbulent evenings—and it proved a fairly successful strategy. Hitler gave Lübeck a wide berth then and later.[52]

The SAP reaction—indeed that of the Left in general, including the KPD and SPD—to its disheartening elections losses was to go into new orgies of internal struggle. Ex-Communists like Paul Frölich demanded that the SAP become a Communist Party. Ex-Socialists accused the radicals of "persecution of heretics" and "dogmatism." Frahm, more out of militancy than out of ideological sympathy,[53] sided with the Communist grouping around Paul Frölich and Jacob Walcher. Except for improvised actions in the provinces, like the Leber evening in Lübeck, there was no sign of a united front.

In the November Reichstag elections the Nazis lost 2 million votes, causing many Germans to think, wishfully, that the Hitler spook was dissipating. The lull was deceptive. Despite the vote, Conservative forces combined to persuade old Hindenburg to appoint Hitler as Chancellor in place of the faltering Kurt von Schleicher. The mighty German Left sank into paralysis—the Left that had toppled the monarchy and chased out the Kaiser in 1918, that had organized and staffed a republic, that had dominated German politics for most of a dozen years, that had built up its own armed formations and squads of toughs, that had brought the German economy to a grinding halt with general strikes. Now it behaved as if it were stupefied, a drugged giant.

When on January 22, 1933, uniformed Storm Troopers flaunted their strength in front of the Karl Liebknecht House, the KPD headquarters at Alexanderplatz in Berlin, the Communist Party officials merely watched from the windows, and the KPD chairman, Thälmann, called it "a victory" for his side. Thälmann didn't even bother to order his security apparatus to hide the secret party personnel files—an oversight that undoubtedly contributed to his own capture by Nazi police less than six weeks later,[54] along with hundreds of other leading Communists.

Why? Even the radical Socialists thought Hitler would be in power only briefly, that Nazism was not a durable plant. "We, too, strongly believed the Hitler regime would only last a short time," Brandt wrote.[55]

On the night of January 31-February 1, two days after Hitler was named Chancellor, Storm Troopers clashed in Lübeck with a group of SPD war veterans organized in the paramilitary *Reichsbanner*. Julius Leber was in the thick of it and during the vicious street brawl was badly injured, his nasal bone slashed through. One of the Storm Troopers was killed.* The Lübeck police, obeying their new masters, arrested Leber, ignoring his putative immunity as a Reichstag deputy.

Frahm helped organize a one-hour protest strike, ludicrous in retrospect but indicative of the feeling at that time that Nazi rule was only tentative. Leber was released on bail and on the condition that he not address the crowd. It was an order he chose to ignore. On February 19, as 15,000 Lübeckers assembled on the broad, icy Castle Field in a renewed demonstration against Nazi domination, Leber, his head still in bandages, mounted a platform and shouted one word: *Freiheit!* (Liberty!)[56]

It was the last time Herbert Frahm ever saw his mentor. Leber, still believing in German justice, went back to jail to stand trial. Although his own grisly fate was still almost twelve years off, already the Storm Troopers, the Gestapo, and the SS were hotly competing to seize, torture, and murder the opponents of Nazism, each group seeking the power of Hitler's ultimate approval. In Berlin alone the *Sturmabteilungen* opened fifty "wildcat" concentration camps for the annihilation of enemies.[57]

In the SAP Seydewitz and Rosenfeld and a majority of the leadership thought the time had come to liquidate the party. They were opposed by a militant minority led by the ex-Communists Jacob Walcher and Paul Frölich. While they debated, the Nazis used the Reichstag fire on February 27 as a pretext to grab every Leftist in sight, including a number of SAP leaders. One of the founders of the splinter party, Ernst Eckstein, was seized on February 28—the day after the Nazis banned the KPD and also banned the SAP press—and tortured to death in the Öls concentration camp only nine weeks later.

Of 17,000 SAP members, only about 1500 followed Seydewitz and Rosenfeld into the attempted liquidation of the ill-starred party. The two men succeeded in escaping to the West. The rest of the group followed a call of the minority leaders to a secret conference in Dresden on March 11, to which Frahm was delegated by his Lübeck section.

"I travelled under my party name of Willy Brandt," he wrote.[58] Herbert Frahm had chosen for himself a name especially common in Lübeck. On the way he changed trains in Berlin and took a look at the sprawling capital for the first time. The downtown area was festooned with Nazi banners, and Frahm

---

*The incident was to play a role in the 1972 federal election campaign, when August Naujock, a former Lübeck police detective, printed thousands of pamphlets charging that Brandt had stabbed to death a storm trooper named Brügmann in the melee that night in Lübeck's Grosse Burgstrasse. Naujock had been a mental patient.

reacted to the metropolitan gaudiness like a typical provincial boy. "Friedrichstrasse looked as vulgar as a carnival, the Kurfürstendamm as ostentatious as the made-up mistress of a war profiteer." (This from a man who was to become the Mayor of that mistress.) But in the workers' district of Wedding, stronghold of Communists and Socialists and assorted Berlin originals, Frahm-Brandt perceived "a strange silence . . . this mute protest touched me deeply. Only here and now did I realize the extent of the catastrophe—much more clearly than I had in Lübeck."[59]

There is a certain journalistic triteness and pomposity about these observations by a youth changing trains in a strange capital. And yet, politically, he was right. The workers of Wedding, the working masses of Germany, were still members of a class society. Their leaders had failed them, and now they went along, in the great majority, with the Nazis—not willingly, perhaps, but in a throwback to the serf mentality of their abandoned forefathers.

The SAP conference met at a restaurant in a Dresden suburb. It started the battered and bruised little band on a program of underground resistance that lasted until the outbreak of World War II. In addition to developing an underground press, the newly constituted Reich leadership of the group decided to set up offices abroad to assist the anti-Nazi struggle. Walcher was sent to Paris, Frölich was delegated to Oslo. The latter, wearing clothes that made him seem an unlikely candidate for a fishing trip, was apprehended by border police at the pier in Heiligenhafen, fifty miles northeast of Lübeck. To go to Oslo in his place, the remaining SAP leaders picked Willy Brandt.

Before he left Lübeck, Brandt saw his former boss from the *Volksbote,* Fritz Solmitz, being hounded through the streets of the ancient Hanseatic town with a placard hung around his neck saying "Jewish pig." Solmitz was deported to a concentration camp, where he died. The young man also spent a few hours in the company of "a girl with whom I was very much in love,"[60] Gertrud Meyer, who promised to join him abroad. Finally, he said goodbye to his mother and to Grandfather Frahm, who still had not forgiven him for quitting the SPD.

There was time left for one more leaflet. The soon-to-be fugitive composed it in the office of a ship brokerage where he had worked for his living since graduation from the Johanneum a year before, and he typed out the mimeograph mat at his desk. The leaflet, which was to have ominous consequences for his Socialist friends, was a call to demonstrate against the Nazis on May 1.[61]

The evening of March 31 he went to Travemünde, half an hour downstream from Lübeck. There, in a bar where he had gone for a beer, he had a brush with a youngster he had known from the Socialist movement, who later had gone over to the Nazis. The acquaintance saw nothing suspicious, but Brandt took no more chances. He hid until dawn in the hold of the small trawler, TRA 10, operated by Paul Stooss, who was then thirty-six years old. The arrangements had been made by the stepfather of the captain, Johann Stooss, owner of the boat and a member of the Lübeck SPD. The elder Stooss had told his stepson simply: "Paul, there's a boy coming tonight, and you take him over, right?"[62]

The stowaway had come aboard with a copy of Karl Marx's *Das Kapital,* a couple of spare shirts in his briefcase, and 100 *Reischsmark* in his wallet. In the early light the boat set out for the Danish port of Rødbyhaven in Lolland, about twenty miles and three hours away. Willy Brandt, the conspirator, was not yet twenty years old.

III:

Outside

Herbert Frahm had been born an outsider. Now, as Willy Brandt, he was moving out of his native Lübeck, out of the land that had been his political, social, and cultural home, aboard a fishing boat in the choppy waters of the Baltic that made him, fantasy sailor of his youth, as seasick as could be. The boy had become his own creation, a self-made man with a certain bravado, with a determination as dogged as it was good-humored to prove himself in a world that was falling apart.

Did he have to go, a mere nineteen years old? It was a question often posed in the latter part of his political career by Germans who remembered how uneven and inconclusive those first months of Nazi rule had been in the spring of 1933. But on April 19, less than three weeks after he had fled, "all the Lübeck SAP people were nailed," his comrade, Heinrich Bruhn remembers.[1] "When I was arrested—I was the treasurer of the SAP—they confiscated leaflets I had with me. They were the last that Herbert had drafted. I got about eight months."

Gertrud Meyer, the lanky brunette who was Willy Brandt's first love, fell into the hands of the Nazi police, too. "She had her first letter from him in her handbag," recalled another Lübeck SAP member, Heinrich Wigger, now a retired railway worker. "On the way to jail she ate it. She was held for three weeks. But she betrayed nothing."[2]

"He was in danger," declared the old SPD Mayor, Otto Passarge. He was already well known in Lübeck, and surely he would have been "nailed," too, by the Nazi police on April 19, 1933. His contemporary, Konrad Scharp, remarked: "Everything was ruined for him at home, all professional opportunities were blocked. They were looking for him. So-called society despised him. What was there to keep him in Lübeck?[3] Besides, he had a task assigned by the SAP leadership—now underground—to build a propaganda center and foreign base for the party in Oslo.

Other Lübeckers were gone or going: Thomas Mann to Switzerland; his

43

brother Heinrich Mann to France; the distinguished jurist of the Prussian state, Arnold Brecht, a Lübeck native, to the United States. On April 1, the day of Brandt's flight, Hitler proclaimed a national boycott of Jewish businesses. The publisher of the *Volksbote,* Erich Gottgetreu, was on his way to Palestine. Fritz Solmitz, the other German Jew on the *Volksbote,* was in one of the first concentration camps. The Nazi terror was in full swing. Communists, Social Democrats, Jews were fair game. A revolution, the "counterrevolution" that no orthodox Socialist believed was possible, had begun with remarkable ease and thoroughness, the Nazis daring to coopt the slogans and even the melodies of the Left for what they called "the national awakening."

Few who were serious about politics had taken Hitler seriously. *Mein Kampf* had been around since 1927 and was reissued in massive editions in early 1933. Brandt, for instance, didn't read Hitler's horribly prophetic work until three years after he had left Germany.[4] Outside the German-speaking lands the prevailing attitude of European intellectuals toward Nazism seemed to reflect literally what Karl Kraus, the great Viennese critic had meant ironically: "Concerning Hitler, nothing occurs to me."[5]

Hardly anyone, it seems, had been ready for Hitler's accession, much less the swift consolidation of the Nazi state. Stalin, whose armed forces were still providing a home away from home for the Reichswehr by allowing them training facilities for pilots and tankers, took refuge in silence. A full year after Hitler took power, the Soviet leader still held the position that Fascism was "merely a militant organization of the bourgeoisie." Lev Trotsky, who had foreseen the menace of Hitler more clearly, was already in his "third exile" on one of the Prinkipo Islands near Istanbul, writing much but not much read. Franklin Roosevelt was busy with his New Deal. Japan had quit the League of Nations to gain a freer hand for aggression. France, with 500,000 unemployed, lurched between strikes by the Left and the coup plots of the right-wing Action Française Italy, with eleven years of Mussolini under its belt, was becoming friendlier with Germany. In Spain Gil Robles formed the Confederation of the Autonomous Right, forerunner of the Fascist Falange. Britain, hard hit by the Depression, developed its own Fascist Party, its Left remaining in disarray. In Austria Chancellor Engelbert Dollfuss consolidated his version of Nazism, complete with persecution of Communists and opening of concentration camps. In all major countries arms budgets ballooned.

The Depression, which so many orthodox Marxists had welcomed as the prelude to the downfall of capitalism, confounded them by precipitating the swift expansion of the radical Right. That growth was evident especially in Germany. The Hitler party in the March 5, 1933, Reichstag elections got 17.5

million votes, or close to 44 percent. Altogether the Communists and Social Democrats received only 12 million votes. With the support of right-wing parties, Hitler was able to ram through his emergency powers, the Enabling Act, on March 23, although the SPD deputies, still permitted to vote, rejected it bravely. The KPD had already been cast into illegality.

Scandinavia was practically the only region in Europe where the impact of the Depression on the political landscape was generally positive. In Sweden a Social Democratic majority in the 1932 elections provided impetus for the "middle way" Keynesian economics of Gunnar and Alva Myrdal, which were soon to be implemented under Prime Minister Per Albin Hansson. In Norway the Labor Party gained almost half the seats in the Storting in the 1933 elections. Under Oscar Torp and Martin Tranmael, Det Norske Arbeiderparti almost immediately shed its revolutionary heritage in favor of working within the parliamentary system. Denmark, as will be seen, already had a relatively stable Social Democratic government. All three countries responded to the perils of mass unemployment by instituting farsighted welfare measures and progressive social legislation. In short, Scandinavia withstood the fierce passions of the politics of misery and remained an archipelago of democracy.

On the island of Lolland, the would-be sailor, Willy Brandt, weak from seasickness, was revived with brandy-laced coffee. He took a train to Copenhagen and called at the office of the Danish Youth Federation. He was directed to the home of Oscar Hansen, a chain-smoking thirty-eight-year-old worker poet who was the "youth editor" of Socialdemokraten, the big newspaper of Denmark's ruling party. The beetle-browed writer, wheezing from a tubercular condition and too much tobacco, had already achieved a reputation as the lyricist of the labor movement, having composed some of the most singable songs later collected in the Arbejder Sangbogen,[6] including "Denmark for the People." Hansen was the kind of man who flew a large red flag in front of his house instead of the ubiquitous national banner, the Dannebrog. Yet it was characteristic of his labor-oriented countrymen that they preferred his national song to the universal hymn of the Socialist movement, the 'Internationale.'"[7] Jens Otto Krag, the former Danish Prime Minister, remembers Hansen as "a very generous man—if you asked him for help he never said no." The Hansen apartment was "visited by young people all day long." The Danish capital in the spring of 1933 was awash with German political exiles and with agents—Communist and Nazi. Krag spoke of "the invasion of German refugees," which "gave us a new ideological experience."[8] Most, like Brandt, moved on. Among those who remained was Ernst Wollweber, the thirty-five-year-old German Communist who had taken part in the Kiel naval mutiny of 1918—the forerunner of the abortive German revolution—and now was the hard-bitten director of the Commintern's Western European terror and sabotage operations.[9]

For the time being the Danish Government was tolerant toward the strangers. The Prime Minister, Thorvald Stauning, was a staunch and popular Social Democrat, and Danish Social Democrats were almost uniformly moderate reformists and strict constitutionalists. But the impact of what had happened in neighboring Germany was strong. "We felt a sense of defeat that Germany had been taken over by Hitler without a fight," Krag recalled. "In our hearts we felt the Social Democrats and trade unions should have done more. But it was difficult because they couldn't rely on the Communists." That which the German refugees had fled they found in Denmark, too: the tensions and bitterness engendered by mass unemployment and Right-Left polarization. Denmark's Communist and Nazi parties were small but active. Krag recollected that for Social Democrats, the prime antagonist was Denmark's Conservative Party Youth: "They had had uniforms—leather boots and shoulder straps—and they talked about 'the main chance' to seize power. They had fights in the streets with the Social Democrats."

As ominous as these parallels may have seemed in retrospect, who could then foresee the range and destructive power of the Nationalist Socialist tidal wave? Much later Brandt wrote:

> Even in Copenhagen I realized how difficult it was to give foreigners a clear picture of the events in Germany. My Danish friends intimated they thought the stories about cruelties in Germany very much exaggerated. The Germans were a cultured people, were they not? Wasn't the judgment of the refugees 'too subjective,' even warped? It must be. Were we not too pessimistic when we declared Hitler would plunge the world into war?[10]

After several days in the Hansen apartment in the borough of Brönshöj, Herbert Willy Brandt Frahm embarked on a packet boat to Oslo. Again he went straight to a newspaperman, Finn Moe, the thirty-one-year-old foreign editor of *Arbeiderbladet,* the powerful Norwegian Labor Party's paper. Moe had been a correspondent in Berlin from 1927 to 1932, so he knew his Nazis. Brandt and his SAP comrades had also advised Moe he was coming. Brandt found him "eager to help a comrade in need."[11]Moe arranged an allowance from a trade union fund for him right away and helped him find an apartment. Volunteering for clerical work in the secretariat of the trade union federation, he was soon receiving thirty Norwegian crowns a week plus a rent allowance. "My life was very modest," he remembered. "But not at all harsh."[12] Nor did the demand by Norway's immigration authorities that he practice "political abstinence" seem to have inhibited his activities. He was appointed head of the Norwegian Refugee Federation, a job that cost headaches rather than backaches, since the number of exiles in Oslo remained small. "Very soon I decided that I didn't want to be a refugee," he wrote. "Much as I was concerned with the sorrows and troubles of my companions in misfortune I realized the necessity of taking roots again. I did not want to be an outsider."[13]

Very soon he was writing for Norwegian publications, too. Less than a month after arriving in the capital, *Arbeider Ungdommen* (*Workers Youth*) published his first article in the Norwegian language in its May 1 edition. In it Brandt described the enormous appeal of the Nazis to a young generation facing unemployment and in conflict with the lament:

> Most young Germans are in the Fascist camp today. Starting with revolutionary sentiments they landed on the counter-revolutionary side. The day of reckoning will come when the soldiers of young Germany see that in their nationalistic fervor they allowed everything to culminate in barbarism. That'll be the day of rude awakening.[14]

He was learning Norwegian in great gulps, discovering a talent with foreign tongues that was to become almost legendary "I had the parrot gift"' he would recall forty years later. "I learn by ear."[15] Within a few months he would be making public speeches in Norwegian. His earnings from journalism soon provided enough to cut him free from the trade union allowance. He could turn out a front-page story containing firsthand knowledge in a new language, and he was busy: writing for newspapers and magazines, tending the Refugee Federation, learning more Norwegian, and cultivating cost with SAP comrades and their sister organization, the Norwegian Labor Party.

Soon, too, he had the beginnings of a new *Nestwärme,* that "warmth of the nest" always so important to him. In June Trudel Meyer was released by her interrogators in Lübeck. She obtained a passport without difficulty and traveled to Oslo to join Willy. The two set up housekeeping together, and Brandt evidently introduced her to some of their new acquaintances as his wife, for she appears in a group picture in a summer frock standing next to him on a sunny porch as "Gertrud Frahm." The photograph, listing him as "Willy Brandt (Herbert Frahm)," was taken in July 1933 at the tiny resort town of Dorr near the long Mjøsa Lake about twenty-five miles north of Oslo. It is contained in the book *Mot Dag og Erling Falk,* about the Norwegian Socialist movement "Toward the Dawn" and its remarkable leader, Erling Falk.[17]

Brandt had been invited to participate in a Mot Dag project that had already been under way for two years: a workers' dictionary (*Arbeidernes Leksikon*). It was a joint effort of Communists and Socialists in a country where the two groupings had intermingled more than almost any others in the world.

Jacob Walcher, the forty-six-year-old SAP leader who had come from Prague on his way to Paris to establish an executive committee for the splinter party's operations from exile, introduced Brandt to Mot Dag. A Spartacist in the Liebknecht mold, Walcher had been chairman of the founding convention of the Communist Party of Germany in 1918-19 and had remained a Communist at heart even in opposition to the Muscovite KPD and after joining the in-between SAP. Willy Brandt looked to him in this "sectarian" phase of revolutionary élan, as he later defined it, and nearly three decades later he could still write of him as "my friend Jacob Walcher."[18]

Walcher is in the photographs taken at Dorr, too, along with Sweden's Karl Kilbom, soon to become a Socialist, and other opposition Communists blown this way by political cyclones of Hitler, Stalin, and Trotsky. They had been brought together in a casual fashion in earlier years through efforts to create some order out of the disarray of the European Left. Still active in this attempt was Heinrich Brandler, a German Communist leader who had been booted out by Moscow. Erling Falk, the founder and leading spirit of Mot Dag, had visited Brandler in Germany in 1932 and had allied his group, as Kilbom did with his Swedes, with something bravely entitled the International Association of Communist Oppositions. Now Brandler was in Norway, too. A chronicler gives a telling picture of exile politics, probably from that same scene photographed at Dorr:

> When Brandler and his onetime party colleague, Jacob Walcher (now with the SAP) split "theoretical" hairs and nearly flared up in discussing what was "truly" centrism, Right and Left opportunism, Kilbom waited impatiently until they finished and then banged his heavy miner's fist on the table and swore pithily that he now understood exactly how Hitler could gain victory: When two people who were in agreement on practically everything preoccupied themselves mainly with scholastics even after having been forced out of their country then he wanted just to write off both of them.[19]

Such exchanges impressed Brandt as characteristic of the exile-émigré scene. He spoke of "daily quarrels which depressed me because of their senselessness."[20] One involving Brandler concerned a Mot Dag man who had just written a book about the Third Reich. Brandler complained that the Norwegian ignored the theses of his Communist opposition splinter, the

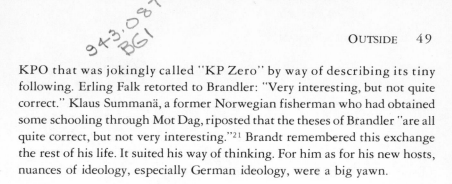

KPO that was jokingly called "KP Zero" by way of describing its tiny following. Erling Falk retorted to Brandler: "Very interesting, but not quite correct." Klaus Summanä, a former Norwegian fisherman who had obtained some schooling through Mot Dag, riposted that the theses of Brandler "are all quite correct, but not very interesting."[21] Brandt remembered this exchange the rest of his life. It suited his way of thinking. For him as for his new hosts, nuances of ideology, especially German ideology, were a big yawn.

With Walcher young Brandt talked SAP politics, but also the practical aspects of promoting party activity in Nazi Germany. "We discussed ways and means of how to strengthen the underground in Germany. Money was needed. Could we get it in Norway? From what sources?"[22]

Alone among the anti-Nazi political organizations, the SAP, which had discerned the Nazi movement for what it was well before Hitler gained power, made the transformation into illegality rather smoothly. It had the advantages of relatively small and controllable numbers, less visibility than the SPD and KPD, the fact that it had been officially dissolved in March 1933 and, finally, the determination of youthful cadres whose demand for a united front was still valid.[23] But it paid its gruesome price. The boldness of young SAP members and their lack of vigilance in distributing anti-Nazi leaflets cost the arrest of ninety-one of them in the Dresden area alone in the spring of 1933. The defendants in the ensuing court case were sentenced to a total of a hundred years. In Breslau, another SAP stronghold, the Gestapo captured more activists in July and, after obtaining confessions by twisting rusty steel springs into their rectums, arrested twenty leading party officials. One month later the Nazi secret police broke up the Berlin underground leadership of the SAP.[24] The dedication of the survivors—there were still 14,000 in 1934—and existence of foreign bureaus and supporters kept the hopeless cause alive. Jens Otto Krag, who was studying in Copenhagen at the time, remembered the visits of a young SAP "illegal" from Germany: "He was named Bob and he came from time to time to recuperate and to pick up fresh printed material. At one point he never came back."

Hitler's *Gleichschaltung* (literally "synchronization," a typical Nazi euphemism) had struck the entire German Left with unmitigated force. On June 20, 1933, the eve of Hitler's ban of the Social Democratic Party, Storm Troopers raided hundreds of dwellings of known Leftists and took away more than 500 persons—many of them leading party officials. Nearly one quarter were tortured and murdered that same night, their faces pressed into sacks of straw to muffle their cries—and if they were still too loud the SS posses revved up their motorcycles to drown the noise. Parallel roundups practically eliminated the SPD inside Germany, although a few young illegals remained active.[25]

The KPD fared no better. Its 300,000 card-carrying members were already "in illegality." But most were well known and easily isolated or seized by the new masters. Ernst Thälmann, the KPD chief, was one of the first to go, seized March 3 with three close confidants, evidently through betrayal. Characteristic of the blind conviction of most German Leftists that Hitler had no staying power, the KPD security officer felt comfortable enough to call Herbert Wehner that night on a regular telephone line to ask if he knew of what was going on. With Thälmann behind bars a struggle for succession opened, and some of the rivals cooperated with the Gestapo in their zeal to wipe out competition. "There was a provocateur-blackmailer practice by top-rank or ambitious people to 'nail' other comrades and 'expose' them," Wehner wrote of this dreadful phase, which he observed as a twenty-seven-year-old member of the German Communist inner circle.[26]

Wehner, who had begun his political career in the SPD and switched early to the KPD, now watched with mounting horror how the KPD literally tore itself to pieces. His unpublished account reads like a grisly passage of the Old Testament. John Schehr, fresh from Moscow with new orders as party secretary was seized in November 1933 in a Berlin apartment along with other KPD officials, tortured, and killed. A rival of Schehr, Hermann Schubert, escaped to Moscow only to be liquidated in the Stalin purges. Another rival, Walter Ulbricht, forty, slipped out to Prague and then moved to Paris. The underground was manned largely by younger Communists, among them Erich Honecker, twenty-one, born a year before Brandt in the Saar coal region. The Gestapo caught him in 1935.

The ravaging of the Left had the double effect of alienating those who stayed behind and survived in the isolation of prisons and concentration camps and those who escaped into the isolation of exile. Kurt Schumacher, forty-four, a World War I veteran whose right arm had been shot off, was picked up in 1933 and thrown into a concentration camp. He emerged bitter and sick twelve years later to lead the postwar SPD. Erich Ollenhauer, the thirty-one-year-old SPD youth specialist, wandered from Prague to Paris to London—uprooted in such a fashion that he found it difficult to strike deep roots in the political earth of postwar Germany. Ernst Reuter, forty-three, the redoubtable SPD Mayor of Magdeburg, was confined in a concentration camp for sixteen months, after which he made his way to Turkey and worked there until 1946.

In Oslo while all this was going on, Willy Brandt—"illegal" in several senses—was learning how to use invisible inks and other paraphernalia of the underground. The Norwegian immigration police still had not granted him a residence permit, and the insinuation by a Conservative tabloid that he was involved in a Finnish espionage affair in the autumn of 1933 made him a public figure in a fashion he could have done without. Only the intervention of Oscar Torp, chairman of the Norwegian Labor Party, saved him from expulsion.[27] Thereafter, he appears to have had no difficulty with the Norwegian authorities in pursuing his SAP activities, which were probably sporadic.

Mot Dag members—there were roughly a hundred in Oslo—had encouraged Brandt to take up studies at Oslo University. After some procedural difficulties he enrolled in the philosophy faculty. A year later, in the autumn of 1934, he received a grade of "good" on his first—and last—university examination. Studies, swimming in the summer, skiing in the winter, and the company of Trudel Meyer made up the bright side of his first year in exile. The Mot Dag people also drew him into the capital's intellectual-social life. He became acquainted not only with locally prominent Leftist writers like Arnulf Överland and Sigurd Hoel, but also with non-Leftists.[28] Despite its growth—Oslo had a population of over a quarter million—the capital still reflected the friendly community spirit that dominated rural Norway. It was a society notable for its monetary modesty and lack of competitiveness. Physicians preferred salaries to direct cash payment.[29] Even in sports "invidious contrasts" were considered gauche and playing down one's accomplishments was almost a cult. These qualities appealed greatly to young Brandt, and he grew to prefer them to the more stratified German system of values.

Mot Dag provided him with a place to work and eat his meals at the organization's small headquarters. Here he was in frequent contact with Erling Falk, whom Brandt recalled as "sort of a high priest of intellectualism,"[30] although Falk had been and was more than that. Falk had gone to the United States in 1907. Along with other Scandinavian immigrants like Joe Hill, he became involved with the revolutionary syndicalist movement known as the International Workers of the World and met Big Bill Haywood of the IWW in Chicago (as had that other Norwegian Socialist wanderer, Martin Tranmael). Falk returned to Norway in 1918 and helped found the worker-intellectual Mot Dag movement and its periodical of the same name in 1921. Active in the Norwegian Labor Party until 1925, he was expelled, joined the Communist splinter group, and left it in 1928 to become a kind of ascetic guru of the Norwegian Left—bald, heavy-lipped, with eagle eyes set back under a massive brooding brow, a cartoonist's delight.

Brandt's encounters with Falk and company may have determined his relationship to "intellectuals" from then on, for he describes himself as being both attracted and repulsed. He spoke of "stimulating hours, literary discoveries, a broadening of my intellectual horizon." This went on for two years, in a period during which Falk's influence in Oslo politics steadily dwindled. Brandt broke with Mot Dag in May 1935, the year the newly moderate Labor Party came to power under Prime Minister Johan Nygaardsvold. Of Mot Dag Brandt wrote, "I left this circle because I could not stomach its intellectual arrogance," and, of Falk,

> with all due respect for his and his friends' accomplishments, I parted from them with the firm belief that in the world of today there is no place for ivory towers to which intellectuals can retire to lead a life of splendid isolation."[31]

During the interlude, however, Brandt had willingly associated himself with the more radical elements of the Norwegian Left, not only in terms of ideas but also in terms of political organizations. He had joined the Youth Federation of the Labor Party soon after his arrival and, under the influence of Walcher and Falk, joined the "revolutionaries" of the Federation's Left fringe. It was a natural outgrowth of his position in the SAP and his own confused politics. "As a young man I thought of myself as a Left Socialist—as Communist in the sense of the *Manifesto* of Marx and Engels," Brandt recalled.[32]

Norway's Left was in ferment. The Labor Party had joined the Communist International after World War I and fomented antimilitary strikes and revolutionary agitation in the early 1920s. Its majority broke with Moscow in 1923, reunited with the Social Democrats in 1927 and, in the election that year, became the largest faction in the Storting. Renunciation of the theory of the dictatorship of the proletariat and a reformist anti-Depression program helped the Laborites win 69 of the 150 parliamentary seats in 1933. By the time the seasick Willy Brandt landed on Lolland, the majority of Norwegian Socialists were moving gradually to the center.

Per Monsen, a Brandt contemporary and friend from those days, sees the Oslo radicalism of the early 1930s in a broad perspective. In a 1974 conversation, he said, "We were very concerned with the defeat of the Social Democrats in Germany, that the Social Democrats and trade unions didn't take a stand of strong physical resistance to the Fascists. It was less a Left revolutionary sentiment than a question of militancy, a question of resistance. He (Brandt) felt at home between the Second (Social Democrat) and Third (Communist) Internationals.[33]

Both Walcher and Falk were attempting to establish links with Trotsky and his followers. Walcher and the SAP's Paul Frölich had called on Trotsky at St.

Palais—near Royan—in July 1933. Falk went to Copenhagen in 1934 to see Trotsky. But the Russian revolutionary had mixed feelings about the splinter representatives, whom he viewed as a distraction from the main task of revitalizing and de-Stalinizing the regular Communist parties—boring from within. There is an exchange of correspondence between Brandt and Walcher from the autumn of 1933 referring to a Trotsky complaint that the Norwegian Labor Party was "no good," and Brandt pointed out later that Mot Dag hadn't bothered to issue a First of May call to the workers of Norway. "Our friends looked at us with astonishment and sadness," he noted. "That was asking too much. Mot Dag never said what one should do."[34]

For Brandt in this period the Norwegian component, the German component, and the international component of his political life, though related in the context of the European Left, conflicted here and there. For the time being he was powerfully influenced by Walcher. In late August 1933 Walcher had brought the exile SAP together with fourteen other splinter groups from eleven different countries in Paris—including the Trotskyite "International Bureau of the Left Opposition" under Trotsky's follower, Erwin Bauer. The general idea was an assembly of the "genuinely Communist" parties aimed at simultaneously overthrowing Fascism and capitalism. The Trotskyites wanted to transform this into an anti-Stalin "Fourth International" right away. But they were outvoted. Instead, the majority formed the "International Bureau of Revolutionary Socialist Unity." A parallel effort was made by the youth groups of the splinter parties, to culminate in a conference aimed at the establishment of an independent (from Moscow) Communist Youth International.[35] Their meeting was set for February 24, 1934, in the Dutch town of Laren, near Amsterdam, and Brandt was to be a delegate to it.

He traveled with a Norwegian identity paper in the company of Finn Moe, representing the Norwegian Socialist Youth, and Äke Ording, thirty-four, also representing the Mot Dag group. They took the boat train from Copenhagen to Germany, going first class as a kind of camouflage. It was a good idea, Äke Ording said in a 1974 interview, since Swedish delegates to the Laren conference were picked up by German border authorities in their second-class coach and turned back. "They didn't think to look for us in first class," he said, recalling the trip with a big grin. Crossing Germany, the train waited in Hamburg, and here the trio from Oslo had time to watch a huge Nazi parade of Storm Troopers—"long columns in jackboots with torches and banners. It was awesome," Ording remembered. They passed on to Laren without incident and spent the night in a rooming house.

In the afternoon while the delegates were preparing for the conference, Dutch police surrounded the house and arrested all foreigners.[36] Four

Germans, including the SAP's Franz Bobzien, a Hamburg teacher, and Kurt Liebermann, a young party official from Dresden, were taken handcuffed to the border of the Third Reich, sixty miles to the east, and handed over to the Gestapo. Bobzien spent the rest of his short life in Nazi prisons and concentration camps, dying, apparently, as a member of a suicide squad sent to clear a minefield in 1941. Liebermann got a six-year prison term. Brandt was spared this fate by the intercession of his Norwegian comrades and because he had his Norwegian papers.

"While they searched us they asked, 'Are there any Germans here? All Germans together.'" Ording recalled. "It was Brandt's intention to tell that he was a German and be brought together with the other Germans. That was shocking to us. A discussion started. Finn and I said we couldn't trust this and the only security is to stick to your Norwegian residence permit. It took quite some time to convince him to take this line. Finally, he agreed.

"We also agreed that all the delegates would try to meet in Brussels at a public school that had a Trotskyite janitor. A police van came and took us to the main prison in Amsterdam. On the way we sang the "Internationale." At the prison we were in a big lockup with all kinds of criminals."[37]

The roundup had apparently been arranged by the Mayor of Laren, a Nazi sympathizer. In the jail, Brandt recalled, a German Trotskyite teased Finn Moe: "What does your King say to this?"[38] Ording, a lawyer by training, learning of the plans of Dutch authorities to dump them all on the Belgian border, raised a fuss, demanding to see the Norwegian Ambassador, the head of the jail, and the chief of police. He did not want the group to become playthings of the border patrols.

"I protested that we had come to a democratic country and expected to be treated accordingly," he said forty years later. "In the end we were allowed to take the train to Belgium." They found the school with the Trotskyite janitor and convened in the basement rooms. The tragically interrupted conference was held in such secrecy that some contemporary chroniclers still believe it took place in Lille, France, as the organizers had led their persecutors to think it would. It was a growing custom of the underground Left to advertise meetings in one country and hold them in another.

Safely back in Norway, Brandt got busy again with studies, with the SAP, with the Norwegian Left, and with refugees. In March 1934 August and Irmgard Enderle, two Walcher allies who had miraculously escaped the Gestapo swoop in Dresden after publishing and distributing the SAP underground paper, *SAZ*, successfully for months under the Nazi noses, reached Oslo. Brandt helped them get living quarters and financial aid until they moved over to Stockholm to establish an SAP bureau there. In April the Youth Federation held a convention in Oslo at which it was supposed to follow the mother Labor Party (DNA) into the moderate reform channel. The radical Left tried to prevent this, and one of its tactics was to put up Brandt as a speaker.

"He was in focus in Norway after less than one year," recalled Oddvar Aas, a Laborite contemporary, "and he had been invited to the convention as a guest from the 'second-and-one-half Internationale.' "

Brandt sat in the visitors' gallery, where his mere presence as an ally of the Left minority that wanted to topple the Federation leadership caused a small tumult. At one point the DNA chairman shook his fist at him, shouting: "You, Willy Brandt, will be thrown out of the country!"[39] Also at issue in the convention was the stance of the Norwegian Left toward the Soviet Union.

"I committed a grave mistake,"[40] Brandt, pro-Moscow in a phase when the majority of Norwegian Socialists were turning inward, wrote of his part in the Left Opposition:

> The Soviet Union appeared to be . . . the target of Nazi aggression—and thereby objectively speaking an ally of the German opposition. . . . In my case it took several years before I overcame the dogmatic narrowness and sectarian elements of my group."[41]

He wrote also of his own "political dilettantism" in those years.

In Lübeck he had offended Julius Leber, and Leber forgave him. Now he was offending his generous hosts, and they forgave him, too. Trygve Bratteli, a DNA moderate who was later to become Norwegian Prime Minister, recalled that a vote to prevent Brandt from speaking at the Oslo convention was "a decision against the Left, not against the person of Brandt." Perhaps they trusted, rightly, in the power of their example. Bratteli would observe four decades later: "I'd like to say that moderate Nordic Social Democracy had a very beneficial influence on Brandt."[42]

Brandt himself thought no single person or party program had a decisive effect on him at this time. "To say I was a radical Socialist or Communist then would be too schematic," he reflected. "I did some doublethink, also in skepticism toward the SAP." Nor was Martin Tranmael a special influence on him, he said in reponse to a query. "He was a great popular leader, and he wrote as he spoke—three words between two periods." He roared with laughter as he recalled some quintessential Tranmaelisms: "Now it is time to do the right thing for everybody for a long time to come." "Eduard Benes (Czechoslovak interwar leader), the prominent states-and-gentleman."[43]

One significant outcome of the Laren-Lille conference was that Brandt's identity became known to the Gestapo; his captured comrades, knowing he had escaped, had named him as the ringleader to avoid more drastic punishment for themselves.[44] Another was a loosely organized independent "revolutionary-socialist" Youth Office, which began publishing *International Youth Bulletin* in Stockholm. Brandt was a contributor to this modest sheet as he was also to the Walcher-line periodicals: *Neue Front (New Front)* hectographed in Paris first as a fortnightly and then printed as a monthly with the slogan, "Organ for proletarian-revolutionary assembly"; *Sozialistische Jugend (Socialist Youth)*; and, for a time, *Kampfbereit (Battle Ready*—the slogan of the SAP members with which they were supposed to salute each other, like "Red Front!" for Communists and "Heil Hitler!" for Nazis). *Kampfbereit* was printed on thin, hard-to-wrinkle paper in small type, for distribution in the Reich, with excerpts from other exile publications, too.

Brandt was learning new tricks of illegality: false papers, codes, false-bottomed suitcases, the stuffing of the bindings of innocent books with propaganda. "Only a small number of our publications reached their destination," he dryly observed. The codes they used were rather simple: Paris was "ADS," a Germany acronym for "on the Seine"; Prague was "ADM," the acronym for "on the Moldau"; and Berlin was "Metro," for metropolis. Brandt remembers "highly unpleasant encounters with righteous Trotskyites" in this work. Brandt found Trotsky himself "interesting, partly fascinating," "terribly righteous." His attempt to visit Trotsky in 1934 was refused with the argument: "He doesn't wish to see you because you are with the Norwegian Labor Party."[45]

Brandt at this time was carrying on a heavy correspondence. "Friends and comrades were scattered all over Europe. The urge to keep our personal relationships alive was as great as the need we felt to exchange our opinions and experiences. Never again have I written so many letters as in the first years of my exile." Not that he was utterly lonesome. "Gertrud helped me and put some order into my rather disorderly life of being permanently on the move from one furnished room to another with a small suitcase holding all my possessions, and the coffeehouses as our meeting places."[46]

He had started out boarding in a single room "with nice people," moved to a *pension,* then to a small apartment house. Toward the end of 1935 Gertrud Meyer found them a larger apartment "simply furnished" near the university library.[47] She undoubtedly loved him, had gone to jail with a piece of his writing in her mouth, had traveled into the unknown to be with him, had shared his uncertain existence in a foreign capital. Per Monsen remembered her as "a typical young Socialist, very bright and very friendly—pretty in a German way, very German, but soft-spoken, and she smiled a lot, the best qualities."[48]

In the summer of 1935 the two of them arranged to meet their Lübeck mothers in Copenhagen, which was aswarm with agents of the Gestapo and the Comintern.[49] The visit was a kind of formalization of their liaison. Of the meeting with his mother, he wrote:

> Two years had passed . . . I could hardly believe that it was not more than two years. I felt much older. My Lübeck childhood was far, far away, no ties bound me to my native town. Certainly I took an active interest in the fate of my friends, and the news of the suicide of my grandfather (that year) had been a great shock to me, bitter and painful. I was also depressed by the knowledge that my mother and stepfather had to endure annoying interrogations and all sorts of chicaneries on account of me. But Mother had not a single word of reproach. I must not worry about her . . . I did what I had to do.[50]

What could a German Leftist do to mobilize force against Hitler? The trouble with the Independent Left was that it had no real leaders and only a vague idea of unity. It also had no headquarters and no money. Some of its members were in Prague, some in Paris, some in Scandinavia. Fascism had its Hitler, Communism its Stalin and Trotsky. And the German Left? Jacob Walcher, the nice guy from Wain in Württemberg who quoted Goethe and Schiller? There was nobody. "The entire German Left had no leadership personality," said Hans Meyer, a journalist who remembered it from the inside. "Paul Levi could have done it, but he was dead. Seydewitz didn't have the stuff. Rosenfeld was a compulsive optimist. Rudolf Breitscheid (of the SPD) was a compulsive optimist."[51]

With Moscow's approval, the German Communists had organized a tremendously successful campaign on behalf of Georgi Dimitrov, the Bulgarian Comintern man accused of plotting to set the Reichstag afire. The brilliant propagandist, Willi Münzenberg, made the Nazis look ridiculous with his triumphant first *Brown Book* in August 1933 and his second *Brown Book* eight months later. Dimitrov, who was much softer than his reputation, was acquitted in February 1934 along with two co-defendants in the Leipzig trial and apparently exchanged for three Reichswehr officers arrested on Stalin's orders for espionage.[52] Despite the decimation of the KPD apparatus and the problems of practicing resistance while remaining obedient to Stalin, the German Communists also managed to secure a front seat on the bandwagon of Leftist unity. It hardly seemed fair. The SAP, which had preached "United Front!" since 1931, was being either ignored or attacked. The SPD took up the cause in early 1934 with a manifesto issued in Prague entitled, "The Struggle and Aim of Revolutionary Socialism." Yet it was the Communist Party, with its shrewd tacticians and the support of the Russians, that had the last word, when in July 1934 at a session in Moscow, the KPD Central Committee issued a resolution for "Creation of a United Front of the Toiling Masses Against the Hitler Dictatorship."[53] Three months later Walter Ulbricht published a reply to the SPD unity appeals calling "For Unity of Action, Against Hitler-Fascism," in the Communist *Neue Weltbühne,* an exile periodical printed in Prague. The appeal caused great confusion because, only two years before, Ulbricht had been the apostle of the anti-unity forces. But the tactic worked. Against the popular successes of the KPD, the Social Democrats and the SAP had pitifully little to offer.

Still, there were some things an activist in exile like Willy Brandt could do. There was the case of the imprisoned SAP leaders—Max Köhler, Dr. Stefan Szende, a Hungarian journalist who had attached himself to the splinter, and twenty-two others. Most of them had been betrayed in August by a spy, and they faced trial in Berlin in late autumn. Brandt participated in an international protest campaign that included a demonstration of 300,000 workers in Paris in October 1934, telegrams from prominent writers, and petitions. Brandt got Brynjulf Bull, a well-known Oslo lawyer to sign the Oslo petition, which was framed in such a way that it looked like an official representation of the Norwegian lawyers' association. It helped Köhler and Szende to get light sentences and leave Hitler Germany—Köhler to Paris and Szende to Stockholm.[54]

Brandt also participated in the ensuing campaign to obtain nomination of Carl von Ossietzky for a Nobel Peace Prize. Ossietzky, the descendant of impoverished Silesian aristocrats, born in 1889 in Hamburg, as a schoolboy gravitated to the Social Democrats. During the Weimar era he emerged as an outstanding journalist whose central theme was antimilitarism. The exposure in his *Weltbühne* in 1929 of Reichswehr budget manipulations brought a charge of treason on his head. After lengthy proceedings he was convicted and imprisoned in 1932. Freed by amnesty at Christmas that same year, he chose to stay in Berlin and continue slashing at the Nazis in *Weltbühne* rather than flee to safety. He was seized in the Reichstag fire roundup, locked up in Spandau Fortress, and then taken to a concentration camp for beatings and torture.[55] A report to the International Red Cross on his maltreatment in 1934 stirred a "Save Ossietzky" campaign that swelled with the support of Thomas Mann, H. G. Wells, Virginia Woolf, and Albert Einstein. Brandt became involved during a visit in January 1935 to Paris, where he attended a conference organized by the London Office of the Independent Labour Party—an ally of the SAP headed by James Maxton and Fenner Brockway. They launched a peace campaign that eventually took in the "Save Ossietzky" cause. When the campaign peaked in a demand that Ossietzky be awarded the

Nobel Prize, the Hitler government became alarmed and the German *chargé d'affaires* in Oslo transmitted a warning not to offend the Reich by honoring "a state criminal." The Peace Prize Committee of the Storting finessed the issue by voting not to give any award in 1935. But in the following year, due in part to Brandt's lobbying with DNA friends who were on the five-member committee, Ossietzky was named. His cause had apparently been helped by the clumsiness of the Nazis in enlisting Knut Hamsun, the distinguished Norwegian novelist who had turned pro-Hitler, against Ossietzky. This move backfired in Norway.[56] Ossietzky was, of course, not released to go to Oslo to receive the prize, but the award compelled the Nazis to soften their treatment of the famous prisoner. Hitler was so infuriated he promulgated a law forbidding citizens of the Reich to accept a Nobel Prize. The Ossietzky affair represented at least a resounding moral victory of the anti-Hitler forces at a time when the Nazis were riding high.

In these years, Norway was being drawn more and more into the ideological contests of the Continent, as the case of Trotsky illustrated. His French stay having been terminated, the outcast revolutionary asked for Norwegian asylum in the spring of 1935. Intercession by Brandt's acquaintance Heinz Epe with the DNA was successful, and the Russian exile arrived in Oslo in June. *Arbeiderbladet* declared that Norway was "honored by Trotsky's presence," and Martin Tranmael extended personal greetings. But there was opposition, too—from the tiny band of Norwegian Nazis led by Major Vidkun Quisling that called themselves the Nasjonal Samling. For a time Trotsky lived in relative peace as a house guest of the *Arbeiderbladet* editor, Konrad Knudsen (who was also friendly with Brandt). But within a year Stalin had begun his great purge trials and Trotsky, one of his principal targets, was heaved into new notoriety. His flaming denunciation of the Moscow purges made the Norwegian Labor Government increasingly uneasy, the more so when the Soviet Government sent a stiff note threatening to cut off trade, if Norway continued to harbor him. Trygve Lie, the Minister of Justice, who was also acting as Foreign Minister, had initially been among those welcoming Trotsky. Now he turned about and ordered him to sign a paper agreeing to self-censorship. A Trotsky interview with *Arbeiderbladet* had been too provocative for Lie's taste, and he was also getting some heat from Quisling's supporters. Trotsky refused to sign, and Lie ordered him interned prior to deportation. In a court hearing, Trotsky accused Lie of "the first act of surrender to Nazism in your own country" and warned prophetically: "The day is near when the Nazis will drive you from your country." He also noted with asperity that the Norwegians were in the midst of campaigning for the release of Ossietzky from a concentration camp while he, Trotsky, was being subjected to "slanders" by Lie. But it was no use. He was deported to Mexico on December 19.[57]

Brandt, who had been rebuffed earlier by the Trotsky circle, learned of all this much later from his friend, Inge Scheflo, one of the exile's Norwegian bodyguards. Brandt himself was out of the country during most of Trotsky's Norwegian tribulations.

In June 1936 Willy Brandt had received orders by mail from "Jim Schwab," the pseudonym used by Walcher, to make his way to Berlin and take charge of the SAP underground called Organization Metro. Again Gertrude Meyer provided decisive help. Though she continued to live with Brandt, a young Mot Dag member, Gunnar Gaasland, had married her in a justice-of-the-peace ceremony to help her obtain the safety of Norwegian citizenship and the assurance of a labor permit. Now she persuaded Gaasland to obtain a passport, which she handed over to Brandt. Another Norwegian friend substituted Brandt's photograph, and he began practicing Gaasland's signature. The passport never failed him.

On his first trip, he journeyed by way of Berlin to Paris to get instructions from Walcher. Hitler's troops had marched into the demilitarized Rhineland on March 7, and the lack of any oppositon from the great powers only whetted the Führer's appetite and caused fresh dismay to anti-Nazis.[58] The European Left had taken some comfort in the surprising victory of the Popular Front in the bitterly fought April 26 national elections in France—one fruit of the united front policy authorized by Stalin one year before and only reluctantly implemented by his satellite parties in Western Europe, if at all. Léon Blum took office June 4 as Premier with a *Front Populaire* Cabinet. Spain's *Frente Popular* republican government had been in power since February and was engaged in the dangerous process of purging the Spanish Army of "reactionaries." All this should have been enough to gladden the hearts of unity-minded SAP members. Instead Brandt found his German comrades in Paris and their putative Left allies plunged into "continual quarreling and wrangling, a rather unpleasant refugee atmosphere . . . this picture of human pettiness.[59]

What happened? In February the SAP had sent delegates to a German *Volksfront* conference that drew 118 representatives of the SPD, KPD, and two other splinters. Heinrich Mann served as chairman of the meeting in the Hotel Lutetia. The German Communists, numerically stronger and stiffened by their orders from Moscow, found new ways to trample on the splinter groups. First they insisted that a German popular front program must include the demand for reconstitution of Germany on a "bourgeois-democratic basis." However transparent and even laughable this may seem as a Communist platform, it was an affront to the really militant Leftists of the SAP and its allies from the tiny International Socialist League of Struggle and the Revolutionary Socialists of Germany. A still sharper dispute loomed with the issue of Trotsky, which the Moscovite Communists determined to use as a club to smash all rivals on the Left. Herbert Wehner, the KPD official who was commuting at this time between Paris, Prague, and border towns where he could meet with underground couriers, spoke of "several positive experiences in working together with Social Democrats and SAP functionaries." Then Walter Ulbricht entered the scene, with the transfer of the KPD's exile Politburo from Prague to Paris. "He wanted to eliminate the SAP functionaries as much as possible," Wehner wrote. "He smashed the beginnings of an agreement on joint assistance for political prisoners (in Germany)."[60] Another sad hour for the German Left—it could not unite even in face of dire need. Somebody always had to come out on top. No wonder Brandt reacted with "a bitter thought" and asked himself: "For that I should risk my head?"[61] Still he had "no regrets" about entering the Third Reich, although, traveling under false colors, "I was not free of fear as I rode with the night train from Paris to Berlin."[62]

Queer, to enter the capital of your own homeland disguised as a foreign student interested in "German science and culture," there to attend lectures at the Friedrich Wilhelm University. One minute the innocent Gunnar Gaasland, the next the conspiratorial Willy Brandt. He took a furnished room with "a nice middle-aged woman," Frau Hamel, on the corner of Kurfürstendamm and Joachimsthalerstrasse in the heart of the fashionable West End shopping district and arranged a *Treff* (rendezvous) with a man in the palatial Wertheim department store on Potsdamer Platz who put him in touch with a chain of five-member cells that made up the Berlin underground of the SAP—still several hundred strong.

Only a few days after his arrival Brandt had an awkward brush with a "fellow Norwegian" who turned out to be a Nazi sympathizer. It happened when he was exchanging "student *Marks*" at the Reichsbank and the clerk pointed to the other student with the "good news" that he was a countryman. Brandt had a hard time shaking him.[63]

In his student guise Brandt spent many mornings at the Prussian State Library, where he worked his way "systematically" through the standard Nazi literature, including *Mein Kampf* and Alfred Rosenberg's racist mishmash, the *Myth of the 20th Century*. Brandt's SAP mission was twofold—to get a picture of the Left underground and its possibilities for resistance activities and to inform the comrades how the party viewed the situation at a time when almost everything seemed to be going the way of the Nazis.

"How could we, under these conditions, keep the spirit of resistance alive?" the comrades asked themselves. "In the big factories there were still cadres of trustworthy comrades. We tried to organize a semi-legal opposition."[64] It was hardly a heroic task, given the nature and size of the scattered band. But it was dangerous enough in a society where betrayal was handsomely rewarded and the secret police were everywhere. Brandt appears to have been well prepared, for he had worked out a ten-point outline as a basis for discussion in the ranks of the illegals. It noted Hitler's war plans and the imminence of war, the "contradictions" in the Soviet Union, and the continuing need for "revolutionary unity." It also preached solidarity with the Soviet Union as "the country without capitalists." Finally, it stressed the need for SAP activists to "work out the best guidelines for the policy of revolutionary socialism" and not stand on the sidelines of the "bolshevist wing of the workers movement."[65] In an essay on "The Practice of Illegality" he observed that "passively sticking together has an eminently political significance. But it has nothing to do with regular illegal revolutionary work."[66]

His head was "full of figures and code words," as he moved from place to place to meet his fellow illegals—in city forests, at movie theaters, "but never inside an apartment."[67] Now and then he would spot someone who knew him as Herbert Frahm from Lübeck or as Willy Brandt the exile. "They kept my nerves under steady tension."

"There were no organized things for me to do," said Brandt of his underground months in Berlin. "It was mainly orientation. I wrote a couple of pieces and did some political things."[68]

He found relaxation, for the first time, in classical music and went often to hear the Berlin Philharmonic, then still one of the world's great orchestras under Wilhelm Furtwängler. It was a Berlin SAP lad who introduced him to concerts. Brandt had known him also in Oslo as "Sverre" and spoke of him as an unusually clever and successful party courier, who apparently died on the Russian front.[69]

In December the SAP called him to Brno, Czechoslovakia, to help organize still another émigré conference, this time with the assistance of the Austrian Socialist theorist, Otto Bauer, who had led the Social Democratic uprising against Chancellor Dollfuss in February 1934. From Brno the group moved to Moravska Ostrava, the big coal town on the Silesian border, for the actual conference. It was less conspicuous. But for security's sake the SAP decided to call it the Kattowitz Convention, naming still another city. The German Communists were doing the same thing, meeting in Moscow and calling it the "Brussels Conference." One wonders whether the Gestapo was fooled.

In Moravska Ostrava Brandt heard for the first time the details of the Moscow trials, the forced confessions, and the executions. "They meant the end of our hopes that the Communists might become our allies and that the Soviet Union might sincerely support our fight for peace," he later commented. "We Leftists had seen in Stalin a trustworthy ally against fascism." Now the world witnessed "his lust for personal power." Yet, Brandt observed, "We still hesitated to admit to ourselves the whole bitter truth."[70] It was a grim session in the border city. Brandt had "little that was good to report" from "Metro" and "the other speakers were not more encouraging." He headed back to Oslo by way of Copenhagen.

In Paris, meanwhile, Walcher and company were feeling the biting wind from Moscow in other ways. He and seventy-one other German Leftist émigrés had just signed a laboriously negotiated joint appeal for a reformation of Germany—the only concrete product of a fragile and ephemeral Popular Front, German-style. The proclamation, dated December 21, 1936, was a mixture of the slightly ridiculous and the considerably sublime.

It spoke of the "sharpened suffering" of German toilers (though the worst of the Depression was over). It vowed nationalization of the arms industry and the big banks (both Hitler had already done in his own way). But it also warned pithily against Nazi preparations for "a new war that will be more fearful than all previous wars," and it called upon all Germans to unite against the Nazis.[71] The proclamation carried the names of sixteen Social Democrats, among them Rudolf Breitscheid, Max Braun, Tony Sender; sixteen Communists, including Ulbricht, Wilhelm Pieck, Wehner, Münzenberg, Franz Dahlem; ten SAP members, including Paul Frölich, Walcher, Brandt; and thirty other personalities including Heinrich Mann, Lion Feuchtwanger, Ernst Toller, Ernst Bloch, Johannes Becher, Egon Erwin Kisch, Arnold Zweig. (Brandt's name, listed as a signator, although he was not present at these meetings, years later led opponents to construe that he had "made a pact with Ulbricht.")

After its Yuletide effort the *Volksfront* quickly returned to pitiless, internecine struggle. The Stalinist campaign against Trotsky, the new archenemy, reached abysmal depths. The next scheduled appeal of the Lutetia Committee collapsed because the KPD demanded a slogan calling for "counterattack against the Gestapo and Trotskyism," and the SAP refused. Walcher commented: "It seems you are more concerned with fighting Trotskyism than countering the Gestapo."[72]

Soon the KPD reverted to its timeworn "Social Fascists" thesis and began denouncing the SAP as "an agency of the Gestapo." A Social Democratic exile publication described the new Communist (Moscow) tactic as: "Every critic a Trotskyite, and every Trotskyite a Gestapo agent."[73]

In Oslo Trudel Meyer had been doing most of Brandt's local SAP work for him. Work? The SAP numbered "nine members and two sympathizers in

Oslo, and two members and one candidate in Bergen." Yet they were apparently very active: distributing 150 or more copies of *Neue Front* among Socialists; collecting for the Ernst Eckstein Fund named in memory of the Breslau SAP leader who had been murdered in a concentration camp in 1933—an average of 100 kroner a month in 1936; sale of the *Marxistische Tribüne,* printed in Paris; work with refugees; seminars; youth programs; liaison with Norwegian Socialists.

Her annual report to the "General Assembly of the O-Group May 1, 1937 (present were eight comrades from Oslo and one from Bergen), would sound like a brave little fable if it weren't for its refreshing frankness:

> Our position in the Norwegian Workers Movement—the leadership of the DNA is mistrustful toward us as it is to the majority of émigrés, especially, probably, because of the experiences of 1934 when Willy operated against the leadership within the Nor. movement. . . .[74]

Later Trudel notes a favorable response to Brandt's suggestion for improving work with émigrés—"émis," they called them and themselves. The activity report also noted "one member in Spain." That was Brandt, who after the conference in Czechoslovakia had spent only a little more than a month in Oslo.

One product of his brief Oslo interlude was an article on underground work in Berlin for the *Marxistische Tribüne,* which appeared in Paris in March 1937 under his name. It carried the reminder, probably from his encounters in his favorite borough of Wedding, that:

> For ordinary people life does not consist of "isms" but rather of eating, sleeping, soccer games, canaries, allotment gardens and other nice things. And don't forget that it was Lenin who proposed that one could put life into the factories with the demand for "tea water." We must learn not always to talk of high politics but clear the way with the appropriate "tea water."

He also recommended taking up "radical" Hitler Youth slogans and carrying them on into Marxist channels.[75]

Gertrud Meyer Frahm Gaasland must have wondered what kind of man she had fallen for. Perhaps Trudel may have thought she was too much of Lübeck and Herbert Frahm for him, not enough of the world struggle and Willy Brandt. He was off again. The Socialist revolution called.

The Spanish Civil War had been under way for over seven months when

Brandt developed the itch to see it. By the time he arrived in Spain the battle was in full flow on several fronts and well behind the lines as the Communists squared off against their Leftist enemies.

He traveled with Per Monsen, the son of the Norwegian Minister of Defense, a sensitive but level-headed journalist just his age. Brandt had two assignments: to send dispatches to Norwegian and Swedish papers from Catalonia, and to cement connections in Barcelona with POUM (Unified Marxist Workers Party), the Spanish sister party of the SAP. He had made the acquaintance of the POUM leader, Joaquin Maurin, at a meeting of independent parties of the Left during the previous May in Paris and remembered him vividly for his anarchist-nihilist approach to the Popular Front propaganda: "We are for the Popular Front because we are against it."

"I was pleased to go to Spain," Brandt recalled. "I wanted to share the experience of what I regarded as the most decisive event since the National Socialists seized power."[76] His friend Monsen said: "He felt the stigma of defeat without resistance. The Austrians had fought in '34, the Germans had not. When Willy went to Spain I think he went to find a new and more vigorous democratic Left. Republican Spain at that time was the only fighting force. I think that is what attracted him."[77]

He and Monsen took a ferry from Kristiansand in southern Norway to Frederikshavn, Denmark, where they missed the train for the next coastal shipping port, Esbjerg. They were traveling light—pasteboard suitcases and a modest joint war chest. Brandt decided on the spot they should take a taxi for 150 miles to catch the next ship. "It cost a fortune," Monsen remembers, "fifty crowns"—but they made the boat. They sailed on deck to Antwerp and took the train, "third class naturally," to Paris, where they put up with Walcher— "one of the father figures Willy Brandt always had, Leber in Lübeck, Martin Tranmael in Oslo, and later Ernst Reuter in Berlin." They slept on the floor.

"We had great comic difficulties," said Monsen. "At the Norwegian Embassy they thought I was taking weapons to Spain with the mysterious student, Gaasland." While Monsen dined at the embassy that day as the son of a Cabinet member should, Brandt was left to munch a sandwich and gulp a beer at a bistro. They went about Paris on foot to save money and on another day, to their delight, discovered a Montmartre restaurant, "Chez Pierre," which advertised *Fromage à discrétion avec vin—20 Francs*. Their translation: as much cheese and as much wine as you could drink for forty cents. Like Vikings they ate up the whole tray of cheese and drank all the wine on the table. When they asked for more "Pierre" had a fit and threw them out. For five days Monsen went every morning to police headquarters to get visa permits for entering Spain by way of France. Brandt was reluctant to appear as

Gaasland. At last they learned the trick, a 1000 franc (twenty dollars) bribe inserted between the passport pages.[78]

The train took them to Spain through the Cerbère-Port Bou tunnel. After a short time in Barcelona Monsen went on to embattled Madrid. Brandt stayed in Catalonia, which was on the brink of a Left-Left war within a war. The followers of Stalin in Spain had already determined that POUM was ripe for liquidation. After all hadn't POUM proposed that Trotsky come to Catalonia?[79]

Like Indochina three decades later, Spain had become a steaming cauldron of blood stirred and fueled by larger outside powers. Hitler sent more than 10,000 men to help Franco's forces, and Mussolini chipped in perhaps 50,000. The Soviet Union helped to mobilize some of the 40,000 irregulars who fought in the International Brigades.[80] Among the latter were about 5000 Germans, the bulk of them recruited by the KPD, which claimed that its Ernst Thälmann Centuria (later Battalion) faced enemy fire for the first time at Tardienta on the Aragon Front in August 1936, a month after the fighting started.[81] (Herbert Wehner in Paris in the summer of 1936 had organized the first 100-man detachment. He had wanted to go himself, but party orders took him instead to Moscow in December 1936.)

Brandt got a room at the Hotel Falcon on the arbored Ramblas Boulevard, two blocks from the harbor. It was also POUM headquarters. Soon he crossed the path of another politically engaged journalist, Eric Blair, who was better known as George Orwell. Brandt says he was aware of Blair's political persuasion, but not of his literary accomplishments at the time.[82]

Brandt was filing a lot of copy to Scandinavia, especially to the Oslo *Arbeiderbladet.* Some of it was firsthand reporting from the front line of Aragon. In his archives there is a tattered carbon of an article entitled "The Battle of Huesca" dated March 1937:

> Our grenadiers attack at the gates of Huesca. . . . It is a black night.
> Fifty of the assault troops have to bite the dust . . . Shelling. The
> Fascists hit better. They have better materiel . . The testament of
> the heroic fighters of Huesca is: Attack on all fronts! Win the war
> and save the Revolution!

It was in another assault on the Franco fortress at Huesca that George Orwell was seriously wounded two months later. Why did Brandt not take up a weapon to fight Fascism and "save the revolution" as did Orwell and so many others of the militant Left? He was frequently asked the question in postwar years. Per Monsen had an explanation: "He is the least aggressive person I know."[83] "Whenever it got dirty Brandt was always a journalist," Herbert Wehner commented. But Wehner, too, like nearly all German anti-

Fascists, was occupied on the political front rather than the battlefront, then and later. In 1960 two right-wing newspapers accused Brandt of having been "a Communist combatant." He observed: "Well, I would not be ashamed if I—like some of my friends at the Aragon front—had defended the cause of the legal Spanish Republic and European democracy."[84] The charge that he had fought for the Communists may have been related to the existence of another "Willy Brandt": Wilhelm Phillip Liborius Brandt, who fought in the Ernst Thälmann Company near Madrid and later became a Spanish citizen and Republican police officer. He was arrested by the Gestapo in 1940 and taken to Dachau Concentration Camp, which he survived. His interrogators there frequently asked him about his activities as "Willy" Brandt in Scandinavia.[85]

Brandt's other "quasi-political task"—his words—in Spain was to expose him to the horrors of the home front. The mortal struggle between POUM and the ever more dominant Communists was taking place before his eyes in the streets of Barcelona.

He had become acquainted with Mark Rein, a gifted young radio technician who was working for the Catalonian Government. The night of April 10 Rein vanished from his hotel, the Continental, leaving all his belongings behind. His friends became alarmed and asked Brandt to help find out what had happened. A rumor went around that Rein had gone to Madrid, but he had not been seen there. Brandt barged into the Casa Carlos Marx and confronted the German Comintern representative, Karl Mewis, who was using the pseudonym Arndt at the time, saying: "You're not so dumb as to let Rein disappear." Mewis, an ambitious Communist with Moscow training, brushed off the question, murmuring, "Maybe it was girls, or the anarchists."[86]

A few days later Rein's father arrived from Paris. Rafail Rein Abramovich, born in 1880 in Daugavpils, Russia, had been a prominent member of the Jewish Bund and was active alongside Lenin in the 1905 Moscow uprising. Later, as a Menshevik (Social Democrat) he parted ways with the Bolshevik leader and was arrested in 1918. He emigrated to Berlin in 1920 where he brought up young Mark as a Social Democrat. He fled Hitler to Paris, where he attached himself to Léon Blum as a publicist. Now the fifty-seven-year-old father listened to the inconclusive reports of Brandt and the others and said only, "Where is my son? Where is my son?" A broken man, Brandt observed.[87] "They probably killed him the day the father appeared," he surmised, relating that he later learned the Communists had abducted Rein, tortured him, and then, "when the case made too great a stir, the Communists decided to liquidate it by liquidating him."[88]

There were dozens of such political murders in those weeks in Barcelona as the Communists moved to destroy POUM. On May 6 Professor Camillion Berneri, an Italian anarchist distinguished for his opposition to Mussolini and

Stalin, was shot down as he was walking home. But why Rein? Was it because he was a vital help to POUM, or because Stalin hated old Abramovich almost as much as he hated Trotsky? Karl Mewis knows, and he wasn't talking even at the ag of sixty-eight. But his 1972 memoir, *On Party Orders,* speaks of the POUM members as "traitors."[89]

Were people like Brandt in danger, too? "Nobody can say exactly," he remarked. "But in the last weeks I went into cover in an apartment arranged by a French friend. I wasn't sure whether the GPU (Soviet Secret Police) was after me." To pay back Brandt for his intervention the Communists began denouncing him as a "Franco agent" and "spy of the Gestapo."[90] These were the first of a series of vilifications that would dog him for the rest of his political life—now from the Left, now from the Right.

"It is not always so," he would conclude almost three decades later, "that opposites cancel each other out. Sometimes they complement each other, or their exponents toss the balls back and forth between them."[91]

"Some things I experienced meant a lot to me," he mused about his Spanish days. "The terrible struggle in the non-Fascist camp, a civil war within a civil war. The Russians who exchanged weapons for political influence. The ruthless liquidation of all who thought independently.[92]

Nor did Brandt revise his skeptical estimate of POUM: "I came to the conclusion that the POUM had taken a false position in almost every practical question." At the time he also accused POUM leaders of "ultra-Left subjectivism" and "sectarian behavior" because of their insistence on coupling the struggle against Franco with a total social revolution and their insistence that "the revolution takes priority."[93] In this respect Brandt was objectively allied with the Communists, who insisted that winning the war came first.

At the time Brandt commented: "We would have to be blind not to see that in the eyes of the broad masses the KP is the most consequential champion of the military exigencies." He also said: "The Russians really want to beat Franco, and without Russian weapons assistance it would have been over long ago."[94] Reflecting decades later, he said sardonically, "When the Communists were right I said so, and that was 'bad.' " Brandt personally liked the POUM men, whom he remembers fondly as "marvelous people, radiating an impulse of liberty."[95] But his political sympathies were closer to Largo Caballero, the Social Democratic leader.[96]

Reading his contemporary political analyses now and comparing his observations to the standard works on the Spanish Civil War, one is powerfully struck with the perspicacity and maturity of the author, who was just twenty-three years old. He had found a vocation of substance in that limbo between professional politics and professional journalism. He was becoming somebody in his own right. There was little comic relief in Brandt's Barcelona days, but he remembered the visit in early May of the Swedish poet, Ture Nurman, whom he found very upset in his hotel. Nurman had been halted by "revolutionary workers" who challenged him as a "class enemy" because he was wearing a hat. Brandt notes that he and his friend, Paul Gauguin, grandson of the painter, "could scarcely keep from laughing."[97] Monsen also related that he and Brandt were "almost attacked" by a revolutionary waiter to whom they had offered a tip.[98]

There were profound frustrations, as when Brandt failed to persuade the POUM youth association to join an all-Left First of May rally. In these and other discussions Brandt used the Spanish he had learned as a fourth language in Lübeck's Johanneum.[99]

From Barcelona Brandt went back to Paris to report to the SAP leadership. It was early July. Although he did not spare POUM from criticism he was harsher in laying bare the actions of the Communists in crushing the Catalonian POUM organization. "Slander . . . persecution . . . blind terror . . . Spain is on the way to becoming a Communist party dictatorship." Walcher agreed with Brandt's view of the POUM, but he was put off by the new anti-Stalin accents of his protégé. For these were identical to the arguments of a new opposition within the SAP headed by Erwin Bauer, the Trotskyite. The dispute was not resolved then or later.[100]

On his way back to Norway Brandt stopped in England to attend an international Socialist congress in Letchworth, the site of the summer school of the Independent Labour Party. Again he reported on Spain, this time in English, and again he faced sharp criticism. An "Italian sectarian" attacked him on the second day, accusing him of helping to kill a Leftist named Kurt Landau in Spain. "Shut up, you mad dog," Brandt shot back. The Italian demanded a translation and when he got it he huffed out of the room. "I still lacked parliamentary experience," Brandt noted. "It was grotesque," he added years later. "Landau kept his munitions in the fireplace."

In addition to extensive public speaking and writing for his newspapers, Brandt accepted a position as a secretary of the Norwegian Spanish Committee, whose Spanish aid drives had substantial results in collecting food and medical supplies for civil war victims.

"Each time I returned to Oslo," he wrote,

> I realized more clearly how much Norway had become my second home . . . Here socialism was felt more and more strongly as a force that strengthened and broadened democracy. I had overcome my former left-socialist position, not my revolutionary élan, but the dogmatic narrowness.[101]

One consequence was his cancellation of the Oslo SAP Youth connection with the Stockholm Youth Office, which had gone too far left for his taste. This was done in Göteborg, Sweden. Shortly afterward he put out feelers to Erich Ollenhauer, the head of the SPD's exile youth, and within a year Brandt's SAP group became an associate of the Social Democratic Youth International.[102]

Although Norway gave him a political version of that *Nestwärme* he craved, he was off and running once more in 1938, visiting Paris and Brussels in the summer and Paris again in the autumn in his dual role as journalist and political activist. Hitler's Wehrmacht had occupied Austria in March, and by September the dictator had wrung the Munich Pact out of France and Britain, authorizing him to dismember Czechoslovakia. The world's radio stations were carrying Hitler's threatening speeches in the newscasts—his melodramatic voice rising to fever pitch as he bit off his words to make them more menacing. The presentiment of a general war was growing. In these months Brandt was also widening his circle of acquaintances among West European politicians: Paul Henri Spaak in Belgium, Hans Hedtoft Hansen and H.C. Hansen in Denmark, all three of whom became Prime Ministers; British Labour MPs; and outstanding trade unionists like Edo Fimmen of the International Transport Federation.

In October he met Erich Ollenhauer who had moved to Paris from Prague with the rest of the exile SPD leadership—almost two years after the KPD had made the move. The SAP was still toying with a five-year-old scheme to establish a "concentration" of Socialist parties that would draw in both Communists and Social Democrats, but had gotten no farther than bitter arguing. Now Brandt was moving closer and closer to the SPD. He took up with contemporaries who had assembled in a grouping called Neubeginn (New Beginning). (It had been Mark Rein's last political home.) Their aim was to be practical and not to indulge in "the politics of old men," as Günter Markscheffel, one of them, recalls. "We called theirs the 'politics of proclamations' and made fun of it. Our concerns were what is coming and the Communists, knowing the Communists would take what they could militarily and try the rest politically."[103] The Communists took something else from the Neubeginn group—the title Freie Deutsche Jugend (Free German Youth), which they had applied to a grouping assembled in July near Paris. It was a loose *Volksfront* association of Communists, Social Democrats, and exile splinters that lasted until the outbreak of war, and Brandt was included. After the war the East German Communists scrounged up the title and stuck it on their pseudo-unitary youth organization of the Socialist Unity Party (in which the minority Communists swallowed the majority Social Democrats under

Soviet compulsion). The first secretary of the new FDJ was Erich Honecker, fresh out of a Nazi prison.

Richard Löwenthal, who was to become a Brandt idea man after the war, remembers Brandt from the Paris visits: "a Walcher disciple with whom we could work closely and on the best of terms. He was sensible—not a sectarian and not naive. Walcher believed Stalin could do no wrong. Brandt didn't believe that. We saw the SAP as willing to cooperate with the Communists on certain points, but not in the underground. They also didn't want to do anything that would compromise their own principles."[104] But the mutations of the Left were endless, as another young German exile proved. Peter Blachstein, a casual SAP member from Dresden who had also been in Spain, turned up in Paris to denounce the Popular Front as "betrayal of the working class." He joined the Trotskyite opposition around Erwin Bauer at this time. After the war he attached himself to Brandt "like a leech," as Herbert Wehner described it.[105]

The German version of the Popular Front had one more fling that ominous autumn in Paris, less than a year away from World War II. It was doomed before it started by those same hatreds, suspicions, jealousies that had beset the German Left since 1913 and, in a way, since the rivalry between Marx and Lassalle. Its members met again in the Hotel Lutetia, which was soon to become Gestapo headquarters in occupied Paris.

"What I remember most vividly was the collapse of the *Volksfront*," said Brandt. "Münzenberg was on one side, soon to be killed by his own people. There was Heinrich Mann sitting down in despair. Leo Bauer (who became a Brandt disciple long after the war and many tragic misadventures) was there from the Communists, and a friend, Alfred Kantorowicz, the writer. They were almost all Communists. 'Is it so? Yes, it is so.' An assembly of ghosts. Wehner wasn't there. He was in Moscow. But he told me years later: 'We knew who was with us, and you weren't.' Heinrich Mann presided. He had tears in his eyes when he said to me: 'We'll never see the seven towers (of Lübeck) again.'"[106]

Mann didn't. Brandt had reason to wonder whether he ever would. On September 3, 1938, under his real name Herbert Frahm, he had been deprived of German citizenship with the publication of the official notice in the German *Reichsanzeiger und Preussischer Staatsanzeiger* of that day. In exile, he had become a stateless person.[107] Even before that happened he had begun to take precautions. Starting in January 1938 he had buried Willy Brandt as far as his articles in *Arbeiderbladet* went, signing them with the pseudonym F. Franke or Felix Franke.

At home in Norway he had time for friends, especially those who were still trickling in from Germany. He had arranged to get a false passport for the SAP youth secretary in the Berlin underground, Herbert George, who arrived early one morning in the Norwegian capital as scheduled. But Brandt wasn't at the station. "He wasn't an early bird even then," George recalled. Brandt turned up about 10 a.m., two hours late. They figured out a cover story for George, since he had no legal papers. Then, because George didn't get his travel times straight, his application for a residence permit was rejected. Brandt used his DNA connections to get him cleared. George sat for a time in Brandt's office and watched him work, smoking a pipe while typing article after article.

You know, Herbert," Brandt said to his friend one day, "I feel like a junk dealer, who trots off each day with his carrying case strapped on. 'I've got an article about this, an article about that. Whaddyou want?'" But he also told George: "Herbert, I'm convinced that someday I am going to play an important role in German developments." [108]

Brandt was still involved with the SAP, although he seems to have felt less and less attachment to the foundering group. Late in 1939, following the Hitler-Stalin pact and the invasion and occupation of Poland, he wrote a situation report for the SAP concluding: "In our circle there is complete unanimity that the Sta(lin) policy of the latest phase has not the least to do with soc(ialism) and stands in screaming contradiction to the interests of the international workers movement." Writing in *Det 20de århundre,* the DNA monthly, he marked with admirable soberness:

> Even if Hitler-Germany should succeed in throwing the bulk of its troops against the West, the Western powers would still be superior in almost every sense . . . In addition the economic and material resources of the United States will probably enter the picture in a few months. Seen thus, a conflict between Hitler-Germany on the one hand and the Western powers on the other must end finally with the defeat of Hitler-Germany. [109]

He also paid careful attention to the Soviet expansion into the Baltic states and the aggression against Finland.

By now, the once Herbert Frahm had drifted apart from Gertrud Meyer. The girl from Lübeck, alone in Oslo much of the time, not fully occupied with Willy's work, had become the secretary of Wilhelm Reich, the remarkable Freudian psychologist who was also a German exile in Norway. She had almost given up hope of a real future with Willy. When Reich decided in 1939 to seek greater safety in the United States, she followed. Brandt's comment on the end of his relationship with Trudel: "The war came between us—but not the war alone." Asked if she had loved him, he replied, with manifest reluctance: "One could surmise it."[110] Neither she nor he said any more about it in public. Evidently she told him she would be back in a year's time. But that was not to be. He was looking elsewhere.

"I almost fell in love in Paris," he said of an affair with a pretty German émigré. "He was always a woman charmer of great quality," said a Norwegian friend, "with the greatest technique of all—patience."

Looking, he fell hard for Carlota Thorkildsen, a fine-featured daughter of a German mother and a Norwegian father. She was almost nine years older than Brandt and "the most completely intellectual woman I ever knew," a Norwegian friend said. Much more intellectual than Willy.

"I was in love," Brandt wrote.

> Carlota was about to become my wife. She was an assistant at a scientific institute connected with the Nobel Foundation. The founding of a family, a home of our own—that was a piece of reality, a certain foothold in the headlong flight of events.

It was February 1940, the height of the "phony war." They went up to the mountains at Eastertime to a hut owned by their friends, the Halvard Langes, from the DNA. "Unreal, this feeling of solitude and rapture?"

They returned to Oslo at the beginning of April. It was to be a month—as other future Aprils for Willy Brandt—of harshness.

Only weeks before he had been listening tolerantly to pacifists. Now, on April 8, the war of wars pressed home to his second home. The news cascaded into Oslo. A German liner had been sunk by a Polish submarine off the south coast. It carried cavalrymen and horses. Survivors said their destination was Bergen. A hundred German naval vessels had passed the straits between Denmark and Sweden. Britain and France sent a note declaring they were blockading the Norwegian coast and mining approaches to harbors. Norway's coastal defense forces were alerted. That day Carlota Thorkildsen learned she was pregnant. That night Brandt spoke to a group of German émigrés and said they might expect an attack by Nazi forces the following day. He came home very late, carrying with him the author's copy of his first book, *War Aims of the Great Powers,* to show proudly to his future wife.

"He was so tired I didn't want to tell him the news," Carlota recalled. "Ten minutes later there was an air raid alarm. I told him during the alarm he was going to become a father. He was happy."

"We had an air-raid alarm that night, but it did not disturb us greatly," he wrote. "Carlota was with child—we took comfort in assuring each other that nothing would happen."

In the morning the telephone rang and rang—a friend who had been trying to get through for two hours—but the lines were down. Did Willy know? German warships had entered the Oslo Fjord, and German troops had landed on the coast.

Herbert Frahm's second exile was about to begin, provoked by the same Germans who had caused the first.

IV:

Double Exile

The Nazi sneak attack on Norway—
one of the most daring bluffs in the history of warfare—placed
Willy Brandt in sudden and very grave danger. He had been on the Gestapo
wanted lists for at least two years, and now the German secret police were only
hours away from his Oslo office and his nearby apartment.

Hitler's invasion plan, a masterpiece of split-second timing, which he had
worked out partially in consultation with the Norwegian traitor, Major
Vidkun Quisling, called for simultaneous capture of Copenhagen and Oslo. At
the same time, landing forces were to take major Norwegian coastal cities—
Bergen, Trondheim, Narvik, and Kristiansand. Copenhagen fell without a
shot to a lone Wehrmacht battalion landed in the heart of the Danish capital
by the troopship *Danzig,* while Luftwaffe bombers roared menacingly
overhead. Norway was a different story, although the invaders were able to
capitalize on the acquiescence and even the support of Quisling followers in
several Norwegian garrisons, and on the widespread disbelief in the Norwegian Government that the 125-year-old peace of the nation could somehow be
broken. The plan called for German envoys in the two Scandinavian capitals
to present ultimatums to their host governments at precisely 5:20 a.m., April
9, 1940, demanding that they instantly accept "the protection of the Reich."
The pretext offered was to prevent occupation "by Anglo-French forces," and
it was reinforced by the threat that "any resistance would have to be, and
would be, broken by all possible means." It worked in Copenhagen, where the
enforcers were already handily on the scene.

But the bluff failed in Oslo, because of the courage of a handful of
Norwegian soldiers and sailors. When Minister Curt Bräuer presented the
ultimatum to Foreign Minister Halvdan Koht in the first light of dawn, there
was supposed to be a German naval task force, headed by the spanking new
heavy cruiser *Blücher,* already landing troops in Oslo harbor. Instead, just
before dawn, the *Blücher* was sunk by the 11-inch Krupp cannons of the

75

Oskarsborg citadel, which guards the fjord narrows about fifteen miles south of Oslo. The squadron was further delayed by damage inflicted on the pocket battleship *Lützow* and the light cruiser *Emden.* A German welcoming party, headed by the naval attaché in Oslo waited for the arrival of the fleet, set for 4:15 a.m. It did not appear. Barely half an hour after confronting Koht, Curt Bräuer was compelled to report Norway's brave response back to his Foreign Ministry on the Wilhelmstrasse. It was "We will not submit voluntarily—the struggle is already under way."

With daylight came a new peril: German bombers and airborne troops. The troop planes, trusty old trimotored Junkers 52s. landed unopposed at Fornebu Airport, a forty-minute drive from downtown Oslo, and by noon had disembarked five companies of light infantry. Other Luftwaffe craft swept over the capital at low altitude, adding to the fear and confusion of the bewildered populace. Leland Stowe, the intrepid war correspondent of the *Chicago Daily News,* was an eyewitness in the Grand Hotel:

> They were five huge trimotored planes with engines wide open, slicing down within five hundred feet of the rooftops across the park—straight toward our hotel . . . No bombs this time, but of course they'd be back. In a few minutes they were; still swooping low, still roaring, still holding thousands of persons speechless and paralyzed on the streets or at their windows.

It was breakfast time.[1] What Stowe saw were probably Junkers 52/3mWs, the 163-mph transport seaplane version of the troop carrier that carried three machine guns, which were extensively used in the Norway invasion. They were not bombers. But they were good for scaring civilians.

The delay of the marine landing force in Oslo Fjord afforded precious time to the Norwegian leadership. Less than five hours after Minister Bräuer had presented his *Diktat,* they were on their way northward. King Haakon VII, the Labor Cabinet, and 145 members of the Storting set off aboard a special train at 7:30 a.m. to Hamar, about sixty miles north of the capital.

Willy Brandt and Carlota Thorkildsen hastily packed and took a taxi to their friends, Dr. Alf and Rakel Sewerin. They parted there.

> Carlota had to stay behind. Norwegian relatives and friends would take care of her; but this assurance did not dispel my worries, nor ease the pain of our parting. Carlota was very courageous—- besides we clung to the hope that our separation would be of short duration: in a few days the allies would intervene.[2]

Brandt was driven further into the suburbs to meet Martin Tranmael, his avuncular patron in the Norwegian Labor Party. With two other party leaders they went by car to Hamar, the long way around through Gjövik, driving across the frozen Mjøsa Lake. They arrived about 10:30 p.m.—three hours after Parliament, in emergency session, had unanimously approved a resolution backing the government and rejecting the resignations of the Cabinet. The escape of the government to Hamar was largely the work of Carl J. Hambro, the resourceful speaker of the Storting.[3]

At the Hamar session Hambro, a Conservative, also proposed a motion that King Haakon and the government avoid capture and establish the constitutional rule outside of Norway if necessary. That resolution was carried unanimously, too. That and the rescue of Norway's gold reserves, twenty whole truckloads of it, were the bright spots of an otherwise dark day. Narvik had fallen. Kristiansand had fallen. Trondheim had fallen. Sola Airfield, with which the Luftwaffe could dominate the entire 1500-mile length of the country, had been seized by paratroops landing outside Stavanger. Oslo fell, too, like Copenhagen without a shot, about 3 p.m. that Tuesday to the 1000 or so troops in the field gray of the Wehrmacht who had been assembled at Fornebu. They marched in three abreast behind two light trucks carrying machine gunners, with General Nikolaus von Falkenhorst at their head, past thousands of astounded Norwegians lining the broad Karl Johansgade. They could have been cut to pieces by any well-armed and determined force. But there was no such force in Oslo with the appropriate orders.

A day later squads of Germans were marching around singing lustily, and on Thursday a Wehrmacht band was playing "Roll Out the Barrel" beneath the trees of the park in front of the Storting.[4] About 4:30 p.m. Major Quisling came on the radio to announce the formation of a new Norwegian Government based on his tiny Nasjonal Samling of imitation Nazis, which had never gotten more than 2 percent of the vote. Quisling, who was fifty-three years old, had served as an attaché in Petrograd during the Bolshevik Revolution. Fascinated by the Russian Communists, he tried to import Red militancy to Norway but was rebuffed by even the Labor Party militants. A tall, blockheaded man of consummate ambition, he made an about-face and became a flaming Fascist, founding his luckless NS Party (the same initials as the National Socialists) only four months after Hitler took power. Through the offices of Alfred Rosenberg, the racist mythmaker, he met Admiral Erich Raeder, who paved the way to secret interviews with Hitler himself on December 14, 16, and 18, 1939. Quisling's thirst for power knew no limits. But his April 9 address, "deposing" the elected government and "ordering" an immediate ceasefire of Norwegian forces—as electrifying as it sounded at the moment—proved to be a disastrous backfire. He was a Nazi puppet, bought and paid, but somehow the strings got tangled. The audience reaction was simple scorn.[5] But the Germans, military and diplomatic, were saddled with Quisling.

The approach of the German assault troops had been signaled to the Royal Government. After concluding the Hamar session, the Parliament and King Haakon fled twenty miles eastward to Elverum and thence another forty miles northeast to the town of Nybergsund, less than one hour's drive from the Swedish frontier. The car carrying Willy Brandt and Martin Tranmael was stopped at the roadblocks of the hastily assembled defensive line erected by Colonel Ruge's officers and volunteers. "We had to leave our car there, and drove then in a truck toward Nybergsund." On the way they were passed by another car carrying Trygve Lie, at the moment Minister of Supplies. A man who had never entertained any affection for Brandt—or for Tranmael—Lie nevertheless told them where they could safely cross into Sweden.[6]

In Elverum King Haakon, asked to do what his brother, Christian X of Denmark, had done, capitulate, refused that request and a parallel demand that he accept Quisling as the new head of government—explaining that political decisions were the business of his ministers. At a tavern in Nybergsund he conferred with the Cabinet and members of the parliamentary opposition, telling them he would abdicate if they accepted the Nazi ultimatum. The government backed him. Norway, free Norway, had decided on resistance. The message was passed to Oslo and then on to Berlin. Hitler's response was in character. He ordered the bombing of Elverum and Nybergsund by some of the 900 aircraft assembled for the Scandinavian campaign. Haakon and his government hid out in the nearby forests, as the bombs and bullets flew that evening. That night Brandt rescued suitcases filled with Oslo Government papers from a hotel room where they had been left behind in the confusion. "What should I do?" he recollects asking himself. "Escape to Sweden? But did I have the right to abandon my Norwegian friends? And besides, was it so certain that Sweden would not be attacked and occupied also?"[7] The snow was still knee high in the woods. For all the protection offered by Norwegian friends he was still a fugitive, and more—a stateless person for the last nineteen months. He had applied in 1939 to Trygve Lie in his capacity as Minister of Justice for Norwegian citizenship and had been told to wait six months. Now it was almost too late. His papers in his apartment had been removed by Carlota or destroyed. But Gestapo men soon ransacked the place. They knew their man.[8]

He chose to stay, trailing the royal party up the stony roads of the Valley of Gudbrand: Hamar, Lillehammer, Ringebu, Sel, Dombaas. For two weeks Brandt helped collect blankets and bandages for Otto Ruge's fighting Norwegians,[9] a ragtag of volunteers and professionals from the three armed services. They waged losing battles against the now superior forces sent by the

Wehrmacht from the Oslo salient to join up with the occupiers of Trondheim in a long-ranged pincer movement; they were also without protection from the air armada launched by Hermann Göring's Luftwaffe. The Norwegians— and Brandt—were clearly hoping for relief from Britain. For a moment it seemed to be coming. Narvik, the hostage of a German landing force, fell to a British flotilla, but then was given up on the spot for reasons of caution. King Haakon was still in flight. On April 29 he succeeded in boarding the cruiser *Glasgow* in Molde Harbor, opposite Aandalsnes.

With a couple of friends from the Norsk Folkehjelp (Norwegian Peoples Aid) of which he had been secretary for the press and for aid to Spanish war victims, Brandt pitched up in the village of Mithet, in the Mittetdal, six miles north of Aandalsnes. At the mouth of the rugged valley on the edge of the deep Langfjord were German troops fresh from Trondheim. At the top was ice and snow. Brandt and his friends debated trying to climb and ski their way to Sweden, more than 160 miles to the east; it seemed hopeless. But in Mithet there was a unit of fifty Norwegian soldiers, some of them volunteers. Luck would have it that two were friends from Oslo: Johan Cappelen and Paul René Gauguin. They advised Brandt to shed his civilian clothes for a Norwegian uniform, the better to escape his Gestapo pursuers. Gauguin, whom he had known in Oslo and also from Spanish days in 1937, decided his was the closest size, although the jacket was too wide and the pants too short. Brandt threw away his Norwegian papers, some of which identified him as Frahm and some as Brandt, and buckled on Gauguin's belt with the cartridge pouches. He also took the forage cap, rifle, and bayonet. "You can speak such good Norwegian that the Germans won't notice," said Gauguin. He was right. It was May 1. The Norwegians in the area had been ordered to capitulate. Brandt, Gauguin, Cappelen, and the others handed over their weapons to a German truce unit without firing a shot. They were taken fifty miles inland to Dovre and interned in a vacated school.[10]

In the next four weeks Brandt passed as a hapless Norwegian soldier, even when he got into a rather touchy political argument with an officer of the guard. In the two "official" versions of his life, the autobiography and the memoir of his exile, Brandt mixes up the rank of the Wehrmacht guard and the time of the incident. In one it is a lieutenant in June and in the other it is a sergeant in May. But the gist of this first exchange with the Germans who fought for Hitler remains the same. The guard notes that King Haakon has fled and calls him "a coward." Brandt retorts: "If King Haakon is a coward then Hitler is a coward, too." There was "rather much excitement" as the guard sputtered threats until a superior came and said: "Let the crazy student alone."[11]

There had been an incident, on May 17, the anniversary of the Norwegian

Constitution, when the prisoners demanded that the Norwegian flag be set at half mast and were refused. They demonstrated. Far to the north at Tromsø, his last wartime station on Norwegian soil, King Haakon was proclaiming on the radio: "This is our homeland and we love it as it is, as it was, and as it will be." The prisoners of Dovre were punished for their insolence, forced to unload bombs from a munitions train. Johan Cappelen, a lawyer chosen as the prisoners' spokesman, protested against this violation of the Geneva convention on prisoners of war. The camp commandant replied in conciliatory fashion and said it wouldn't happen again. "And he kept his promise," Brandt noted. "In the German Army there were Nazis—and Germans."[12] It was a pretty soft life as prisoner-of-war camps went. They were allowed to buy food at nearby farms and to listen to the BBC. But Brandt was in a deep depression:

> The debacle, Hitler's victories in east, north and west seemed to secure his power for many years to come. The future was without hope. What could I expect? I let my life pass before my eyes and decided with all the superiority of my twenty-six years that it had been a failure.[13]

The journalist-politician accustomed to a Norwegian-German-Socialist audience was a prisoner of the people he had been struggling against for more than seven years. But he had not reckoned with the nutty twists of the Nazi minds who imagined that Norway, because it was "Nordic," would automatically side with its fellow Aryans from Germany. Conciliation was still the dominant theme of the occupiers, even though General von Falkenhorst had published reprisal threats when two young resistance fighters tried to blow up one of Oslo's major bridges on April 13. At the beginning of June Brandt and his comrades were set free, Brandt getting a pass and a railroad ticket to his "hometown Oslo." He went to the home of Dr. Nicolas Stang in suburban Bygdo and, who should open the door? Carlota.

"Instantly all the pain and sorrows of the past weeks were forgotten. A few days later our happy reunion was over. I had to go on."[14] He dared not move about in a city where he could fall into the hands of the Gestapo. So he journeyed to the wooden summer cabin of another friend, Per Borgersen, who had been with him on Norsk Folkehjelp. He stayed there more than a month, a hermit on an island in Oslo Fjord, visited occasionally by Carlota, by Borgerson, and other friends. Borgersen was able to draw the arrears of his Folkehjelp salary out of the bank—so he had no money worries for the moment. He remained deeply disturbed, however, about what to do, and he seems to have given consideration to getting into the fight against Hitler. But as what? And where? And how, for a man who had no military training whatsoever? "I am grateful that fate did not put me before the decision of conscience to fight with a weapon against my fellow Germans. The decision, however it might have sounded, would have been tragic, yet never a disgrace."

King Haakon had been evacuated from Tromsø on June 7 aboard the cruiser *Devonshire* along with the Oslo Government, beginning five years of exile. An Allied expeditionary force of 25,000 had driven the Wehrmacht out of the Narvik region only ten days before. But now, with France crumbling before the onslaught of Hitler's Panzer spearheads and Stuka bombings, the Allied force was hastily withdrawn. Otto Ruge, now a general, had to surrender the remaining Norwegian units to the Germans. As yet there were no Norwegian resistance forces in action. Brandt noted "uncertainty" and "readiness to capitulate in rather wide circles in the summer of 1940." He was too well known to travel about the country without jeopardy to himself or to his companions—"and I surely did not like the idea of remaining idle." So it was decided that he should flee to Sweden to work as a journalist—"also for the cause of a free Norway."[15] He set out at the beginning of July by car up the Oslo Fjord and then fifty miles by train to Kongsvinger and on to a spot five miles from the Swedish frontier. He got food from a Norwegian army reservist and then, with a guide, hiked the last few miles to the border unapprehended by German patrols. At twilight of the third day of his flight he crossed into Sweden, where, at the first military post, he reported himself as a political fugitive from Germany.

He was taken to Charlottenberg, only five miles inside Sweden, for interrogation. Did he know any Swedes who could vouch for him? Again the network of international Socialist acquaintances came to his rescue. There was August Spangberg, deputy of the Riksdag, whom he had met three years before in the midst of the POUM-Communist street clashes of Barcelona. Spangberg journeyed to the small house near the Charlottenberg railway station where Brandt was interned and obtained his release. On their way they stopped in an old castle at Beggä, which was being used as a labor camp for refugees. There he met Ernst Paul, a forty-three-year-old Sudetenland Social Democrat who had spent almost a year taking care of German political refugees. He reached Stockholm "as a free man," thanks to the intervention of Spangberg, Paul, and others like him. In the Swedish capital he immediately got together with the other exiles from Norway, above all with Martin Tranmael, who was running an émigré office of the Norwegian Labor Party. Another Oslo Social Democrat, Halvard Lange, was there, too, and Brandt soon became very friendly with Inge Scheflo, the Socialist son of the elderly Norwegian Communist-turned-Socialist, Olav Scheflo. That summer Brandt, Tranmael, and others from Oslo paid their last respects to Erling Falk, the grand old Norwegian radical, who had come to Stockholm for medical treatment after several strokes. Brandt had last seen that short-lived patron about 1935 in the office building in Oslo that had once been Mot Dag headquarters. Falk died July 31, 1940. It was Tranmael, then sixty-one years old, whom Brandt in 1974 remembered most affectionately. For example:

> He was fanatically antialcoholic, which was something you had to see in connection with the workers' movement. Alcoholism was the most severe problem of the Norwegian workers, especially the loggers who made up the bulk of the labor force. But Tranmael knew I liked a drink, and one time in Stockholm when we met in a restaurant he went and fetched me a *schnapps*. That was an extreme instance of his kindness.[16]

He lived at first in a *pension,* working on articles about the battle for Norway, which were to form the basis for a new book. He also renewed contact with German émigrés, among them his old SAP comrades, Stevan Szende and August and Irmgard Enderle, by whom he was "heartily welcomed."[17] Brandt's friends from that time remain devoted to him to this day. They were the best kind of friends a person could have—helpful in time of need, loyal yet never uncritical. He probably felt closer to them and more at home with them in the tribulations of exile than he ever would in his native land, even in the latter German years when his living was easy—those special bonds created by nearness of danger, by the knowledge of interdependence, which tend to melt away in the comforts of peacetime and in the liberty of one's own home. Certainly some of those friends are convinced that: Szende, Per Monsen, Oddvar Aas, Inge Scheflo. "I have many friends and contacts in Germany," he would tell Monsen after the war. "But all of my real friends are in Norway." By the same token he sensed a deep obligation to them. "I felt bound in honor and duty to keep the Swedish and foreign press informed about events in Norway," Brandt wrote of these months, and he kept that pledge.[18] "He was *the* most important spokesman for Norway in Sweden," said Eric Loe, editor of *Arbeiderbladet.* "Five books in the war—one a year—and hundreds of articles."[19]

Soon after his arrival in Stockholm Brandt received his Norwegian citizenship papers from the government-in-exile in London. It gave him a security and a legitimacy he had lacked for seven years, although it did not blunt the sting of being "outside." If he did not waste time on self-pity or blame others for his fate, he was sensitive to the plight of the banished.

> It should not be forgotten that the Germans in exile had a particularly rough time. They bore the burden of defeat without a

fight, often living in difficult financial circumstances and, for a long time, foreign democracies were more inclined to respect or fear Hitler than to listen to the warnings, let alone the demands of Hitler's opponents.[20]

Every German exile had his own special identity crisis. Nor was it a new phenomenon in German politics. In the loneliness of his forced exile in Paris, Heinrich Heine wrote on January 24, 1837:

> He who has lived his days in exile, the damp cold days and the black long nights, he who has ever climed up and down the stairways of the strangers will grasp why I reject the suspicion concerning (my) patriotism with wordy indignation.

A century later, from California, Thomas Mann wrote an acquaintance: "You didn't know it, the heart-asthma of the exile, the uprooting, the nervous terrors of homelessness.

Brandt's exile was less heart rending, if only because he was young—not yet twenty-eight years old—vigorous, and surrounded by well-wishing friends. He had work, and he had the relative safety of an accepted citizenship. Above all, he had an audience, which was more than Heinrich Mann, Arnold Schönberg, or Bertolt Brecht could claim as émigrés in the United States. But he was also Herbert Frahm again on his Norwegian papers, to the surprise of those who had known him only as "Willy Brandt."

In December 1940 he and Inge Scheflo decided to return to Oslo. They wanted to see firsthand what was developing in the way of civil resistance and underground action against the Nazi occupation. Brandt also wanted to see his first-born child, Ninja, who had come into the world October 30 in the Norwegian capital.

The resistance movement had been slow to form. Undoubtedly, many Norwegians were numbed by the fall of France and the ensuing battle of Britain. Things were going Hitler's way. They were also confronted with a puzzling political landscape where loyalties were torn between a government-in-exile and a group of Storting members in Oslo who tried to retain control of civilian affairs. But the German governor wanted a Nazi Norway, as he made clear in a September 25 speech. His first instrument was a system of commissioner ministers, chief among them a Quisling aide as Commissioner Minister of Interior. Soon after they attempted to nazify a number of Norwegian institutions. Now the spirit of civil resistance gathered strength. The entire Supreme Court resigned after declaring Reichskommissar Terboven's decrees illegal. In a spirit of ecumenism church leaders got together to defy attempts at spreading National Socialist ideas. Teachers organized to prevent acceptance of a loyalty oath to the new order. Meanwhile, the first couriers were arriving from Britain to help organize armed resistance by partisans.[21]

Brandt and Scheflo had cultivated several senior officers of neutral Sweden's army, and through them they obtained a permit to visit the border region. As in prewar days Brandt used a doctored pass, this time the one that belonged to Konrad Knudsen, the *Arbeiderbladet* editor who had provided a haven for Trotsky four years earlier.[22]

They took a train across to Göteborg and another northward eighty miles to the frontier area. Swedish soldiers escorted them to the border itself and after trudging over frozen ground they found a guide on the Norwegian side who led them past iced-over lakes into the large town of Halden. From there they took a train again, straight to Oslo. Brandt wrote:

> Illegal border crossings were nothing new to me. Nor was I any longer the amateur conspirator of the early days of the Nazi regime. Nonetheless it was much easier for me to travel in Norway than it had been in Germany. There at every step I had the feeling of being in an enemy country. In occupied Norway I felt much safer.[23]

Still, it was an evil time. The Gestapo was well entrenched and could now reckon with partial assistance from the Quisling-dominated police force. Quisling's Nasjonal Samling now had 20,000 members, thanks to an influx of opportunists. Informers were everywhere. It was as the Wise Woman had forecast in the 1000-year-old Völuspå lay:

> Brothers shall fight and fell each other
> And sisters' sons shall kinship stain.
> Hard 'tis on earth with mighty whoredom,
> Axe-time, sword-time, shields are sundered,
> Wind-time, wolf-time, ere the world falls—[24]

Brandt-"Knudsen" found Carlota and Ninja safe and healthy, and he arranged to receive them in Stockholm as soon as his daughter was strong enough to travel. They had Christmas together. Brandt dared not move about much in daylight, but in that season it was dark most of the time. He met friends in the protection of the night, at the home of a fellow journalist. He also met some of the men and women of the new Norwegian resistance, among them Einar Gerhardsen, the former Mayor of Oslo, who was now simply a municipal employee. Gerhardsen asked with apparent surprise: "You are the comrade from Sweden about whom my friends have written me?" and Brandt replied: "You, of all people, are the one in command here?" Gerhardsen was arrested in 1941 and sent to a concentration camp, and the journalist who had arranged the *Treff* was captured while trying to sail to Britain.[25]

Brandt returned in January of 1941 to Sweden by the same route without incident but with fresh information and impressions about his second homeland under the Nazi heel. That and the successes of Hitler's arms in Yugoslavia and Greece—a prelude to operations in Africa and the invasion of Russia—depressed and even frightened him. Of neutral Sweden, he wrote:

> the danger threatened that this Scandinavian country, too, would be overrun. In my papers from the year 1941 there is a carefully worded application for entry into the U.S.A. It says: "Swedish authorities have advised me to leave Sweden. In the event Sweden's situation should become more exposed, there is no guarantee for my personal safety. My German citizenship was taken away and I have certain information that the Gestapo has tried to trace me in Norway."[26]

(Evidently neither Brandt nor the Americans pursued this application.)

Another January 1941 arrival in Stockholm was Herbert Wehner, the KPD official, who had been sent from Moscow to inspect the work of the Comintern relay station for the underground apparatus in the Reich run by that slippery striver, Karl Mewis, and to prepare for his own entry into Nazi Germany to participate in resistance work. He was glad to go. To get away from what he called "the Procrustean bed" and the humiliation of Moscow exile at a time when some of his best comrades were dying as victims of Stalin and some of the worst comrades were spending their waking hours justifying the Hitler-Stalin pact. Among the latter was Walter Ulbricht—Wehner called him "Wulbricht" in a characteristic name game he played all his life. Ulbricht had emerged at this time from the fratricidal struggles of the German Communist leadership as Stalin's choice to run the KPD.

During the great purges Wehner had been interrogated in April 1937 by the NKVD—about Trotskyites and the 1933 Gestapo capture of Ernst Thälmann. For the next nine months he and his first wife, Lotte, watched the cold terror stalk down the halls of the Hotel Lux, where they were quartered with other exile Communists from Central Europe. One after another the NKVD seals went up on the doors of their arrested countrymen and party comrades; Wehner's number came up again in December 1937. He was taken off to the Lubianka prison for a night of questioning as a potential "enemy of the people." Then in the spring of 1938 he was handed a forty-two-part questionnaire, the construction of which led him to believe it was based largely on denunciation by KPD comrades, some of whom were even then being arrested and liquidated. The investigation continued until mid-July 1938, and a month later Georgi Dimitrov, the Comintern chief, told him to resume his regular duties. But as Hitler and Stalin drew closer together, Wehner had cut down his propaganda writing to the obligatory minimum. On the eve of the Molotov-Ribbentrop nonaggression treaty of August 23, 1939, he was advised by his chief at Radio Moscow: "Anti-fascism at any cost could easily become a provocation."[27] It was at this point that he had asked to be allowed to return to Germany to work underground, a request that was granted seventeen months later.

"I wanted out, away from all the ambiguities," Wehner wrote.

> I wanted to be directly in the struggle against the enemy, whose essence I believed I knew more about than some of the political dignitaries. That this enemy was strong, I knew. I knew, too, that he was stronger than Russian politicians imagined. . . . Again I came under the spell of the old idea I had cultivated in the early days of illegality, to steer the bungled development of the movement into new channels from within the country.[28]

He left behind him his party pseudonym, Kurt Funk, traveling as "Svensson." He also left behind his wife, Lotte, a dainty little woman, who pleaded: "Don't leave me to die in this country!"[29] Later, when Wehner was in Sweden and expelled from the party, she would marry Erich Wendt, a German Communist who had been deported for a time to the interior for some political lapse. Wendt's wife, another Lotte, surnamed Kühn, had taken up meanwhile in the corridors of the Lux with Walter Ulbricht, whom she later married. Funk-Svensson-Wehner, arriving by way of Estonia, remained underground in Stockholm. He had no contact whatsoever with the exiled German Social Democrats. Nor was he aware of the presence of the twenty-seven-year-old Frahm-"Franke"-Brandt, six years his junior.

Brandt was writing under the name Brandt, but to guard his anonymity he had taken on his old identity as Herbert Frahm. Carlota was astonished when she arrived with Ninja in the spring. "I had to get used to being called Frahm," she remembers. "I had never heard the name before."[30] But the Swedish authorities had learned of his secret excursion to Oslo, and he was arrested when he appeared in police headquarters to apply for an extension of his residence permit. He was kept in custody three days. The Stockholm police charged him with participating in illegal political activity—on behalf of a "belligerent" power, the Norwegian Government-in-Exile. He received chilly treatment because he refused to tell how he had penetrated the border zone.

Again, friends came to the rescue, foremost among them Martin Tranmael, the man Brandt had described eight years before in an SAP circular as "The Norwegian Louis Blanc—a hopeless mixture of reformism, pacifism, revolutionary phrases. . . ." Tranmael mobilized his friend Gustav Möller, the Swedish Minister of Social Welfare and the father of a trailblazing Swedish social reform program, and Brandt was swiftly sprung from jail. He wrote: "In any case we didn't take it out on the Swedish authorities and didn't run to the press if difficulties arose for us out of the more or less understandable interest in maintaining neutrality. It didn't occur to us to chide Sweden."[31]

But the incident showed he was not immune. Nor were any others of the 50,000 Norwegians and 3500 Germans who had sought asylum in Sweden. The Stockholm Government's neutrality policy had its limits, too. It had a pact in 1940 with Germany to ship Swedish iron ore by way of Narvik to the Reich, and Swedish naval vessels provided escort for Germany freighters in the Baltic. From 1941 to mid-1943 Sweden allowed whole divisions of the Wehrmacht, complete with weapons, to cross the territory of the kingdom on the way to the Finnish front. The Swedish state police were meticulous in overseeing the activities of the political émigrés, many of whom were kept for a time in labor camps for surveillance. In the early war years the Swedish police controls also showed touches of rank anti-Semitism in the handling of émigrés, especially those from Germany and Austria, who made up the bulk of the German-speaking exiles in Sweden. In one flagrant case an Austrian Jew was turned back by the Swedes at Trelleborg and forced to return on the ferry to Sassnitz.

Brandt had briefly been a war correspondent in Spain. Now he was a war journalist, a prolific one. His next two books were published in Swedish in 1941: *Kriget in Norge (War in Norway* and *Norge Forsätter Kampen (Norway Fights On)*, a two-volume reworking of his newspaper articles. The texts were published by the reputable house of Bonniers. His first book, on war aims, of which he had only the Norwegian author's copy, would serve as raw material for a later work, *After Victory*. Of the early books—he wrote four on Norway alone during the war—Brandt spoke very modestly years afterward: "They were more registering of facts than original works."[32]

He had come to Sweden "without anything." But within a year he had established himself quite comfortably. He and Carlota married soon after she arrived with Ninja. They settled in an apartment near Ole Jödal, deputy editor of *Aftontidningen,* the Social Democratic paper, which was a principal consumer of Brandt's articles. Later they moved to a larger dwelling in the suburb of Hammarbyhöjden. It was "paid for from journalism," Brandt said. "We lived better off than workers—for those times we lived well." Carlota was earning, too, working for the Norwegian Legation.[33] He wrote in 1942 to an exiled friend:

> My wife and my daughter Ninja came here a year ago. The little one is just 20 months old and we have a lot of pleasure from her. We live a bit outside of town in a pretty newly built house. I have no reason to complain. Now and then one really has a bad conscience to live a comparatively normal life and in such a neutral country.

The Frahm-Brandts were so well off that they could afford a maid. She was a shapely blue-eyed blonde with a warm smile. Rut Hansen had been born twenty-three years before in Hamar, one of four sisters, and was "completely Norwegian."[34] She met Willy and Carlota at one of the innumerable Stockholm parties held by exiles, and the tall, slender German-Norwegian caught her eye. She also needed a job, and she apparently spent more than a year in the Frahm household before acquiring a secretarial job in the press office of the Norwegian Legation. In Stockholm Rut had married Ole Bergaust, a railroad worker who had been in the Norwegian resistance and then fled to Sweden. He had contracted a severe case of tuberculosis, and was hospitalized. She and Brandt began an affair sometime in 1944.

This duality in his personal life was reflected in almost everything Brandt did. Committed to Norway, he was also committed to Germany. Writing books, he was also engaging in daily journalism. Still an active member in the Norwegian Labor Party, at the same time involved in new efforts at reviving international Socialist organizations. Did all appear to him strands of the same skein? Of his political-journalistic activities he would say: "The main aim was to get rid of the Nazis."[35] And "Hitler took away my homeland twice. I worked for a free Norway and a democratic Germany."[36]

Together with a Swedish journalist he opened a news agency in 1942—the Svensk-Norsk Pressbyra in downtown Stockholm. Entry of the Soviet Union and then the United States into the war—followed by the Allied victories at Stalingrad, El Alamein, and Midway—gradually eased the situation of anti-Nazi émigrés, including ventures like the press agency. He had also taken up with his old comrades from the SAP, that scattered band of militant idealists held together all these years by resolutions laboriously copied on onionskin paper. There were perhaps thirty of them in Stockholm and a few more in Göteborg. But his interest lay less in sociability than in Socialism and with them he began in 1942 to discuss the future of Europe in what they called the International Group of Democratic Socialists. "I had come to the Social Democratic world in Norway aged twenty and a Left Socialist," he recounted. "There I became more of a democratic Socialist and still more of one in

Sweden."[37] The SAP's Jacob Walcher had gone to New York and was making his peace with orthodox Communism. But in London, SAP exiles, including Brandt's friend Herbert George, joined a "unity front" with the exiled SPD leaders around Erich Ollenhauer. The Stockholm SAP members followed this example.

The initiative for the international "working group" of Socialists had come from Martin Tranmael, assisted by Brandt. They first convened on July 2, 1942: some Norwegians, some Germans, some Swedes, an Austrian, a Czech, a Frenchman. Brandt spoke:

> Anti-Nazism and neo-nationalism are progressive factors as long as the war lasts. But at the speed with which the end of the war is nearing we feel that this doesn't suffice as a basis for reconstruction . . . The contradiction between democratic and revolutionary socialism need not arise again if one thinks of the real problems lying ahead. . . . It is not unthinkable that one can attain a united Europe. . . . It's more probable that creation of regional units will represent an intermediary stage on the way from dispersal of nations toward a comprehensive European and international order.[38]

Some of these ideas and some of the men debating them had an impact on the formation of politics in Europe for the next three decades after that first Stockholm meeting. "We didn't want to play 'International' in Stockholm," Brandt commented in 1974. Yet from that deliberately modest beginning there emerged the postwar Socialist International, or "Small International" which, in the 1970s, could boast the linking of governing Social Democratic parties in West Germany, Austria, Sweden, Norway, Denmark, Britain, and Israel. The connection was personified by Brandt as Social Democratic Chancellor of the Federal Republic of Germany and Bruno Kreisky as Social Democratic Chancellor of Austria. Kreisky (who had also been married, during his Stockholm exile, to a Swede) was active from the beginning in the "International" discussions. Another participant was Gunnar Myrdal, the noted social economist, who became quite friendly with Brandt at this time. Nor was the circle confined to Europeans. Later meetings were attended by Willi Smulowicz, representing Palestine, and by Victor Sjaholm, a railroad union representative from Montana who was stationed in Stockholm as labor attaché of the American Embassy. Brandt functioned as secretary of the group, which convened nine times from September 1942 to May 1943 and regularly thereafter. The group established contact with like-minded Socialists in London—first by letter and then by dispatching members to meetings of the Fabian Society—and concluded that "the initiative for reconstruction of the

Socialist International must come from the English labor movement . . . the Labor Party," because it was the only group substantial enough in wartime Europe to take on the task.

But the Stockholm group was concerned with current wartime developments as well as the postwar era. Brandt noted that one of the discussions in 1943 dealt with the first detailed reports of mass extermination in gas chambers by the Nazis in Poland. They urged that "no opportunity be lost to save the lives of Jewish people." At the same time they expressed sympathy for construction of a "Jewish national home in Palestine."[39] The information on Nazi gassing had been assembled by one of the group's members, Dr. Maurycy Karniol, envoy of the Polish Government-in-Exile. Fritz Tarnow, the senior member of the German Social Democratic group in Stockholm and a former Reichstag deputy, "refused to believe in the truth of those reports." Brandt commented: "Personally, I never doubted them. The song of the youth movement, 'Man is good,' has, I am afraid, no more validity than the saying, 'Man is a swine'; the truth lies somewhere in between."[40] This concept of an intrinsic human polarity—now tending to good, now tending to swinishness—became the essence of Brandt's innermost view of his fellow man. It was a view he rarely disclosed, especially in the latter years of his political career, when the public was confronted only with one or the other tip of his psychological iceberg: Now Brandt-the-optimist, and then Brandt-the-skeptic.

He also had to contend with a vicious attack from the underground press of the Norwegian Communist Party. In early August 1943 the paper *Friheten* printed a lengthy article "revealing" that Willy Brandt was in reality "a German with a dubious background," an informer who had delivered Communists into the hands of the Gestapo, and one of "the bitterest enemies of the Soviet Union within the workers movement." The Norwegian Communists further denounced him as "an adviser to the POUM" in Spain who "fraternized with Trostkyites," and they claimed he was cool to the concept of "guerrilla war in Norway" against the Nazi occupiers because of his German origins. Brandt retorted with an "open letter" published in various illegal papers in Oslo in which he insisted that he had never made a secret of his German nationality—"and I have no reason to be ashamed about it." He went on to point out that he had "participated actively in work against Nazism for years" and that "the Nazis took away my fatherland and Hitler my citizenship." He explained that he could not have been "an adviser to the POUM" because "POUM people didn't listen at all to my occasional suggestions," and he denied fraternizing with Trotskyites. Finally, he wrote: "I am a supporter of a gathering together in the international workers movement." Whatever illusions he might have entertained about the possibilities of Socialist-Communist "unity" before the war were burned away by the "disgusting" attack of August 1943.[41]

The accusation that he was "soft" on resistance against the Nazis was doubtless prompted by the third of his six Stockholm books, *Guerillakriget,* published in late 1942 by Bonniers. The book dealt not only with historic examples of guerrilla warfare, but also the problems it raised for international law. He wrote, prophetically

> Nations fall back on the "primitive" forms of struggle of earlier times to hold their ground against modern military and political means . . . There are many signs that the last phase of the current war will be marked by extended guerrilla struggles and national uprisings.

Two decades after his *Guerrilla War* had served the Communists as a pretext to assail Brandt, it was used against him by West German reactionaries in political campaigns. Brandt was accused by propagandists for the Christian Democratic Union who had never read the text of composing "instructions for the treacherous assassination of hundreds of thousands of German soldiers" and a "handbook for Norwegian resistance fighters."[42]

The file he kept of slanders and libels was thickening, and he was facing criticism from another direction. Trygve Lie, the man who had banished Trotsky from Norway, was sitting in London as Foreign Minister of the government-in-exile, stewing about other Norwegians, particularly Tranmael and his friends. Lie had associated himself early on in the war with the extreme anti-German views of Sir Robert Vansittart, who carried his campaign from the Foreign Office (where he had been Permanent Undersecretary of State) to the public in articles, speeches, and the two books, *Lessons of My Life* and *Black Record.* Vansittart, and to an extent his Norwegian disciple, held that Germans were *inherently* evil and that "the great mass of Germans have developed in the course of three to four generations into a nation of violent, organized and wild aggressors." To overcome the "German national character" he recommended an occupation of "at least seventy-five years" and elimination of German heavy industries. Trygve Lie reflected similar thoughts in statements and messages directed against Tranmael and Brandt, whose Stockholm circle had begun to express different, Socialist views about the future of Germany. In his waspish memoir Lie wrote:

> Meanwhile I had become rather fed up with the attitude adopted by leading Norwegians in Sweden. At first they had tried—since they were forced to stay in Sweden—to defend Sweden's neutrality as

best as possible; later they had given the kindest explanation one could possibly give of Finland's participation in Hitler's war against our allies. But in my opinion it was going too far when they now seemed to be more concerned about Germany than about Norway's interests and about how to win the war.[43]

The Lie-Vansittart line—they were not the only ones promoting the stiffest terms for the German nation—spurred Brandt to put together another book, probably his best: *Efter Segern (After Victory)*. Published in 1944, again by Bonniers, it took up some of the same themes he had developed in his first—unpublished—book about war aims of the great powers. In it he dwelt at considerable length on the questions raised by "Vansittartism," answering them in part with quotations from Churchill, Roosevelt, Stalin, and Léon Blum. He went to argue: "The anti-Vansittart attitude starts from the premise that war must be conducted against Nazism and the conditions from which it sprang. Once can hate a system and its representatives without directing hatred toward the nation involved." Brandt also recommended that postwar occupation of Germany should not consist of an administration operated exclusively by the visitors or, at the other extreme, an administration with "the character of a Quisling regime." He continued: "Democratization of German society can only be accomplished in cooperation with German democrats and in connection with German democratic traditions." He avoided committing himself irrevocably on postwar Poland's final boundaries or on the problem of the 3 million Sudeten Germans, suggesting that a federative or supranational solution would be preferable in both cases. "In the struggle against Nazism, nationalism was a very important positive element. In European reconstruction work it can become a very negative factor."[44] Another thread running through the book was Brandt's preoccupation with the Prussian tradition as a "negative" factor in German history. It was a subject on which he spoke elsewhere, too. In the book it was Prussia "playing the role of the mighty fortress of reaction and militarism," and "Germany submitting to this Prussia." He continued, "The Junkers and the Prussian military class determined German politics in the last analysis. Brandt hardened these views of Prussia later, to the extent that he would write of "Prussian militarism topping off Nazism" and of "arrogant, brutal representatives of Hitlerite Prussian Germany."[45] It is practically the only German tribal attitude that comes through in all of his exile writing. One senses a breath of his Mecklenburg forefathers languishing as serfs under the knout of Prussian and Mechlenburg overlords and of the non-Prussian Free Hanse city of Lübeck where he grew up.

The Vansittart program also moved him (together with other German émigrés) to write a pamphlet, "On the post-war policy of German Socialism." Its most important conclusion was:

> The international balance of power will have changed essentially. None of the truly European states will be counted among the leading great powers. Germany will play the role of a second-rate power. It will be the task of German democrats and Socialists to represent the right of their nation to self-determination in the framework of an international organization and to secure its means of existence. It cannot be their task to struggle for regaining of German supremacy on the continent.[46]

For all his increasing concerns about Germany, Brandt was still wondering about a Norwegian variant for his life. One late night in Stockholm in 1943 he sat watching the sun rise with Oddvar Aas and Walter Taub, a Czech-German friend and asked, almost rhetorically: "What do you think? Should I be active in Norwegian politics?"

"No," said Aas. "One day someone will shout, 'You're not a good Norwegian, you are still a German.' You are too German, Willy. So stay a German."[47] In mid-December 1943 he contracted hepatitis, which laid him low for his thirtieth birthday on the eighteenth and for many weeks thereafter. It postponed completion of *After Segern* for almost two months," as he wrote Jacob Walcher in March 1944.[48] In August he would write Walcher again: "I'd like to tell you about my daughter, who will soon be four. She gives me a lot of pleasure." But his relationship with Carlota, burdened as it was by competition from a younger woman, was not easy. Before the year was out, he had broken with his wife:

> In large measure the pressure of external circumstances—the outside world—may have hastened our mutual alienation. Life in exile puts every human relationship to a severe test. Finally we had to admit to each other that there was a wall between us and we could not break it down. I had a feeling of guilt. Was it not my fault? Should I have married at all? Politics is a stern master. I would always find it difficult to lead a normal family life. Had I the right to bind myself to a woman, to ask a woman to put up with the hazards and uncertainties of my existence? I was in conflict with myself . . . We parted without hard feelings.[49]

Carlota Thorkildsen Frahm's recollection was less complicated: "We separated again in 1944, in 1948 we were officially divorced."[50]

A friend of both commented: "Willy exchanged the intellectual Carlota for the proletarian Rut. He didn't get warmth from Carlota, but challenge. He got warmth from Rut. There was disappointment on Carlota's side, for sure. But not hatred."

Brandt made support payments for Ninja regularly thereafter; Carlota supported herself.

Herbert Wehner's life in Stockholm had reached a turning point, too. He had been apprehended February 18, 1942, in the bedroom—under the bed— of a party comrade, a woman Communist, presumably on the tip of an informer. He had been on the verge of exposing Karl Mewis, a Komintern *Rezident,* as an incompetent boaster, and he was close to completing preparation for his own secret trip into the Third Reich to participate in the German Communist underground. But his plans were aborted. As he tried desperately to twist out of the grasp of the Swedish state police, more and more of his comrades in illegality were seized. In June the KPD declared him a "renegade" and a traitor to the movement. Wehner spent twenty-nine months at hard labor in penal institutions, finally being released through the intervention of Swedish politicians in late 1944. While incarcerated in 1943 he sent a postal card greeting to Charlotte Burmester, the émigré widow of a KPD comrade from Hamburg who had been tortured and finally murdered by the Nazis. Frau Burmester and her son and daughter had made their way to Sweden after she had served time in a concentration camp herself. She replied with a parcel of food, and out of their correspondence grew love.

Lotte and Herbert arranged to meet at a little railway station, but they missed each other. She entered the corner cafés singing, "Herbert Wehner, Herbert Wehner," until driven away by the proprietors. Then she bicycled across the town waving a handkerchief, still singing, "Herbert Wehner. . . ." Near a forest a voice said in German, "Who is that?" She turned and saw a man in a telephone booth. It was Wehner. "Then it happened," she said. They married at the end of the war.

Herbert Wehner had entered prison a Communist. He emerged a Socialist, "a convert," as he would say later—"a child once burned," bitter to the point of obsession, yet determined to help his people avoid the mistake he had made at such great personal cost and possessed of a dedication to find a proper home in this world for Socialism, for Germany and for himself—in unison.[51]

In the period 1943-44 Willy Brandt's interest in German affairs was concentrated on two related developments: First there was the internal resistance against Hitler that had developed out of the rather elite and conservative army officer-churchman-intellectual grouping known as the Kreisau Circle, named for Kreisau, the estate of the principal organizer, Count Helmuth von Moltke. The second interest was in the potential for a unity program of German Socialists, that old SAP dream, in resurrecting the defeated German nation. The connection between the two was personified by Julius Leber, the intrepid Social Democrat from Lübeck who was the only major figure of the Left involved in the plot against Hitler led by Moltke and Colonel Claus Schenk von Stauffenberg. Leber did not care for the political program under discussion in the Kreisau Circle. He found it "not constructive enough." But he did care about getting rid of Hitler, whatever the cost. Would their plot succeed, asked his wife, Annedore? "I don't know, and it doesn't make any difference," he replied. "I have only one head to lose. I know of no better cause than this for which to risk it."[52]

The chief political figure of the anti-Hitler conspiracy from early on was Carl Friedrich Goerdeler, the former Lord Mayor of Leipzig. A large man with pronounced ascetic leanings, Goerdeler had been an ardent monarchist and later a dedicated right-wing nationalist with strong roots in Prussian Protestantism. One of the flaws in his thinking, shared by some of the leading officers, was that a post-Hitler German leadership could somehow strike a deal with the Western powers and keep up the struggle on the Eastern front against the forces of Stalin. But it was too late for that. Only in the last months before the *Putsch* was finally attempted did some of the Kreisau men, notably Stauffenberg and Adam von Trott, conclude that Leber, rather than the sixty-year-old Goerdeler, would be the more desirable leader.

Significantly, Leber sounded out the German Communist underground leadership in Berlin in early 1944 about their intentions if Hitler was toppled. He conferred with two KPD men on June 22, 1944, in the home of a physician in East Berlin. A third man advertised as a reliable Communist was also present. He turned out to be a Gestapo agent. At a rendezvous scheduled for July 4 the KPD men were arrested. Leber, who had stayed away because of suspicion that the rules of conspiracy were being broken, was picked up by the Gestapo the following morning and slammed into jail for secret police interrogation.[53]

Brandt had been informed about the general nature of the Kreisau Circle and its intentions in early 1943 and in more detail in the winter of 1943-44 by a leading member, the profoundly religious Theodor Steltzer. The Wehrmacht had assigned Steltzer to direct the German transportation system in Oslo, and this office took him occasionally to Stockholm where he met Brandt. Through Steltzer he was able to meet the German Foreign Office Counselor, Adam von Trott, who visited Stockholm briefly in June 1944, bringing a message from Julius Leber. The news that Leber was participating in the *Putsch* electrified Brandt and virtually dispelled his sharp skepticism about the worth of an uprising led by Hitler's Wehrmacht officers, the bulk of them Prussians. He was thrilled to learn that Leber, after four years in a Nazi concentration camp and almost six years in conspiracy against Hitler, had essentially the same vision of Germany's immediate future as he himself had developed: unconditional surrender and no separate peace with the West. In their two Stockholm meetings, von Trott asked Brandt if he would place himself "at the disposal of the new government." It would appear that Brandt said yes. He also asked on Leber's behalf whether the Western powers and the Soviet Union could be approached to learn whether a successful uprising would permit them to accept the new government as a legitimate spokesman for Germany. Brandt had already sketched out the nature of the anti-Hitler conspiracy for John Scott, the *Time-Life* correspondent, on April 19, 1944, and he was in touch with members of the United States Embassy.[54] The approach to the Western side, one of the many made by the Kreisau men— some of them by von Trott himself—was easily accomplished. But when Brandt arranged a meeting thorugh Tranmael with Alexandra Kollontai, the Soviet Ambassadress, von Trott drew back—apparently fearing betrayal. Still, Brandt was exhilarated:

> Some of my closer political friends regarded Leber's alliance with the officers and conservatives as wrong and dangerous. They were afraid that the Right Social Democrats might let themselves be used as a facade for reactionary forces. I contradicted them vehemently. The formulas of the time before Hitler seemed to be out of date. I had full confidence in Leber's judgment and in his political instinct.[55]

Von Trott was scarcely back in Berlin when Leber was captured. It was a terrific blow to the conspiracy, the more so since it prompted von Stauffenberg to rush ahead his plans to plant a bomb in Hitler's headquarters to July 15 in hope of freeing Leber before he was tortured into revealing the plot or was executed.[56] Hitler's sudden absence at his East Prussian "Wolf's Lair" at the last minute forced a replay on July 20 with disastrous consequences for coordination of the rest of the *Putsch* actions.

Brandt recalls being "moved to tears" by the news of Leber's arrest, and one believes him.[57] That and the subsequent failure of the *Putsch* virtually wiped out his association with the July 20 plotters. Of the leading men of Kreisau only Theodor Steltzer and two others survived the wave of Hitler's vengeance. Brandt would see Steltzer and Leber's widow again in peacetime.

Brandt remained active in émigré politics in the closing months of the war. His SAP comrades formally merged with the Social Democratic Party of Germany in October 1944. He retained membership in the Norwegian Labor Party and, curiously, in the Norwegian Seamen's Union. The International

Socialist discussion group was in the process of establishing itself formally as the Socialist Internationale, with membership from eleven countries, and he was still its official secretary. (In this function he noted such details as the cost of sharing a "tea snack" per member: "2.25 crowns—Butter and bread ration tickets to be brought along."[58]

His prominence as a war journalist and author provided him an entree in the embassies of many a foreign government. In addition to the Americans, who seem to have cultivated him quite a bit, he was also seeing the British, who were rather cool. Later it was revealed that the British Secret Service had put together a dossier on Brandt that held him to be "unreliable" because he had contact with Communists and with the Soviet Embassy. Among the Communists he saw briefly was Karl Mewis, who had been arrested six months after Herbert Wehner by the Swedish State Police and interned for a year. The way Mewis tells it, "Willy, the German Norwegian, sought contact with me." He also claims that he and Brandt not only agreed on most political questions but also arranged to work together on printing leaflets to be sent to occupied Denmark.[59] Brandt later described the Mewis account as "false."[60]

Nevertheless, there was a taste of "socialist unity" to some of his activities and, indeed, some of his old SAP comrades were propagating the establishment of a "Socialist Unity Party of Germany." One of them was apparently Max Seydewitz, that friendly Leftist gasbag who had been a co-founder of the original SAP and was now a fellow exile in Stockholm. Two years later Seydewitz was in Berlin attending the establishment, under Soviet aegis, of the KPD-SPD merger, which took on the same name, Socialist Unity Party (SED).

Early in 1945 Brandt and the other Stockholm émigrés learned of the attempts by Folke Bernadotte to rescue some of the thousands of Scandinavians held prisoner by the Nazis. In secret communication with Heinrich Himmler in February the Swedish count succeeded in persuading the SS Führer to assemble deported Danes and Norwegians under care of the Swedish Red Cross in the Neuengamme Concentration Camp near Hamburg. In April Himmler released these and a group of deportees who had been confined in the women's concentration camp at Ravensbrück to Sweden. At the end of April a group of 3500 Norwegians was released, among them several old friends of Brandt from Oslo.

When Brandt learned of a new meeting on April 24 between Bernadotte and Himmler in Lübeck he rang up Nazi occupation headquarters in Oslo. It was the evening of Sunday, April 29, three days after Mussolini had been executed by Italian partisans and the eve of Hitler's suicide in the bunker of the Berlin Reich Chancellery. Brandt was put through to Skaugum, the palace of the crown prince, which was the residence of Reichskommissar Terboven.

Terboven asked who was calling, and when Brandt identified himself, the Nazi governor handed the receiver to SS Obergruppenführer Wilhelm Rediess. In this unique long-distance call, Rediess confirmed that Norwegian political prisoners were about to be released.

> Rediess: "As far as that has been discussed between the Reichsführer SS and Count Bernadotte it is being prepared."
> Brandt: "But can one reckon with immediate action?"
> Rediess; "Yes, yes, as far as the agreement between the Reichsführer SS and Count Bernadotte is concerned this is in preparation."
> Brandt: "In view of the latest events in Germany can one expect an announcement of the occupation authorities in Oslo?"
> Rediess: "No. Is that clear, yes? (click)."[61]

That was the last the world heard from Wilhelm Rediess until his death ten days later. Some of the 6000 Norwegian prisoners in the Grini camp near Oslo were released in the following days. On May 3 the leaders of the Hjemmefront—the underground Home Front—issued a proclamation calling for public order and the avoidance of unnecessary clashes with the Germans. In the evening of May 8 the German commander-in-chief, General Franz Böhme, signed the capitulation order for his 310,000 troops in front of a British brigadier. In the same hour Rediess shot himself in the head. Terboven had the corpse taken to his bunker and there he blew himself up. Already the streets of the Norwegian capital were filled with jubilant citizens celebrating victory.

Willy Brandt was jubilant, too, but he was celebrating in the quieter atmosphere of Stockholm. From Oslo, where he had spent the previous ten months running an underground newspaper, Inge Scheflo called his friend:

"Willy, where are you? What are you doing? When are you people coming back?"

"What do you think?" Brandt replied. "I am a German. You know the mood against Germany."

"Thunderation!" Scheflo bellowed. "Are you crazy? Come back right away! Otherwise it's Hitlerism in reverse." Reflecting many years later on this, Scheflo mused, "It was his tact. He was German and a Norwegian citizen, but he wondered whether it would be tactful to appear right away—after all, Lie had accused him of being 'too German' and said, 'Blood is thicker than water.'"[62]

Two days later, on May 10, Brandt arrived in Oslo. "My Norwegian citizenship was more to me than a mere formality. Consequently I felt certain obligations which I could not simply shake off."[63]

The war he had foreseen twelve years before was over, and with it his compulsory exile. His double-banishment was halved. But he remained a Norwegian citizen for the next three years. That, too, was an aftereffect of the rule of Hitler.

V:
Roads to Berlin

When World War II ended, those Germans who were destined to assume for their nation the job of rebuilding after Hitler were scattered across the blasted face of Europe—and in utter obscurity. So complete was the devastation of the German polity that within or without the frontiers of the Reich there was scarcely a German left who could presume to eventual power.

Willy Brandt and Herbert Wehner were in Sweden. Erich Ollenhauer was in Britain. Konrad Adenauer was just emerging from what he called "inner emigration" at his home in Rhöndorf on the Rhine. Kurt Schumacher, with ten years in four different concentration camps behind him, was free from Nazi house arrest in Hannover. Erich Honecker, the militant young Communist, escaped from a prison detail in the confusion of the seige of Berlin after serving a decade in Brandenburg Penitentiary.

Of the anti-Nazis who survived the Hitler era in various forms of exile with a will to return to German politics, only Walter Ulbricht, the career Communist, was already in business and in Germany. He had landed with nine other German Communists in a Soviet Army transport at a temporary field north of Frankfurt an der Oder early in the afternoon of April 30, 1945— the day of Hitler's suicide in besieged Berlin, fifty miles to the west. The initial assignment of the "Ulbricht Group": Seek out reliable Communists, Social Democrats, and other "progressive citizens" to reestablish a German civil administration. The Communists were not to assume a leading position immediately, Ulbricht cautioned.[1]

Power in the defeated Reich was exercised by the victors—the Soviet Union, Britain, and the United States, soon to be joined by France. The country was divided into four occupation zones under protocols signed the previous year in London and Paris. But for the apparent exception of the Russians, none of the wartime Allies had given thought to the structures of postwar administration. The land lay desolate: cities smashed, highway bridges blown, crops unplanted, hunger and looting spreading as millions of uprooted Germans and freshly liberated inmates of concentration camps and forced labor camps swarmed across it.

At Yalta in March Stalin, Churchill, and Roosevelt had agreed on indefinite occupation of Germany, but little more. For a time in late 1944 Stalin had sung in the chorus of those demanding the eternal "pastoralizing" of Germany, reducing her powerful industries to nil: Britain's Robert Vansittart, America's Henry Morgenthau, France's Henri de Kerillis. Now his triumphant forces were busy gathering in massive reparations, removing entire factories and railway lines to Russia. In the mind of Stalin one thing was sure—what the Soviet Army conquered, it would retain. His country had paid a blood tribute of 6.5 million fighting men and women and 10 million civilian lives in less than four years of war (4 million Germans died out of a total of 40 million killed of all nationalities). But for the rest his attitude was ambivalent. Reparations were fine, as was chasing the Junker landowners off their estates. But how was a German working class to assume power under Soviet aegis if there was no place for them to work? Did Stalin still believe, as he had told a Polish politician, that "Communism fitted Germany as a saddle fitted a cow"? Was he still thinking of Germany as a whole, instead of Germany in pieces? Whatever the case, Ulbricht and his comrades proceeded—correctly—on the assumption that the Soviet dictator wanted Communist authority established in that part of Germany held by the Red Army. Following the precepts of the murdered Trotsky and Lenin's brief 1920 example—the attempt to export revolution to Poland and "probe Europe with the bayonet of the Red Army" in the "political vacuum" of Germany, as Willy Brandt described it in 1945,[2] the German Communists were the first to gain legitimacy from an occupation power.

On June 11, 1945, scarcely one month after the unconditional surrender of the Nazi regime, the Communist Party of Germany was created in Berlin on the authority of Order No. 2 of the Soviet administration. Ulbricht remained a backroom boy for the time being, light years away from becoming Stalin's proconsul. Wilhelm Pieck was designated head of the provisional KPD leadership, while Ulbricht became one of the sixteen members of the Central Committee.

Had Willy Brandt opted for the Communist variant in Germany, he probably could have returned swiftly to the Soviet zone. To enter the Western zones was still difficult, and illegal, for the political émigrés. The Enderles, August and Irmgard, slipped into Bremen by August without permission from the British or American occupation authorities. Other former comrades from the SAP were heading for East Berlin, Max Seydewitz included.

Willy Brandt continued to commute between Stockholm and Oslo, initially as a correspondent for Swedish newspapers. He spent the last three weeks of May in Oslo, then several weeks in Stockholm, then more time in Oslo. He was doing Scandinavian things, helping organize relief operations for Germans and Norwegians; he published a pamphlet about the trials of Quisling and his aides. But his mind was on occupied Germany. "I am most certainly not a German nationalist," he wrote on August 14 to Walcher. "For years I have opposed those who believed everything depended on keeping the old frontiers. But I regard the arrangement reached in the East in its present form as unreasonable." It was only a few weeks after the conclusion of the Potsdam Conference attended by Attlee, Truman, and Stalin; Brandt wrote also to the Enderles: "I make an unequivocal reservation in regard to the frontier arrangement in the East, which in my opinion goes much too far."[3]

The Poles had been accorded administrative rights over the huge territory that had been part of the Reich as Pomerania, East Prussia, and Silesia, and Brandt immediately saw that it would soon be incorporated into Poland. Soon after he noted that "none of the occupation powers has presented a program as yet for the final solution of the German question although all are certainly aware that 'total' occupation can only be a temporary condition." He went on: "Most noticeable is plainly the contrast between the fraternization ban of the Western allies and the collaboration propaganda on the Russian side." He was struck also by the fact the Russians had authorized creation of "anti-Nazi parties" while, "with the Western allies the tendency is dominant to treat the Germans as a Nazi totality whose master race mentality should be driven out with toughness." At the same time it was clear to him that "Nazism is not completely overcome."

> As a regime it is destroyed. As a spiritual pestilence we find it or a mentality related to it in the heads of many people, I'm sorry to say. No one can imagine that Europe will become healthy from one day to the next. It needs a fundamental healing. (But:) Europe doesn't play the same role in the world as before. Germany and Italy have been eliminated as great powers. France's role as a continental great power no longer enjoys unlimited recognition. . . . the Soviet Union is on stage alongside the U.S.A. as a decisive world power.[4]

About this time he wrote to an Austrian friend, "Well, I will always feel the closest bonds with Norway. But I have never given up Germany. It would be more comfortable to retreat to the Norwegian position. But I cannot make that decision." He went on to tell of the activities of Bruno Kreisky, still in Stockholm, and to describe the situation of Ernst Paul, the Sudeten German

Social Democrat, as "especially tragic" in view of the expulsion of the 3 million Sudetenlanders from Czechoslovakia then under way.[5]

Brandt also heard from Martha Kulhmann, his mother, and replied:

> My dear Mother! Your question, when I am returning, can't be answered yet. The return of political refugees will move faster now. The Americans, especially, but the English authorities, too, are interested that people outside return and join the administration and help with the reconstruction of the trade unions. In this framework I ought to have a possibility of return. I still have a couple of things to do in Norway which I can't simply leave lie. But one of these days I'll show up.[6]

He was itching to get back to Germany. But how, and where, should he go? Legally, he was now a Norwegian, just as Thomas Mann was an American. In October he persuaded a number of Swedish and Norwegian papers to send him to Germany as their correspondent at the International Military Tribunal in Nürnberg to cover the trials of the remaining Nazi leaders. He flew to Bremen in a British plane and immediately got in touch with the Enderles, who had found employment at the newly licensed *Weser-Kurier.* There he met Senator Adolf Ehlers, formerly of the KPD, now of the SPD, and Mayor Wilhelm Kaisen, an SPD stalwart. Irmgard Enderle remembered that Brandt appeared in "a Norwegian uniform," which was required for correspondents at that time.

> He brought us a lot of things: coffee, flour, powdered eggs, chocolate, cigarettes, all the things you couldn't buy in Germany then. He had a whole rucksack full of them . . . He asked us then for advice whether he should keep his name Willy Brandt. He had become accustomed to it in the years in which he had lived only as Willy Brandt. We told him not to call himself Frahm again.[7]

His Bremen hosts arranged for him to be driven the three hours' distance to Lübeck, and along the way he noticed the keen contrast between the ugly rubble of the cities and the relatively unspoiled countryside. It had been more than twelve years since he left his birthplace, and now he spent only one day there, mostly with his mother, stepfather, and stepbrother—the latter had been drafted as an anti-aircraft orderly in the last days of the war at the age of seventeen.

He had presents in his rucksack for them, too. He also saw that Lübeck was "no longer the town of seven spires; the churches and the historic buildings of the city had suffered much."[8] Indeed, the Hanse capital had been the first struck by a massive night raid of the Royal Air Force. The attack on the eve of Palm Sunday 1942 by four-engine bombers rained tons of explosives and incendiary bombs on Lübeck. "I saw how everything caught fire in the clamor all around, the railroad terminal, houses in Lindenplatz, in Moislinger Allee (next to Brandt's birthplace), in Lindenstrasse, in the city," an eyewitness recorded. "Then the Petri Church was burning, Marien Church, the Graben. Fires ran like snakes through all the streets."[9]

The first impressions made him reflective. His half-brother was "perplexed and lost . . . a typical representative of the new generation." But "I could not have said which depressed me more: the indifference with which each spoke of his horrible experiences—without raising his voice, in parentheses so to speak—or the bitter complaints about the occupation." Just the same:

> Nobody reproached me, nobody brought up the argument that abroad I had had a better life. Yet, I had to admit to myself that my lot had been a much easier one. Certainly, in exile I had not rested on a bed of roses, but through my own work I had made my living, I had had the chance to learn and to widen my horizon.[10]

From Lübeck he journeyed to Nürnberg, another devastated monument to the awesome and the awful in Germany's recent and ancient history: a city of Hans Sachs and Albrecht Dürer, memorable medieval buildings, the renowned Christmas Market and toy industry, gingerbread, and, beginning in 1933, the monstrous Nazi Party rallies of Hitler. The Führer had fixed on Nürnberg as a link to Germany's mighty past, the site of imperial conventions. Nürnberg, too, had been chosen in 1935 as the place to announce his notorious anti-Semitic decrees comprising the "Law for the Protection of German Blood and German Honor" at a rally engineered by Albert Speer and eerily illuminated by thousands of torches and searchlights. Nürnberg had become a spiritual home for Nazism, and it was as such that it was selected as the venue for the prosecution of the vilest crimes of modern times in the persons of twenty-one surviving Nazi leaders.

Willy Brandt watched, listened, and reported the war crimes trials with considerable detachment, it appears, although "the factual reports of what had happened in the occupied countries and in Germany, in the concentration and extermination camps made one's flesh creep."[11]

The indictment was handed to the defendants in mid-October. All were charged with guilt in the most horrifying excesses of Nazi rule, including genocide. Writing a comment for the trial proceedings on October 17, the eve of the official handing down of the indictment, Speer, Hitler's architect and later his chief of forced labor operations, the exception admitting his culpability among those in the dock declared: "The trial is necessary. There is a shared responsibility for such crimes even in an authoritarian state."[12]

Brandt's reaction was almost identical to Speer's at this time. He wrote:

> The Germans must carry the responsibility. Responsibility however is not the same as guilt. Those who do not feel guilty and are not guilty of the Nazi crimes cannot—if they want to go on working in this nation and make it better—withdraw from the consequences of a policy which the greater majority of the nation acceded to. They cannot place themselves outside the community of responsibility.[13]

At the same time, he wrote, even German anti-Nazis would be "out of their minds if they did not admit their share of the *co-responsibility* (Brandt's italics) for Nazism—disregarding the fact that they could not shirk off the consequences of the Nazi war and murder policy even if they wanted to." These observations made during the Nürnberg hearings he set down in a book published in 1946 in Norwegian and Swedish entitled *Forbrytere og andre-Tyskar* (*Criminals and Other Germans*). Like most Germans, and a few non-Germans, Brandt had mixed feeling about the Nürnberg trials, or at least about some aspects of their methodology: "I was not one of those who on principle criticized the decision to put the chief culprits of the Hitler regime on trial in an international court of justice and to call them to account for their crimes against humanity." However inadequate, it permitted an insight into the criminal practices of the Nazis and how "power can be abused in a highly developed country ruled by totalitarianism." But it might have helped to have the accused tried by "representatives of the 'other Germany.'" Another problem raised by the Nürnberg proceedings was that they "did not administer justice impartially."[14]

Still, the trials were an accomplished fact, and Brandt had become accustomed to waste little time dwelling on the inevitable. Rather, his interest lay in weighing the consequences of such events for the future. At the time there was much talk of "collective guilt," which was a kind of postvictory spillover from the wave of anti-German feeling given expression by the Vansittarts and Morgenthaus. Brandt's response:

> The Nazis—in Germany and other countries—are *guilty*. Nürnberg has laid bare a guilt complex that outstrips the wildest imagination. The guilty are not only party leaders and Gestapo terrorists, but also the groups of Junkers, big industrialists, generals, bureaucrats and professors who participated in unleashing the

terror and the war. These groups must be eliminated and their social influence taken away. . . . The Nazi opponents . . . are not guilty. But they cannot escape co-responsibility for Hitler's coming to power. They cannot avoid the consequences of the Nazi murder policy. They must realize that their actions will be viewed with mistrustful eyes for a long time. They cannot expect to receive a blank check. . . . Between the Nazis and the Nazi opponents lies the great mass of the more or less indifferent. Their responsibility is great. But there is no sense in heaping a disproportionate guilt upon them. A guilt feeling that one attempts to impose from outside is not the happiest start for reeducation. . . .[15]

The Germans were not "predestined to be a nation of criminals"; they were, rather, "in many respects an immature people." Now, in defeat, there was an opportunity "to grow into a genuine unity." There was room for hope because the "community in woe is not the worst soil for a new patriotism," and "perhaps even German culture has still a task to fulfill," however bold that might sound "so short a time after Maidanek, Belsen and Auschwitz."

Brandt noted that German attempts at unity across frontiers were viewed with extreme skepticism abroad. But if such sentiments were implemented by

reliable anti-Nazi forces with a correct foreign policy orientation they could be something quite different, namely, a contribution to the securing of peace. The Nazis made the attempt to Germanize Europe in their fashion. Now is the time to Europeanize Germany. That won't work by chopping it up, or by playing one German group against another. The problem of Germany and Europe can only be solved through a bringing together of the West, the East— and that which lies in the middle. It can only be solved on the basis of liberty and democracy.[16]

All this was addressed primarily to a Scandinavian audience. More than a decade later, when Brandt became prominent in German politics, it would serve as grist for his detractors, who called it a "damnation of Germandom," and the "book of German ignominy." Often his attackers would distort the title and make it *Germans and Other Criminals* or even, in 1975, *Germans and Other Murderers.*[17]

Brandt was one of the very few Germans accredited by the Allies to cover the trial, although he was officially listed as a Norwegian. When the disparity became known, there was some trouble. "The British Secret Service objected to Willy Brandt," Oddvar Aas recalls. "When he was at the Nürnberg trials they found out he was not Willy Brandt but Herbert Frahm. But he had so many Allied friends that they extricated him."[18] Except for the Christmas holidays, which he spent in Oslo, Brandt remained in Germany until February 1946—most of the time attending the trials. In Nürnberg he got acquainted with some of the surviving Social Democrats. Early in January he attended a meeting of SPD leaders in Offenbach and was introduced to Kurt Schumacher by Erich Ollenhauer. In nearby Frankfurt he also met Willi Richter, later chosen as chairman of the German Trade Union Federation.

Despite the continuing ban on political organization in the Western zone a lot of activity had developed—in large part because of a political counterforce emerging under Russian aegis in the Eastern zone. Unburdened by scruples or prejudice, the Soviet Military Administration authorized the reestablishment of political parties—as long as they were "anti-Fascist"—sure in the knowledge they could be manipulated or, if necessary, coerced.

Within two weeks after the first troop contingents of the Western Allies arrived to take up their posts in Berlin and participate in an Allied *Kommandantur,* the Soviets authorized the establishment of a "Unity Front of anti-Fascist-Democratic Parties" comprising the KPD, SPD, a Christian Democratic Union, and a Liberal Democratic Party. It was the first step toward a "united" Left under Communist domination, although parallel steps were under way in Czechoslovakia, Hungary, Rumania, and Poland. The days of harmony were limited. By autumn the Russians were humiliating the CDU leaders to the point of stealing the trousers of one while he was on a speaking tour. By Christmas they had compelled a co-founder of the CDU to quit.[19] The Social Democrats in the Soviet zone fared a little better, but not for long. They were living on time borrowed by a small group of SPD men who believed so fervently in the need for unity of the Left after the Nazi debacle that they risked meeting halfway with the Communists. Chief among them was Otto Grotewohl, a former Reichstag deputy from Braunschweig.

The activities of the Berlin KPD and SPD were well known to Kurt Schumacher at his provisional office in Hannover, and he viewed them with great suspicion. It was characteristic of the occupation situation that when the Grotewohl group sought to meet with the Schumacher group in the autumn of 1945 they got permission immediately from the Russians, but not from the Western Allies. The meeting was convened October 6 in Wennigsen, a Hannover suburb. On arrival the Berlin delegation of three was told by a British liaison officer that there was no room for them in the conference hall. Schumacher kept his distance. When Grotewohl appeared again, Schumacher let him do most of the talking. Perhaps, as an experienced SPD man observed, he also saw Grotewohl as a possible rival for chairmanship of the national SPD.[20] Or worse, as the puppet of a Soviet-manipulated Leftist unity movement throughout occupied Germany.

Other factors were at work. In November the reconstituted Communist parties of Hungary and Austria suffered humiliating election setbacks at the hands of Social Democrats and bourgeois parties. Immediately, Wilhelm Pieck, the KPD chief, opened a vast "unity campaign" in the Soviet zone designed to swallow the SPD, which had much broader support than the German Communists. Grotewohl went along hesitantly at first. Then, as the Communists promised rewards, he grew more enthusiastic. Ploy and counterploy followed. On Pieck's seventieth birthday, January 3, 1946, the Communists heaped him with honors in the State Opera House, and Grotewohl declared in the name of the SPD: "To you, dear Wilhelm Pieck, we offer a handshake, a handshake that should have meaning not only for today, but one that should last so long that the hands do not part."

It was the Communists, however, who had the steel in their grip that foreboding day. On January 6 Schumacher declared to a group of West German SPD officials in Frankfurt that their part of the party "does not want to be a blood donor for the weakened body of the KPD." Now the Russians forced the issue in their zone, compelling the SPD in Thuringia to raise the call for unity and set a date for its realization. At the end of January Grotewohl was ordered out to Soviet headquarters in Karlshorst and told to push unification of the two parties at all cost. The man who gave the secret order was Marshal Georgy Zhukov.

What was the hurry? The Communists had had enough of elections they couldn't run themselves. In Hesse local elections on January 20 the KPD got only 4.6 percent to the SPD's gain of 41.4 percent. All across the Soviet zone SPD officials found themselves under extreme pressure to get on the unity bandwagon. Some were arrested and sent to the reopened camps at Buchenwald and Sachsenhausen. Others were spied upon, in Weimar and Wittenberg, in Halberstadt and Jena. On February 8 Grotewohl made a desperate dash to Braunschweig to bid once more for legitimation from the West SPD. Without success. Schumacher asked if under pressure Grotewohl would consider simply dissolving the Eastern SPD. But Grotewohl had committed himself to the Russians, and on February 11, before a crowd of more than 1000 Social Democrats and trade unionists, Grotewohl issued the call for SPD-KPD merger by May 1—in the Soviet zone alone. It was a first step toward deliberate separation of East Germany from the rest of Germany, to be followed by many more on both sides.[21] He met with scorn.

Grotewohl's colleague, Gustav Dahrendorf, skipped to the West three days later. The game was over for the SPD in the Soviet zone, and very nearly in Berlin itself. The dream of unity once shared so passionately by Willy Brandt was coming true, but in the distorted mirror image of the Communists.

What about Berlin, the greater part of it occupied by troops of the United

States, Berlin, and France? The bulk of the Berlin SPD members adamantly refused to go along with a merger. Kurt Schumacher came to the divided city February 20 to offer support to a group of mostly younger party officials who were planning to go their own way. Led by Franz Neumann, forty-one, and Otto Suhr, fifty-one, the antimerger Socialists got help from British occupation officials and some Americans, too. The Americans had to act stealthily because their primary order was to get along with the Russians at all costs. But with the blessing of the senior political officer, the young Americans of the military government did what they could to block the merger. "Sometimes it was just a matter of giving out food," Louis Wiesner recalled almost thirty years later. "George Silver had his whole apartment full of parcels for the Social Democrats. We had to do it out of our own pockets." The Americans also tried to the end to turn Grotewohl and Erich Gniffke away from a merger. Wiesner went so far as to talk to Walter Ulbricht for hours and remembers him saying: "We are going to bring about unity of Germany no matter what you say."[22]

A day after his call on Neumann and Suhr, Schumacher sounded out Grotewohl, who had just rammed through a merger decision in the SPD central committee at headquarters in East Berlin. Accompanied by an armed British Army captain, Schumacher appeared at Grotewohl's home in the American sector. With Grotewohl's concurrence he addressed the central committee saying that merger was desirable but impossible as long as the German Communists were "tied to one of the occupation powers." With his British escort Schumacher also ventured across to the Soviet sector to inspect SPD headquarters. It was all very polite, but neither the East or the West Social Democrats were in a position or a mood to compromise. On March 1 the SPD opposition in Berlin cast down the gauntlet, challenging Grotewohl in a turbulent delegates' conference. When Grotewohl rose to speak for the merger with the KPD, he was shouted down: "You didn't ask us!" and "Go back to Karlshorst, Otto!" and "You are a splitter!" Whistles shrilled. Boos were bellowed. Grotewohl pleaded: "We can't have Nazi methods." To no avail. Franz Neumann called for a showdown vote. One month later the Berlin opposition organized the referendum, despite a prohibition in the Soviet sector, and got 80 percent of the SPD ballots. A week later the opposition reconstituted the Berlin SPD in a Zehlendorf schoolhouse with a borrowed typewriter and a table given them by sympathizers.[23] Grotewohl and the Communists went ahead with the fusion schedule and poured eight tons of leaflets—printed on paper specially "donated" by the Soviets—into the fray. "It was painful," Wiesner remembered, "you could see these men like Grotewohl crumbling under Soviet pressure." Grotewohl's rump SPD held a "Fortieth Party Congress" in East Berlin's Theater am Schiffbauerdamm on

April 20, while the KPD held its Fifteenth Congress nearby in the Admiralspalast playhouse. They came together on Easter Sunday, and Grotewohl and Pieck repeated their handshake, with Ulbricht watching. Their clasped hands were chosen as the symbol of their newly established Socialist Unity Party (Sozialistische Einheitspartei Deutschlands or SED). Together, they moved into "The House of Unity," a hastily refurbished building that had belonged to a Jewish mail-order merchant before the Nazi takeover. Grotewohl got a villa in a northern borough, next to the Soviet commandant and Ulbricht and Pieck, safe behind newly strung barbed wire and Red Army guards. Their SED had 1,298,415 members, of whom 53 percent had been sucked in from the SPD.[24]

There were celebrations—on May 1 the SED mobilized half a million Berliners for a "unity" parade—and parties in a short-lived honeymoon atmosphere. Grotewohl's lifelong friend, Erich W. Gniffe, who hung on as a senior party official for two and a half more years, recalled an evening affair where he and a KPD man played a practical joke by frenching the beds, knotting pajamas, and hiding Walter Ulbricht's house slippers in a rainspout. "Where are Walter's slippers?" Ulbricht's Lotte pleaded. "We don't like that at all."[25]

Germany, to reverse the dictum of Karl Clausewitz, is a country where politics is nothing but the continuation of war with other means.[26] One ignores this reality at one's peril. The formation of the SED was, in reality, a declaration of war on the rest of Germany's politicians and nascent parties, a declaration of war against the three Western occupying powers as well.

The message from the East was not lost on Kurt Schumacher, nor on the more foresighted Western occupation officials, especially the British. Schumacher was hastily authorized to stage a convention of the free SPD in Hannover from May 9 to 11. He had not been idle, and among the 258 delegates were representatives of the newly formed SPD organization from the Western sectors of Berlin, as well as of all three West German occupation zones.

Willy Brandt attended in the double capacity of reporter-delegate, representing his Scandinavian papers and the Norwegian Labor Party. Per Monsen was there with him: "It was the first postwar convention of the SPD, and it was held in the Hanomag (motor vehicle) Hall. It was the first time he heard Schumacher, a vitriolic speaker who called the Communists 'those red-lacquered Communists' and criticized the (Western) Allies. He was a nationalist who didn't want a new stab-in-the-back legend. He called the small powers 'these also victors'—a good phrase. And he said that only when the Russians are east of the Oder-Neisse line could Germany be safe. Willy didn't like Schumacher from then on. He said afterward that Schumacher had the wrong approach to be nationalist."[27]

Like him or not, Schumacher had been elected chairman of the first postwar political party established on a confederation basis in the western two-thirds of Germany. The Free Democratic Party did not achieve this until 1948, and the Christian Democratic Union only in 1950.

Willy Brandt, a tall thirty-two-year-old in a Norwegian Army uniform with a correspondent's patch on his shoulder, called on Schumacher after the party congress at his office in the Jakobstrasse. Schumacher's secretary, Annemarie Renger, then an attractive war widow of twenty-six who was also nurse to the ailing chairman, recalled in 1973 that "Schumacher said to me, 'That's a remarkable young man. If he came back you could do something with him.' He knew of him as having been with Leber and in the SAP. He wanted him. But one got the impression Brandt didn't feel very good about the Germans. There was a certain reserve. That's subjective of course. But it didn't seem after his talk with Kurt Schumacher that he would come back, although that was not impossible. But Schumacher got the impression Brandt caught fire. He was a very good-looking young man who impressed everyone without your knowing why. He's not my type. Almost shy toward women. Not a conqueror, but one who seeks protection from a woman. Not at all the male conqueror."[28]

Brandt recalled: "I wanted to do something. But I was also wary and critical."[29] Schumacher had asked him to return and join in the grim but exciting work of reconstructing the devastated land, the first of many offers. Brandt asked for time, exercising a quality of deliberation—or hesitancy—that was to be a hallmark of his political life. But it would appear he caught the Berlin bug from Schumacher then—he had been closely watching the events in the former Reich capital.

From Oslo he had written Erich Ollenhauer on April 30:

> . . . In the trade union area an initiative should come from our side for interzonal cooperation. That way we can overcome the isolation of our comrades in the East to a certain degree. In any case we can't look on them as "traitors" even though they have decided under the given conditions for a policy that we hold to be ominous.

At the end of the month he also wrote Jacob Walcher, still in New York exile:

> It is indisputable that the Socialist Unity Party in the East Zone is something far different from what we had striven for as the outcome of our unity policy. What decides it is that the creation of

the Socialist Unity Party was pushed forward with undemocratic means and in part even with violent methods.

A zonewide land reform was under way with the dispossession of the great landowners, Brandt noted and added:

> Delight over the structurally progressive changes in the East Zone is fundamentally diminished by the fact that a "new type of democracy" is being practiced which has hardly anything to do with democratic basic rights and even shoves aside the elemental requirements of democratic formation of opinion within the workers movement. The democratic basic rights however are not questions of expediency. They are basic questions of the first order. . . . Forced merger undoubtedly contributes to hardening of the zonal borders. This effect will not be softened however many appeals the Socialist Unity Party makes. For the Western powers but also for the Western workers movement the SED policy represents a function of Russian foreign policy. It calls for countermeasures. The result will be a deeper split rather than the so necessary stronger unification. For my part I draw the conclusion that now more than ever one must allow the SP (Social Democratic Party) to get as strong as possible in the West.[30]

Brandt also noted that

> At the party congress in Hannover the Berliners were the heroes of the day. After thirteen years Germans had had the opportunity to make a political decision freely, and they had voted for freedom, and they had voted for freedom in spite of all the allurements and threats from the East, in spite of many a disappointment about the lack of understanding in the West. Now one ought to be in Berlin, I thought. With "one" I meant myself.[31]

But he was not to reach Berlin for another eight months. The divided city was still the preserve of the four Allied powers, and they were not about to let exiles sample the entrepot yet. Instead, Brandt turned north to Lübeck, where he spoke at a rally organized by local SPD leaders. Monsen was there, too: "He drew a big crowd. Brandt decided to be antinationalist. He gave a conciliatory speech about Germany's obligations and did not share Schumacher's nationalist feeling. We were greatly surprised that he got great cheers, more than the usual, more than those who took the nationalist line."[32]

Stopping in Nürnberg again to write a few more reports on the trials,

Brandt then headed for Oslo and a vacation. From the Norwegian capital he wrote Jacob Walcher:

> I haven't made a final decision about my future work. Several proposals were made to me in Hannover. But I want to be financially independent of the party if possible. In Lübeck, where I spoke on May 20 for the first time in 13 years I was very warmly greeted and the comrades would like it if I came there. Perhaps I'll do it even though I have the feeling it would be plenty tight for me there.[33]

He told Walcher he had also been offered various German press jobs and was "very tempted" by a proposal that he take over a news agency. The same day Brandt wrote Walcher he also sent a letter to Schumacher, advising him that packages for Germany gathered by Swedish charities were piling up in Lübeck because of "stalling" by German customs authorities (a service notorious then and for years later as a refuge of ex-Nazis.)

Then he went on a long vacation to Sogne fjord in Norway to sift the prospects for his future and talk them over with his companion, Rut Hansen Bergaust, the girl from Hamar who had captivated him. Sogne fjord was the place where he had made his first political speech in Norwegian in 1933.[34]

In August Brandt was back in Germany and in demand. He again conferred in Hannover with Schumacher, who urged him to return. Other exiles were on their way or already resettled in Germany. In Bielefeld, where he went to report on the founding congress of the Western zone German Trade Union Federation, he met Max Brauer, just back from the United States and soon to be chosen the SPD Mayor of Hamburg. Brandt stopped in that great port city, too. There for the first time he made the acquaintance of Herbert Wehner, who had become an editor of the *Hamburger Echo,* an SPD paper, and a disciple of Schumacher.

Northern Germany was the British zone, and Britain had a Labor Government well disposed to the SPD. Fritz Heine, who had come back from London with Erich Ollenhauer and was in charge of press affairs for the SPD executive told Brandt that the two German press agencies DENA in the American zone and DPD in the British zone were about to be transferred from military to civilian control. Would he be interested in a top job? He was enthusiastic enough to travel to Bad Nauheim for a talk with the Americans about taking on DENA. "A captain talked to me; he regarded me as too far Right, too close to Schumacher, and too negative to the Russians. Then, Heine said, try DPD, but the British didn't reply."[35] Not at once, at any rate. Brandt went back to Lübeck and to Kiel, where Theodor Steltzer, one of the July 20 conspirators against Hitler, had become governor of the state of Schleswig-Holstein. For the second time Steltzer offered Brandt the post of Mayor in Lübeck, explaining that he wanted Otto Passarge to take over the state interior department. Brandt politely begged off, although "it was not easy to say no." Later, he admitted that Lübeck "seemed to me a bit provincial" and that "presumably I would have quickly found it too confining."[36] He had grown accustomed to bigger cities.

While in Lübeck Brandt got together with Annedore Leber, the widow of Julius, whom he had not seen since 1933. They gave a joint interview to the *Lübecker Freie Presse,* in which Brandt said:

> In my opinion Germany will not arise again and will not be able to maintain herself if she fails to find an adjustment with the East as well as the West, regardless of an East or West orientation. Therefore it would be an ominous policy to commit herself to (only) one of the powers.[37]

He took time in Lübeck to write a reference—a document he signed "Willy Brandt-Herbert Frahm"[38]—for Emil Peters, a Socialist who had been his illegal contact man in Germany during the Nazi era and had participated in his escape to Scandinavia in 1933. Brandt also went out to Travemünde to find Paul Stooss and thank the fisherman once more for the assistance.[39] Then he returned to Oslo to wait for word from the British on the DPD editorship.

He had made up his mind to return to Germany, but the where and the when and the what were still undecided. On September 28 he spent an evening with his old friend Halvard Lange, who put a new iron into the fire. Although recognizing Brandt's desire to reenter German affairs, Lange proposed that he join the Norwegian foreign service. There was a press attaché post open in Paris, and Brandt was tempted enough that night to say, "Okay, for a year."[40] But he was still committed to speak at an October election rally in Lübeck, where his SPD friends were also pressing him with arguments like: "As the successor of Julius Leber you can make a good start too, from Lübeck . . . We must have you."[41] Nor had Brandt entirely written off the DPD. Sure enough, a telegram from Hamburg arrived with a job promise. Then on October 19 he again saw Lange, who had just returned from a trip to France, and this time the Foreign Minister said that although Paris was still open, he would prefer Brandt go to Berlin to observe the development of the East-West problem.

"I said yes," Brandt recalled. "Berlin—this decided the issue; I had made my decision." Lange cleared it with Prime Minister Einar Gerhardsen. There were some details to straighten out: The bureaucratic pecking order called for the post of press attaché in the Norwegian military mission in Berlin to be filled by a captain; Brandt insisted on the rank of major, "because of the pay scale."[42]

The assignment had several merits: He could go to a place that really interested him in a capacity that would give him protection and freedom of movement; it postponed an unquestionably agonizing decision whether to resume being wholly German; it was also an awesome compliment and expression of trust in him to send a German native to represent Norwegian interests in Germany. Still he had fleeting doubts, which he conveyed a few days later to Stefan Szende in Stockholm by letter:

> The Berlin proposal was a middle way for me. I know I disappointed my Lübeck friends deeply. But I will have a direct contact with German developments, and follow them better from Berlin than from a Western provincial city, and also be able to help German as well as Scandinavian friends. I only had to obligate myself for a year . . . Do you agree with the decision I have made?[43]

On November 1 Brandt addressed a circular letter to a number of friends explaining why he had taken the Berlin assignment: "As you know I have been engaged for years simultaneously in German' and 'Scandinavian' causes. Those were and are not contradictory." He added that his inner feeling for the German Socialist movement remained the same and that he felt he could serve the cause as well in this post. "Commitment and obligation to European democracy and international socialism override secondary matters of form and questions of my own personal position. In this sense I am your Willy Brandt." Annedore Leber replied: "We are delighted. It doesn't matter in what form you come to us. We know the person who is coming." Other friends wrote in a similar vein.[44]

He spent Christmas with Rut and then set off for Berlin, where he took up his duties on January 17, 1947. Rut agreed to join him in the spring. Just as well, because it was one of the coldest winters in memory, and Brandt, while he had access to good rations, was quartered modestly. "He lived a very poor life, in two rooms," said Oddvar Aas, who visited him then. But better than that of the bulk of the Berliners. Berlin was a city of the dead and the dying that terrible winter. Some of the Germans expelled from the East, 9 million from Poland and 3 million from Czechoslovakia, were arriving dead, too—fifty-three frozen to death on trains from the Oder-Neisse region in the Christmas week alone. The Berlin *Tagesspiegel* carried notices that began: "Found starved and dead in their beds . . . the seventy-three-year-old pensioner Gerhard Z . . . the forty-six-year-old Anna K . . ., the fifty-nine-year-old Bertha O . . ., the one-year-old Joachim D." The cold held the city in its grip until March when, in the middle of the month the temperature suddenly shot up by forty-five degrees in three hours, bringing floods and hundreds of new tuberculosis cases.[45] "Craters, caves, mountains of rubble, debris-covered fields," Brandt noted, "no fuel, no light, every little garden a graveyard, and above all this, like an immovable cloud, the stench of putrefaction.[46]

Another émigré, Ernst Reuter, had arrived in November from exile in Turkey after overcoming a lot of difficulties with British occupation authorities in the expectation of being offered the post of Mayor of Berlin. But things were not that simple. There was another candidate, and, besides, the Communists in the still unitary city government were dead set against Reuter. They remembered him as a militant Social Democrat and, more to the point, one of their own who had changed his mind about orthodox Marxism-Leninism. (Reuter, as a young Socialist imprisoned by the Russians in 1916, had become a successful People's Commissar of the Volga German region in 1918 on behalf of the new Bolshevik Government and from 1919 to 1922, as "Ernst Friesland," a leading figure in the German Communist Party.) "Is a Turk going to be mayor of Berlin?" asked one of the Soviet-run papers.

The answer was no. Reuter took a post as a city councillor with responsibility for transport and power. As such he felt the brunt of Allied displeasure in dealing with the critically cold winter. Three thousand factories had closed for lack of fuel and power, and the electricity had to be shut off for as long as ten hours a day. In trying to make the best of a bad situation he clashed occasionally with the Russians and Americans, at one point because the electricity was cut off in the Allied offices of the Rathaus. Reuter observed cooly that it would do them good to freeze their rears for once.[47]

Brandt met Reuter in the small Zehlendorf home of Annedore Leber on one of those icy days that winter, and there was an affinity immediately between the two returned exiles, the elder fifty-five and the younger thirty-two. "From the very first moment I felt that Reuter and I understood each other very well," Brandt wrote. "He remained young at heart and young in spirit. This made him a comrade of the seekers and strugglers. We came from completely different social environments. But we not only had the same aim, we also traveled the same road."[48]

Brandt was made welcome in German Social Democratic circles and well beyond. Louis Wiesner, who as an Office of Strategic Services analyst had followed Brandt's career since 1943, remembered him from this period as "tremendously keen, dedicated, and shrewdly anti-Communist—certainly very impressive with his sincerity and easy grasp of the political situation."[49]

His old friend and onetime mentor Jacob Walcher turned up in Berlin, too, arriving about the same time as Brandt. When they got together at last Brandt found him espousing not only the cause of unity and the combative merger of SPD and KPD, but also the cause of the Soviet Union, as if he were back in his Spartacus days at the end of World War I and nothing at all—not his participation in the KP-Opposition in 1928, not the founding of the SAP, not the Hitler-Stalin Pact, not the subjugation of Socialists in the Soviet zone— had happened. "Despite our friendly feelings for each other we were advocating diametrically opposed political convictions," Brandt wrote. Walcher joined the SED and was briefly rewarded with the editorship of the Communist trade union paper, *Tribüne*. But he was too independent a soul, despite his persuasions, and soon he was cast into obscurity along with most of the other ex-SAP figures who tried the Soviet zone route.[50]

Brandt mixed with other Communists, too, some of them Russians. As Oddvar Aas was to observe in this regard: "He was never a Communist. But I think he liked to discuss with Communists."[51] Once as press attaché he accompanied a conservative Norwegian journalist to the Soviet sector to call on Wilhelm Pieck, the aged Communist figurehead leader whom Brandt described as "a monument of himself." The only unrehearsed moment in the interview as far as Brandt could tell was when the Norwegian asked about the reopening of concentration camps in the Soviet zone. Pieck replied: "If you only knew what letters I receive from comrades whose sons have vanished. But we have no say in this matter. This is solely the business of the Russians.[52]

He was busy enough, sending at least one report a day to Oslo, circulating among the horde of newsmen in an effort to find writers interested in Norwegian information, organizing collaboration between German and Norwegian news agencies, helping visiting journalists and, incidentally, trying to market in Germany his latest book about the Nürnberg trials—a project that failed for lack of printing paper. Evidently, one of Brandt's biggest concerns was a dispute between Norway and the German fishing industry, which was seeking to override prohibitions against catching whales and using trawling nets in the rich Norwegian coastal waters. An Oslo paper singled out Brandt for sharp criticism on this issue, accusing him of not representing Norwegian interests. In a lengthy report to his superiors Brandt ventured the guess that as soon as the Germans were better fed the controversy would die down.[53]

Busy, but lonely. He was glad enough when Rut joined him in April. She had been working for an Oslo illustrated magazine, and now she had an assignment in the Norwegian military mission. Her husband had died of tuberculosis the previous year, and she was free—the girl who had lost her father at age three, worked in a bakery and as a seamstress at fifteen, and gone briefly underground as a member of the Socialist Youth at twenty.[54] "A proletarian," Per Monsen recalled, "with an elementary school education. But always a lady. For two years in Berlin she remained silent in the presence of Germans. She didn't know the language. When she began she spoke well. She gave Willy the nest warmth he sought."[55]

The currents of international politics were shifting, and soon Berlin, still horribly ravaged by the war, was being pounded by new waves stirred up in the contradictions of occupation policies.

Winston Churchill had already set the tone of the East-West dissension in his Fulton, Missouri, speech of March 1946, accusing the Soviets of ringing down an "iron curtain" in front of Eastern Europe. General Lucius Clay, the American military governor, gave a foretaste of opposition to unitary occupation economic policy in May 1946 by ordering a stop to the dismantling of industries in his zone for shipment to the Russians. In a further step toward separation he and the British military governor, Sir Brian Robertson, agreed in September on joint economic development in their zones.

The suspension of reparations for the Soviets from the Western zones and the coordination of bizonal economic policy were measures taken more out of a desire to protect assets than a desire to offend the Russians. But the Russians were intensely suspicious.

Soviet policy on Germany was ambivalent to the highest degree. On the one hand the Russians were professing to treat Germany as a whole—not just for the sake of reparations but also in political terms. Their German Communist clients were dispatched as frequently as possible into the Western zones to plead the cause of unity. On the other hand Soviet practice in the Soviet zone was separatist: starting with dispossession of large landowners in September 1945, continuing with nationalization of big industrial enterprises and the gradual throttling of political opposition to the Communists. In short, Soviet policy was riddled with contradictions.

The factor that probably resolved these contradictions was the Germans themselves—even in that early stage of relative impotence. This was most evident in Berlin in the wake of the first and only democratic election held in the entire city after the war. The SED, for all the influence and material benefits it enjoyed in the Soviet sector, got only 19.8 percent of the October 10, 1946, vote, while the SPD, cut off from its Eastern sector base for almost six months, got 48.7 percent. At stake was the city council, and there was no mistaking the will of the Berliners in an election that drew nine out of ten eligible voters. That rebuff hardened the determination of the Soviets to secure their zone with methods proven by Stalin.

The struggle over German unity had only begun, and Berlin was one of the prizes. Eastern and Western occupying powers showed themselves capable of tactical retreats, usually at the expense of their German clients. Generals Clay and Robertson made it clear they meant business with their economic coordination by implementing their agreement on January 1, 1947, and strengthening it five months later with the creation of a Bizone Economic Council. The Soviets responded a fortnight later with their own German Economic Commission, strictly a Soviet zone operation.

In practical terms the division of Germany was going on before the very eyes of those who were nominally working for unification. Much of the impetus for separation came from outside—non-German—factors: the enunciation of the Truman Doctrine in March 1947 with its combative anti-Communist policy in Greece and Turkey, the offer of massive American assistance for economic recovery in Europe made in June 1947 by Secretary of State George C. Marshall. Stalin registered both as threats to his newly won empire and reacted by forcing the pace of communization in Eastern Europe (though there were still many detours ahead on the road to total German division).

The Western sectors of Berlin were to feel the pinch of East-West contradictions in several ways. In April, for example, Mayor Otto Ostrowski was asked to step down by his own party, the SPD, because he couldn't handle the job. In June Ernst Reuter was elected to succeed him, 89-17, in a secret ballot of the city council. But by employing some legal tricks the Soviet commandant succeeded in vetoing Reuter's acceptance. The American delegation in the Allied Control Council—still the supreme governing body in Germany—accepted the veto without protest, continuing to obey orders to get along with the Russians. So Berlin's acting Mayor for the next year was Louise Schroeder, with Reuter at her side as a loyal aide.

This was the milieu in which Willy Brandt was moving, still the outsider and still obliged for ceremonial occasions to put on his Norwegian major's uniform with its "civilian officer" patch on the shoulder. But he was already heavily engaged, subjectively, with the SPD—with the Berliners around Reuter and with the West German apparatus headed by Schumacher. With Rut he attended the Second Party Congress of the SPD at the end of June in Nürnberg, where Schumacher declared that Germany needed the Marshall Plan and the Social Democrats adopted resolutions calling for the establishment of a new German republic as a federal state—a proposal American Secretary of State James Byrnes had aired the previous year. There was still a lot of Marx in the SPD program, however, with guidelines calling for a massive land reform—nobody to own over 240 acres—and a planned economy.

From Nürnberg the couple journeyed eastward to Prague for some fun, but also to see what was happening in a country where the Social Democrats and the Communists were supposed to be getting on well together. It was a critical moment for Czechoslovakia, which was still enjoying a modicum of democratic government. So easy going was the atmosphere that President Klement Gottwald, who was also the Czechoslovak Communist Party leader, airily declared approval of the Marshall Plan and its aid promise for his country on July 4. But three days later he was summoned to Moscow and given a terrible dressing down by Stalin himself; Czechoslovakia was forbidden to attend the forthcoming Marshall Plan Conference in Paris.

A few months later Brandt wrote down impressions of that Prague summer:

> It was not at all the case—to be truthful—that open terror reigned then. There was a lively discussion of the questions of the day in the press, in Parliament, in meetings and in evening discussions on Wenceslaus Square . . . Many Czechoslovakians lived under the impression they were part of a new national revolution which would create the basis for a socialist republic. . . . Again and again one heard that they wanted neither to exclude themselves from the Western cultural community, nor from Western trade. They hoped to be mediators between the East and the West.

But he also noted that "the Communists had learned how to obtain numerous advantages for themselves, not the least in the area of propaganda."[56]

Back in Norway at the end of August Brandt was asked by Foreign Minister Lange whether he had plans to get into German politics, and Brandt replied that the question was "not on the agenda."[57] A few weeks later, however, it was. In Hannover Schumacher urged him again to return to German affairs and offered him an interesting post in Berlin as representative of the SPD executive in the divided city.

The post was held by Erich Brost, an SPD man from Danzig with whom Brandt had become friendly in previous months. Brost, a professional newspaperman, wanted to get back to his trade, and in October he, too, urged Brandt to take the job. It was an enormously tempting offer, for it afforded not only an intimate connection with both the Berlin and the West German SPD officials, but also with the Western Allies and with remaining SPD sympathizers in East Berlin and the Soviet zone. Loosely connected with the "liaison office" was something called the SPD East Bureau. It had been set up by Schumacher with the help of the Berlin Americans. Nominally, the task of this *Ostbüro* was to maintain contact with and assist SPD loyalists in the Soviet zone. It later developed a more sinister purpose as a spy center, and its financing was to pass to the newly established U.S. Central Intelligence Agency.

Brandt wrestled with himself for weeks. "The months in Berlin allowed the decision to ripen in me to dedicate myself entirely to political work in Germany," he wrote.[58] His decision was complicated by the fact that Gunnar Myrdal, who headed the United Nations Organization's Commission in Geneva, had offered him a press job at his side in September. Brandt confided to Inge Scheflo his doubts and his pangs about abandoning the citizenship and the service of the country that had been his home for all his adult life, beloved Norway:

> There were various reasons why I waited so long to make a decision. The most important was that I found it hard to "give up" Norway. You know yourself that it was much more for me than a formality to become a Norwegian citizen. Norway and the Norwegian workers movement formed me. That is something about which I am glad and thankful. . . . I will take all the good with me that I experienced in Norway and with my Norwegian friends.[59]

Reinhart Bartholomäi, a shrewd SPD official who worked on the Brandt chancellorship election campaigns, reflected in 1973, "Why did he hesitate? Well, he wasn't sitting on his suitcase. He was young. He was asked to become a German again. He got the call to become a German. He *knows* why he is German. He chose it. The rest of us were just born into it."[60]

In the end it was Berlin that did it. Berlin and Germany and the SPD. "Liaison man," he recalled more than a quarter of a century later, "that interested me. It didn't have to be a great temptation."[61]

Kurt Schumacher was genuinely interested in Brandt, for pragmatic reasons and more. He told Annemarie Renger: "We could use him, Brandt, with his good connections to the (Western) Allies. He would be a good thing for Berlin." His own relations with the Americans and British were none too good, Schumacher acknowledged. The situation for the SPD and for the non-Communist Germans was becoming more precarious as Soviet pressure on the Western sectors mounted every day. Brandt was an almost ideal candidate for the liaison job. But to Mrs. Renger there was still more—"a certain wooing of Willy Brandt by Kurt Schumacher," she observed.[62]

Brandt did not respond in kind to Schumacher's blandishments, which must have gone against his Norwegian grain. "I didn't humor him," he remembered. "I told him, 'I never gave up my independence, and I don't to you, either.'[63] Schumacher was somewhat astonished by this reserve. Mrs.

Renger remarked: "Kurt Schumacher couldn't bear it when someone was not captivated by him. He had such a strong personality that he practically conquered people with his fascinating pull and couldn't imagine anyone resisting it." But the two men reached agreement, and Brandt won from Schumacher the right to offer his own opinion in the party councils in the event of disputes between Hannover and Berlin.

His next obligation was to write to Foreign Minister Lange and ask for release from his contract. He did so tenderly on November 7 in a letter that began, "Dear Halvard":

> The issue is not so simple as if I was choosing Germany instead of Norway. The way I see it is that I can and must do something more active for the ideas I hold, and that such an effort is necessary particularly in this country. . . . Political work in Germany means communing with all sorts of people with whom one doesn't have much in common . . . But it cannot be helped. I know that the solution of the German problem depends on decisions that will be taken on the international high politics level. But there is much that must be done in Germany, in the interest of Europe, democracy and peace . . . You should know that I really have no illusions. But I want to try to help Germany be brought back into Europe and if possible to become part of that third force that is necessary to avoid the greatest catastrophe of all time. It is fairly certain that I will experience disappointments, perhaps more than that . . .[64]

So it was done. A day later he wrote to Myrdal to thank him for his offer and explain what he had decided. He also wrote to Haakon Lie, secretary general of the Norwegian Labor Party, to express his "innermost gratitude for all that the Norwegian workers movement has given me for the further journey."

Soon the news spread along the strange and far-stretched network that was the German political emigration: Brandt was going home to occupied Germany, to an important job in the SPD. In Stockholm and Oslo some jealous souls reacted by launching an intrigue against him. They passed messages to Schumacher alleging that Brandt was "an SED man in disguise." As proof they submitted that he was continuing to meet Jacob Walcher in Berlin, and they noted that he had supported the cause of "a unitary socialist party."[65]

Brandt heard of the suspicions cast on him from Erich Ollenhauer and Franz Neumann. The intrigue came close to blocking his appointment at the last moment. "Schumacher was prejudiced because of what these people said about me," Brandt recalled.[66] On December 22 Erich Brost returned from a visit to Hannover and conveyed Schumacher's suspicions to Brandt, who was appalled. The next day he wrote a five and a half page letter to the SPD chairman beginning, "Dear Comrade Schumacher":

> . . . I have reason to fear that you have acquired a distrust which would put successful cooperation into question . . . I have decided to write you in complete frankness about the intrigues woven against me in the last weeks among Scandinavian émigré circles . . . I would be glad to have your answer in hand soon. It would be better to settle it once and for all rather than let a murky situation drag on.

He went on to explain precisely what he had done and thought during his exile years, saying, he had "not the least reason to hide anything or to be ashamed." He added that Schumacher was surely aware of the "lunacies to which the emigration mentality could sometimes ascend," and that "this doesn't bother me much any more." Just the same, "I don't have any desire to look on quietly when somebody spits in my face." Brandt also pointed out that, "I didn't press for a certain job and I don't want to do that now." In conclusion, he said: "Let me assure you that I have never been a simple yesman and I hope I never will be. But I have learned a long time ago how to fit in and to work with full force for our cause from the position allotted me."[67] It was the letter of a man outwardly modest but inwardly proud.

The letter sufficed to remove Schumacher's doubts about his political reliability, and the rest of the formalities went quickly. Brandt concluded his Norwegian press attaché service January 1, 1948, and filed his final report to Oslo four days later—his four hundred seventeenth in less than twelve months. He was already in harness for the SPD.[68] Four months later he resumed German citizenship.

Norway had been a mild mistress. Germany was demanding from the beginning. He would have liked to have kept both loves simultaneously and instantly available. Nor was there ever any doubt which was the sentimental favorite. But "duty" called, as he wrote Scheflo. Years later he would tell an interviewer somewhat grumpily: Nobody said I had to go around Germany in 1945. I could have stayed in Norway."[69]

As a native of what had been the free Hanse city of Lübeck, a separate entity that became part of the new state of Schleswig-Holstein under Hitler, Brandt had to go for his renaturalization to Kiel, the state capital. The certificate was issued to Herbert Ernst Karl Frahm "called Willy Brandt." Not for another year did he take out papers in Berlin eradicating his given name in favor of the *nom de guerre* he had chosen for himself. It was a choice that caused him to reflect again and again as long as he lived, even though he rationalized it to the point where he observed that his own mother after her marriage bore the Frahm name no more.[70] It was also to cause him pain.

"In Berlin he was a new star," Mrs. Renger recalled. "People knew right away who he was. He had a name already. Nobody knew what would become of him, but he had something about him. The Berliners saw him as a beau. He was livelier there, less complicated in Berlin than later."[71]

Berlin had already entered its own liveliest times. In the Soviet zone the Communist grip was tightening, despite the fact that the unpopular Walter Ulbricht had very nearly missed being elected to the secretariat of the SED at a September congress. Unabashed, Ulbricht started the SED on a new course of discipline, switching it from a mass party to a "Marxist-Leninist militant party." He also announced the formation of a "Central Administration of Interior" to watch over East Germany's 17 million citizens and to supervise the prisons where more than 2000 Social Democrats already languished.[72]

In the Western zones Lucius Clay and Brian Robertson announced the intention on January 8 to expand the competencies of the bizone economic administration to include political functions—a further move toward a federal state. A week later the Soviets retorted by applying controls to traffic moving on the *Autobahn* between Berlin's Western sectors and the Western zones. "Is this a dress rehearsal?" Berliners asked. "Are the Americans going to stay in Berlin?"[73] On January 24 the Russians stopped a British zone train for eleven hours, demanding to control identity papers, and by April they were holding up Western military trains and German freights. There was a smell of blockade.

Elsewhere, matters were worse. In Czechoslovakia the Communists took over all power in a bloodless coup that was concluded after five days on February 25. That same day the Soviet Union confronted Finland with a demand of accession that would have made Helsinki a satellite capital and came close to swallowing the Finns, too.

The Czechoslovak developments provided Brandt with a unique opportunity. Kurt Mattick, a forty-year-old SPD aide to the Berlin party chairman, asked Brandt to make a speech about what had happened in Prague, including the mysterious death of Foreign Minister Jan Masaryk. "I asked him to talk to Berlin party officials, and he was outstanding," Mattick said. "That was his entry into Berlin politics and after that he was much in demand as a speaker."[74] Brandt called it "The Lessons of Prague," and the fifteen-page address was a scorcher:

> Woe to the victors of February 24, 1948. They put their political opponents behind bars by the hundreds, yes, by the thousands. They robbed some of the deputies, the elected representatives of the people, of their mandates. They beat up editors and took over their newspapers. They dismissed judges and university professors who

wouldn't cooperate. They called on high school pupils to denounce their fellow pupils and teachers. . . . To socialize the plumbers and the barber shops they establish the proletarian dictatorship and Red terror. Old Marx would turn in his grave if he knew (laughter, applause) if he knew what bald foolishness one created in his name. But we say as German, European and internationalist Social Democrats and we say it so loud that they can hear it in Prague and perhaps a bit further: If that which took place in Prague is supposed to embody socialism, then we have nothing more to do with that socialism. . . .

He went on to recount the fate of Social Democrats under the Russian boot in Hungary, Rumania, and Bulgaria and declared: "I tell you, comrades, he who gets involved with the Communist unity front perishes in it. . . . Czechoslovak, German, European liberty is not lost as long as there are people to whom liberty is worth more than anything else their creator gave them." He was interrupted fifty-seven times with applause and approving calls from his listeners.[75]

It was Brandt the tribune, at his very best. Less than four months later it was Berlin's turn to face the implacable Stalin, and Brandt had a resolution to draft for the Berlin SPD that set him and the party squarely with the West.

The currency in all of occupied Germany was still the old *Reichsmark*—just about the only remaining connection with prewar Germany. But there was much more money in circulation than goods to purchase. This didn't bother the Russians, who merrily printed more and more and resisted attempts of the Western Allies to initiate a currency reform from mid-1947 onward. Inflation set in.

By April the Western Allies had determined to establish a federal state in their zones and to make it stick by devaluing the *Reichsmark*. But on May 20 Ludwig Erhard, the Bavarian professor who headed the Administration for the Economy in Frankfurt, declared it was impossible to include Berlin in the West zone reform and suggested a special currency for the former Reich capital. The Berlin representatives, including Ernst Reuter, protested bitterly and got some backing from American financial experts who pointed out, nevertheless, that without special arrangements, a new West zone currency would turn Berlin into "a hole in the East." through which the hard money would spill. In a compromise move the Western Allies started printing up new notes with a "B" stamped on them for use in Berlin, but for the moment General Clay let the *Reichsmark,* with all its inflationary effect, remain the currency there. Reuter threatened to launch a campaign calling on the Berliners to "refuse Russian money." On June 18 the Western Allies announced their currency reform would take effect two days later, without Berlin. That same day the Russians stopped all private traffic on the access routes to the Western sectors of the city. Furthermore, Marshal Vassily Sokolovsky, the Soviet military governor, declared the new currency prohibited, under penalty, in the Soviet zone and all of Berlin. The Soviets had already walked out of the Allied *Kommandantur* on June 16, but now, three days later, they were laying claim to the whole of the city. It was on a Saturday that, in haste, Willy Brandt drafted a resolution for the Berlin SPD leadership, and issued it that afternoon, blaming the Soviets for failure of attempts at an all-German currency reform and declaring Sokolovsky's proclamation "invalid" for the Western sectors.

On Monday, June 21, initial reports of the enormous success of the West zone reform came in. The 10-to-1 devaluation had almost eliminated the flourishing black market overnight. On their side the Russians readied countermeasures, closing the Soviet zone banks on Tuesday and issuing their new currency—it was a paste-on tab to be attached to the old *Reichsmark* at first, giving it the Berlin soubriquet *Klebemark* ("sticker mark")—the next day. Now the wartime Allies went their separate ways—the Western commanders forbidding the use of the new *Ostmark* in their sectors and the Russians declaring the *Westmark* invalid in theirs. On June 24 the Western Allies introduced the new *Deutschmark* into West Berlin.

That same morning the Soviets began their blockade, stopping all land traffic to West Berlin, cutting off deliveries of bread and milk, coal and electric power from their zone. It was the hour of Ernst Reuter, a man who had seen it coming for months and who now addressed the "people of Berlin"—80,000 of them on a soccer field—calling on them to resist enslavement. He was still only a city councillor, and one who had stirred resentment among the Western Allies. But to the beleaguered citizens he instantly became a rallying point for defiance. Brandt was at his side, not only in his capacity as the SPD liaison man, ut also as an admiring though scarcely visible confidant. He participated with Reuter in a conference that week with American occupation officials, who indicated it might be possible to supply Berlin by air transport through the three twenty-mile-wide corridors granted the Western Allies by the Russians in 1945. Reuter was skeptical and replied: "But we will go our way. Do what you can do. We will do what we feel obligated to do." He told the same to General Clay June 25. On June 26 the Americans began "Operation Vittles" with initial flights of thirty-two Dakotas carrying about 120 tons into Berlin. By July, using bigger Skymasters, the shipments reached 1500 tons a day. In September the Berlin airlift reached 7000 tons daily, and by April 1949 over 8000 tons, with transports landing almost every minute—the equivalent of 1200 railroad freight cars. Eighty men died in crashes connected with the airlift, thirty-one of them Americans.[76]

Willy Brandt was working day and night. He was kept hopping for Reuter and Schumacher, and he also was corresponding regularly for *Arbeiderbladet,* his old paper in Oslo. Per Monsen, who visited him in the airlift days, provides a vignette: "Brandt would have a glass in the evening and then say, 'Sorry I've got to work,' and then sit down and write for *Arbeiderbladet* until four in the morning—terrific working discipline.[77]

He and Rut had moved into a modest home on Trabener Strasse. Behind them was a large railroad yard, now virtually silent because of the blockade of trains from the West, and in front was the idyllic Halensee, a lake covering about fifteen acres in the borough of Wilmersdorf. He used the house for his contacts with East German SPD members who were seeking help. A Soviet zone lawyer, Günther Nollau, who had specialized in "defending democrats" caught in the toils of Communist courts, recalled visiting Brandt "in the second half of 1948":

> The Communists were reducing parity in the SED by involving SPD officials who resisted in criminal cases. One fine day after I had handled several such cases one of them said, "You defend people from the SPD and you ought to go to West Berlin to see Herr Brandt." I asked, "Who is he?" and was told he took care of such cases on behalf of the West German SPD. I said, "All right, I'll go." I liked to go to West Berlin to eat, to buy clothes. I took the *Reichsbahn* [train] from Dresden and checked to see if I was being followed by the K-5 [acronym for the secret police]. In Halensee a man came to the door at the Trabener Strasse 200-and-something and said, "I am Brandt." We talked over the cases. He impressed me with understanding for the situation of secret work. He didn't ask one to take risks. A humane attitude. I had the impression he was more experienced in conspiratorial work than I was. An intelligent type. He struck me as a person who had a special grasp of the situation of people like us and worked with human warmth to help.[78]

Nollau had been with the Soviet zone CDU, an association that Brandt welcomed because it prevented the Dresdener from being identified by the Communists as part of the hated SPD. Two years later, when Nollau's number finally came up on the wanted lists of the East German secret police and he escaped to Berlin by a hair's breath, Brandt was there to help him. Nollau had been confronted by a phony murder charge fabricated by the Communists out of a hunting accident, and the West Berlin police locked him up pending investigation. Nollau recalled: "I alerted Brandt and he reappeared and helped me in a very nice way."[79] The assistance enabled Nollau to get a job in the West German Interior Ministry through CDU friends and launched him on a career in intelligence work that was to bring him together again—in awful irony—with Chancellor Brandt in 1973.

Despite the swelling airlift West Berlin was almost like a medieval city under siege. There was no newsprint for the press. Electric power was cut off as much as twenty-two hours a day. Food for many citizens consisted of dried potatoes and powdered eggs. Suicides multiplied.

Willy and Rut were better off than most, with parcels arriving regularly from friends in Scandinavia. They received a strong new petroleum lamp from Sweden, and he brought in a kerosene stove from West Germany. They took comfort, too, in the legendary dry humor of the Berliners, who were already calling the airlift food transports "raisin bombers" (one of the enormous piles of war rubble had already been dubbed "Mount Junk").[80]

Throughout the summer the Soviets and the Western Allies quarreled about currency, food, East-West trade, and all the other issues related to the first Berlin crisis. Move and countermove on the Berlin chessboard: General Clay recommended an armored probe along the main access road to Berlin July 10 and was overruled by President Truman; the Russians held out the tempting offer of food supplies for Western sectors; a week later the British and Americans broke off interzone trade and established a separate authority in their sectors; on August 2 the ambassadors of the three Allies in Moscow had an informal interview with Stalin. All the while protests were fired off on both sides. Finally, at the end of August the four powers met again in the person of military governors in Berlin at the Allied Control Council. The Communists, in their sector, were impudent enough to instigate riots those very days, forcing Reuter, among others, to sneak out of the back door of the new city hall in East Berlin to avoid the toughs. For a few days the West Berliners and their new Western protectors had the impression the Communists would attempt a *Putsch* by armed demonstrators. It wouldn't have been that difficult with only 6500 Allied troops in the city. With this in mind Reuter asked West Berlin workers to participate in a test demonstration and was surprised to draw 50,000. When the SED strongboys made new trouble at the city hall, he called another demonstration, and this time, 350,000—many of them from East Berlin—showed up on the broad field before the ruins of the old Reichstag. The Russians arrested five of them, while Reuter spoke:

> Today is the day the people of Berlin raise their voice and call the whole world, for we know what is at stake in the negotiations in the Control Council Building and in the stone palaces of the Kremlin . . . In all this wheeling and dealing we Berliners don't want to be an object of barter. Nobody can barter us. Nobody can negotiate us.

Nobody can sell us. It is impossible to make a rotten compromise on the backs of such a brave, decent people. You, nations of the earth. You, people in America, in England, France and Italy. Look upon this city and realize that you dare not give away this people, cannot give it away . . .[81]

It was an appeal that echoed around the world.

Three days later Reuter was in Düsseldorf attending the Third Congress of the West zone SPD and talking the same bold stuff. He called Berlin "the island, the showcase of freedom," phrases that stuck in the mind like nails. In the balloting for the new party executive he was elected with 332 of the 357 votes.

Willy Brandt was also a candidate for the ruling executive, without his knowledge. He had been put up by friends, including Ollenhauer, and he probably would have made it except for a denunciation by Peter Blachstein, his onetime comrade from the SAP who had gone Trotskyist in Spain and then taken a rightward turn when he reached Stockholm as an exile. A Saxon from Dresden, Blachstein turned up in Düsseldorf now and accused Brandt in a closed session of "mysterious affairs" during the Spanish Civil War, suggesting that he was responsible for the death of Mark Rein Abramovich and perhaps Kurt Landau, too (see Chapter III). "They dragged me into it," Herbert Wehner who was in attendance as an aide to Schumacher at Düsseldorf, recalled with contempt.[82] When it came to the vote, Brandt withdrew his name from the list.[83] Later, when Brandt's political star was in ascendency, Blachstein stuck to him "like a leech," as a man who had listened to the Düsseldorf accusations said later with mouth-wrinkling disgust. It paid off. As Foreign Minister, Brandt would appoint Blachstein Ambassador to Yugoslavia.

The fall brought a new problem for Willy and Rut. Rut—already six months pregnant when the blockade started in June—was heavy with child. It was time to get married. Willy appealed to the Norwegian military mission for help. There was a Norwegian Army brigade stationed in the British zone. It had a chaplain. Wouldn't he perform the ceremony? No, the chaplain was sorry, but he was an ordained minister of the Lutheran State Church, and he was not about to perform nuptials for a divorced man living in Berlin sin. In Rut's eighth month a solution was found, a major in the Norwegian brigade in the Harz who was a pastor in private life. He was airlifted to Berlin in a Royal Air Force plane. The simple ceremony was performed at the Norwegian mission on the edge of the *Tiergarten* with only a few Scandinavian friends present. Per Monsen served as best man. When it was over, Brandt made a short speech and then, overcome by emotion, wept tears of joy.[84] There was to be no mention of the wedding date in the official Brandt literature.

On October 4, with a foretaste of winter in the air, their first son was born in a hospital chilled and dim for lack of fuel. Brandt noted: "Peter came into the world by candlelight—a real child of the blockade."[85]

There are such things as ideal careers in politics, where the rise to the top is easy and quick. But that is the stuff of young, newly independent countries. Germany was old and defeated. Adenauer was over seventy when he set out on his postwar career. Erhard, fifty-one. Reuter, fifty-nine. Brandt was only thirty-five, and he had seen a lot already. To be in Berlin during the blockade was to undergo a kind of baptism, not a baptism of fire, but of privation and danger. It toughened the hides of the majority of the Berliners and made them resilient enough to withstand future threats from the East. By being there with Reuter Brandt won a kind of acceptance from the citizenry that was to last him all his political career. He became a Berliner, and that was a proud distinction accorded to few strangers. Clay would become one in his way, and Maggie Higgins, the dauntless foreign correspondent of the *New York Herald Tribune*. Britain's peppery Brian Robertson, too. So, too, France's General Jean Ganeval. In the summer the French commandant authorized the building of a new airport in his sector at Tegel. It was completed in ninety-two days. The only hindrance was a group of tall radio masts that belonged to the Soviet sector station. He ordered them destroyed. When an outraged Soviet officer demanded how he could do such a thing, Ganeval responded deadpan: "With dynamite and French sappers." *Voila, un Berlinois!*

For Brandt the experience of the blockade had a decisive personal impact. He wrote:

> The Berliners demonstrated their allegiance to common basic values; their knowledge that they stood for each other; the determination they manifested in the defense of justice and freedom of speech and press; their acceptance of individual responsibility. All that reminded me of the admirable resistance the Norwegians had offered nine years before against all attempts to break their will and their spirit. As I felt then that Norway had never been greater than in the time of its hardest distress—just so I experienced now the real greatness of Berlin.[86]

He had always felt a wanderlust and he always would. But the sense of solidarity made almost palpable by the blockade gave him a feeling of belonging again. He had found a home again, in the middle of Germany, among those tangy, tingling, sometimes nasty, always sharp-witted, racy, bluffing, snooty people, the Berliners.

VI:
Island and Mainland

The 1948-1949 blockade transformed Berlin's Western sectors into a kind of island in the sea of Soviet power and, at the same time, made the Western occupation zones of Germany into the nearest free mainland. The effect in international politics of the day was almost tidal. None of the occupation powers, including Stalin's Soviet Union, had contemplated the permanent division of Germany and the separation of the rump capital of the Reich from its natural hinterland as the logical consequence of victory over Hitler. No. The Western Allies had imagined an untroublesome, if shrunken, Germany "reeducated" gradually toward obedient and useful membership in a future community of nations. The Russians evidently dreamed of a Germany—and perhaps a whole Europe—eventually subject to Communist rule and Soviet domination. Both sides were motivated by missionary urges deeply rooted in their respective traditions. Both were clearly surprised to find their opponents, and the Germans themselves, resisting—even when resistance was very costly. In this respect, the isolation of West Berlin and the following division of Germany were historical accidents, however much they were facilitated by the lack of unison among the war victors and the German people themselves about what Germany had been and should be.

This was the political fluid in which Mayor Ernst Reuter and his young aide, Willy Brandt, found themselves at the beginning of 1949—and it was jelling fast in the winds of the Cold War.

The occupation anomaly of Greater Berlin, the metropolitan capital established in 1871, was breaking apart under the blows and counterblows of East and West. Reuter's personal security was endangered whenever he went to a session of the magistrate in the Soviet sector, and in October 1948 he was persuaded not to go across again. On November 15 the Soviets declared him "dismissed" from his city council post. The Western commandants rejected this unilateral move. City elections were due, but the Russians instead set up their own magistrate with a renegade Social Democrat, Friedrich Ebert, the roly-poly son of the first Weimar Republic President, as Mayor. West Berlin stubbornly held its own elections in December. The SPD got a convincing 64 percent, and on that basis Reuter at last took office as Mayor of Berlin (West) in January 1949.

There were new problems. West Berlin needed an additional power station, and the heavy generators had to be cut in half by blowtorch before they could be flown in. A new fire department had to be established. Stores were meager in the still-besieged city. Even Mayor Reuter used his ventures westward to stuff his briefcase with potatoes and sometimes coal briquettes.[1] Reuter's message to the Berliners that winter: "It is cold in Berlin. But it is still colder in Siberia." There were 2000 students who had fled Humboldt University in the Soviet sector (together with SPD stalwarts like Otto Suhr). They founded a free university in the American sector, and Reuter persuaded the venerable Friedrich Meinecke to be its first rector. The half-city was in dire need of money. It was getting 40 million *Marks* ($10 million) a month from the American and British zones and 50 million *Marks* in American counterpart funds. But what was West Berlin's status to be?

The Western zone military governors had constituted a parliamentary council in September with a view to creating a federal government in their occupation region. Reuter attended as a representative of West Berlin. This brought him into conflict with the newly designated president of the council, Konrad Adenauer, who wished from the outset to keep the Berliners at a great distance. It was a twofold struggle. Adenauer, old but full of strong Rhenish juices, had bent his Christian Democratic Union in the direction of a highly decentralized federal state; the SPD was demanding a strong central state authority. Again siding with the Western Allied majority and with his own preservative instincts, Adenauer rejected the idea of including Berlin in the new West German federation. It was his bow to the neighboring French, as Reuter later concluded. But it was also tinder for domestic strife.

The blockade had the effect of sharpening the political contest among the citizens of postwar Germany, so much so that their feeling for nuance was numbed. Brandt himself reflected the black-white vision of the moment in a speech at an SPD meeting in Berlin in January, when he denounced Soviet Communism as "an octopus" and added, "You cannot be a democrat today without being anti-Communist, although anti-Communism is not the only criterion of a democrat."[2] That was fine for Berlin and Berliners. But in West Germany Adenauer was already simplifying the East-West struggle in his speeches by tossing the Social Democrats into the same basket with the Communists. His was a powerful appeal to a people who had just survived another form of dictatorship, and he had working for him the traditional distaste of some Western Allied leaders for anything that smacked of Socialism.

In that same address Brandt commented on the potency of Germany's "restorative" forces—an almost euphemistic usage for the renewal of old pillars of German society: church, industry, and aristocracy. This was another political fact of blockade and postblockade Germany, much to the disadvantage of the Social Democrats. The Soviet offensive in Central Europe suddenly halted the efforts of thousands, perhaps millions of Germans to come to grips with their immediate past. Instead, they were diverted into a simplistic anti-Communism already sickeningly familiar from the Hitler era and, for the rest, into the comfortable habits of the pre-Hitler bourgeoisie. Annemarie Renger remembered it this way: "Normally, after what had happened with Hitler we should have gotten an SPD government in 1949, with such a strong leader as Kurt Schumacher. There was a need to do something else. Then suddenly, with the blockade, we saw we didn't have to change and could stay the way we were. We pursued our own personal interests, with a bad conscience that we had gotten off so easily."[3] This was to become the raw material of the social-critical novels of Heinrich Böll and Günter Grass on the one hand and the self-satisfied *Wirtschaftswunder* mentality of the dominant Conservatives on the other. It also drove the SPD leadership, or most of it, into a desperate hedgehog position for years to come; they were forced to man outmoded trenches with the weapons of the past: class militancy and socialization slogans. The shift in priorities was evident, too, in Brandt, the young man who had regarded himself as "a left Socialist, as a 'Communist' in the sense of the *Manifesto* of Marx and Engels,"[4] now saying a democrat had to be anti-Communist.

Since August of 1948 the Western Allies had been talking desultorily with the Russians—up to the level of Stalin himself—about ending the Berlin blockade and a Western counterblockade of Soviet trade. At the same time the Allies pushed ahead with redoubled energy to establish a civilian government in the Western zones and to erect a Western defensive alliance. It was that Creation over which Dean Acheson and President Truman presided. What they were doing was not lost on Stalin. In January 1949 he and his aides had begun signaling a retreat—the Soviet leader in an enigmatic statement to an American reporter and Walter Ulbricht in a speech declaring that Berlin was *not* part of the Soviet zone.[5] (He had said the opposite before.) But the Allies were not to be seduced. The idea of an Atlantic alliance was broadcast that same month, and the plans for a West German state went ahead, too.

The central issue between Schumacher and Adenauer, between the Socialists and the Conservatives, was the nature of the state to be. The SPD wanted to stress its temporary, provisional character, Adenauer its permanence. Schumacher also held out for a strong centralized government. In the end, he won, particularly on the point of establishing a parliamentary constitution that contained a "constructive no-confidence vote," a regulation providing that no Chancellor could be voted out of office without the assurance that his replacement had an adequate number of parliamentary supporters to assure solid rule. This rule was not to come into use for twenty-three years, but when it did it proved to be a source of tremendous strength for the practice of democracy in Germany.

By springtime of 1949 establishment of the West German state and the North Atlantic Treaty Organization, as well as the conclusion of the blockade of Berlin, were on parallel tracks. The Berliners were caught in between, and Mayor Reuter set off to London, Paris, and Washington to put before the Allies his case for the inclusion of his half of Berlin in the German Federal Republic. The French said *"non."* Otherwise, his journey was well worth it in terms of influencing official and public opinion. At the time he was the best-known German on the international scene.

The Atlantic Pact was published in March and signed in April that year. The secret deliberations on ending the blockade between the American diplomat, Philip Jessup, and the Russian, Jakob A. Malik, were successfully concluded with an agreement in New York in May, including a face-saving device for the Russians—a new Big Four Foreign Minister conference in Paris. On May 12 the blockade was officially ended, having lasted 322 days. Eleven days later, the West German Parliamentary Council adopted the basic law authorized by the Western Allies, thereby establishing the Federal Republic of Germany.

These were heady days as the Soviet tide ebbed. In the chapter on the blockade in his biography of Reuter, Willy Brandt wrote:

> For the struggle of Berlin to become a turning point of the history
> of post-war Europe one thing was necessary beyond the factual
> conditions—that the historical moment found at the head of the
> threatened city a moral personality of the rank of Reuter.[6]

The emphasis on the moral quality of leadership was not new with Brandt, but with the tutoring of Reuter it became an essential theme of his own political career.

Almost overnight the political landscape of Germany changed. Konrad Adenauer, with his powerful position as president of the Parliamentary Council, suddenly found himself in command of a viable political base for the elections now set for August. With the end of the blockade Reuter and his followers found themselves deprived with equal abruptness of their dominant issue. Bonn, not Berlin, now became the fulcrum of German politics. Brandt described the change thus:

> Many Allied authorities moved to Frankfurt or Bonn. My contacts with high Allied officials, originally my main task, lost their importance. In addition, my relations with Schumacher were not as good as before. He had the impression that I, instead of representing the (SPD) Executive, had become Reuter's man.[7]

Brandt was again being wooed. Schumacher offered him a candidacy for the first Bundestag (Parliament) from a safe district in Schleswig-Holstein. Reuter urged him to stay at his side in Berlin and take a post in the Magistrate to duplicate his own experience as a young city official in the Weimar Republic. Brandt turned down both these offers. "Reuter was visibly disappointed, maybe even a little angry with him for letting him down."[8] Brandt had his eye on Bonn—but as a freshly baptized Berliner. He wanted to participate in the strange new relationship between the island and the mainland, which was partially captured in the dialect ditty composed for a popular radio cabaret show entitled "Der Insulaner" ("The Islander"). The refrain, which Berliners listened to and sang for the next decade, went (in liberal translation):

> The islander doesn't lose his cool
> The islander doesn't praise the fool. . . .
> The islander hopes for the day
> On which his island joins the mainland far away.[9]

Unfortunately—and inexplicably in the context of most other nations—the feeling toward the island capital was scarcely reciprocated in the mainland of West Germany, least of all by Adenauer. There was even some resentment among West Germans at having to contribute extra tax money to the support of Berlin. Perhaps there was also a deep-seated suspicion of a capital from which two world wars had emanated, not to mention a distrust of big-city big mouths among a population mostly accustomed to small-town traditions. Besides, who of the West Germans had even glimpsed the metropolis since the war, cut off as it was? Adenauer didn't come to Berlin until 1950, and then only because it was a state obligation.

The Bundestag elections of August 14, 1949, had given Adenauer's Christian Democratic Union parties a slight edge over the SPD. Would he have lost if the Berlin blockade was still in effect and Reuter still the man of the hour? Together with the vote of the newly established Free Democrats and the tiny German Party, the seventy-three-year-old Rhinelander assembled half the deputies of the Bundestag. By one vote, his own, he was elected Federal Chancellor on September 1. A long period of darkness settled over the SPD.

The Christian Democratic Union had based its successful campaign on the promising economic prospects opened by the currency reform and on the necessity for German integration with the West. The Social Democrats had emphasized the priority of German reunification, and they continued to do so. The "Western" Adenauer was pitted against the "Eastern" and more nationalist Schumacher, the one from the Rhineland and the other from East Prussia. Schumacher's nationalism—a sagacious Frenchman called it "preventive nationalism"—had two related motives. He told friends that after what had happened to the SPD with its "internationalist" policies in the Weimar era, the party could never again afford to be overtaken on national issues. He also feared that if the field were left open to others, a dangerous new nationalism could develop on the Right.[10] Honorable, but not very realistic—particularly the drumming for reunification of the split country. He, the amputee, did not see his amputated countrymen were concerned first of all with getting around on one leg aided by a Western Allied cane, rather than with the dim and distant hope of getting the other leg sewed on again. Here Adenauer was the shrewder politician by far.

Reinhart Bartholomäi, the young SPD man from Swabia, saw it in terms of what might be called psychogeography: "Modern German history begins with the French Revolution. The trauma for the German intelligentsia was the figure of Napoleon. Hegel, Schiller, Goethe, were all enthusiastic supporters of the French Revolution. Then they saw the terror and turned away horrified. . . . In 1813 the victory against France in Germany was also the defeat of enlightenment. Afterward, throughout the entire nineteenth century, an intellectual East wind blew through Germany, and there was a struggle between Anglo-Saxon French enlightenment and Russo-German mysticism. It lasted until Heinrich Mann, who made the first intellectual opening to the West. . . . I am astounded when I read the books of the 1920s—those that my father and grandfather dismissed as 'superficial English fluff,' and they were talking about the pragmatism of William James. They loved Dostoevsky's lonely hero, who has to lose to be great. It was un-German to win, and in the war the German *Landser* (equivalent of the American GI) felt closer to the Red Army than to the Americans or English.

"What was new after the war was the Western influence, the opening to the West. . . . It influenced a whole generation—the press, the students. In the SPD it came from the second-generation emigration—Reuter and Brandt, who had a vision of a different Social Democracy, reformist, pragmatic, without ideology. But with certain moral assumptions."[11]

Although this West wind filled the mainsails of Adenauer, it only fitfully caught the jibs of the Reuters and Brandts; Schumacher, their helmsman, was still beating against the breeze with the bulk of the party as crew. The SPD chairman, bent on total opposition to Adenauer, doubtless feeling cheated out of a rightful place in the leadership of the new West Germany, militantly swung the party against some prized policies of the Western Allies—the establishment of West European unity and a corresponding defense organization with German participation. As a result of this conflict of interest between the Berlin-SPD and the Hannover headquarters, the Reuter group had developed its own SPD foreign policy even before the first Bundestag election.[12]

"Brandt didn't like Kurt Schumacher's Europe policy," Annemarie Renger recalled, "nor the confrontation with Adenauer. He was for cooperation with the other parties, and he regarded Adenauer as more of a mental power than Schumacher did. This, too, created a distance between them. Schumacher felt that certain reserve of Brandt toward him—that he was not completely in agreement with his policy and thus not completely loyal."[13]

Brandt saw himself as "between Reuter and Schumacher—and I got it from both."[14] But he had opted for the Bundestag, and evidently Reuter decided to make the best of it with Brandt, who went to Bonn as one of eight Berlin delegates to the West German Parliament—permitted to speak, but not to vote. (In fact, he did not make his maiden speech until the following year.) Just as West Berlin was the poor relative of the Federal Republic—"the Cinderella," Brandt called it—so the Berlin deputies were the step-children of the Bundestag. This was largely Adenauer's work, for the Americans had indicated they would be willing to allow Berlin to become the twelfth state of the Federal Republic if the Bonn Government would only agree. Of the position adopted by the Adenauer party, Brandt wrote: "They were afraid of the Social Democratic votes of Berlin."[15] By way of excusing himself in a Bonn meeting with Reuter, Adenauer said he was preoccupied with more important questions than those of the Berliners at the moment—for example, the prevention of dismantling of the foundry in Duisburg-Meiderich by occupation authorities.[16]

The constituting of the Federal Republic of Germany had another little-noted consequence, it seems, at the time and for a long time afterward. On October 7, only a month after the two houses of the Bonn Parliament convened, the Soviet occupation officials authorized the founding of the German Democratic Republic (DDR), complete with a Peoples Chamber and a separate constitution. The fact that few eyebrows were raised in the West was probably attributable to the forced-march communizing of the Soviet zone that had preceded the formal erection of a state apparatus. Already in

January 1949 the SED had been transformed into "a party of the new type"—
that is, Marxist-Leninist. Socialization of industry was advancing swiftly.
Centralized economic planning had begun. Military cadres numbering 10,000
had been formed by the end of 1948. The Free German Youth organization,
led by Erich Honecker since its inception in 1946, was now on the way to
becoming a duplicate of the Soviet Komsomol. In short, every essential
element of the East German society had been set on a Communist course.
Walter Ulbricht, the watchdog who presided over this transformation, still
remained in the background. (At the time of the founding of the DDR he was
a member of the ruling SED Politburo, and he took on the additional post of
Deputy Premier.) It is noteworthy that in his 1960 autobiographical chronicle
Brandt did not even mention the founding of the DDR. His 1957 Reuter
biography devotes less than a page to the event, and then mainly to cite
Reuter's response: "If I were Federal Chancellor I would go to Berlin and
establish the Federal Government here."[17] Adenauer was not amused.

By the end of 1949 Brandt at last acquired a firm footing in the Berlin party
apparatus. Though he had been at Reuter's side for well over a year and was
apparently his favorite understudy, too, he had annoyed the Schumacher
group in the Berlin group, headed by Franz Neumann, the previous spring. At
a city SPD congress Brandt had pointedly criticized the neutralist ideas with
which some of Neumann's people were toying, and he clearly identified
himself with Reuter's pro-Allied foreign policy. Now, however, he was
assigned the chairmanship of the party local in the residential borough of
Wilmersdorf. This was the base from which Willy Brandt set out to conquer
the Rathaus of West Berlin. It took him eight years. From the beginning he
had some huge advantages, the protection of Reuter, his own realism, and,
another priceless asset, the editorship of the SPD newspaper, *Sozialdemokrat*. Still, these were relatively quiet years in what had become a backwater of
international—and German—politics. Not until the Cold War ice thickened
around the island of Berlin would he again find a platform for prominence. As
Brandt observed, "Most of the foreign correspondents moved to Frankfurt or
Bonn—Berlin was no longer 'interesting.'"[18]

Despite the airlift and substantial financial assistance coming from West
Germany, the isolated city still had grievous problems: Half of its labor force
of 600,000 was unemployed, and many thousands more were on welfare.
While much of the war rubble had been cleared away, little had been
constructed in place of the lost buildings. Nor was it easy to find support for
the cause of Berlin in the increasingly conservative capital on the Rhine. Only
with the backing of the American high commissioner was Reuter able to
obtain for his city about 10 percent of the Marshall Plan funds designated for
Germany. Reuter, with Brandt as his spokesman in the Bonn Bundestag, also

had to struggle for the establishment of at least some federal institutions in West Berlin. Berlin was still in a political limbo, and Reuter's renewed efforts in the spring of 1950 to get its acceptance as a state of the Federal Republic were rejected by Adenauer. "I supported him with all my strength,"[19] Brandt said of Reuter and his initiatives. But the Berliners had to content themselves with gradual inclusion into the legal, social, and fiscal system of the Bonn Government, without formal acknowledgment as an integral part of the republic. This was finally accomplished in 1952, with the adoption of the so-called "third transition law" in the Bundestag—creating parallels in all essential government functions.

It was not simply a situation of Bonn versus Berlin. There was also the battle developing in the SPD itself between the Schumacher and the Reuter groups on a range of issues. Ernst Reuter had had difficulties with Kurt Schumacher long before the Berlin blockade had ended over the usual Berlin-Western zone issues, compounded by the problem of what Western Germany was to become. Not helping the situation was the fact that Schumacher lay terribly ill in Hannover, the one-armed leader suffering from having had a leg amputated in September 1949. It had not been easy to reach Hannover from Berlin or Frankfurt or Bonn, when the British and American authorities made the Germans wait for hours to get interzone travel permission. (Brandt remembered, not without bitterness, being denied use of the washrooms reserved for the Allies at one airport.)[20] Now the battle was spreading in Reuter's backyard, where Franz Neumann, the Berlin party chairman, opposed the Mayor. The contest came out in the open at the SPD convention in Hamburg in May 1950.

At stake in Hamburg was the SPD's position on West German foreign policy with regard to German participation in the proposed Council of Europe. The Schumacher executive sponsored a resolution calling on the Bonn Government to stay out of the Strasbourg organization on the ground that it represented a union of Europe's "reactionary" forces. Brandt spoke up:

> I don't really think we can go so far as to say that we can only really take part when there is a possibility of Social Democratic solidarity in Europe. Naturally we would prefer such a development, just as it would be desirable in Germany. But. . . . I believe that a "*Ja*" must be said to Europe and all its beginnings, which are represented in the economic area by the OEEC (Organization of European Economic Cooperation) and perhaps will develop politically in Strasbourg.[21]

But Schumacher was dominant, and the convention voted overwhelmingly against "Europe." Neumann commanded a majority of the Berlin delegates in support of Schumacher. Brandt was among the eleven delegates—six of them Berliners—who opposed the resolution.

It was not just in foreign policy that Schumacher demanded "total opposition" to the Adenauer party. He was also pushing domestic policies that were frankly Socialist. Even Wehner, who was loyal to Schumacher, privately criticized his views on the economy. "The entire Schumacher economic policy was dilettante," he observed much later. Nevertheless, for him, Schumacher was "an incomparable personality and not to be substituted in a people who sinned for twelve years—he took the old Social Democratic dogmatism, the belief that the change will come, and overcame that, developing a *state* concept, the *Lassallean*. Then we became interesting as a party." At the time Wehner regarded himself as Schumacher's "lightning rod," and so he kept silent. "I often had to go to Berlin when Neumann and Reuter were fighting," he said, "and I had to avoid taking sides because I saw how unhealthy it was."[22]

Brandt had no such obligations and felt free to criticize. In July 1950 he picked up the theoretical arguments of his Norwegian Socialist friend, Torolf Elster—pleas for a "Socialism free of dogma" and concentration on pragmatic reforms and presented them as a "modern and flexible" recipe for German Social Democrats.[23] About this time an article appeared in the Norwegian press that was critical of Schumacher's personal style and of his Europe policy. Mrs. Renger recalled: "It was an event that brought tensions in their relationship almost to a tearing point. Schumacher was sure it was from Willy Brandt, or that the information was from him, or the inspiration. Then he learned it was not. But that did not bring him away from the idea that it was intentional, and it hit him hard inside. There was an exchange between them either by telephone or letter but no meeting afterward for a long time— weeks. There was a rift.'"[24]

On top of this Bandt had somehow stirred an antipathy in Neumann so strong that the Berlin party chairman once confided to a friend that he "could not stand the sight of Brandt." Jupp Braun, a Neumann deputy who later worked under Brandt, told an interviewer in 1963 that Brandt also irritated elder comrades "simply through his appearance."[25] Brandt was well aware of it. "Some people think I tried to topple this deserving man, who had such a clear political line. But I told him early on that I wanted to help him. For one reason or another he refused to trust me."[26]

There were elections in West Berlin on December 3, and they reflected a new situation. Reuter was not presented as the SPD's main candidate; rather the Social Democrats campaigned as a party. A certain normality had returned to Berlin. The lights were on. The buses and subways were running. The stores were full. Unemployment had begun to recede. The blockade was an eighteen-month-old memory. "Heroes on Furlough," was a tabloid headline about Berliners. The Conservative wave that was at its peak in West Germany lapped at Berlin, too. The SPD took a bad beating, pulling 44.7 percent of the ballots, 200,000 votes less than in the election of 1948. Franz Neumann told a city convention of the party a month later that the SPD should take the consequences and go into opposition, as it had done in Bonn. It was a proposal that would have made Neumann stronger than an ex-Mayor Reuter, and the decision was postponed. Reuter was given a free hand to negotiate a coalition with the candidate of the Christian Democratic Union and the Liberals, Dr. Walther Schreiber, and he brought it off on January 18.

Neumann hadn't given up. At another special convention of the SPD on January 31, he openly attacked Reuter's thesis that Berlin was dependent on integration with the West:

> If it is so that that support Berlin gets is a means to an end, that it is provided only on the basis of certain preconditions, then it would be a policy just like that of the Russians. The only difference would be that the Russians do it with hobnailed boots and the other with pressed pants.[27]

It was a pithy phrase, and for years afterward Germans would speak of Americans as "Russians with pressed pants." Neumann grew bolder, as Kurt Mattick remembered it. "He wanted Berlin to keep its back free toward Bonn, and he would have given Adenauer the opportunity to split off Berlin. He also raised impractical demands in terms of financial and social policy. Things that were impossible. That's when Willy Brandt got into the act."[28]

Noting that the occupation powers were preparing a new Foreign Ministers conference on what to do about Germany and a peace treaty, Brandt observed:

> It is not a matter of indifference who will speak for Berlin during the period of the four power conference. . . . The real problem is not coalition or opposition, the real problem is to master Berlin's affairs in a responsible fashion, proceeding from the factual situation, and then, to activate the party.[29]

When it came to a vote, 167 of the Berlin SPD delegates opted for coalition, and 105 supported Neumann's opposition proposal. It signified the formal birth of two wings in the Berlin SPD that beat against each other with mounting ferocity until 1957.

Brandt concluded that to get ahead he would have to labor in the fields of the Berlin SPD, and so he made the rounds of Berlin districts—to Reuter territory in Zehlendorf and Steglitz, to Neumann territory in Kreuzberg and Neukölin. "I really did work at the grassroots level," he recalled, "all over Berlin, day after day and night after night. There is a point in politics where you say to yourself, 'Do I, or don't I? I did it, I developed a *Fraktion* (faction)."[30] As an ex-Communist, Herbert Wehner remembered that, too: "He maneuvered in a faction, chess moves. He always had a faction, wherever he was. He always did the same. Look! I was a Communist, and I never joined a faction. Not then, and not in the SPD. For I knew, that is the end of a party. Only one survives. That is the history of Marxism."[31]

Per Monsen visited Brandt in those days, when his old friend was "fighting for his political life." He remembers driving through the *Tiergarten* with him in a taxi and Brandt telling him of Neumann's intrigues and the struggle with Schumacher. "You probably don't know it," he murmured to Monsen, "but I am very thin-skinned. Sometimes I feel like chucking it all." Monsen also recalled: "I was embarrassed to talk Norwegian with him. But he was not. He said he didn't care. He wanted to be himself. He's never done anything he didn't think was honorable and true to his political opinions."[32]

Rut Brandt was pregnant again, and on June 3, 1951, their second son, Lars, was born. The godfather chosen for Lars, as for Peter, was Brandt's SPD friend, Günter Klein, the first Berlin senator for federal affairs in Bonn. The two had worked closely for years as Reuter men and then drifted apart. Thirteen years Brandt's senior, Klein was a Prussian lawyer who had made a brilliant career in business. In his political capacity he was the man who did more than any other to push through the legislation linking the social-political system of West Berlin to that of the Federal Republic. The cooling of his friendly ties with Brandt was attributed by friends of both in part to Klein's own stubborn self-assurance and in part to Brandt's surrounding himself with a new circle.

As a deputy of the Bonn Bundestag and a member of its Foreign Affairs Committee, Brandt was spending many weeks of the year in the West German capital. There, as was his custom, he sought diversion in lively company after the often dreary hours of parliamentary work. In the spring of 1951 he made the acquaintance of a redhead from Cologne. Susanne Sievers was a thirty-one-year-old divorcée who had landed in the secretarial pool of the Bundestag. She was handsome, in a strong-featured way. Herbert Wehner remembers her being sent to him with a recommendation from the interior minister of North Rhine-Westphalia as "somebody who was clever." She turned up in

Wehner's office and announced: "People say I have the prettiest thighs in Bonn." Wehner recalled: "I could only laugh—this whore."[33] But Brandt was interested in the shapely Susanne, and they began to see each other. Now in the Carlton Bar, now in the discreet elegant restaurant of the Adler Hotel in Godesberg, now in her apartment on the Reuterstrasse. They exchanged letters—hers passionate, signed "Puma," his amiable and signed "Bear."

Susanne Sievers was immensely ambitious. With the support of a Bonn journalist she began putting out the *Bonner-Informations-Briefe,* or BIB for short. It was one of those intimate little periodicals, purporting to give inside stories that flourish in many a capital—like the Kiplinger Letter. She gloried in the name she had given herself, "Madame Scandaleuse," and among her conquests she numbered Carlo Schmid, the ranking SPD intellectual, and Franz Josef Strauss, the stubby Bavarian who was becoming the powerhouse of the Christian Social Union. Such a woman was bound to attract the interest of others, particularly the intelligence network of the German Democratic Republic. She was recruited, apparently by agents of the year-old Ministry for State Security, during a visit to the Leipzig Autumn Fair. It was a relationship that ended less than a year later, in her arrest in East Berlin and a prison term of more than four years. Presumably, she had tried to work both sides of the German fence.[34]

The Brandt-Sievers affair lasted more than a year. What was there to it? A woman journalist who knew and admired Brandt for many years remarked: "Nothing. He was bored after a day's work and wanted to have some drinks and fun, and women were fun. I know dozens of men like that." One of his other admirers, Dolly Franke, wrote him in those years: "At 16 you were already a far-seeing politician and your path was already clear for you. There was nothing but politics. . . . You were my first acquaintance with the opposite sex and in the course of the years you have acquired a halo that would lose some of its glitter on closer acquaintance."[35]

The conflict between the Reuter and Neumann wings of the Berlin SPD simmered on, heated to boiling every few months by friction over every sort of issue—a plan for unifying the coal and steel industries of France, Germany, and the Benelux states; the relationship of Berlin to Bonn; Franz Neumann's familiar argument that the West Berlin SPD should follow the federal SPD into opposition; the question of rearming Germany. But for Neumann, these issues merely served as pretexts for his main desire—to get rid of Reuter and make the Berlin SPD conform at last with the mother party in Bonn.

On April 3, 1952, he rounded up his twenty-two SPD deputies in the House of Representatives to vote against a Reuter policy declaration—that is, to topple him. The Mayor was waved by CDU and FDP votes and the remaining twenty-nine SPD deputies who backed him. A close call. The breach of voting discipline was unprecedented, and it provoked the calling of a new SPD convention. Brandt spoke later of "long and bitter quarrels" among his Berlin comrades, as well as "open and hidden conflicts."

In respose to the Neumann offensive, Reuter asked Willy Brandt to run for the Berlin party chairmanship in May against Neumann. Brandt, who said, "I belonged among Reuter's closest friends," accepted, even though, "I knew I could not win."[36] The choice meant that Reuter had settled on Brandt as his successor, and it seems that Schumacher acknowledged this, for he did not oppose the contest. Still, it was daring to go into a struggle with the knowledge of certain defeat. Though Brandt would lose other contests at higher levels, challenging Neumann for the Berlin party chieftainship may have been the bravest of all his political ventures.

Even the dispatch of Ollenhauer to Berlin to smooth the feathers of the rival wings failed to head off the battle. Neumann was full of confidence, but he had not counted all the votes. When Brandt presented a resolution favoring continuance of the Berlin coalition with Mayor Reuter at the head, the Neumann wing mustered only 135 of the delegates, against 150 for Reuter. But he got satisfaction in the following vote on the chairmanship, beating Brandt 196 to 93. That was the beginning of the end for Neumann. Brandt had a larger concept, and he was younger and more resilient than the big bear from Berlin-Reineckendorf. The conflict practically paralyzed the Berlin SPD for a time, and none of the leading men wanted to take the deputy chairmanship next to Neumann. Reuter and Brandt decided the best tactic was to avoid strife, and they sidestepped any tangle with Neumann for many months afterward.

In July Brandt had a long talk with Schumacher, who was by this time a very sick man. "Did he have a foreboding of death?" Brandt asked himself. "On the one hand he criticized the stubbornness of a certain type of party functionary and demanded a greater intellectual independence; on the other he defended the yes men . . . I had the impression that he himself was aware of these contradictions and that he suffered from them."[37] Brandt then went on vacation to the hills around Hamar with Rut and the boys. Schumacher died August 20, while Brandt was still in Norway. Erik Loe, an editor of *Arbeiderbladet*, got in touch with Brandt, who was still the paper's regular Berlin correspondent, and Brandt hastened down to the capital that same day to write a *Nachruf* (an obituary). "It was his most important article, a very big article, a very important political document, and he worked very hard on it," Loe recalled. "His correspondence was balanced, although his position was difficult, because in his heart he didn't agree with the policy of Schumacher."[38] Brandt wrote later that Schumacher's death was a "heavy blow for the Party, a grave loss for Germany . . . In spite of the criticism that his autocratic leadership and some of his decisions deserved, Schumacher's integrity, his will power, his idealism, were a great asset for the Federal Republic, for the German people."[39]

The passing of Schumacher eased the position of Reuter and Brandt, because it deprived Franz Neumann of his one big ally. When the post-Schumacher SPD held its federal convention in Dortmund in September, he avoided confrontation. Brandt was not even mentioned as a candidate for the party executive this time around and, when he spoke to the assembled comrades, did so with extreme caution. West Germany shouldn't simply refuse to participate in a Western defense system, he said. But the possibility of withdrawal in the event Germany could achieve reunification in liberty should not be excluded.[40] Ollenhauer, a man of reason and decency—but uninspired and uninspiring—was chosen as Schumacher's successor in the chairmanship.

Throughout these years the Soviet Union and the Western powers were locked in global combat. In divided Korea there was the real war. In divided Germany it was a shadow war—more and more a struggle fought between German deputies of the great powers. The battles cost few lives, but the very absence of clearly defined fronts envenomed the atmosphere all the more. In retrospect, one might assume that the underlying motive of Stalin's policy was defensive in character, that he was merely trying—however, aggressively—to protect what he had gained in the war. But to the Western leaders the Berlin blockade and the Communist invasion of North Korea were clear signs of expansionist intentions. Their response was to look to their own common defenses. There were sufficient excuses. The Russians had applied pressure on West Berlin's land access routes with harassing controls on truck and train shipments, sometimes stopping traffic for days at a time. Communist agitators sent out by East Berlin caused violent disturbances in West German cities. There were kidnappings in the West of political figures deemed hostile by the Communists—thirteen in 1949, forty-two in 1950, thirty-six in 1951.

Herbert Wehner, denounced by East Berlin as a "traitor" and "renegade" traveled with an armed guard because he had good reason to fear for his life. The American and Soviet intelligence services were marshaling small armies of covert agents, saboteurs, and professional killers throughout Germany—many of them former Gestapo and SS men desperate to avoid punishment for their crimes as Nazis. The U.S. Central Intelligence Agency was running an espionage stable of barely ex-Nazis, the Gehlen Organization, under former General Reinhard Gehlen, who had been Hitler's East Front spy chief. But the Americans were also sponsoring and directing such diverse storefront operations as the SPD's East Bureau, the "Investigation Committee of Free Jurists," and the sabotage-oriented "Battle Group Against Inhumanity." The Russians responded in kind.

Gehlen also used his growing power unscrupulously to penetrate what he deemed to be "unpatriotic" German political organizations, chiefly the SPD. He systematically built up "compromising" dossiers on the leading Social Democratic politicians, including Wehner and Brandt. That was against his orders. But he himself admitted that he only obeyed orders that pleased him and dodged those he disliked when he could.[41]

The impact of the spying, kidnapping, and threats showed up in the political life of both parts of Germany. Fear was greater than at any time since 1933. The witchhunts provoked by Senator Joseph McCarthy in the West had their deadlier counterpart in the East: the persecution of Communists branded by Stalin as "Titoist" agents and, worse, those accused of working for "American imperialism." In East Germany alone more than three hundred Communists were rounded up as putative members of a ring run by the dreamy American Leftist, Noel H. Field. One of the victims, Leo Bauer, had been an acquaintance of Willy Brandt during the Paris "unity front" days before the war. He was dragged to Siberia under a death sentence, only to be released to West Germany in 1956 with six years of confinement behind him.

Willy Brandt faced an actual threat from the Communists because of his associations with East German SPD members, so he did not risk traveling to West Germany on vulnerable land routes. Instead, until 1955, he used airplanes. Only Reuter drove to and from West Berlin on the *Autobahn,* assuming correctly that the East German authorities would not tamper with such a well-known politician.[42]

Against this background, it was small wonder that the Western leaders, including the Germans, looked skeptically, even scornfully, upon Stalin's new peace bid of March 10, 1952. In his note to the three Western Allies, the Soviet leader proposed the reunification of Germany on the basis of neutrality. Coming on the eve of the conclusion of a treaty designed by the Western Allies to give West Germany a large measure of sovereignty, the note betrayed less than altruistic intentions. Like Soviet maneuvers aimed three years before at holding off the establishment of the Federal Republic of Germany, it appeared to be a delaying tactic. Only the Social Democrats seemed to think it worth probing Soviet intentions. In the Bundestag Herbert Wehner spoke of the "burning interest" of all Germans to know what was behind the March 10 note, and he warned of "the danger of slamming the door." Brandt, too, "regretted that no attempt was made to put Russian sincerity to the test,"[43] though he was also skeptical. But the Western negotiating machinery was running in high gear, and on May 26 the Bonn Government signed the general treaty with the three Allies, coupling it the following day with the commitment to rearm West Germany in the signing of the European Defense Community pact in Paris. With those two acts the basic orientation of West German policy was set and sealed for decades to come—reliance on American security guarantees and dedication toward integration of West Germany into a larger European whole.

The mustering of West Germans into a new army was still four years off, delayed in large part by the collapse of the European Defense Community concept and its substitution with a German contribution to NATO forces. But debate on the remilitarization issue wore on, linked as it was to the perennial question of German reunification.

After warning that a "Cold Peace" might perpetuate the divison of the continent and of Germany, Brandt said, in a December 1952 Bundestag discussion:

> We must awake the satisfied and the fatigued, the lazy and the complacent, and never stop asking ourselves whether German policy has really done all it could do to concentrate all the forces of our nation on one decisive point and to imbue the people with a boundless will to win the struggle for the reunification of Germany.

Five months later at an SPD convention in Berlin he spoke up for "a more effective system of defense," adding: "The Kremlin must know quite clearly that a Federal Government led by Social Democrats would conduct not an impotent policy, but a collective policy of the Western world." Four years earlier he declared that a democrat had to be anti-Communist. Now the man who had bitterly denounced the armaments of the Weimar SPD twenty-three years before was earnestly defending a large-scale defense effort. He had come a long way.

Stalin's death in March set off a chain of events that ended with a hardening of the fronts in Germany. It was a most peculiar sequence. Many a dedicated Communist wept for the dictator and then began to tremble in his skin. Would the West seize the opportunity and attack? Among the quavering was Erich Honecker in East Berlin.[44]

The program for Accelerated Construction of Socialism had been largely a failure, with its wasteful collectivization campaigns and its unsuccessful attempts to mobilize the masses. There were grim shortages of consumer goods, mounting vigilance campaigns, and increased efforts to draft young people into military and paramilitary formations. Ulbricht's response seemed paradoxical: He demanded tighter discipline than ever, countering the very recommendations of his Soviet superiors. A struggle for the succession was under way in Moscow, and he surely knew his enemies and rivals were assembling in Berlin as well. Undeterred, he rammed through a decision to raise work norms by at least 10 percent and announced it on May 28—a measure technically justified, but politically incendiary. A movement calling for workers to put down their tools spread during the next days, and on June 16, several hundred employees of the Peoples Own Union Construction Enterprise stopped work at the huge Stalinallee housing project in the heart of East Berlin and began a demonstrative march to trade union headquarters. Soviet tank units on the sector perimeter were already on the alert. Over the next thirty-six hours the rebellious mood spread across the entire DDR, partly by word of mouth, but much more through excited reports on the American-sponsored radio station in West Berlin.

On the morning of June 17 hundreds of thousands of East Germans joined in what was briefly a national uprising, calling for "free elections" and demanding that Ulbricht *"der Spitzbart"* (the goatbeard) quit. At ll:10 a.m. a youth clambered to the top of the Brandenburg Gate and tore down the red flag of the Communist movement that had flown there since 1945. It was replaced with a Federal German flag. Fifty minutes later the first shots were fired. Soviet tanks moved into the downtown streets. At 1 p.m. the Soviet Commandant declared martial law. A similar state of emergency was imposed in 121 DDR cities soon after.

Altogether several hundred East Germans were killed during the short-lived uprising; twenty were shot on the spot, and 1400 persons were sentenced to a total of 4100 years. The Western Allies stood idly by as the East Germans shook their fists and threw stones at the Soviet tank squadrons. Almost miraculously, Ulbricht survived the debacle, though he fled Berlin, probably in a Russian tank. In retrospect, he seems to have known that a far more decisive fight was going on within the walls of the Kremlin at that moment; Lavrenti Beria, the secret police chief, was bidding for Stalin's power. On June 30, less than two weeks after the worker uprising, Ulbricht awarded himself the Hero of Labor medal on the occasion of his sixtieth birthday, for he knew, well ahead of the announcement nine days later, that Beria had been arrested. The wily German suffered a few bruises from the uprising—he was now "first secretary" instead of "secretary general" of the SED. But late in July he was able to deliver a counterblow to his party rivals, the secret police chief, Wilhelm Zaisser, and the *Neues Deutschland* editor, Rudolf Hernnstadt. They were stripped of all offices and honors as "enemies of the party" and "defeatists." Erich Honecker now moved up as Ulbricht's number-one boy.

In Bonn the response to the uprising was a mixture of righteous wrath (Adenauer) and forlorn hope (the SPD opposition). All parties in the Bundestag agreed on July 1 to make June 17 a national holiday, with Herbert Wehner stressing the fact that it had been an uprising principally of workers. Wehner, Reuter, and Brandt persuaded Adenauer to organize a Care package action to help the East Germans, and in July more than 2.8 million packages were distributed through West Berlin. In the Bundestag discussion Wehner spoke of Brandt for the first time as "my friend." It was a signal of a future alliance.

In his Bundestag address Brandt presented the uprising as a bugle call in the struggle for German unity: "The struggle for reunification in freedom has precedence over all plans and projects in foreign affairs," he declared.

> The workers in the Zone have recognized the moment when spontaneous actions could be started. Now it is our task in the Western world to recognize the moment when the German question can—if at all—be solved on the international level. . . . We are armed with skepticism. But despite skepticism and mistrust we believe that negotiations ought to be attempted, and the attempt must be made swiftly. . . . We demand more activity, more clarity, more determination in the struggle for German unity in peace and freedom.

Brandt, Reuter, Wehner, Ollenhauer—the SPD got its answer to these expectant pleas less than three months later in the second federal election. Adenauer had campaigned with a poster that depicted a slant-eyed, vicious looking Soviet soldier and the slogan: "Because of Him—CDU!" The fright caused by the brutal Russian suppression of the June 17 rebellion was unquestionably an elemental factor at the polls on September 6. The West German electorate didn't want vague reunification hopes, à la SPD. It wanted safety, à la CDU.

"Adenauer *with* the CDU," as the aged Chancellor had presented himself, won 45 percent of the vote, a gain of 14 percentage points over 1949. The SPD lost ground.

Twenty-three days later, following a series of massive heart seizures, Ernst Reuter died in Berlin. He hadn't bother to consult a physician until it was too late, certain that he would have been told to take it easy.

Brandt got the news by way of Oslo. *Arbeiderbladet* reached him at his home in Halensee and asked for a quick obituary. Brandt rushed to Reuter's home, hardly believing his ears. That evening, walking back through Zehlendorf "benumbed and troubled," Brandt saw scores of candles lit in the windows and remembered that Reuter had asked his fellow Berliners to light candles for their missing loved ones at Christmas. "The Berliners wept wherever they received the news," Brandt recorded.[45]

On October 1 Brandt was chosen to give the eulogy in a memorial service at the Knie, the big intersection near the Charlottenburg Palace, which was named Ernst Reuter Square that day. "You have been at the same time our teacher, cheerleader and friend," he said, and he was speaking for himself, as well. "You never doubted the victory of freedom. Therefore you were able to inspire those who worked with you, the whole population. . . ."[46] Later Brandt would mention Reuter in the same breath with Leber as permanent influences on his life, both in their interpretation of Socialism and in their moral stamina. Leber would have been sixty-one had he lived. Reuter was sixty-four when his baton was passed to Willy Brandt, who would soon turn forty.

An immediate consequence of Reuter's death was the collapse of the all-party coalition in Berlin and the subsequent rule of the CDU and FDP for more than a year. But opposition proved to be of little benefit to Neumann, the Social Democrat who had sought it so long. When Brandt challenged him again for the Berlin party chairmanship in May 1954, the vote was a cliffhanging 145 to 143 for Neumann. The challenger was feeling his strength from several sources: He had inherited Reuter's bright mantle; the federal SPD was doing none too well. At the Berlin state convention Brandt openly attacked "neutralist" tendencies and, at a later session, he called plainly for German rearmament and participation in the Western security system. [47] This was treading on German eggshells. Neutralism was no German virtue, and to suggest that an opponent was "neutral" came close to insult. Clemens von Brentano had written:

> To hate or to love
> None in the world is above
> There is no choice at all
> The Devil remains neutral.

Two months later the national SPD held *its* convention in Berlin and the main theme, again, was the military question. It took a certain daring to speak out against the soaring trend toward neutralism or pacifism for what was clearly a minority view, but Brandt did not flinch. Pointing to a recent poll that had shown only 12 percent of West Germans considered reunification the top policy priority, Brandt observed that the tendency toward sharper division would continue. This obliged the SPD to consider what should be done in terms of defense policy: "We cannot, to overstate it a bit, convene a special Party congress on the third day of mobilization, so to speak, to make a decision." He continued:

... As difficult as it may seem we have to get done with the problem of the relationship between democratic order and armed power. Otherwise we won't be able to manage the problem of democracy at all. The Left in Germany failed to solve this problem the last time. . . . We cannot stick our head in the sand today in the face of these unpleasant problems. . . .[48]

The protocol shows that Brandt got "applause" and "lively applause" for his remarks, as had Herbert Wehner in a more cautious contribution a few minutes before. But when it came to the election of the new party leadership on July 23, Brandt fell thirty-three votes short of the number required for acceptance in the new executive. Franz Neumann and Wehner were both elected. Writing of the defeats later he observed: "I had in the meantime gained some appreciation in spite of a strong hostility on the part of some functionaries."[49]

In the face of Neumann's bitter opposition, Brandt was chosen president of the House of Representatives after the December 8 elections in West Berlin, replacing Otto Suhr, who had become Mayor on the strength of a one-vote SPD majority. A kind of truce followed. The peace was welcomed by Brandt, who, in addition to his continuing journalistic efforts and his parliamentary duties, had begun a major literary project. Together with Richard Lowenthal, his friend from the émigré Left, now a British subject and correspondent for the London *Observer,* Brandt conceived an enormous political biography of Ernst Reuter. With the blessing of Reuter's widow, Hanna, and with full access to his papers, the two set to work, Lowenthal writing the first six chapters, and Brandt finishing most of the remaining seventeen.[50] When completed in the spring of 1957 the book came to 760 pages—a labor of love and also a thoroughly persuasive account of a complex man. "Through this work I have learned much for my own political activity," Brandt said.[51]

Brandt was attracting attention elsewhere as well. He had already won the sympathies of Americans in Stockholm during the war, and less emotional officials of the intelligence services also kept files on him in Washington, since Brandt did not fit into their ordinary categories of Germans. Now, as the leader of the "reasonable" people in the SPD, he was thinking and doing things that appealed to Washington policy-makers. They invited him to Washington in 1954 in a group of other amenable Social Democrats—Carlo Schmid, Fritz Erler, and Günter Klein. It had become the custom to invite the up-and-coming, as well as the established German politicians to the United States; Reuter had made three American trips in five years. The journey took the four as far afield as Texas and Boston, and for Brandt it was the beginning of a long and warm relationship with many Americans on their home ground.

A trip to Yugoslavia followed in 1955, and that, too was a country to which he would often return.

Although still in the minority, Brandt steadily broadened the base of his support in the Berlin SPD throughout 1955. It was, as Reinhart Bartholomäi would describe it later, with a phrase borrowed from the Radical Left, "Willy's long march through the institutions."[52] In May there was still another Berlin state party convention and, once more, the familiar Brandt-Neumann contest over arms and armies. The Berlin party chief pointed to shifting international arrangements: Austria had won her sovereignty from the Russians after years of negotiations; Khrushchev made the Soviet Union's peace with Tito's Yugoslavia; another four-power conference in Geneva was scheduled. In this atmosphere didn't the German future look more promising? he rhetorically asked. Brandt's reply was firm. Germany could not be compared to the smaller states, as much as she might admire their situation. Germany had too big an economic and military potential. The axis of the balance of power plainly ran through the middle of Germany, and therefore she could not function as a buffer state. "We ought to know that you can't resign from Europe and the world as if it were a bowling club," he concluded.[53] Neumann was reelected chairman of the Berlin organization and Brandt became his—despised— deputy, for the first time. He was picking up valuable support.

Brandt's view had not prevailed in the SPD as yet. But he was correct in his vision. In July, at the Geneva summit meeting, Premier Nikolai Bulganin had unveiled a prospect of German reunification in the framework of a European security system, following negotiations between East and West Germany. Passing through Berlin on the way back to Moscow, Khrushchev declared that nothing could be accomplished in the direction of unification at the cost of the DDR. To cement this the Russians signed a treaty with East Germany on September 10 granting the DDR a measure of "sovereignty." Chancellor Adenauer had already arrived in Moscow the day before to negotiate the release of thousands of Germans still detained by the Russians ten years after the war. In exchange for taking up diplomatic relations with Moscow, he won the liberty of more than 20,000 Germans. But from then on the Russians made plain they intended to deal equally with the two German states, and their political proposals indicated that they expected to have one Germany (East) as a vassal and the other Germany (West) as a neutral. Nor did that change much in the next score of years. Brandt was keenly opposed to the Soviet suggestion that West Germany recognize the German Democratic Republic. He and his fellow Social Democrats still called it "the zone," and its government, "Pankow," after the East Berlin borough in which President Wilhelm Pieck had lived for a time. In this respect and in others he was really much closer to Adenauer than to Ollenhauer. Though it was virtually a breach of party discipline, he approved of West Germany's joining NATO in 1955 following the French torpedoing of the European Defense Community.

Brandt was taking on more and more of the work of Otto Suhr, who was ailing. He was writing a book. He was still busy in the Bonn Parliament. So he finally gave up his contract with *Arbeiderbladet* in Oslo. He visited Scandinavian friends in Oslo and Stockholm in March, and in the Swedish capital he explained that while opposing recognition of "Pankow," he favored the idea of opening direct talks with the East German leaders. There was nothing to fear, he said, since the West had the better arguments.

Brandt attempted to carry these softened thoughts into the next national party convention at Munich in July and found a disappointing echo. Neumann had been intriguing against him again, and the bad feeling Brandt had stirred two years before with his arguments on military policy were still alive. He lost when it came to the critical balloting for the national party executive, while Neumann swept in once more. A hard blow—especially when Fritz Erler, whose arms policy coincided with his, was finally voted in. Brandt was ready to move up. As Kurt Mattick remembered it, he had developed "a personality and a natural authority to integrate others. He had learned much from Reuter in administrative and state leadership. Until then Brandt was a journalist. It had to grow in him. He recognized the Berlin job as a political office, as Reuter had and Suhr, too."[54]

In August Susanne Sievers showed up in his office at the Schöneberg Rathaus. Brandt had intervened with Adenauer to help get her released after serving three years of a five-year sentence. She apparently thought the old relationship would again catch fire.[55] But Brandt had a different view of the old relationship; he didn't want a new one. She went on to Bonn and very swiftly became a militant anti-Communist—and anti-Social Democrat. In time she lowered her sights.

Khrushchev, the maker of spectaculars, had stunned his comrades at the Twentieth Party Congress of the Soviet Union Communist Party (CPSU) in February by denouncing the crimes of Stalin. A few weeks later the Cominform was dissolved. Copies of his secret speech were circulating throughout East Europe, that tightly policed but otherwise loosely organized Soviet empire. Combined with wretched physical circumstances and the increasingly isolated situation of Stalin's Eastern European disciples, the mixture became volatile, particularly in Poland and Hungary. After the East German uprising in 1953, Ulbricht was prepared to handle any and every threat. Restless workers? "Arrest the ringleaders." Restless students? "Beat them up." Intellectuals? "Arrest them." Rivals in the party? "Dismiss them."[56] His newly established *Nationale Volksarmee* was ready. So, too, his secret police and his two-year-old Factory Fighting Groups. Nothing was left to chance. When the echoes of the June riots in Poznan and the October storm in Budapest reached East Berlin, Ulbricht was ready.

Brandt had been watching the spreading rebellion closely, and, like other Germans, he spoke hopefully of the possibilities for "Titoism" and "Gomulkanism" in the ranks of the SED. But given the peculiar mechanics of Central European politics, things were to turn out quite differently for them.

Soviet tanks crushed the incensed rebels of Budapest in pools of blood and 8000 smashed bodies on November 4, after ten days of revolution. A wave of revulsion spread across Europe, reaching Berlin, where the Germans remembered their own abortive and pitiful defiance of Soviet armor three years earlier. On November 5 hundreds of thousands took to the streets. A rally was scheduled at the square in front of City Hall in Schöneberg. Ernst Lemmer, that good and decent man from the CDU, was shouted down. Neumann got hisses and boos. Brandt was there, but not on the program. Calls came from the crowd: "To the Brandenburg Gate!" "To the Soviet Embassy!" "Russians go home!" Brandt reached a microphone and steered one large group to the Steinplatz, where there is a memorial to the "victims of totalitarianism." There, with Rut at his side, he led the crowd into singing the "Good Comrade" song, as moving a tribute as there could be to the fallen Hungarians. Then a new report reached the standby police detail: Another large group was storming north toward East Berlin. (Both these sites were over two miles from the original rally, quite a distance on a chilly November evening.) Willy and Rut sped through the *Tiergarten* and reached the mob a few yards from the border. Just beyond stood *Volkspolizisten* armed with carbines and supported by a scattering of Soviet tanks. Sweating despite the cold, Brandt spoke again through the police car microphone, urging calm on the raging multitude and warning them that they could very well play into the hands of the Russians if they got out of control. Indeed, there had been game plans by Ulbricht's men for launching an occupation of West Berlin in the event of a "provocation" that night.[57] Again Brandt intoned the "Good Comrade" song. Altogether he spoke to the Berlin public four times that night, the last from the top of a police car in front of the Brandenburg Gate, where he asked the crowd to join him in singing the German national anthem. "In political situations it is useful to know that my German countrymen are fond of singing," Brandt commented later with the wryness he found most suited to his sense of humor. He added: "That evening certainly helped Rut and me to win the hearts of the Berliners."[58] By almost all accounts it did.

Klaus Schütz said that "when he got this night under control," it was an "outstanding point" in Brandt's political career.[59] Franz Neumann pressed his lips together "in wordless fury."[60] Brandt had stolen the show.

With Mayor Suhr mortally ill and sinking before their eyes, Brandt and Neumann carried their rivalry into its final phase, now above ground, now underground. Experienced and hardened by his numerous knockouts at the hands of Neumann, Brandt avoided a clinch with his adversary. Neumann argued at a new Berlin party congress in January 1957 that the latest Soviet setbacks cried for new initiatives from the West. Brandt remained skeptical. He appears to have sensed, as Adenauer did, that the cruel retaliation of the Russians in East Europe and the concomitant passivity of the West—despite all of Dulles' resounding proclamations of "rollback"—were auguries for status quo. Not that he approved of Adenauer's superloyalty to the West, which reached a pinnacle in his demand for atomic arms for the newly established Bundeswehr (federal army). Instead, he concentrated his fire on Neumann's superficial treatment of domestic affairs, quoting Reuter liberally and calling for a policy of "great spiritual and moral impulses. . . . for performing daily tasks."[61] At the next state convention of the SPD Brandt again avoided the atomic weapons issue, devoting his foreign policy arguments to saying that if the Russians wanted West Germany to leave NATO they should think about withdrawing their troops from East Germany, Czechoslovakia, and Poland. It was a harmless kind of chess. But he knew what was in the wind for his party in the next elections. Two weeks after Mayor Suhr's death of cancer on August 30, the voters presented the bill to Ollenhauer, Neumann, and the others for their four years of utopianism on the issues of reunification, armaments, the situation in East Europe, and the temper of the German people. Adenauer and Brandt, from their different vantage points, had seen reality. The CDU won over 50 percent, while the SPD creaked from 29 to 32 percent.

The Communists in East Europe, with their almost helpless maneuvers, had helped elect the Conservatives in West Germany again. That suited Ulbricht perfectly, and it helped Brandt in his way, too, for the accommodating attitude of the SPD leadership had been completely disavowed. So, too, were Brandt's detractors, who had launched the first major campaign of denunciation against him that summer. Brandt felt compelled to launch a civil suit to protect himself against the "vicious attacks" and "veritable campaign of slander" involving his émigré past.[62]

With the Mayor's office vacant, Brandt became eligible for high office at last. Neumann's month-long search for another candidate was in vain. He failed to lure Erler and Schmid to Berlin. When Adolf Arndt, a brilliant economics specialist, learned of Neumann's intentions, he too, turned down the offer. From Bonn came the odor of conviction that the national party had fallen on its face twice now in critical election battles. It was time to give a fresh group of Social Democrats a chance. The Neumann wing was already broken, and Brandt was the obvious man in this situation. The Berlin SPD nominated Brandt to the office of Governing Mayor 233 to 26, with 22 abstentions at a convention on September 30. Three days later the House of Representatives elected him 86 to 10 with 22 abstentions. Brandt was Mayor of the biggest city between Paris and Moscow, the former Reich capital, and still *the* German city. He had done it with some help and some luck, but also with a lot of hard work of his own. He had spent most of the time operating between the island and the mainland. Now it was the island that he won and that won him. It had taken him eight years; he was not yet forty-four years old. "It was a heavy burden," he wrote. "But . . . nobody forced me to shoulder this burden."[63]

VII:

The Front-Line Mayor

Brandt made Berlin glitter," Herbert Wehner observed in 1973. "He gave it a role for the young."[1] Brandt's accession to the post of *Regierender Bürgermeister,* or Governing Mayor, signaled a generation change not only in Berlin, where he succeeded Otto Suhr, almost twenty years his senior, but also in the Social Democratic Party as a whole. The title was a crutch chosen in 1950 to uphold West Berlin's peculiar status as a rump city and a kind of rump capital. Ultimately the city was a ward of the four Allied commandants (with the Soviet on permanent self-imposed furlough). *Regierender Bürgermeister* was something less than *Oberbürgermeister,* the equivalent of the English Lord Mayor, because of the continuing occupation limitations, but a good deal more, too, because Berlin was a state and the *Regierender* its Governor. With its huge population, relative to other German cities, and its historic role in the center of modern German politics, being Mayor of West Berlin was a formidable calling— comparable in American politics to being Mayor of New York.

Up to Brandt's time there had been another limitation on the SPD Mayors. None, including Reuter and Suhr, was in command of the Berlin party organization, which remained the preserve of Franz Neumann. Now Brandt set out to eliminate this handicap. He was favored by the changing currents in the SPD as a whole. In Bonn, for example, the SPD Bundestag deputies responded to the humiliating September election defeat by picking three new parliamentary leaders to serve under Erich Ollenhauer. Against Ollenhauer's express wish they chose Carlo Schmid, Herbert Wehner, and Fritz Erler—all three men with reputations for a flexible, undoctrinaire approach to politics.

Brandt's campaign to drive Neumann from his last citadel, the Berlin party organization, had the marks of a general staff plan. It proceeded on two levels: in the press and in the party locals. For an entire month—November 1957— the Brandt stalwart, Kurt Mattick, carried on harsh, polemical exchanges with Neumann in the columns of *Berliner Sozialdemokrat,* later the *Stadtblatt,* the

SPD paper of which Brandt had been the editor under Reuter. At the same time Brandt's operations chief, Klaus Schütz, who was to become Mayor of West Berlin, canvassed Berlin's twenty district SPD organizations for support. Schütz built up a card index file on the 290 delegates to the upcoming Berlin party convention, where the chairmanship would be contested again. Using this system the Brandt team figured out various approaches to the different groups of delegates on the basis of their "political views." The combination worked. Even before the convention Berlin newspapers were carrying reports that reminded one observer of a soccer series. Stories about SPD district organizations were headlined "Now 8 to 4 for Brandt."[2] In addition, Brandt was obtaining friendly notices from the newspapers of Axel Caesar Springer, the young Hamburg press magnate whose outlook was basically arch-Conservative. Years after the fray Willy Brandt remarked: "I made a *Fraktion* (faction) to become chairman. It was very arduous."[3] By the time the convention opened, Brandt had won the support of twelve of the twenty Berlin districts and 73 percent of the 2500 branch members. Neumann went down fighting. Before the final vote in the convention on January 12, 1958, he beseeched the delegates to reflect on their Socialist "traditions" (his wing was already known as "the Traditionalists") and declared that "some comrades have written off too much of the program of Social Democracy." Reiterating the familiar anti-NATO and antirearmament line of the Ollenhauer leadership, he appealed for tighter party discipline. His was a two-front strategy: "On the offensive against restoration in the West, on the offensive against totalitarianism in the East." Brandt's uncompromising reply was, in its way, a beacon aimed at the horizon of the SPD in Germany: "There is a natural contradiction between Social Democracy in itself and that which it represents in the responsibility of government." It was one thing to sun the body of the party in the mild rays of opposition—quite another to expose it to the extreme weather changes of governing by itself. "I am of the opinion that the party could even use a bit livelier internal democracy." Then, with a sideways glance at another sign of how things were moving in the national SPD, Brandt said: "We want to follow the example of Hamburg, not of Bonn." (A few days before the Hamburg SPD had won a state election after expressly rejecting any help from party headquarters in Bonn.) When the debate was over, the Berlin convention of January 1958 elected Brandt as the new chairman with almost 56 percent of the total.[4] Within four months Brandt had acquired two commanding posts in the SPD.

Just before the convention Brandt had received and accepted an unusual invitation to meet the Soviet commandant, Major General Andrei S. Tchamov at his headquarters in Berlin-Karlshorst. It was a classic Russian performance.

Brandt was treated to caviar and insults, vodka and tirades, smoked salmon and, finally, compliments. Tchamov accused him of harboring anti-Communist spy headquarters in West Berlin and then praised the rapid reconstruction in the Western sectors. Brandt answered the insults firmly: "I came to make a courtesy call, not to sit in the dock. If you want to make charges I can tell you about secret police brutalities, kidnappings and other things in your zone that merit your attention. . . ." It was the first official contact of a high West German official with the Russians since Adenauer's visit to Moscow in 1955. Though nothing came of it, and despite the sharp criticism Brandt underwent afterward in West Germany, the three-hour exchange seemed to whet the appetite of both the Mayor and the Soviets for more of the same. Brandt wanted to establish, as he told the SPD convention, that he for one was prepared to talk to the Russians.[5]

Brandt went to Karlshorst in the knowledge that he would soon be traveling to the United States, and he undoubtedly calculated the juxtaposition of the two trips. His second American journey was largely the work of Eleanor L. Dulles, an indefatigable woman who had won her position as head of the State Department section on Berlin Affairs out of sheer ability rather than any help from her brother, the Secretary of State. Eleanor Dulles, already over sixty but as lively as a debutante, had made her mark on Berlin by organizing relief packages for the East Germans after the June 17 uprising and helping to raise funds for a Free University dormitory as well as for the new Berlin Congress Hall. Now she argued with her superiors at Foggy Bottom that it would be a boon for Berlin to get the new Mayor to visit Washington. The idea was rejected again and again.

"There are hundreds of thousands of mayors in the world, and he is just a mayor," said Martin J. Hillenbrand, who was to be appointed U.S. Ambassador to the Brandt government fifteen years later.

"But there is only one Berlin," Eleanor Dulles shot back. "And we are doing everything within reason to build up the morale of Berlin."

In the end she got her way by "maneuvering it so they had to do it—I had no power except when people were looking in the other direction," she explained. "I spread the news around that Willy Brandt was going to be Chancellor one day." He was welcomed February 10, 1958, by John Foster Dulles with the words: "You have infiltrated the American Government by way of my sister."[6] The next day Brandt had an audience with President Eisenhower, who was recovering from his stroke and responded to his questions about reconstruction in West Berlin. (The victorious wartime general had at least that much in common with his Soviet counterpart—wanting to know what had happened to the wreckage they had wrought.)[7] Brandt also gave a press conference and made a speech during this visit; he was becoming a desirable commodity for the press and the public beyond the confines of Germany. Visits to London and Paris, and his homes away from home in Scandinavia, followed.

In the months after Brandt acquired the levers of power in Berlin the West German political scene was dominated by a countrywide debate on atomic weapons. It reached a peak in a 37-hour Bundestag debate covering five days in March. At issue was whether the Federal Republic armed forces should accept—if offered—nuclear arms. In one sense a repetition of the earlier contest over putting Germans in uniform so short a time after the terrible war, in another respect the debate was an allegorical argument about the still underage German republic and whether its civilian virginity needed to be protected from the rapacious designs of Mars. Arms and armies had twice raised the German nation to heights of conquest and plunged it into depths of defeat in the space of thirty-one years. Was this trip necessary? In the spring of 1957 a group of eighteen German nuclear physicists had urged German renunciation of all atomic arms and scolded Chancellor Adenauer for describing tactical nuclear weapons as merely "a modern development of artillery." Now, a year later, the Social Democrats were attacking Adenauer as "the atomic death Chancellor." The stage was set for one of those classic German bearpit battles. Epithets zinged across the dimly lit hall: "Headhunter!" "Filthy baiter!" "Provocateur!" "Poisoner!" There were walkouts, challenges to duels, accusations of godlessness—M.S. Handler of *The New York Times* was moved to observe: "God is a controversial character in Germany."[8] Before the debate was over the SPD carried the campaign against weapons further in a "Fight Atomic Death" protest meeting in Frankfurt, complete with manifesto signed by the writers Heinrich Böll and Erich Kästner and the churchmen Martin Niemöller and Helmut Gollwitzer. There were loud calls for a general strike, which Erich Ollenhauer seemed to think was too much. The strike threat was quashed, and in the end the CDU majority voted to accept atomic arms.

But the anti-atom campaign sputtered on, and it came near placing Mayor Brandt in an awkward position. Having already exposed himself as an opponent of the Bonn party headquarters on defense policy, he left it to his aides Kurt Mattick and Joachim Lipschitz to argue his point of view at the convention.

Brandt followed the same tactic of discreet silence on emotion-laden foreign policy issues at the next SPD national convention in May at Stuttgart, where the bannered slogan was: "Hands Off Atomic Weapons!" It was the path of wisdom at a meeting where the first day was dominated by the premiere of a fullblown antinuclear "Cantata" directed by the venerable

"Do your own dirty work," Brandt told his SPD colleagues after losing the 1965 Chancellorship election to the Conservatives. To the right are Herbert Wehner and Karl Schiller.

November 1966: Brandt takes over the desk of the German Foreign Minister.

Chancellor Brandt with his small coalition. Seated clockwise from Brandt: Heinz Kühn, Carlo Schmid, Walter Scheel, Wolfgang Mischnick, Hans-Dietrich Genscher, Josef Ertl, Karl Schiller, Alex Müller, and Helmut Schmidt.

Brandt at Erfurt: (top) leaving the train station with Willi Stoph; (bottom) the crowd breaks through the security cordon; (right) Brandt at the window of the Erfurter Hof.

photos courtesy of the author

DPA, UPI

At the Warsaw Ghetto memorial, December 7, 1970. "Just an attempt to help a lot of people."

J. H. Darchinger

Brandt placed considerable value on his relationship with Yugoslavia's President Tito, whom he saw frequently over the years.

From *Publik*,
a liberal Catholic
paper.

Wehner and Brandt, in tandem but not always a team.

J. H. Darchinger

Leonid Brezhnev comes to the Federal Republic of Germany in 1973.
The Russian regarded Brandt as "a serious man."

Victory smiles. Willy and Rut at 10:30 p.m., November 1972, in the Chancellery bungalow after winning a second term.

Foto-Service

MARKUS

cartoon by Markus in *Ster*

"If they go on growing, you will have to talk to your tailor, Willy."

In the background, Günter Guillaume, the sleeper spy who rarely slept or slipped, March 1974.

Resignation, with Wehner and Karl Wienand, before the SPD *Fraktion*.

Brandt didn't want roses . . .

Erwin Piscator, the Expressionist theater director of the Weimar period. When Brandt finally did speak, on the third day, it was mainly about internal organization questions. Only at the close of his short statement did he hint at what he had in mind for the future of the SPD:

> A large party such as this must be self-assured, must have a healthy will to power and distinguish itself with the clarity of its message, must be open to all the currents of the times. Not just a universal reform club, but a political party that wants to shape the destiny of a people, a state that has the confidence to do that.[9]

He was rewarded two days later with election to the party executive as the nineteenth of twenty-nine candidates chosen. After the cabal of 1948—of which he was not even aware a quarter of a century later[10]—and successive defeats in 1954 and 1956, he had finally gained entry to the inner circle of the Social Democratic Party. It was his third advancement in eight months, and the shifts in the SPD promised more. At Stuttgart the party adopted a moderate policy line on defense issues and on that bugbear of the bourgeoisie: nationalization. At Stuttgart, too, Herbert Wehner emerged as the most dynamic and one of the most popular leaders. He gained only twenty-one votes less than Erich Ollenhauer in the elections for the executive and was chosen as a deputy to the chairman. The outlines of a new leadership were taking shape. Finally, in another move foreshadowing the future, the Stuttgart convention adopted a resolution declaring the SPD's willingness to "enter into talks with the governing authorities of the Soviet Occupied Zone, if it could serve to relax domestic tensions and ease the condition of the population."

This bid marked a considerable step beyond the cold-shouldering stance of the ruling Adenauer Conservatives toward the East German Communist leadership, although it fell far short of what Ulbricht was demanding: "the international legal recognition of the German Democratic Republic." The DDR had been pronounced "sovereign" by the Soviet Union in 1954, and this was reaffirmed a year later in a bilateral Moscow-East Berlin treaty.

The Bonn Government's response to the Soviet moves toward anchoring the sovereignty of the East German state was to pronounce anathema on any country that took up diplomatic ties with East Berlin. This so-called Hallstein Doctrine held the Federal Republic of Germany to be the sole legitimate German state. So, when Yugoslavia accorded full diplomatic recognition to East Germany in October 1957, the Bonn Government broke off relations with Belgrade.

On several occasions in 1957 Walter Ulbricht made guarded offers of rapproachment between East Germany and West Germany; he spoke of eventual "confederation" of the two German states. But the offers were coupled with extravagant demands for socialization of West Germany and were consequently ignored in Bonn.

In 1958 the Soviet Union, emboldened by the consolidation of the Khrushchev leadership, the development of hydrogen bombs, and the first Sputnik, began to replace words with deeds in the German question. Ulbricht, too, was feeling more confident after eliminating the last of his major rivals in the Socialist Unity Party leadership in February 1958. Inklings of the new trend came in May, when the DDR suddenly announced it was imposing customs duties on the heavily used canals linking West Berlin with West Germany and, again, in August, when the Soviet Union declared that Berlin was "the capital of the DDR" in a note to the United Nations.

On October 27, in a geometric progression, Ulbricht declared that the Soviet-American agreements of 1949 on Berlin were "invalid"—and, with them, the guarantees of access to West Berlin. Moreover, he demanded a "normalization" of the situation of West Berlin. One of the major abnormalities of this time was that East Germany appeared to be in the process of bleeding to death through a large artery opened to West Berlin. Since the founding of the German Democratic Republic in 1949 more than 2.2 million citizens had fled "the first German Workers and Peasants State"— most of them by way of that city. In 1958 more than 200,000 East Germans turned up as refugees in the West.

Ulbricht's October threat was amplified a fortnight later by Nikita Khrushchev in Moscow with a pugnacious speech that contained the boast: "A new power relationship has developed now in the world. The mighty Socialist camp is growing and gaining strength. . . ." Then, after accusing West Germany of becoming more militaristic, and the Western Allies of using West Berlin as a base for subverting the DDR—both more than half-truths— he declared: "Plainly the time has come that the powers who signed the Potsdam Agreement renounce the vestiges of the occupation regime in Berlin and make it possible to create a normal situation in the capital of the DDR." By implication Khrushchev was laying claim to *all* of Berlin for the DDR, a grasping gesture that Ulbricht would lovingly repeat on auspicious occasions until his death more than a decade later.

The Khrushchev speech sent a tremor through the capitals of the West. When John Foster Dulles was asked about its implications for West Berlin at a press conference on November 26 he replied that the Western Allies might very well find it possible to regard East German authorities as "agents" of the Soviet Union, should they be assigned to man the checkpoints on the Berlin access routes. It seemed an astonishingly conciliatory approach from the Western knight of the Cold War, and Mayor Brandt's initial reaction was to suggest that Dulles was yielding to Communist "salami tactics." In retrospect it appears that Dulles had taken correct measure of Khrushchev's threat as being largely bluster. He didn't feel really provoked—yet.[11]

The large provocation came from Moscow on November 27, 1958, in the form of identical notes to the United States, Britain, and France concerning "the situation of Berlin." The notes opened with a cascade of bombastic charges interlaced with dripping sentiments. Berlin had become "a fuse in the vicinity of the powderkeg." It was linked with West Germany, which was in the process of dangerous remilitarization. The Western Allies had "broken" the Potsdam agreement by setting up a separate West German state and thereby caused the split of Germany into two states. Therefore, the Soviet Union considered the occupation agreements "obsolete," and, because the Western Allies had "violated" the 1945 Potsdam agreement, they had forfeited their occupation rights under the 1944 London protocols. Rushing on, the notes reminded the Allies that the Soviet Union still favored a "peace treaty with Germany" as a whole and that neutralization of Germany should be a prerequisite. Barring acceptance of that thesis, the Soviet Union felt compelled to eliminate the "only" vestige of four-power occupation control in Germany—that in Berlin. (There were, in fact, other vestiges that the Russians jealously protected—particularly the reciprocal stationing of military observers in West Germany and East Germany.)

West Berlin, the notes said, had become a *Frontstadt*, a "front-line city" employed by the West as "a springboard for espionage, diversion and subversive activities" tantamount to "indirect aggression" against the Soviet Union and East Germany. (Ulbricht and his propagandists were already speaking of West Berlin as the base of "eighty spy organizations," and they were probably half right. Moreover, both the Russians and the East Germans were smarting still from the uncovering in 1956 of tunnels bored from the American sector of West Berlin into the DDR to tap the telephone cables running down to the Soviet Army headquarters at Wünsdorf. That was a CIA operation, as many of the others were. No question about it, Berlin—all of it—*was* a huge nest of spies in those days, as the latterday nonfiction espionage literature of both East and West has made abundantly clear.)

Finally, the notes presented the Soviet conclusions in the form of an ultimatum. Unless the Allies would consider a Soviet proposal to transform West Berlin into a "free city" with neutral status "similar to Austria," the Russians would take unilateral steps transferring remaining authority to East Germany. The "free city" could benefit from generous Soviet Bloc trade and investments, and it could stay "capitalist." But unless the West agreed to negotiate, the Soviet Union would make its own moves to create the new "free city" at the end of a six-month period of grace.[12]

The notes launched what was popularly known in the press and in some diplomatic circles as the second "Berlin crisis"—following the first by only ten years. It also caused new anxiety to many West Berliners. (My landlady, an attractive fortyish woman who had a large flat in a fashionable Grunewald street, asked me to terminate my residence. She had survived the terrors of the Nazi era as a Jewess hidden by gentiles and the rigors of the Berlin blockade. Now she said: "I want you to leave. If the 'Ivans' come, I don't want any 'Ami' around the place." Many West Berliners made emergency plans to move to West Germany. "I packed them all," said Packer-Atze, a leading figure in the West Berlin moving van business, "the big ones lost their nerve when Khrushchev spoke, and I was booked up for months.")

It was a time for cool heads, and one of them belonged to Mayor Brandt. He perceived the situation as "an artificial crisis" and, after dispassionately analyzing the content of the notes for the Berliners, he declared that same day:

> The Berliners won't allow themselves to be disconcerted by this. They will work on at the reconstruction of the capital of Germany and make their contribution to the guaranteeing of legitimate security in Berlin and the maintenance of a free democratic order. The people of Berlin have confidence in their friends around the world at this time.[13]

The Khrushchev ultimatum also provided Brandt a bit of unexpected assistance in the campaign for elections to the Berlin House of Representatives, only ten days away. The West Berliners rallied to the polls in the biggest turnout since the war: almost 93 percent of the eligible voters. It was a triumph for Brandt's SPD—its 52.6 percent the best showing since the Reuter election during the blockade.

A week later Brandt was invited to attend a meeting of the three Western Foreign Ministers convened in Paris prior to the annual NATO Council sessions, and there he spoke on the situation in West Berlin. Afterward the Allies, together with the West German Foreign Minister, issued a declaration rejecting the Soviet ultimatum as "unacceptable" and reiterating their rights in Berlin and "determination" to uphold them.

The crisis whistled on in a blizzard of diplomatic meetings and notes: the Allies' wintry replies to Moscow on the eve of the new year, a Soviet draft of a German peace treaty in January. In the meantime the Russians and East Germans had become somewhat frightened of their own boldness and began making anxious inquiries of Western diplomats and correspondents.

("Something could go wrong—something bad could happen," a Soviet political counselor said to me in late December with what appeared to be a genuine concern.) Possibly the Russians had already learned of the National Security Council meeting in the White House, where General Maxwell Taylor, himself a certified "Berliner" from blockade days, had proposed an armed thrust by American forces down the land access routes.

Spring came, sweet and green, melting away the frozen threat of the six-month ultimatum. Instead of a confrontation, the Khrushchev bluff produced a conference—this time a gathering of the Soviet and Western Foreign Ministers in Geneva, with the East German and West German Foreign Ministers attending as observers. The Berlin deadline of May 27 came and passed, almost unnoticed as the diplomats diplomated from May 11 to June 20 and again from July 13 to August 5. Out of it all came Khrushchev's September summit meeting with President Eisenhower and the "Spirit of Camp David," which was probably what the Russian had sought from the very beginning.

In his first campaign as Mayor, Brandt presented himself as a moderate reformer. Nothing was permitted that smacked of "socialization" slogans or of Marxist class struggle. He insisted on "modesty" and claimed no special credit for the SPD in the comprehensive effort to rebuild isolated West Berlin. He also forbade any campaigning by firebreathers of the Bonn SPD leadership. This won him not only the sympathies of voters traditionally committed to bourgeois parties, but also the vocal support of Axel Springer's influential Conservative papers, and of Springer himself, who would speak a dozen years later, with the bitterness of unrequited affection, about "Willy Brandt, to whom I was close for many Berlin years. . . ."[14] With the resounding victory of December 7, 1958, in his pocket, Brandt went before his party comrades at the end of the month and proposed continuance of the SPD coalition with the CDU in Berlin. It was not the CDU that threatened Berlin's life and liberty, he argued, but the Soviet Union. "This is not a contest with an Adenauer ultimatum, but with a Russian ultimatum against Berlin," he continued. "For those who would rather see Americans and Khrushchev sit down at a table today instead of tomorrow it shouldn't be such an absurd thought that Adenauer and Ollenhauer talk to each other, too."[15] The requirement of the moment was "the unity of all democratic forces." He got the backing of his party.

But the clocks were running on different time in the Bonn SPD, as became evident in mid-March, when the federal SPD brought out a hastily drafted, wide-reaching "Deutschland Plan" for attaining reunification in the course of a drawn-out process of reducing tensions in Central Europe. Troop cuts would be followed by disarmament, and the countries of the region—East and West

Germany, Poland, Czechoslovakia, and Hungary—would withdraw from respective military alliances. Berlin would keep its special status until solution of the Germany question, which should begin with an "all-German conference," the establishment of joint economic institutions, and constitution of a kind of governing assembly. Only then would all-German elections be held. The biggest lure in the plan for the Communists was the proposal to treat East Germany and West Germany as equals, although the DDR comprised only 26 percent of the population of divided Germany. Indeed, the Deutschland Plan, drafted largely by Herbert Wehner, although six other Bonn SPD officials had a hand in it, bore many resemblances to the confederation and peace treaty schemes proposed in the previous twelve months by the East Germans and Russians. Moreover, Erich Ollenhauer, the SPD chairman, had conferred for two hours with Premier Khrushchev in East Berlin on March 9 at the end of the Soviet leader's whirlwind tour of East Germany. That meeting had no effect on the SPD draft, except to make it more suspicious in the eyes of its critics. Willy Brandt, returned from a month-long "world journey" three days earlier was invited to see Khrushchev, too, in the East Berlin Embassy. His old friend from Stockholm emigration days, Bruno Kreisky, acted as the middleman. But he declined, probably on American advice. Khrushchev had just threatened to sign a separate Soviet treaty with East Germany, if nobody else wanted to join in the effort, which moved Brandt to comment: "All that Khrushchev would achieve with that would be to marry himself."[16]

The Deutschland Plan was presented with great fanfare on March 18, and the echo was a universal raspberry. Adenauer branded the plan "capitulation" to Soviet demands and coined the phrase: "With Wehner into the abyss." East Germany's ruling SED rejected fundamental elements of the SPD proposal out of hand—especially that regarding West Berlin—and sidestepped other awkward questions. But some of the sharpest criticism came in secret party councils from Wehner's comrade to be, Willy Brandt. "When we were drafting the Deutschland Plan, Brandt shot sharply at me for the first and only time. He shouted, 'It was just an act of desperation.'" Wehner added, in retrospect: "We wanted to raise the German question, not because of Germany, but because of (the threat to) Berlin. But he was swimming on the Berlin wave."[17] So the Germany plan was stillborn, and, while Brandt loyally refrained from assailing it in public, his silence helped to dig its grave. By the time Ollenhauer arrived in Berlin to attend the SPD state convention in late May the national party chairman was already speaking of it as merely a "working paper." Brandt used the occasion to voice thanks in the spirit of Reuter, for the generous support given Berlin by the federal SPD *and* the Adenauer government in the current crisis. Then he politely condemned the

Deutschland Plan as useless and, if it were to be used, "fatal." His fellow Berliners reelected him chairman of the state SPD with an overwhelming 70 percent of the delegates; the Neumann wing dissipated.[18]

The "Berlin wave" of which Wehner spoke carried Brandt halfway around the world that year. During a rain-soaked ticker-tape parade on New York's Broadway he was cheered: "Hi Willy!" "Good luck, Willy!" In Washington Eisenhower tired to engaged him in small talk about gardening and intercontinental rockets—two subjects totally alien to Brandt—before addressing the Berlin problem.[19] A mortally ill Dulles received him, too, and then Brandt went on to Springfield, Illinois, to deliver the anniversary speech on the one hundred fiftieth birthday of Abraham Lincoln. He used the occasion to suggest to his audience that the "house divided" in Germany was not unlike the cutting in two of America in the days of the Emancipator. The experience of Lincoln Day moved Brandt profoundly. He called it the "high point" of his trip, and he took home a bust of Lincoln for his office desk. The next leg took him to Japan and to India, where Jawaharlal Nehru counseled "patience" to the young Mayor attired in an impeccable white suit and a characteristically dreadful tie covered in a bold rhombic pattern. He was on his way to becoming what a German paper had called "the best-known mayor in the world." More and more people were talking of him as "the next Chancellor of Germany." He had that about him, a certain radiance, a sense of promise of something more, something uplifting. On his 1959 trips he also had Rut with him, a person who had her own glow. "An inestimable help to me," Brandt wrote a year later. "Her naturalness, simplicity and charm made her an excellent ambassador of Berlin."[20]

In several ways Berlin was the most exciting spot on earth in those days. Despite the undercurrent of apprehension set in motion by the deadline crisis—about 30,000 West Berliners moved to West Germany—there was an almost palpable thrill about the place: East German refugees passing silently through the city at a rate of 11,000 a month; North Koreans journeying half way around the world from Pyongyang to see South Korean relatives who had come the other way from Seoul to the only city where a meeting was possible; the cabarets full of biting wit and songs; the nightspots packed with revelers and spies; smuggling of everything from Polish rugs and Russians atlases to American drugs and French essences. Decadent? A bit. But full of new life, too. Apartments were being built at a rate of 23,000 a year. Industrial production reached nearly $2 billion annually, five times the amount of the yearly subsidies provided to Berlin by the Bonn Government. More was coming with an $8.4 million expansion of the Siemens electrical company and

Axel Springer's big new press building at the very edge of East Berlin. The Free University, begun so modestly under the leadership of Otto Suhr in 1948, had grown to 11,000 students. The city had luster. Threat or no threat, Berlin was the only East-West metropolis of the world with the advantages of both—and Brandt was its best-known figure.

There was a turnabout, too, in the attitude of West Germans toward Berlin. From 1953 to 1956 citizens of the Federal Republic were required to add a two-pfennig Berlin contribution stamp on their letters. The income, along with parallel imposts totaling $1.7 billion, went to support West Berlin. The Berlin stamps were so unpopular that on one occasion a car bearing Berlin plates was plastered from grill to trunk with them in a West German city. But by May 1959 when Brandt inaugurated a Berlin solidarity appeal with the sale of little silver lapel pins featuring the Brandenburg Gate and the legend, "Open the Gate!" more than 14 million symbols were vended in only a few weeks. It was the kind of popularity that made Adenauer's CDU begin to wonder who was running things in Germany. A CDU man in the Adenauer Foreign Ministry was instructed to prepare a secret study of Brandt's Berlin impact; he came to the conclusion that the Bonn leadership should work to "cut down" the role Berlin was playing in German politics because "Brandt is becoming an anti-King," rivaling the authority of Adenauer himself. "But it was too late," Herbert Wehner observed much later.[21]

Brandt was working at a devilish pace in these months. Part of it was just plain work, for as Governing Mayor he served on the boards of trustees of the Free University, the Technical University, the (state) Bank of Berlin, and the Berlin Electric Company. He was called on to preside at the opening of trade fairs and the eight-year-old International Film Festival—these in addition to his state and federal party and government tasks. But he was also obviously intent on milking the "Berlin Crisis," however artificial it might be, of all its political potential. He had seen Eisenhower and de Gaulle, and Khrushchev had asked to see him, the front-line Mayor.

When he took office, Brandt vowed "to spend at least one hour every day with my family." He soon learned, "I could not keep this promise very often." When he did get home to the small house near the waters of the Schlachtensee and began to complain about his hard life, Rut would cut him short: "Please be quiet. You didn't want it any other way."[22] Rut manifestly enjoyed the lights, music, and merriment of official occasions, and she cut a very smart figure. When she dressed up, it was almost like a little girl putting on her mother's ball.gown and high heels. But she made no pretense of being anything other than a practical-minded housewife. She was not ambitious.

Willy was. He had begun to compose a 287-page autobiography "as told to"

Leo Lania, a German-American. Lania, born Lazar Herman, had been an anti-Nazi journalist who escaped to the United States by way of France in 1940 and worked for the Office of War Information. The manuscript bears the marks of intense haste—there was no foreword and no index. Yet in its frequent understatements, its repeated admissions of gloom ("depression," "deep anxiety and grief," "my grief," "benumbed and troubled"—mostly at the deaths of friends), its constant use of euphemism, it is purely Willy Brandt. Lania was at most a transcriber. "Make no mistake," Klaus Schütz observed. "Willy worked very hard on the manuscript."[23] But why an autobiography at age forty-five, not a biography? After all, Adenauer had been the subject of several popular biographies already, and he would wait to write his autobiography until 1965, when he was retired. There were, as so often in Brandt's way of doing things, several reasons. On the surface was the obvious appeal of capitalizing on crisis fame and creating a durable reminder of what he and Berlin meant to the world. The book was to be published more or less simultaneously in Germany and the United States in 1960 as *My Road to Berlin,* with the subtitle: "The autobiography of the crucial mayor of Berlin and the biography of his crucial city." Besides, he knew already he had a good chance to go farther in German politics, much farther. The last chapter was auspiciously entitled "My Credo."

There was a second, deeper reason. Brandt had been maligned continually since 1937 by political adversaries, now as a Communist, now as a Fascist. There was no reason to imagine that he would lack for enemies in the future in a nation where the political smear was cultivated as if it were an art comparable to that of Albrecht Dürer. At the time he became Mayor in 1957 East German publications had issued lengthy vilifications of Brandt, reminiscent of the disgusting Ulbricht-inspired broadsides against Social Democrats during Hitler's rise to power. One of these called him "a deeply alien element for the German workers movement" and added:

> Brandt has never in his entire development stood for the interests
> of the working class, but always allied himself with its enemies,
> whether in the Nazi period as an emigrant in Scandinavia
> harmonizing with Trotskyite circles, or in his postwar political
> activity in West Berlin in chummy unity with the Adenauer CDU
> . . . He denies the revolutionary traditions of the workers
> movement, just as he does the fundaments of scientific socialism.[24]

Thus, *My Road* was at once a retort to past slanders and libels and an anticipation of new ones. Careful reading of what he said—and what he did not say—would provide anyone who was really curious with all that was really worth knowing about Willy Brandt.

Finally, it was *his* story, covering his life in eleven countries. Much of it only he could relate, and, as a seasoned journalist, he undoubtedly felt better qualified to tell it than anyone else. Besides, his previous books had helped him along in his career. Why not one more?

Willy Brandt had written to Kurt Schumacher in 1947 that he was "not a yesman," and he wasn't. By the same token he was not a nay-sayer in the postwar Social Democratic sense of *total* opposition to the governing powers He preferred the role of man in the middle. As he would observe almost proverbially, when his own period of administration was over, "He who gives up the center sacrifices his ability to govern." The SPD had spent twelve Hitler years in banishment and was now in its thirteenth year of opposition on the national level—still a party full of old-time ward heelers, functionaries, *apparat* time-servers. Its membership had dwindled steadily in the years of repeated defeats, from 875,000 in 1947 to 534,000 at the beginning of 1959—a loss of 39 percent. It had lost two federal elections to the Adenauer Conservatives. In those days, when the SPD had some jubilee to celebrate, it was still the custom for local party veterans to brush off their best black suits and hats, seize their venerated red flags and their black, red, and gold banners of German patriotism and march, singing the grand old songs of the workers' movement: "Brothers to Sunlight and Freedom" and "When We Stride, Side by Side." As if it was 1880, the Kaiser and Bismarck were still in power, and Marx and Engels still alive. It was touching, even moving. But it had less and less to do with German workers or what was happening in Germany. The time to change was already overdue, and the SPD already had a foretaste of what to do and how to do it with the party organization triumphs in West Berlin.

The Social Democratic Party wheeled on its axis—the German labor movement—in the most improbable place, the congress hall of Bad Godesberg: the Rhineside home of retired generals, old Nazis, Rhenish papists, and other addicts of the ferric spa waters of meanminded German Conservatism. "The diaspora," as one SPD official branded it. "Little Potsdam," as some of the townspeople proudly called it. There, in the shadow of those eerie hills haunted by Nibelung heroes and dragons, the SPD held a special convention from November 13 to 15, 1959, to discuss and adopt a new "basic program." The preparations were made in great secrecy, for the party was about to undergo basic surgery. It was cutting Karl Marx, who had studied in neighboring Bonn 123 years earlier, out of the SPD's programatic body. It was abandoning nearly a century of commitment to being exclusively a "workers' party" in exchange for broader appeal as a "people's party." It was taking a new look at the problems of "modern society" in the light of "the second industrial revolution." It was trading ideology for pragmatism.

Like most trailblazing developments the Godesberg Program had many fathers. The man who drafted most of it was Willi Eichler, a sixty-three-year-old Social Democrat who had emigrated during the war to France and Britain and was close to Ollenhauer. The economic section, committing the SPD firmly to a free-market economy and discarding nationalization schemes, was largely the work of Dr. Heinrich Deist, a protégé of Herbert Wehner. The unconditional *ja* to military defense of the state of West Germany's alliance commitments was attributable in part to Fritz Erler. Brandt had participated in the drafting sessions and was, in several senses, the practical father of the Godesberg Program. He had been pleading the cause of realistic reform politics for years, ever since his association with Ernst Reuter. Moreover, he had put it into practice and won not only a thumping election victory as Mayor of West Berlin, but also the majority of the state party organization. He had, additionally, gained the attention of large sections of German and international public opinion. Finally, he was young and not used up. In his opening address endorsing the draft program Ollenhauer said, with a nod to Brandt: "It fills all of us with special pleasure that our Berlin comrades have actively participated in the discussion and formation of the draft."[25]

Accordingly, when Brandt rose as one of the first to speak at the congress hall, he was greeted with what the protocol registered as "lively applause"—a rare accolade. In his brief statement he called the new program "a timely message that will help us in our work and make it harder for our opponents to deal with a caricature instead of the reality of German social democracy." It showed that "the party has the courage and the strength to appear as that which it is." Then, noting that the SPD leadership was beset with doubt whether it was right to conceive a new program in a still-divided country he said:

> There is no absolutely hopeless situation. Hitler didn't have to come to power, the split of Germany does not have to become petrified, and the Federal Republic doesn't have to be suffused with a perverted Kaiser Wilhelm mentality.

He concluded:

> We want to take over the political leadership of the state with the unconsumed energy over which this wing of German politics disposes, and we *will* take over.[26]

But the program needed something more to win the minds of the party faithful whose faith was undergoing a change before their very eyes. The man who pounded it through, the *Pauker* (kettle-drummer), was Herbert Wehner. He, too, had entertained some doubts about the efficacy of the new program at that time, as had Brandt and others. Some thought he became a wholehearted supporter only in late October 1959 for higher party reasons.[27] (Asked once how Wehner would respond to a critical decision, Brandt wet his index finger and held it up, as if to the wind). In Wehner's own recollection his reasoning went like this:

> It came about that we presented ourselves better and buried the things that were false. Godesberg didn't come overnight. I was no born Social Democrat. Ollenhauer, a reasonable person . . . I taught him and others. I had to say it crudely: "Social Democratic counterfeit politics." Either you capitulate or you march beyond, which you cannot. . . .[28]

At Godesberg he spoke more than most of the delegates, four times in all, and at length, using his popularity, his prestige, and even his troubled past as a Communist to persuade the doubters and waverers:

> I belong to the burned. I know from the bitter experience of the days of the Weimar Republic—I learned much under the blows of dictatorship and have much to pay back for that today and do it for this party—for the very reason that I belong to the burned who once out of discontent and falsely understood radicalism, had to gather bloody experiences through the circumstances—whereby I don't want to say anything against radicalism; I interpret it as Marx once did, to try to grasp things by the root. Dear comrades, I am of the conviction that Marxist thinking and Marxist methodology are inexpendable for our Social Democratic Party . . . But I turn against the presumption of exclusivity. I turn against it out of bitter personal experience because I am of the opinion that Marxism as a doctrine is neither party-forming nor beneficial in the sense of what we should want social democracy and democratic socialism to be, if as a doctrine, as a teaching structure it should be imposed on a party as solely valid. That is in the nature of the matter. Believe one who was burned!

Then Wehner explained what the Godesberg Program should mean in everyday terms:

> We must prove to the broad public that we are striving for a general order—that is my understanding of the real territory of politics—which discriminates against no rank or group of the

population. That is a breakthrough to a basically different handling of power in the state than is the case today and probably for some time to come in this struggle. . . . [29]

With these statements, Brandt and Wehner made an objective alliance—in a short time, more than that.

The SPD was in a tremendous ferment, more so, perhaps, than at any time since the 1920s, or the days of Bebel, Kautsky, Liebknecht, and Rosa Luxemburg. It was midterm in the third Adenauer administration, and the younger SPD men were looking toward the next election in 1961. Brandt conferred with Helmut Schmidt. Schmidt remembered: "We got into a conversation, the two of us, about the impossibility of coming up with Ollenhauer as a Chancellor candidate again. We also agreed the two of us should strive to present Carlo Schmid, because we had the idea to keep Ollenhauer as party chairman."[30] Schmid, a big rumpled South German intellectual with a warm heart and a witty tongue was, by the latest poll, the most popular man in the SPD—the kind of man it was hard to get mad at. He was sixty-two years old. But when the comrades came to put him into the wringer he waved them off: "I know what I can do—I can do quite a lot—but there are also things I can't do, in any case not as well as another. I am lacking a lot of qualities that a Chancellor candidate must have." One of the things he named was his ruined marriage to a wife who would not divorce him. "I know another who has better qualities than I," he went on, "Willy Brandt."[31]

Brandt himself wrote shortly after the Godesberg convention:

> I regard it as specially important to formulate a program and to develop a policy which could facilitate our efforts to assume the responsibility for governing the Federal Republic. The new program of my Party, which was accepted in November 1959, was a decisive step in that direction.[32]

He was ten years away from the Chancellorship, but it was a correct prognosis. (He was in a prophetic mood, too, when interviewed in mid-December. After remarking that the Western Allies could have been more resolute in dealing with the Soviet Union, he observed: "I don't think we should try to steer toward a perfect Berlin solution, but there are a number of practical improvements one could discuss with the Soviets."[33] He was puffy from fatigue then and nervous, snapping off the heads of matches and fiddling with the stems.)

The last phase of wheeling the SPD around to face the new world was performed alone by Wehner in a speech on June 30 during a Bundestag debate on foreign policy, where he called on his fellow Germans to "look ahead."

Whatever was going to happen in the politics of divided Germany would happen slowly, he warned. Therefore it behooved free Germans to pull together in questions concerning the essence of the nation. It was a scarcely muffled appeal for a bipartisan foreign policy on the issues of common interest: the sanctity of West Berlin, belonging to the West, opposition to Communism, concern with the destiny of the 17 million East Germans, and the need to contribute to military security. Then, having absorbed the I-told-you-so hoots of the governing party, Wehner killed off the Deutschland Plan for good. He emphasized: "Off again, on again, the Deutschland Plan is not a plan that faces decision anywhere, and can no longer be one." Finally, he cautioned that in the politics of a country like the Federal Republic "a hostile relationship ultimately kills democracy."[34] It was the speech of a stateman, and it was at the same time an express endorsement of Willy Brandt. The national SPD had swung around to adopt his foreign policy concepts. "Godesberg would have been a placard if I hadn't drawn the consequences in that speech," Wehner said much later.

Brandt's candidacy for Chancellor, already rumored at Godesberg several months before, was out in the open by late January, although he turned away questioners with a noncommittal laugh as late as May. But one more monumental struggle took place in the SPD leadership before the decision was reached. The opposition was led by Max Brauer, the Hamburg Mayor who had been in exile in the United States during the Nazi years. "There was fanatical resistance to the Brandt candidature," Wehner recalled. "I put him up and I boxed him through."[35]

Brandt was widely called "the boy wonder," although he was almost four years older than that other promising candidate, John F. Kennedy. But at forty-six he seemed a mere babe in comparison to the eighty-four-year-old Adenauer. Brandt and his supporters counted very much on the youth bonus, on the vote-getting appeal of a new look. He dispatched Klaus Schütz, who had studied political science at Harvard, to observe the Kennedy-Nixon campaign and bring back helpful ideas.[36] The German elections were still a year away.

On August 25, the day after he was officially nominated by the full SPD executive to the Chancellorship candidacy, Brandt made a highly unorthodox visit to East Berlin. He called at the headquarters of the shrunken and beleaguered SPD local in Friedrichshain. It was a first-class provocation to the Ulbricht leadership. Not only was this traditional workers' district the last resting place of the Socialist martyrs, Karl Liebknecht and Rosa Luxemburg, it was also the locus of Stalinallee, where the construction laborers had marched seven years earlier to set off the June 17 uprising. The Ulbricht press had already expressed strong objections to the union in Brandt's person of the West Berlin mayoralty and the West German Chancellorship candidacy. Now he was in their midst, "cheered and applauded" by hundreds of East Berliners.[37]

Five days later the East Germans slapped restrictions on the land access routes to West Berlin, stopping "militarists and irredentists" heading for a rally of refugees and expellees from former German eastern territories. In the next five days more than 1000 West Germans were turned back at control points on the *Autobahnen* and railways. Ulbricht went on televison warning West Gemany to negotiate a new Berlin settlement "in time." 'On September 8 his government announced that West Germans would be barred from East Berlin unless they carried a special permit. An omen. The clocks had begun to tick for Berlin again. West Germany's response was muted except for perfunctory protests. A scheduled meeting of the Bundestag in West Berlin was postponed out of deference to the Communists. A threat to stop the $500 million annual trade between East and West Germany was aired.

Brandt was on the road again—to Greece, to Israel, to Italy, with a call on Pope John XXIII. He seemed to be better known and more popular abroad than at home. As if to underline this, Norway's King Olav had presented him the Grand Cross of the Order of St. Olav in the spring.

The next party congress was set for Hannover, the "archdiocese of the SPD" as Klaus Schütz called it. The SPD was on the upswing, with 650,000 registered members—perhaps a reflection of hopes stirred by the Godesberg Program and the candidacy of Brandt. But Brandt did not speak until the third day of the five-day convention and, when he did, it was to make clear his thoughts about the longstanding issue of atomic weapons. His was a short plea for general disarmament. He had spoken, he said, "so that no one should have the feeling tomorrow that he has bought a pig in a poke—in politics hot potatoes are there to be grasped, whether it is fun or not." But the candidate did not say a word in the discussion about the domestic questions that were the main concern of most German voters. Nor did Brandt make a dent in the executive to which he had belonged for two years. He hadn't spent much time in Bonn and had no base in party headquarters there. When the time came to reelect the executive, he tied for twentieth place with young Helmut Schmidt. His candidacy for Chancellor was not something he had earned on the rungs of the party hierarchy; it was something handed him on a platter in the hope he would know what to do with it.

But there was no mistaking the enthusiasm of the comrades at Hannover when Carlo Schmid presented Brandt as "the captain of our team" saying, "the second half of the century must be represented by people who are under fifty at this time" and reading "The Hannover Appeal" with the peremptory conclusion: "Willy Brandt must become Federal Chancellor!" A minute later he was confirmed by unanimous vote and welcomed to the platform "with tempestuous applause."

In his acceptance speech Brandt struck some notes that were new for German ears and that he would come back to again and again in the rest of his political career:

> Our people must reconcile itself. Certainly we must differentiate between guilt and error. We all know about the terrible crimes of the past. But we know, too, how much idealism was misused and there is nobody who is free of error. . . . In this spirit we must confront the past in that we acknowledge it with all its elements. To let the grass grow is no useful therapy. We must face up to our history and this history did not begin in 1949. Nor did it begin in Bonn on the Rhine. . . . We here are proud of the almost 100 years of history of our party. It experienced the glory and misery of our fatherland, but we, too, are a part of German history. That which comprises Germany today originates from many sources. Otto von Bismarck and August Bebel, Friedrich Ebert and Gustav Stresemann, Julius Leber and Count Stauffenberg, Ernst Reuter and Theodor Heuss—they all belong to this nation. But no silence can make the terrors that are bound to the name of Hitler forgotten. All that belongs to our history. We must see it as a unity. . . . We are all one family. That is why our nation must make peace with itself. That is what I want to work for with all my strength.

Brandt also declared his intention to develop a "self-assured Eastern policy," so as to overcome "the ideological trench warfare," adding, "I know that I am in harmony here with the newly elected American President, John F. Kennedy." He had already announced his intention to call on Kennedy in March 1961.

In his Hannover speech Brandt also touched on one of his own sore spots: the recurrent whispering campaign suggesting that he was everything from "illigitimate" to "a traitor." The smears, some of them originating in East German propaganda mills and the rest in Bavaria, were circulating in printed form as well. Far from deflating the insinuations, his recently published autobiography, with its explicit passages about his childhood and political development, served only to pump up new campaigns of slander and libel. "Dear friends," Brandt told the Hannover convention, "the chancellorship candidate of the German Social Democrats will have to prepare himself for some maliciousness. I've already gotten a strong foretaste of the dirty brew that is being cooked up." Then, reciting how he had come to the name he had carried for twenty-eight years, he remarked gently, "I do not have a simple life behind me. I had to clear my own path and I had to learn a lot." When he was done the ovation lasted for minutes.[38] The SPD at last had a program *and* players.

The new year started meanly for Brandt. He was involved in a legal contest with an extreme right-wing publisher, Dr. Hans Kapfinger, who had printed a series of libels and innuendoes about the new SPD standard-bearer. In his *Passauer Neue Press* and *Rottaler Anzeiger*, Kapfinger drew attention to "the emigration problem in the opposition party." He accused Brandt of having worn "the uniform of the Norwegian resistance" and asked whether he additionally had "fought alongside the Red Spaniards" and, did he "fire on German soldiers . . .?" He also noted that "the emigrant Wehner put up the emigrant Brandt as the SPD candidate." It got worse. The *Deutsche Zeitung* of Cologne repeated these thoughts and added some more, including a distortion of the title of his 1946 book, *Criminals and Other Germans*. The new version was *Germans and Other Criminals*. Brandt had won a libel case against similar allegations in 1959. He went to court again. But what was there to do when Franz Josef Strauss in a February speech on his Bavarian homeground of Vilshofen asked rhetorically of him: "What were you doing those twelve years outside Germany?" In one of his counterattacks Brandt noted that Wilhelm Stuckart, the Nazi official who had signed the order depriving him of citizenship in 1938 had been the Nazi superior of State Secretary Hans Globke of the Adenauer Chancellery. It was shortly before the trial of Adolf Eichmann began in Israel on mass-murder charges, and in the Bundestag Fritz Erler asked on March 8 how the Conservatives could condone attacks on Brandt's anti-Nazi past while condemning Eichmann's crimes. Adenauer replied that in the case of political emigration, "summary condemnation would be as wrong as summary glorification." That was four days before Brandt arrived in Washington to meet President Kennedy for the first time. "Hateful attacks which I had to face at home threw a certain shadow over my trip," he observed.[39]

On the face of it, Brandt's call on Kennedy was a bit presumptuous, if not unconventional. He was but a Mayor and a contender for the top political office in his country. He was preceding Chancellor Adenauer to Washington by a month. Yet Brandt and the narrowly elected Kennedy represented the new generation in international affairs. They also had some things in common aside from their age group. Both had worked as journalists (Kennedy had been in Berlin briefly in 1945 as a correspondent for

International News Service), and both had made their political careers through timely rhetoric. Both had personal charm. Both had charisma.

Their meeting in the White House lasted about forty-five minutes. They talked first of Berlin, of course, and Brandt stressed that the Soviet free-city campaign was directed not only against the people of West Berlin, but also against American prestige and credibility. The President reiterated the determination of the United States to hold its Berlin positions. But they did not go into details. Kennedy wanted to hear about East Germany. (Refugees were escaping to the West at a rate of 15,000 a month—two-thirds of them by way of Berlin.) He informed his guest about plans to increase American conventional forces. They also discussed the domestic issues of the forthcoming German elections. (Brandt had with him his new press spokesman, Egon Bahr, a Berliner whose foreign policy commentaries for RIAS had impressed him. Bahr had joined the SPD in 1957, the year Brandt became Mayor.) Brandt assured Kennedy that foreign affairs issues would not burden the election campaign, since the SPD had more or less made peace with the CDU in that area. It was apparently a very cordial session. "The President wished me luck in a manner that was more than flowery politeness."[40] There was a joint communiqué underscoring Kennedy's commitment to "the freedom of Berlin," and Brandt left confident that his city's future was safe. Before he left the capital, however, he heard the Cassandra voice of Foy Kohler, then director of the Bureau of European Affairs at the State Department, warning that a new Berlin crisis might begin in August. Kohler had guessed this on the basis of various events scheduled in Europe, including the Bundestag elections in September and the next Soviet Communist Party congress one month later.[41]

The German problem, the problems of Germany, had always looked different from other vantage points. From afar, it seemed the relatively simplistic problem of keeping the Germans peaceful and content—untroublesome. From the perspective of neighbors, Russia to the East and France to the West, it was a problem of holding down Germany's military potential. But *inside* Germany the problem was one of competing ideologies and power allegiances—with all that meant for the daily lives of families and generations on the crowded ground of a divided country.

Khrushchev was demanding a German peace treaty and threatening to settle separately with East Germany, because he wanted to give legitimacy to the East Berlin Communist Government before West Germany got hold of atomic weapons. He said as much to Walter Lippmann in spring 1961. Besides he had the uncertain menace of an independent Communist China at his back. Kennedy, who was plunging into the Bay of Pigs debacle, wanted calm in Germany so that he could think out his plans for a proper balance of United States military forces and then move gradually toward détente with the Soviet Union. While seemingly contrary, one goal of both Khrushchev and Kennedy was ultimately the same: stability in Central Europe.

But there was the other factor of scarcely calculable instability. Nearly 200,000 citizens of Ulbricht's East Germany were fleeing West in 1960, and the rate was rising month by month.

The idea of sealing off West Berlin with some kind of barrier had been around since 1952, when it was aired in East German Communist councils by Erich Honecker.[42] Ulbricht evidently began harping on it to Khrushchev in 1958, and he repeated his demand for action at the meeting of eighty-one Communist and workers' parties in November 1960, claiming that West Germany was "systematically recruiting" skilled East Germans to flee. In March 1961 he directed Honecker, his national security official in the Politbüro, to begin assembling the material and the men for one of the greatest construction projects of the century.[43] But when Ulbricht asked for permission to barricade West Berlin "perhaps with barbed wire, too," on the evening of March 29, Khrushchev stalled. They were meeting in Moscow together with the Communist chiefs of Poland, Hungary, Czechoslovakia, Bulgaria, and Rumania—all of whom were shocked by Ulbricht's request. Khrushchev let it come to a vote, and the hands raised, five to Ulbricht's one with Khrushchev abstaining, overruled the East German for the moment. Khrushchev said he wanted to test out Kennedy first. Meanwhile he would cut the risk by reinforcing Soviet troops in the East Europe.[44]

The next deadline for Khrushchev's separate peace treaty came in mid-April and passed without event. But the repetition of Ulbricht's demands on the West, aired in his press, caused an alarming spurt in refugee escapes, and nearly half of them were under twenty-five years of age. It was 30,000 by the end of February, over 70,000 by the end of May.

On May 10 the NATO Council, meeting in Oslo, named "three essentials" for which the West would shoulder the burden of Berlin: the presence of Western Allied troops in West Berlin, access of the Allies to West Berlin, and the survival of the West Berliners. When Egon Bahr read the text on a teletype ticker in the Schöneberg Rathaus he hastened to Brandt and said: "That's almost an invitation to the Soviets to do what they want with the East Sector."[45] There had been no mention of *East* Berlin in the NATO communiqué.

It was the same when Kennedy conferred with Khrushchev in Vienna on June 3 and 4. In his rough-and-tumble manner the Soviet Premier declared he would sign that separate treaty in December and handed Kennedy a written memorandum to this effect. Then the West would have to deal with a Soviet-backed DDR about West Berlin. "If you want war, that is your business," Khrushchev snapped. Kennedy replied that while the United States could not prevent the Russians from doing what they wished in their own area of power, he would not allow the Communists to tamper with *West* Berlin and its access routes. Again, no mention of East Berlin or Berlin as a whole. For Kennedy was preoccupied now with the specter of nuclear war, as Khrushchev perhaps intended. A surprising turnabout, considering that it had been the Americans, for more than a decade, who had waved the bomb around in moments of crisis. Kennedy went home bitter and depressed. Khrushchev's estimate of him at the time: "weak and irresolute."[46] It was similar to Adenauer's judgment after visiting Kennedy in April: "a choir boy." But in Khrushchev's case the conclusion was probably decisive in swinging him behind Ulbricht's plan for cordoning off West Berlin. The preparations under Erich Honecker's guidance were running full blast, including night exercises for the military and paramilitary units that would shortly take up the frontier positions. Ulbricht was leaving nothing to chance. On June 15 he called a rare "international press conference" in the grand hall of the House of Ministries, that same building stormed by the East Berlin workers in 1953, with its back to the West Berlin boundary.

"Does the creation of a free city mean in your opinion that the state frontier will be erected at the Brandenburg Gate?" asked a shrewd reporter. "And are you determined to draw all the consequences from this fact?"

Ulbricht replied, "If I understand your question to the effect that there are people in West Germany who desire that we mobilize the construction workers of the capital of the DDR to erect a wall, *ja?* Uhh, I am not aware that such an intention exists. No one has the intention to build a wall."

He had spoken the magic word, "wall," and a little later he remarked that in a free, demilitarized city of West Berlin, the refugee transit camps would have to close down and the air traffic would be controlled by the DDR. The desired effect set in: escapes en masse, the kind of panic that made the CIA and other observers question the cordoning off because it might lead to a new uprising, an explosion. On the same day Khrushchev made public his new free city ultimatum in a speech. There were over 19,000 refugees in June; in July, the month in which both Khrushchev and Kennedy bolstered their defense budgets, it was 30,444. In early August they were coming at a rate of 1,524 a day. The people who fled knew what was up, even if they had not penetrated Honecker's tight security girdle. They had heard Ulbricht say "wall" and murmur something about closing down the refugee camps, and they had heard Kennedy talk in somber terms on July 25 about the sanctity of West Berlin. Over and over again the examiners in the Berlin refugee transit camp at Marienfelde heard the same explanation, that people had decided to escape "before it is too late."[47]

Since mid-May Brandt had been almost constantly on the campaign trail, from town to town, village to village, escorted in Mainz by twenty-five red-sweatered motorcyclists, elsewhere by motor cars. "Willy Brandt Is Coming!" the big posters proclaimed. Klaus Schütz had persuaded him to try an America-style approach of grass-roots electioneering up to but not including the kissing of babies. He wore a dark gray homburg for dignity (wearing out three on the road), but he shook a lot of hands and signed a lot of autographs. Schütz called it their "Germany tour," and they made their own private joke about it, asking "Where are the Germans?" In Nürnberg they found Franks; in Munich it was Bavarians; in Stuttgart, Swabians; in Aurich, Frisians; in Cologne, Rhinelanders . . . "But where are the Germans?"

"It was a decisive breakthrough," Schütz insisted. "Not so much with the population at large, but with the Social Democrats. Many saw the candidate for the. first time in their villages; they had never seen Schumacher or Ollenhauer. Brandt was put in touch with ordinary SPD members, and this was significant. Up to then the idea had been that voters should come to the candidate. We saw that we had to go to the voters. Journalists made fun of us. They asked, "Why Aurich? Why Rosenheim? You have no candidates there."[48] It was uphill. The polls consistently showed old Adenauer well ahead.

Brandt was in Berlin briefly on June 17, the eighth anniversary of the worker uprising, to tell an audience of 100,000: "We shall never surrender!" He added: "Without a doubt we are heading toward a new test of nerves. We will stand up to it because we have good friends." He was back again on July 4, July 9, July 20, and August 7—warning that the West would have to come up with its own constructive proposals for a Berlin solution. He was aware of the critical nature of the situation, but he could not have known what a sticky mess that so-called Allied contingency planning really was or the lack of unity even inside the Kennedy Administration—where some were reviving Lucius Clay's old idea of an "armed probe" along the access routes by American armor, while others talked of the atom bomb, and still others thought the best course was to do nothing at all.

Little wonder the news of the deployment of East German and Soviet forces around the boundaries of West Berlin on the night of August 12-13 caught him, literally, asleep. He was in a special car on the express train from Nürnberg north to Kiel, when an urgent telegram was sent him by his chief aide. It reached him at the station in Göttingen shortly after 3:30 a.m. East German troops had already torn up paving stones on several Berlin streets, stopped subway and elevated trains, and begun setting up barbed-wire barriers.

Sleepy-eyed, Brandt stepped into a car at Hannover a half-hour later and was driven to the airport. The first plane for Berlin left three hours later. His chief aide met him at the Tempelhof Field at eight o'clock, and the two drove to the Brandenburg Gate and the nearby Potsdamer Platz, once at the heart of the metropolis. They faced uniformed East German factory guards standing elbow to elbow, armed with submachine guns. The only Western Allies in sight were three British military policemen. A man grabbed his arm: "When are the Americans coming to put an end to this nightmare?" Brandt had to shrug.[49] He was staring numbed, not only at an accomplished fact, but at the beginning of one of the most masterful political-military defense works of modern times—in the planning for five months, authorized in secret by the Warsaw Pact chiefs in Moscow eight days before, and now in execution since midnight. Ulbricht had boasted in June that you could not "call the tune without paying the piper," and that day he was the piper.

Three years before Brandt had instantly seen through Khrushchev's bluff, and it gave him room to maneuver. He could afford to talk back then and to stretch a bit in reassuring his 2.2 million West Berliners. It had brought him international fame and approval. But now? It was no longer a bluffing game, and his credit in the Western casino was suddenly next to nil, except for the temper and temperament of his fellow Berliners. That much he could wager. But did anybody who counted care? Like Brandt other German and Western leaders had been caught napping literally and figuratively. Adenauer had rolled over in his bed when he received an intelligence estimate that the Communists would stick properly within their borders. Secretary of State Rusk would say similar soothing words to Kennedy and let him go off sailing at Cape Cod. In Bonn the American Ambassador went to watch a baseball game. In Berlin the U.S. mission officials set out for golf, tennis, and swimming. The chief political officer for Eastern affairs rubbed his hands with satisfaction as he told colleagues his reaction to the East German barriers: "Well, gentlemen, I guess that clears up the situation."[50] But to the east, north, south, and west of Berlin the Soviets and East Germans had mobilized over thirty divisions, ground-to-ground rocket units, portions of the Baltic Fleet, and some airborne units—all under the command of Field Marshall Ivan "The Tank" Konev. Willy Brandt, who had seemed to have so much at his command a few hours and months before, was suddenly empty-handed. From a protagonist he had been transformed into a supporting actor, the victim of larger forces in the drama of Berlin.

Brandt met with his assembled senators in the Schöneberg Rathaus at 9:30

a.m. His friend, Joachim Lipschitz, senator for interior, presented details of the barricades including the fact that the East Germans had reduced the number of crossing points between East and West Berlin from eighty-eight to thirteen and blocked cross-city public transportation. Together they drafted a statement:

> The Senate of Berlin raises the accusation before the entire world against the illegal and inhuman measures of the splitters of Germany, the oppressors of East Berlin, the threateners of West Berlin. The cordoning off of the Zone and the Soviet Sector from West Berlin means that the barrier wall of a concentration camp will be drawn through Berlin. The Senate and population of Berlin expect that the Western powers undertake energetic steps with the Soviet Government.

At this stage and for weeks afterward it was the consensus of the Allied military and political leaders that the Berlin barriers had nothing to do with them and their rights—but only with the stanching of East Germany's refugee outflow.

The three Western commandants called in Brandt at 11 a.m. at that curious vestige of four-power occupation control, the Allied *Kommandantur* in Dahlem. They kept him waiting a quarter of an hour. Brandt was boiling with anger. After their formal salutation he exploded: "You let Ulbricht kick you in the rear last night!" Frigid silence. Then the commandants told Brandt to come to the point. He declared: "What happened last night is an illegal breach of the existing four-power agreement concerning free movement in all of Berlin . . . The least that has to be done is that your governments must immediately protest sharply and emphatically in Moscow . . ." More silence. "You must do something!" Brandt then urged them to at least send Allied patrols to the East Berlin sector border. They unanimously refused on the ground this would turn the affair into an international political contest. Instead, they ordered Brandt to send West Berlin policemen out along the boundary to prevent clashes. Meanwhile, they would "consult" their governments. Brandt withdrew in helpless rage.

The West Berliners who had begun their Sunday as a day of rest and relaxation began streaming to the sector borders. Here and there clashes developed as they tried to remove the newly planted barriers. Some were menaced by bayonet-wielding East German troops backed up by menacing tanks. As the number of incidents between West Berliners and East German border guards mounted that evening, Egon Bahr muttered to Brandt: "We've been sold, but not yet delivered." Brandt reportedly commented: "*Kennedy haut uns in die Pfanne.*" (Kennedy is making mince meat of us.) All that stood against the East German armored units and infantry that night were some West Berlin policemen carrying small Belgian pistols and billy clubs.[51] "Kennedy reckoned with an entirely different sort of crisis," Brandt concluded[52]—at a later date.

The 11,000-man Berlin garrison, more than half of it American, was kept in its barracks the next day, too. Late in the afternoon, having called off his election campaign appearances for the next two weeks, Brandt spoke to his House of Representatives and to a news conference. He urged the Berliners to be "calm and reasonable." On the other side of the barriers—nobody was calling it a "wall" yet—Walter Ulbricht was congratulating his officers and soldiers on his new frontier and the acquisition of 155 square miles of no-longer-disputed territory.

On August 15 the first Allied patrols showed up along the twenty-eight-mile sector border dividing Berlin. But they did not attempt to test the blocked crossing points. That morning Brandt was informed of how Chancellor Adenauer had spoken of him the evening before in an election rally in Regensburg, a Bavarian Catholic stronghold: "If there is one person who has been treated with the greatest consideration by his political opponents, then it is Herr Brandt alias Frahm. . . ." Brandt was stunned, and he walked wordlessly out of his session with the senate. Later he issued a statement: "Chancellor Adenauer thought it right to attack me . . . in the lowest way while I was carrying out my duty in Berlin."

German politics was never a gentle sport. It is, rather, something akin to the *Hetzjagd* of German hunters. Candidates were quarry. Did the skin of the *Politicker* toughen with the years? Not Brandt's.

Earlier in the year a note was passed to Fritz Heine, who had connections with the British Secret Intelligence Service from his exile days in London, alleging that Brandt's missing father was "a Russian or a Bulgar." Heine confided in Wehner, who turned to Ollenhauer. What to do? "Show it to him," Wehner advised. "There are some things you have to trample out with your feet."[53] But, of course, Brandt knew the real identity of his father; this attack was something he could shrug off.

What he could not shrug off was an assault from a new quarter, prepared by Susanne Sievers, his onetime Bonn girlfriend. She had become involved in journalism once more, this time with the coldest of cold warriors in the Bavarian Christian Social Union, whose chairman was her old boyfriend, Franz Josef Strauss. She wrote for the *Freiheitsglocke* (*Liberty Bell*), a publication of the Associaton of Victims of Stalin, often attacking Social Democrats. Her protector for a time was a Strauss aide who ran a virulent anti-Communist organization called Save Liberty. One of the politicians most active in it was a young man named Rainer Barzel. When a counterintelligence tip warned against Susanne Sievers, she was summarily dumped from the Victims of Stalin, but she continued inveighing against Social Democrats. The SPD responded in kind, and she wrote Brandt a threatening letter saying that if he didn't put a stop to it she would "lose patience." Some Bavarian intriguers learned of this and offered to publish her personal account of the old affair with Brandt in time for the 1961 election campaign. She agreed and went to work with a scandal specialist, Hans Frederik. Their book was published under the pseudonym Claire Mortensen, and it was entitled . . . *Da war auch ein Mädchen* (. . .*There Was Also a Girl*). Only a last-minute court action enjoined Frederik from distributing the book, which contained photocopies of Willy's "Puma-Bear" correspondence with Susanne. But there were extras that circulated like the wind through the Federal Republic.

There was more: A certain Professor Schwartz of Greifswald University had broadcast that "We will prove Brandt worked in Norway for the Gestapo." A Soviet propagandist calling himself Burnov was broadcasting on the Volga station to soldiers in Germany that Brandt had been "a French agent who became a Gestapo spy." In East Germany there was also a variant calling Brandt an agent of the CIA.[54]

Everything seemed to be turning against him. After walking out of the senate session Brandt received Edward R. Morrow, director of the U.S. Information Agency and a Kennedy friend. Murrow had spent the afternoon in the company of Axel Springer who had inspired the fellow journalist to put his friendship to use in persuading the President how serious the Berlin situation had become. Murrow had just sent a cable to Kennedy, and now, showing a copy of it to Brandt, he urged the Mayor to get in touch with the White House. Brandt sat down and wrote Kennedy but decided to sleep on what he had written.

On the morning of April 16 units of the *Volksarmee* and East German construction workers began mortaring the first cement blocks of what was to be the real Berlin wall. Brandt telegraphed a copy of his letter to Kennedy. The tone was dry, but the text crackled with tension:

> The measures of the Ulbricht regime, supported by the Soviet Union and the rest of the East Bloc have almost completely destroyed the remains of the four-power status. Whereas earlier the commandants of the Allied powers protested already against parades of the so-called *Volksarmee,* this time they have contented themselves with a tardy and not very powerful step following the

military occupation of the East sector by the *Volksarmee.* The
illegal sovereignty of the East Berlin Government has been
acknowledged through acceptance . . . I regard this as a grave
turning point in the post-war history of this city. . . .

He went on to warn that inactivity and pure defensiveness could cause a crisis
of confidence among the West Berliners toward the Western powers and stir
the East Germans to adventurism. "After the second act there would be a
Berlin that resembles a ghetto," he continued, "Then we would experience
instead of a refugee movement to Berlin the beginning of a flight out of
Berlin." He pleaded for "political initiative"—perhaps the proclamation of a
three-power status for Berlin while continuing to demand restoration of four-
power responsibility, perhaps an appeal to the United Nations on grounds of
human rights violations, and, at least, a strengthening of the American
garrison in Berlin. "I estimate the situation to be serious enough to write you
this frankly, as is only possible among friends who completely trust each
other."

"Trust?" Kennedy stormed when he received the message. "I don't trust
this man at all. He's in the middle of a campaign with old Adenauer and wants
to drag me in. Where does he get off calling me a friend?" He authorized
Pierre Salinger to tell the Washington press that the President had "not yet
decided" whether to reply. The White House was even more annoyed when it
learned that Brandt had told a mass rally of West Berliners of his note to
Kennedy. For the next twenty-four hours Brandt was terribly alone in a fickle
world of swirling tensions, facing new foes at every turn. Was he all wrong?
Had he lost his touch?

The rally in front of the Schöneberg Rathaus on August 16 drew one in nine
West Berliners—a crowd of 250,000. Brandt spent the entire morning
scribbling his address. *Bild,* the Springer tabloid, had carried the banner
headline: "THE WEST IS DOING NOTHING." Now the Berliners appeared
carrying homemade posters: "Doesn't the West Know What to Do?"
"Betrayed by the West?" "Where Is the Chancellor?" "Where Are the
Protective (Western) Powers?" "Bang the Drum, Willy!"

"What should I tell them?" Brandt murmured. "Nobody could speak in a
way that would satisfy the people." He was somber but there was something
of the fighter in him, too:

The Berliners have a right to know how the land lies. The people of
this city are strong enough to stand the truth. The Soviet Union has
given its mastiff Ulbricht a bit longer leash. It has allowed him to
march his troops into the Eastern Sector of this city. It has
empowered him to break international law. The tanks moved into

position to stop the mass flight from the Zone have mashed the valid four-power status under their treads. . . .

I turn at this hour consciously to fellow countrymen active in the authorities and organizations of the Zone regime. Don't let them turn you into scoundrels. Be humane wherever possible. Don't shoot at your own countrymen. . . .

This city desires peace, but it will not capitulate . . . But peace has never been saved by weakness. There is a point where you have to recognize that you cannot retreat one step. This point has been reached.[55]

But the only cheer he got was when he announced he had written Kennedy. Egon Bahr ordered the city hall's imitation of the Philadelphia Liberty Bell—a gift of the United States after the blockade—to be rung. It drowned out the cries of hotheads calling for a march on the sector border.

There was a change in the political climate of Washington during the night. Kennedy was persuaded to alter his view. Murrow's message helped, but so did the counsel of Marguerite Higgins, the old Berlin hand, and, in the end, Brandt's letter itself. Even the leaking of the full text of the letter to a Frankfurt newspaper by Adenauer failed to halt the shift.[56]

On August 18 Kennedy wrote a firm but conciliatory reply on pale green White House stationery and handed it to Vice President Johnson to deliver personally in Berlin. He said he had read Brandt's letter "with great care" and "I want to thank you for it." He also said,

I understand entirely the deep concerns and sense of trouble which prompted your letter. . . . Grave as this matter is, however, there are, as you say no steps available to us which can force a significant material change in this present situation. Since it represents a resounding confession of weakness, this brutal border closing evidently represents a basic Soviet decision which only war could reverse. Neither you nor we, nor any of our Allies, have ever supposed that we should go to war on this point. Yet the Soviet action is too serious for inadequate responses. . . .

Kennedy then politely rejected Brandt's proposals as "mere trifles compared to what has been done," adding, "some of them, moreover, seem unlikely to be fruitful even in their own terms"—with particular reference to the suggestion of three-power status for West Berlin. But he would order "a significant reinforcement of the Western garrisons." He closed after three pages, saying "It is my own confidence that we can continue to rely on each other as firmly in the future as we have in the past. With warm personal regards, Sincerely, John Kennedy." It was marked "SECRET."[57]

As Lyndon B. Johnson prepared to fly to Germany, Willy Brandt appeared in Bonn before the Bundestag to make a special address on the situation created by the barriers, and a presidential command reached the United States Army garrison at Mannheim ordering a 1500-man battle group to move in convoy to West Berlin.

Brandt spoke crisply for less than fifteen minutes in the Parliament, assuring the Adenauer government that his Berliners had not lost confidence in Allied guarantees of their liberty but again demanding "political initiatives" that went beyond the formal protest lodged by the Western powers in Moscow the evening before. Looking ahead, he observed:

> The abandonment of our countrymen will not take place. We are one people that also has its self-respect. Right and morality oblige us to hold this point of view. This attitude arises from our democratic conviction, for without this untouched and unflinching stance we would ourselves pave the way, out of weakness or opportunism, toward a new nationalism. And no one to whom peace is worth something can wish that.[58]

It is the art of the politician to turn a setback to his advantage; it was an art in which Willy Brandt was getting a lot of practice. The policy of the West in divided Germany was in a shambles. Gone its illusion of eventual reunification through a policy of strength including atomic threats. Gone its dwindled hope for free elections. Gone, for a time, the possibility of negotiated accommodations with the East.

The Communist-made barriers now hardening into a formidable wall crushed the illusions. In hindsight, some West Germans would observe much later that an independent German *Ostpolitik* had its origins in the minds of Willy Brandt and Egon Bahr that morning when they woke up to find their city finally cut in half and Western Allies unwilling to stick up for all their own rights or to afford ultimate protection to their wards in Berlin. Of course Brandt had been proposing a down-to-earth *Ostpolitik* for years. He was doing so now in his first post-August 13 speeches. What the barriers wrought, perhaps, was the clearer realization that German politicians would have to come up with their own ideas—because nobody else was going to do it for them.

The Berlin wall became the high-water mark of Soviet Communist militancy for more than a decade. Without question its overwhelming success—not even a peep of protest from the West for three whole days— encouraged much more military mischief: in the Congo, in Indochina, in Cuba. Khrushchev's implantation of missiles on that Caribbean island was a direct consequence of his Berlin triumph. But the missiles were withdrawn, and some other advances eventually turned into retreats. The Berlin wall stayed and grew. Like the Warsaw Pact invasion of Czechoslovakia in 1968 it was essentially a defensive measure, albeit with definitely offensive overtones. Within a few days Ulbricht was calling it his "anti-Fascist protective wall." Its concrete blocks, antitank ditches, barbed-wire rolls, raked fire fields, watch towers, electric trip wires, and pillboxes were aimed inward against his own people, not against potential Western assaults. The wall was designed to protect not the people of East Germany but the Communist system imposed on them. It would lose significance only in inverse ratio to the strengthening of the Communist system in East Germany.

Konrad Adenauer was still scornfully mocking Willy Brandt as "Herr Frahm" in election rallies when he learned that Vice President Johnson was on his way to Berlin, accompanied by Kennedy's specially appointed adviser Lucius D. Clay. Perhaps he had misjudged the temper of Washington and of his electorate. He asked whether he might fly to Berlin with Johnson and Clay, an act he had glaringly avoided all week. When Brandt heard of this, he told an American diplomat in Berlin that if Adenauer came to town after abusing him as "alias Frahm," then "stones will fly." The American sent an advisory note recommending Adenauer stay in Bonn.[59]

When Johnson and Clay arrived it was Brandt who welcomed them, and what a welcome! He had mobilized 300,000 Berliners to line the streets from Templehof Airport to Schöneberg Rathaus. Clay's eyes grew moist. Johnson handed the Kennedy letter to Brandt later in the evening. No matter its coolness to some of his proposals. Johnson was there, and 1500 American troops were on their way. He was being listened to again. That evening Lyndon Johnson outdid himself in self-indulgence. Where did those handsome shoes come from that Brandt was wearing? Leiser-Berlin. "I'd like to have a pair, too," said the Vice President.

"But it's Saturday and the stores are closed," Brandt replied.

"Mister Mayor, you said you wanted action instead of words. You, too, must act."

Next morning Johnson received a pair of Leiser slippers and a twenty-four-person coffee set from the Berlin Porcelain Factory, which he had also admired. It was Sunday, a week after August 13, and Colonel Glover S. Johns, a hero of the hedgerow battle of St. Lo, commanded his men to roll. He was connected by radio telephone with the White House, where President Kennedy was anxiously awaiting news of the completion of the troop movement. At the candy-striped barriers of Marienborn, the westernmost checkpoint of the Soviet forces on the main East German highway to Berlin a

Russian colonel started to count the men and the vehicles. To help him, Colonel Johns asked his men to climb down and line up. Johns wanted to move his men 110 miles to Berlin as swiftly as possible. Reports were going to Kennedy every twenty minutes. When the first unit of the Eighteenth Infantry Regiment, Eighth Division, reached West Berlin in mid-morning, Kennedy "felt as if the crisis had reached a turning point," an aide observed. By the thousands West Berliners turned out to welcome the convoy, throwing flowers and blowing kisses. Johnson and Brandt were at the boundary, too. Meanwhile, General Clay, the airlift hero, was taking a half-hour drive around East Berlin and being hailed by East Berliners as well. At the end of the day Brandt issued a statement:

> I am completely satisfied. We have the full confidence of the President. The President is determined to keep West Berlin secure. I can say that West Berlin's freedom could only be lost through a military attack by the Soviet Union. I do not believe we are facing a war. West Berlin remains free.

Then he, Johnson, and Clay repaired to the roof tavern of the two-year-old Berlin Hilton and sipped whiskey. Johnson took off with his new shoes and his porcelain at 5 a.m.

The wall was growing higher and thicker with every passing hour. Although many more tests of right and will stood before the Western Allies and Brandt's Berliners, the worst had passed: the possibility that Western laxness would tempt the massed Communist military formations to move against West Berlin itself. The isolated city was now under the protection and the watchful eye of the United States President.

Chancellor Adenauer finally reached Berlin a full nine days after the East Germans had thrown up the first barriers. It was all Franz Amrehn, Brandt's CDU coalition partner, could do to persuade the Mayor to shake hands with Adenauer at the airport. The rest of the reception was equally frosty. A banner strung above Hanger No. 9 at Tempelhof read: "Hurrah, the Savior Is Here— Too Late." When he drove alone through the worker borough of Wedding, which was also Brandt's election district, people on the streets shouted "Willy! Willy!" at him. At the Marienfelde Refugee Camp someone had scribbled a verse on a wall:

> The election is so important for him
> That coming to Berlin is much too grim.[60]

He turned around after eight hours and flew back to familiar and comfortable Rhenish haunts for more campaigning. That same day the East German authorities reduced the number of crossing points through the mounting wall from thirteen to six and began charging visa fees for civilian entry into East Berlin.

Adenauer had taken a beating because of Berlin. But the wily old man was not through by any measure. His CDU was still far ahead in the polls, and there were many West Germans who felt it was unwise to switch chancellors in the middle of a crisis, even though Brandt clearly had the sympathy of the Americans. The Chancellor left nothing to chance. He had denied Brandt the opportunity of wider exposure by refusing to debate him on television. When Khrushchev made a blistering attack on the Bonn Government on August 31, Adenauer turned it around immediately with an election poster that proclaimed: "Now We All Know—Khrushchev Demands Adenauer's Ouster!—In This Threatening Hour the German People Stands Firmly Behind Konrad Adenauer—The German People Will Give Khrushchev the Right Answer on September 17!"

Brandt, too, attempted to use the balcony of Berlin to his advantage. He resumed campaigning in West Germany a week after the Johnson visit but only from his base in West Berlin. "We flew out mornings and campaigned during the afternoons and evenings," Schütz recalled. "Then we went back to Berlin for the night in those English two propeller planes we chartered." It was exhausting, and it showed in his face. There were deep furrows below his eyes and around his mouth. "I am tired," he told his audiences. "But I will bear up." As for Adenauer, Brandt refrained from the gutter tactics; "I don't want to attack him personally," he told an audience in Essen on September 12. "All I want is to wish him a quiet life in retirement."[61]

The vote was something of a surprise for everyone. Adenauer's Conservatives polled a disappointing 45.3 percent. Brandt's party got 36.3 percent, and the Free Democrats expanded to their best-ever showing of 12.7 percent. The CDU was humbled to the extent of having to seek a coalition government.

Brandt was balked, but he did not feel crushed by the September 17 vote. He was content in knowing he had done his duty in a severe test. "Despite the many difficulties, it brought my political friends and me 2 million additional votes."[62] Herbert Wehner was almost jubilant: "Compared to the Federal election of 1957 the lead of the CDU over the SPD was exactly halved on September 17—in the number of votes and in percentage terms."[63] For the moment Brandt was still the front-line Mayor, and there he would remain for another five years. There was work enough and resonance enough for the man who stood at the Berlin barricades. In time the fronts would shift a bit and with them his opportunities.

VIII:
Barriers to Breach

Far from resolving West Berlin's problems, the erection of the Communist wall sharpened them for an entire decade. Far from resolving West Germany's political struggles, Adenauer's fourth election victory, with his loss of parliamentary majority, created new ferment that lasted for eight years. Everywhere the barriers dividing the playing field of Germany shifted. The task facing the politician-players was to determine exactly where the barriers now were and then to figure out ways of breaching them.

Only one day after the 1961 elections Willy Brandt made a bid to Chancellor Adenauer to form an all-party coalition government. Brandt argued that a "government of national concentration" would be the appropriate reply to the Communist offensive. Besides, he had himself demonstrated in Berlin that in time of need—from the 1958 Khrushchev ultimatum onward—it made sense to govern in coalition. It worked rather well in West Berlin. Why not the Federal Republic? The arithmetic of the election was such that the SPD could have become the dominant party in coalition with the Free Democrats, but that variant was flatly excluded by the very person of Erich Mende, the vainglorious leader of the Liberals. Mende, former professional officer, winner of the Knight's Cross, and reportedly a taker of big-industry bribes was committed to Conservatism. The only real question of moment was how much Adenauer could cut down Mende's demands by flirting with Brandt. The Chancellor conferred in secret with the Berlin Mayor on September 22, allowing Mende to dangle for more than a month. In the end Mende compromised, and once more Adenauer was chosen Chancellor in the Bundestag with FDP support. From then on the Free Democrats gloried in tipping the scales of West German coalition politics. The idea of a "big coalition" had at last been formally broached, however. Its acceptance, at least as a hypothetical possibility by all concerned, opened up the coalition question in new terms—the CDU with the SPD or the SPD with the FDP. Barriers were coming down, creating new opportunities and new uncertainties in West German politics.

Willy Brandt now had three constituencies: his Berliners, the SPD voters of West Germany, and the friendly supporters he had acquired on the international scene since 1958. Without a base in the Federal Republic other than the SPD barracks, Brandt was particularly dependent on resonance in West Berlin and abroad for his future impact on the West German electorate. Thus, he repeated his pledge of the previous spring that he would leave only to exchange the post of Mayor for that of Chancellor. His international audience too remained loyal. At the end of September twenty-three U.S. mayors flew to Berlin carrying messages to him. As Mayor Hayden Burns of Jacksonville, Florida, put it: "American support for Berlin goes down to the grass roots."[1] A week later Brandt was in New York to receive a Freedom House award and to speak in several forums for Berlin.

He was quartered in the Hotel Sheraton-East where President Kennedy, from Washington, had been trying to reach him all afternoon by telephone. Finally, it was arranged that they should talk the next morning, October 7, long distance. When the telephone first rang however, it was the Schöneberg Rathaus calling from Berlin to report that Rut had borne him their third son, Matthias. She had been pregnant again in a critical phase of her husband's career. Rut took such events with the stoicism of the North. "Oh, I am rather tough," she would say after another difficult period. "Not hard, but—if I know I have to go through something then I manage it."[2] Brandt replied with a telegram, musing: "Strange, the kind thoughts one sends across the ocean cost nothing but the arid words of a telegram do."[3]

In the talk with Kennedy a few minutes later Brandt told the President his Berliners were counting on a long-term arrangement guaranteeing their security. Kennedy said there was nothing as yet in sight, but that was what he wanted, too.[4] He also wanted to know about the reception of his special emissary, Lucius D. Clay, who had arrived in West Berlin on September 19 as a kind of morale-booster but with a nebulous watchdog function in the American chain of command.

There was more than enough to watch in Berlin, and Clay, too, was being watched with suspicion and envy by generals and diplomats who feared he had come to undercut them. The ugly atmosphere in the city was amplified by daily tragedies at the expanding wall. East German border detachments were clearing out apartment houses situated directly on the sector boundary. To escape their clutches dozens of East Berlin residents leaped into the West from the third- and fourth-story windows, sometimes after agonizing wrestling matches with *Stasi* plainclothesmen before the eyes of helpless West Berliners on the streets below, and sometimes jumping to their deaths when they missed the outstretched safety nets of the West Berlin fire department. Elsewhere, East Berliners swam the chilly border canals and rivers, and still others hurdled the barbed-wire barricades amid hails of submachine gun bullets.[5] West Berliners were decamping, too—at a rate of more than 1000 a month in August and September—to the Federal Republic.

The response at the U.S. Mission on Clay Allee, the broad boulevard named for the airlift hero, was nonexistent. There a group of fatigued American officials huddled in the bombproof bunker, frightened, most of them, by the piece-by-piece encroachment of the Communists and equally afraid of risking a swiftly escalating conflict with Soviet power, should they dare to retaliate—say by ramming holes in the nascent wall or even moving to rescue East Berliners trapped at the very frontier and in deadly peril. Some Americans—General Clay among them—thought the West should be prepared to "die for Berlin," but they were in a distinct minority in autumn 1961.

Clay had gotten off to a very bad start with some off-the-record remarks—speculating about a future political arrangement in which East Germany might also be involved to secure the stability of West Berlin's access routes—which were reported in a garbled version by an Associated Press correspondent. To counter accusations by the German press that the United States was reneging on its commitments (the Springer mass circulation tabloid, *Bild,* appeared with the 3-inch scare headline: IS GERMANY BEING SOLD OUT?" and an editorial entitled: "Can We Still Trust Our Friends in the West?") Clay persisted in demonstrating that U.S. forces could and would exercise their prerogatives. The crunch came in late October, not only in the war of East-West nerves at the Berlin sector borders, but in the test of Clay versus the faint-hearted in the U.S. Army and State Department. East German border guards turned back the American Chief of Mission at "Checkpoint Charlie" because he declined to respond to their request for identification papers. General Albert Watson, the American commandant, thought the best response was for American civilian officials to avoid East Berlin altogether; the Pentagon backed him. Clay was outraged, and he called Kennedy to protest.

For a moment the President hesitated. But here was a plain and simple provocation that could end the same way as a unilateral peace treaty, with the East Germans determining which Americans went where, and how, in the middle of a country conquered in part by American might. Kennedy ordered military measures to back up American rights. Beginning on the morning of October 25 with U.S. bayonets and tanks deployed to back up the right of entry of American diplomats into East Berlin, it ended seventy-six hours later, after a day and a night of tense confrontation between American and Russian tanks standing almost muzzle to muzzle at the crossing point. Clay won his point by compelling the Russians to take the ultimate responsibility for their wards in East Berlin. But the high-risk showdown cost him his last scrap of authority.

Brandt sensed that Clay was rapidly becoming a minority of one and, also, that the hardy general was not one of his greatest fans. There was a *bon mot* about him attributed to Clay: "The nongoverning Governing Mayor of Berlin." Clay was also reported to have characterized Brandt as "a Socialist who doesn't believe in Socialism."[6] But in his conversational book about these difficult months Brandt was most generous in his remarks about the general, calling him "a good friend and helper." Although he felt that "there was something curious about the relationship between Clay and Berlin, Berlin and Clay," he refrained from criticism.

The East Germans and Soviets continued to probe the Western position throughout November and December, while at the wall and behind it in East Berlin and East Germany agonies continued. There were shooting incidents, some of them fatal, and tragic escape attempts every week. American tanks still lurked in the vicinity of the Friedrichstrasse crossing point. Inside East Germany dissidents were being rounded up and harshly disciplined. Gangs of young Communist toughs menaced householders whose television antennas were positioned to pick up West German transmissions. The suicide rate rose in Berlin and East Germany.

From the vantage point of West Berlin it was not apparent that the Communist offensive had lost its momentum. Viewed from afar, however, without the burden of emotions created by the daily reminders of Berlin's individual woes, it was clear from the increasing diplomatic traffic that the crisis tensions were gradually winding down.

Brandt was attuned to this trend, and he took up where he had left off before the campaign for the Chancellorship, attempting to steer his 2.2 million West Berliners to a safe anchorage. There were efforts on the American side to persuade the Bonn Government that Soviet guarantees for West Berlin could be extracted in exchange for eliminating the constitutional link between the city and the Federal Republic. Brandt would have none of that, he told the Bonn Parliament on December 6, serving notice that the Social Democratic opposition would block any such move by denying the necessary two-thirds majority. There were proposals, too, that the West should try to negotiate with the Russians on the Berlin issue only. Again Brandt took a negative position, arguing, as he had before, that such vital issues could not be solved "in isolation" from the larger problems of divided Germany. He addressed the three Western Foreign Ministers prior to the NATO ministerial meeting in Paris, warning them against "rotten compromise" on the Berlin question. When it seemed this diplomatic shadow boxing was at an end, he resigned his Bundestag seat to devote more time to his mayoralty. He was rewarded for his efforts during the year over the Christmas holidays with a handwritten letter of loyalty from Herbert Wehner: "You can always count on me when it is a matter of making a truly consequential reform party out of this party, and to develop it further as such, and you can always count on me in confronting those who think it suffices just to put on rouge."[7]

He had lost a big election. But he had been the Mayor of West Berlin in a time of crisis, and he had won more than 11 million West German votes. The party, his first and last home, would not—perhaps could not—push him out of the door. Social Democrats were not accustomed to changing candidates like shirts, or race horses. Besides, Willy Brandt was something phenomenal in the SPD leadership. He appealed, and not only to Germans.

The Berlin crisis evolved throughout 1962 on two widely separated planes. On the practical, everyday level there was the physical menace to West Berlin and its emotional consequences. In the three air corridors to the West Soviet MIG fighters were buzzing airliners and Allied military transports in a harassing action calculated to underscore a Russian claim to control of the airspace. On the ground around West Berlin would-be refugees were being shot down at the barriers and left to bleed to death—one just before the turn of the year and another in April. Allied directives prevented Western patrols from crossing into East German territory—even into the few square yards that divided possible life from certain death—to rescue them. Concurrently, the Berlin crisis was being acted out in international diplomacy in Moscow, Washington, Bonn, Paris, and London. Early in the year the United States had proposed an "International Access Authority," with East German participation, as a means of overcoming the threat to West Berlin's lifelines. The Soviet Union expressed limited interest in the plan but linked any concessions to fulfillment of its longstanding demand that West Germany be denied nuclear weapons.

Brandt's task in this complex setting was that of the tribune. He had no levers of power at his disposal other than his voice as an expression of the will of the Berliners. He could speak out, as he did February 17, warning the Russians against their "war of nerves" in the air corridors. He could also broadcast Berlin's message through the many notables coming to see the city with the new wall in its middle. Britain's Foreign Secretary Alexander Douglas-Home was there in January. Bobby, Teddy, and Ethel Kennedy came in February. Berliners on both sides of the barriers thrilled to have the Kennedys in their midst, and they turned out in droves. The personal greetings conveyed by the Attorney General from his brother to Brandt and the Berliners were the kind of morale-boosting they needed, along with his assurance: "An armed attack on West Berlin is the same as an armed attack on Chicago or New York or London or Paris, and we stand by you." Bobby was so taken by the warmth of his reception that he kept a Berlin bear on his desk in Washington and a large photograph of himself with a crowd of Berliners on his wall.

Brandt was intent, of course, on holding his lines open to President Kennedy, whom he had come to view as a kind of *Schicksalsbruder,* a comrade in destiny. The connection was all the more important because Chancellor Adenauer had set himself at cross purposes with the young President, not only on the question of Germany's future Eastern relations, but also on the question of France's policy under President de Gaulle. Adenauer's deliberate leak of an American position paper, torpedoing negotiations with the Russians on Berlin and related issues before they were even moving on the diplomatic seas,[8] angered the Kennedy Administration so much that when Secretary of State Rusk came to Germany a little later he declined to take Adenauer with him to West Berlin.

Brandt was scornful of these maneuvers, and he took the occasion of the national SPD convention at Cologne in May to say so:

> They attacked American foreign policy in public after agreeing to it internally. That has nothing in common with (real) foreign policy. . . . We say, the Federal Republic must cultivate and further develop a relationship of trust with the United States. There is no alternative.

He was in top form at the convention, his speech crisp and clear and his portable aura polished to a high shine. The Adenauer era was "nearing its end," he noted, alluding to the vow of the old man to quit after two years of coalition with the FDP's Mende. "We have destroyed a legend," he continued, the legend that Bonn and the leadership of the Federal Republic were a privilege of the (Christian) Union Party." But he also soberly assessed the shifts in German politics as "long-term developments" and not something "that could be changed in the course of a few months." He left open the door for further efforts to form a CDU-SPD coalition. Although skeptical—"The leadership of the Union parties has never really learned to share responsibility with others"—he declared: "There is no black, and no red, but alone a German Federal Republic. . . . All citizens and all parties are called upon to participate in the competition for the best and worthiest solution of the social challenges." The SPD, he boasted, was a "stabilizing factor participating in the shaping of the Federal Republic—conscious of responsibility and ready to bear responsibility."

The most memorable part of his May 27 address was devoted to foreign relations:

> Germany does not stand as close to the hub of world events as we might like to imagine today. A different question stands at the center of interest today: how to make a formulated agreement out of the silent pact that there should be no great war, so that the avoidance of the great war can be guaranteed according to human standards . . . The German question is only interesting for the great powers insofar as they can be made aware of it. . . . The Federal Republic must escape from the twilight. Two things are needed: First, we have to develop our own proposals and not leave the burden of thinking solely to those who bear the most extreme risks . . . The Federal Republic must first of all lose the taint of wanting to profit from the East-West conflict. In reality a lessening of tensions—as endlessly difficult as that may seem—is the most important condition for realizing our self-determination . . . The division of Germany is the result of Hitlerism and the consequence of the conflict between East and West. Reunification can only be regarded as realistic in connection with a changed relationship between East and West. We must contribute to such a change for the sake of peace and our national destiny . . . In the meantime we will not and may not give up hope of a possibility of achieving (at least) a minimum of permeability of the wall. . . .

The applause was loud and long,[9] and in partial recognition the convention elected him deputy chairman of the party along with Herbert Wehner. Brandt got an overwhelming mandate—298 of 312 delegate votes; Wehner 232. Ollenhauer was endorsed for what was to be his last year as chairman. The Brandt-Wehner tandem became a formal reality at Cologne.

The same day of his Cologne speech another East German was slain at the wall by the Kronprinzen Bridge across the Spree in a hail of thirty shots. In August Brandt had scarcely returned from a month's vacation in Norway with Rut and the three boys when there was another appalling border incident, this time within view of Checkpoint Charlie. Peter Fechter, an eighteen-year-old East Berlin mason who had been working on Walter Ulbricht's new State Council Building slipped away on his lunch hour and attempted to climb the wall with a friend. He was felled by submachine-gun fire and lay bleeding to death within arm's reach of West Berlin, where scores of people watched in helpless horror. General Watson ordered his men at the border to stay on their side of the wall, until Peter Fechter succumbed. There were demonstrations that night in West Berlin, larger ones the next day. One of the placards addressed the Americans: "Protective Power? You Tolerate Murder—You Abet Murder." The Russians, too, came under fire. West Berliners began stoning the buses that carried Russian soldiers to a Soviet war memorial in West Berlin. Brandt noted: "We had to make plain what was possible in Berlin, and what was impossible. People had to understand that the legal basis of four-power responsibility still existed in the Western view, but that actual guarantees ended at the wall." A campaign of explanations was carried into the factories and office buildings.[10] Not a pleasant job for an elected Mayor of "the bridgehead of freedom."

The Soviet leadership took the uproar over the Fechter shooting and another border killing six days later as a pretext to tighten the vise on West Berlin. They sent armored vehicles into West Berlin, threatened to stop United States military patrols on the highway to Berlin, abolished the office of the Soviet commandant in East Berlin, and renewed buzzing of Allied aircraft in the Berlin corridors. All this was part of a larger plan. Unbeknownst to Brandt and the Berliners, Khrushchev and his military advisers were embarking on a global adventure to test the will of the West again. A year before Khrushchev had been proven right in his estimate of an irresolute West with regard to the Berlin wall. He was feeling bold. This time he reached with one hand to the familiar locus of Berlin and, with the other hand, 5300 miles westward to Havana. By late August there were over 3000 Soviet technicians on Cuba building new military installations, including guided missile sites. The first reports of troop concentrations around Berlin reached Western ears early in September.[11] Presumably the Communist strategy reckoned that a squeeze on the one teat might produce milk on the other, or both.

At first it seemed that the primary Russian thrust was toward Berlin, and Brandt was alert to this. "I simply cannot grasp why everything should at all times depend on Moscow," he told a German interviewer. "It is an unsatisfactory state of affairs that the West does nothing but wait for Khrushchev's moves."[12] He went on to elaborate a thesis that "in reality there is only a three-power responsibility for West Berlin," excluding the Russians. Four weeks later Defense Secretary Robert McNamara, returning from West Germany, declared the United States was ready to use nuclear arms to protect vital interests in Berlin. The storm fronts were on the move.

Brandt set off for the United States again, to be a marshal in New York's fifth annual Steuben Day parade, then to the Harvard School of Public Administration to deliver two lectures, and finally to Washington. In Cambridge he spoke on the "Ordeal of Coexistence" and, against the backdrop of looming war clouds he conjured a vision of Germany as "a sort of testing ground where the ability and readiness of the great powers to solve difficult international problems in a reasonable way and with an acceptable coexistence concept are put on trial." He added that the experience of Berlin had shown "moral capitulation" was not the answer. But "if the choice was unavoidable to bring human or national interests into harmony, we would have to place the human interests more in the foreground than the national."[13] This was a foretaste of a concept he would develop further in later years.

Kennedy had the Harvard lectures on his desk when Brandt showed up at the White House on October 5. Brandt's thoughts on Germany and coexistence, unusual as they were, coming from a German politician, coincided with his own. But with a new crisis confronting them their discussion centered on immediate dangers and possibilities. A new Communist push on Berlin might stir an uprising in East Germany, Brandt suggested, and in the case of armed conflict Ulbricht's *Volksarmee* was not an altogether dependable fighting force. Kennedy noted that the West's contingency planning for Berlin was in poor shape, without anything resembling unanimity on how to respond to this or that probe from the East. They also discussed the feasibility of an access authority, perhaps under a four-power umbrella, and a West Berlin referendum—both means for compelling the Communists to negotiate rather than take unilateral action. Finally, Kennedy mentioned Cuba. Despite the pressure from extremists to take "drastic steps," he wanted to avoid strong measures in the Caribbean because of the "threat to Berlin." On October 16, a week after Brandt's return to Germany, the first aerial photographs of Soviet rocket bases on Cuba were made available to the President. Six days later Kennedy addressed the world about the dual Soviet threat—to Cuba and to Berlin—and his determination not to give way. He articulated his commitment to "the brave people of West Berlin" and readied an armed probe up the highway from West Germany, coincident with the naval blockade of Cuba. He and Brandt exchanged several messages of mutual reassurance during the next nervous week. Kennedy had at last found the right mixture of firmness and ability to compromise, Brandt noted. As a result the Cuba missiles were withdrawn and the Berlin threat removed.[14]

International tensions were in full bloom when West Germany was faced with a major domestic political crisis. The Free Democrats had quit Chancellor Adenauer's coalition when it became known that Defense Minister Franz Joseph Strauss had engineered the *Spiegel* affair—the arrest of Conrad Ahlers, a reporter for the nosy news magazine who had disclosed some federal army shortcomings, and a police raid of *Der Spiegel*'s Hamburg premises on October 26-27. Not even Strauss's resignation on November 30 mollified the FDP, and Adenauer was forced to weigh a coalition with the Social Democrats—this time seriously. Adenauer authorized emissaries to sound out Herbert Wehner, and on December 3 the Chancellor formally opened coalition negotiations with Erich Ollenhauer. During the next six days the Adenauer party was torn between the need to keep a presentable successor for Adenauer and the desire to revise the electoral law so as to eliminate the small but noisome Liberal Party. The determining factor lay in the CDU, where the supporters of Ludwig Erhard rallied behind the man they wanted to follow Adenauer as Chancellor.[15] Mende could accept that alternative, and Adenauer finally formed his fifth Cabinet, with five FDP ministers, on December 14. But it was close. Had it gone the other way, Willy Brandt might have been Vice Chancellor in mid-December 1962.

A month later Nikita Khrushchev came to Berlin to attend the sixth convention of Ulbricht's SED. He was in a defensive mood after his retreat from the Caribbean and mounting troubles with the Chinese. Willy Brandt signaled that he would not be averse to meeting the Soviet Premier this time, and an invitation arrived from the embassy. "This time I'll fight for it," he told friends. The afternoon of January 17 he called Chancellor Adenauer and got his approval. But in the Berlin senate, Franz Amrehn, his deputy mayor from the CDU, turned on him and insisted: "If you go, I go." Amrehn would quit the coalition rather than stand by and see the Mayor confer with the Soviet leader. At the last minute, about 6 p.m., Brandt relented and stayed in West Berlin a second time. It ran against his every instinct, but at 9 p.m. he told waiting reporters that he did not want to stand before Khrushchev as the remaining partner of an enterprise that had just collapsed.[16]

In elections in West Berlin exactly one month later the SPD gained almost 62 percent—112,000 votes more than in 1958. The CDU lost by a comparable number and got about 29 percent. In reprisal, Brandt formed a new coalition, though he had no need to do so, with the Berlin FDP. The landslide strengthened his hand even more in the federal SPD. Willy was still a winner. With an eye to the next federal elections he turned over the bulk of his administrative duties to his new deputy mayor, Heinrich Albertz, and his Berlin party chairmanship to his trusted aide, Kurt Mattick.

He was thinking, too, of the additional work facing him in connection with a visit by President Kennedy scheduled for late June. There had been a lot of back and forth at the White House before the trip was finally arranged. Kennedy had taken note of President de Gaulle's success in wooing the West Germans—his triumphal tour of the Federal Republic in September 1962 had emboldened the Frenchman to veto British entry into the Common Market in the following January, against American wishes. Adenauer and de Gaulle concluded a friendship treaty the same month. Even Mayor Brandt had found it opportune to hail "close and sincere Franco-German cooperation" after visiting de Gaulle in April.[17] Kennedy wanted to show the flag in Germany and his own special red, white, and blue charisma. His political and security advisers warned against the venture, on grounds of personal and strategic risk. However, enthused by Bobby Kennedy's report of his Berlin reception and the welcome there for other Kennedys, the President overruled the doubters. The Germany trip was on. As for West Berlin, he had a two-year-old invitation from Brandt and Brandt's additional reminder that Nikita Khrushchev had visited East Berlin several times.[18] Brandt touched down in the United States for few days in mid-June—speeches in New York and St. Louis and an honorary degree from Harvard—and got a briefing from Dean Rusk on Kennedy's new "strategy for peace" before zipping home to be a co-host for the President.

The Germans had long been accustomed to subjugation by their own rulers, but only seldom by foreigners. Now, in the eighteenth year of military occupation, they had learned the lessons of colonial subjects immemorial—to make prisoners of their masters, prisoners of love, or something resembling it. Kennedy's German tour from June 23 to 26 was a bath in alien affections: flowers, fanfares, and fireworks. Bonn, Cologne, Frankfurt, and, the high point, Berlin. Brandt was on hand to soak up the New Frontier rays from the beginning and was rewarded with a breakfast *tete à tete* in Bad Godesberg. Kennedy had spent some time with Adenauer, of course, and heard the Conservative Chancellor assert that the Social Democrats were "not reliable," that they could "try to make a deal with the Russians"—shades of the secret Rapallo Treaty of 1922! He was curious about this the next day when he met Brandt again in Berlin. But in the rapture of the reception in the old Reich capital such dark reflections were fleeting. Kennedy surfed near the crest of a majestic wave of approval. It moved him, and he worked on his short West Berlin speech up until the last minute. Brandt and his aides had made sure there would be a good turnout. But even they were astounded by the biggest rally ever in front of his Rathaus. Kennedy had General Clay at his side again, after a year of humiliation for the American who so loved Berlin, and the President praised him again and again. Then he said that 2000 years before it had been the proudest claim of all to say, "I am a citizen of Rome," that today the proudest phrase of the free world was, "I am a Berliner." A few minutes later he declared in tones of a Roman senator: "Therefore, as a free man I am proud to say, *Ich bin ein Berliner.*" It was probably the most emotional moment of his political career, and, at the end of it, he confided to an aide, "As long as we live, we will never experience another day like this." He had conquered Berlin, and the Berliners had conquered him.[19] It was good for

Brandt. Kennedy had developed a special relationship with the Berlin Mayor that put old Adenauer in a twilight shadow.

Would it have made a difference in the German elections a year later if Kennedy had lived? Probably. In Brandt's thinking "The great day for Berlin"—the living Kennedy who had only five months to live—entrusted the Germans with a global task: "To participate in a policy which has the goal of overcoming sources of tension step by step. Naturally we must take part in this." He also remarked that

> the number one man of the West had declared that freedom was indivisible and he told the world that our generation of Germans, eighteen years after the war, had earned the right to be free, and that our people could lay claim to the right to live in unity, in a good sense, with everyone.[20]

These were themes he had touched on for many years, but now Brandt had incomparable endorsement from a powerful friend from abroad.

There was one other thread linking the two: the politics of the labor movement. Fritz Erler had visited Kennedy in May, and they had spoken of limited role Erhard would play in Germany and of the newly elected leader of the Labour Party in Britain, Harold Wilson. Kennedy conjectured that "the day of the Christian Democrats" in Europe was passing and a new phase was beginning in which German, British, and Scandinavian Social Democrats would play large roles.[21] Three weeks afterward Brandt polished the labor-Social Democratic link by attending a six-country meeting of trade unionists and Socialists in Stockholm including Walter P. Reuther from the United Automobile Workers, Hubert H. Humphrey, the Democratic Senator who participated as a representative of the Minnesota Democratic-Farmer-Labor Party, and Premier Tage Erlander of Sweden.

While Brandt was promoting his ideas in Stockholm, Egon Bahr, his aide and intimate, was doing the same in darkest Bavaria. The West Berlin press spokesman had been invited to speak on July 15 at the Evangelical Academy in Tutzing. His address became a kind of benchmark in the Brandt-SPD approach to Central European politics, mainly because of two phrases Bahr employed. One was *Wandel durch Annäherung*—"transformation through rapproachment"—describing a way of easing the sclerotic condition of the German split. The other was "a policy of small steps," which was also a Brandt usage. They coincided with Brandt's call for "permeation" of the barriers raised across the map of Germany and of Europe, a message that he had articulated in his Harvard lectures and that was now available in his latest book.[22] Bahr's *Wandel durch Annäherung* acquired a lasting place in the German political vocabulary.

A loosening up was discernible, too, on the Communist side. The Russians signed a partial nuclear test ban agreeement August 5 in Moscow, and Nikita Khrushchev went off to Yugoslavia to renew and strengthen ties with the onetime outcasts of the international Communist movement. But the venturesome spirit was not dead in the sixty-nine-year-old Soviet leader. On October 10, nearly a year after the Cuba missile contest, he authorized his border troops in East Germany to stop a United States military convoy at the Marienborn control point, 110 miles from West Berlin. The Americans refused a demand to get out of their vehicles and be counted. Two years before it had been a request with which Colonel Johns, in a hurry to get his battle group to Berlin, had complied. Now it was an order. A tug of war ensued, with Kennedy and Khrushchev the opposing anchormen at each end of a rope stretching 4873 miles from Washington to Moscow. After forty-eight hours and some prideful strutting between American and Soviet infantrymen, the Russians gave way and let the convoy pass into Berlin. A bluff, but a big one, and the first time the Berlin contingency planning by the United States had been put into practice. Brandt remarked a few weeks later: "War threatened in these October days. We reckoned any minute with a big bang at the gates of Berlin."[23]

Two deaths jolted Brandt in the last weeks of 1963. Both the shooting of Kennedy on November 22 and the decease of Erich Ollenhauer on December 14, after a protracted circulatory illness, strongly affected his political future. Kennedy had been living proof of generational change in the politics of the West and the viability of a fresh approach to international affairs. Ollenhauer was the last rallying point of the SPD old guard, a vivid symbol of its *Arbeiterverein* (workers' association) origins. With Kennedy gone, Brandt was on his own as a representative of New Frontier policies. With Ollenhauer gone, the SPD was freer to become what Brandt and Wehner had already charted as the future course of the party—an undoctrinaire reform organization appealing to all ranks of German society.

Brandt was among those attending the Kennedy funeral on November 25, and afterward, Jacqueline Kennedy asked him to visit her at the White House. She had heard that the large square in front of the Schöneberg Rathaus had just been renamed John F. Kennedy Platz. "How could you do it?" She asked softly, and then answered herself, "It's good that you did it." They talked of Berlin and what it came to mean to John Kennedy. Bobby Kennedy accompanied Brandt to his car and said in farewell: "He loved Berlin." As at the deaths of Julius Leber and again of Ernst Reuter, Brandt assumed a kind of moral-political obligation to the deceased. Concluding his memoir of his meetings with the Kennedy family, published in 1964, he wrote: "The torch of hope for a tormented mankind that slipped from the hand of John F. Kennedy must be carried on."[24]

Brandt was chosen acting party chairman immediately after Ollenhauer's death, and on February 16, 1964, he was formally elected to the post at a special SPD convention in Bad Godesberg. With Hamburg's Max Brauer again opposing him in unrelenting bitterness, he got 320 of the 334 delegate votes. Fritz Erler, the only serious rival for the chairmanship, received 319 votes as deputy chairman, and Herbert Wehner took the tandem deputyship. At last Brandt was both the chief of the party and its standard bearer as the candidate for Chancellor. His only nod to his predecessor as party chairman was a simple observation in the foreword to the SPD Yearbook for 1962-63: "Erich Ollenhauer remains for us a model of loyalty to ideals and fulfillment of duty." It was shortly after the hundredth anniversary of the Social Democratic Party, and Brandt continued: "This jubilee presents to the public the picture of a party that has completed, programmatically and in fact, a process of transformation toward becoming a party that is open to all strata of the nation."[25]

The SPD had changed profoundly in the course of four years. But the CDU was changing, too, against its will. Adenauer kept his promise to the Free Democrats and resigned October 11. Five days later his long-time deputy, Erhard, whom Adenauer had long since judged and found wanting, was installed as Chancellor in Bonn. He was saddled with a weakened Cabinet and, for the first time, a Vice Chancellor from the coalition—Erich Mende.

Willy Brandt's "small steps" had begun. On December 5 he received a letter from the East German Council of Ministers, indicating that it might be possible to arrange visits of West Berliners to their relatives in East Berlin. More than half the Berliners on each side of the wall had relatives on the opposite side, and nearly all of them had been cut off for twenty-eight months. After some initial friction Brandt received a go-ahead from Chancellor Erhard and authorized negotiations by a subordinate that concluded after seven rounds with a Christmastime passes agreement. From December 19 to January 5 more than 1 million crossed into East Berlin to see relatives. A wave of criticism followed in the right-wing press of West Germany, alleging that the deal implied "recognition" of the East German Government. But for the Berliners, humanitarian considerations were dominant and nearly everyone looked forward to more visitor pass agreements.

Throughout the spring and summer of 1964 there were other numerous signs that the Soviet leadership felt the time had come to make new peace overtures to West Germany. In June Erhard let the Russians know that if Khrushchev wanted to come to the Federal Republic he would be welcome, and in July, Aleksei Adzhubei, Khrushchev's journalist son-in-law, called in Bonn and was told the same thing. By early September it seemed that Khrushchev was ready to come. But he had apparently acted too hastily, and his flirtation with West Germany was to play a central role in his overthrow on October 14.

Still the conciliatory moves from the East continued. The DDR gave permission for its pensioners—men sixty-five and over and women of sixty— to visit relatives in West Germany. A new agreement for Berlin visits was settled, and in the fortnight spanning the end of October and the beginning of November some 600,000 West Berlin visitors were registered in East Berlin. There was a catch, of course: The East Germans wanted some official recognition and some money out of the arrangement. They began demanding that Berlin visitors change a minimum of three *Marks* (seventy-five cents) a day to enter the Soviet sector. West Germans were supposed to change five *Marks* a day. But the main point was that Germans were meeting Germans again. Understandably, Brandt made the passes agreements a theme of his address at the next regular convention of the SPD in Karlsruhe in late November:

> What concerns us next in the German question is making things easier for people and step by step changes. That was the point of the struggle for the passes . . . I hope it will come to further steps, if we don't allow ourselves to be held up by nitpicking. To hell with politics if it isn't there to make life easier for people instead of making it harder for them (strong applause). And what is good for the people in the divided country is good, too, for the nation. Official Bonn is scarcely aware that in recent months our nation has experienced the greatest all-German get together in years . . . I would be pleased if in the coming year, despite the domestic political tussle, we were able to bring off the necessary common sense to grab hold of these problems together in the interest of the people and in the interest of sticking together in national questions . . . You might say these are all just little steps. I reply: I'd like big ones more, but small steps are better than no steps.

There were other accents in Brandt's speech—some of them stronger than before, as in his friendly words about the "social" teachings of the modern Catholic and Protestant churches. Herbert Wehner had already done a lot of spadework in the garden of God. The ex-Communist had become a believing Christian and a registered Lutheran. Five weeks before the party convention

Wehner preached a sermon in Hamburg's ancient Michaelis Church to unbelieving multitudes. His was a political faith, as Luther's had been in part. But it was a faith nonetheless. Brandt, the self-seen nonbeliever, was no churchgoer either, and would never be one.[26] But he could recognize social concern when he met it.

Haunting Brandt and Wehner was the dilemma of another coalition choice after the 1965 elections. They were aware that as popular as Ludwig Erhard seemed to be, the CDU alliance with the Free Democrats was creaking under the strain. Franz Josef Strauss was out but not down—still ruling his Christian Social Union in Bavaria—and powerful enough to start party loyalty procedures against the emissary who had dared to negotiate with Wehner a year before about a possible CDU-SPD coalition. Brandt assured the Karlsruhe delegates: "After all that has happened there will be no place for him in a federal Cabinet headed by me. Joining up with Herr Strauss is thus not a matter for debate."[27] Strauss had long since become the bogeyman for the SPD, and at Karlsruhe one of the district delegations had submitted a resolution to the convention declaring him to be "intolerable for German politics." Wehner protested: "Children, do you have to do him the honor of making him the subject of a party resolution?"

It was a rather quiet convention. Brandt, Wehner, and Erler were overwhelmingly reconfirmed in their party posts. Afterward Brandt presented a shadow Cabinet, his future government in the event he won election. It included Erler and Wehner, of course, but also Professor Karl Schiller, his hotshot economist from Hamburg; Alex Möller, a successful businessman in his own right; Helmut Schmidt, who had demonstrated organizational talent in taming a destructive flood in Hamburg; and Käte Strobel, a tough little woman who had become a legislative expert on price policies. Brandt was especially generous in praise of his two deputies: the "brilliant" Erler and, Herbert Wehner, "a motor of many cylinders—the forward thrusting force in the small and large questions of organization and policy—with all his edges, he has become very dear to our hearts." Rut and Willy had visited Herbert and Lotte Wehner the previous summer—the first and only time—at their vacation retreat on the Swedish island of Öland, and in the fall Brandt told an interviewer who asked about his relationship with Wehner: "It took a little time 'til we got closer to each other as people. We have become good friends.'"[28]

The SPD was growing, now boasting 700,000 members—half of them workers. From Karlsruhe, election prospects looked bright, and Brandt boasted, "It is certain that we can win." He was looking better, too, younger at fifty than at forty-eight. He was getting more exercise, and he looked trim. But the Berlin crisis years had taken a toll; his eating and drinking habits and his chain-smoking had also left marks.

Away from the convention hall, Brandt's 1965 election campaign had an air of doom almost from the beginning. Even before it was all over there were journalists and political analysts arguing that the chemistry of Brandt versus Erhard was such that the Berlin Mayor could not possibly emerge from the retort as the dominant element. "Against Chancellor Erhard . . . the wrong candidate with the wrong propaganda," said an Erhard man, and he was right.[29] An image study done for the CDU before the campaign showed Germans thought of Erhard as a kind of father figure, or a priest, or even a "prince of the church." Brandt came off as a roughneck or a climber.

Ludwig Erhard had spent sixteen years in Bonn, and he was known far and wide as "the father of the *Wirtschaftswunder*" for his role in the 1948 currency reform. He was sixty-seven years old, a picture of comfortable German prosperity, thick set, white haired, usually puffing a big cigar—a kind of man difficult to dislike. Adenauer, however, hated him for his apparent helplessness in the face of complicated political decisions. But in the relative calm and contentment of West German life over the previous two years Erhard seemed the epitome of solidity. "Sure is sure," ran his campaign slogan, a variant on the Adenauer parole: "No Experiments!" He was mightily assisted with the by-now familiar underground CDU campaign picturing Brandt again as a wartime traitor and a Red.

What could Brandt do? Berlin had been his destiny, and Berlin, in the West German mind, conjured up visions of uncertainty, threats, risks. It was all very well to have the brave young Mayor there standing up to the Commies, standing off the West Berlin hotheads. But what advantage was that for a Chancellor in Bonn? There was a flurry in early April when the East Germans retaliated against what they termed the "illegal" convening of the Bundestag in West Berlin. Some of the Bonn deputies were turned back when they tried to drive through to the split city. Brandt himself was refused the right of transit on April 4. Was this a benefit for the West German campaign? Besides, he and his aides had already agreed that it was not the occasion to go to the hustings on foreign policy issues.

True, his handlers, chief among them Klaus Schütz and Egon Bahr, had abandoned the Kennedy campaigning mold, which had never fitted Brandt or Germany anyway. No more the sporty suits and the hats and the white convertible. No more the emotional appeals for "blue skies over the Ruhr," as in 1961. But they stuffed him full of ecological, technological, and scientific phrases just the same as part of their domestic issues package.

Horst Ehmke, then a thirty-eight-year-old SPD lawyer, remembered him coming to Freiburg im Breisgau, the university town: "He had drunk a lot on the train, and Schütz told him to talk about science and he started off: 'The technology gap . . . up there is the Sputnik. We have to get into space, too.' Then he lost the thread. Suddenly he roared: 'The Federal Republic is not a great power, but a great power of the spirit!' I was sitting next to two masons, and one said to the other, 'You know how Willy speaks? As though he has to shit bricks.'"[30]

Wehner had pleaded with Brandt to divest himself of his Berliners and try to adapt himself to the different ground of the Federal Republic. But he wouldn't hear of it. "He did exactly the opposite," Wehner growled. "It was all Berlin. I could do nothing but clench my teeth."[31]

The Berliners had talked Brandt into another innovation—enlisting some of Germany's successful writers as drummers for the SPD. Günter Grass, who had published two best-sellers, *Dog Years* and *The Tin Drum,* showed up at the Karlsruhe convention and became an SPD supporter on the spot. He began campaigning for Brandt on his own in July. By August there were ten fairly well-known authors pitching in for Brandt with gags and slogans. Erhard mocked them as "little *Pinschers,*" a phrase that stirred great waves of indignation among the German intelligentsia, who were rather a conceited lot anyway. But Erhard probably garnered more votes from this exchange than Brandt. For Germans—unlike Americans, British, French, and others—were slow to change especially so in their unique situation of division, semi-occupation status, and unresolved history. Willy Brandt and his intellectuals were out of step in almost all respects.

He had spoken during his annual spring visit to New York of the need for a German "national identity." "No people can live without pride. This is as true for Germany as it is for any other people."[32] That was all very well. But at that time the Federal Republic had just taken up diplomatic relations with Israel, and all but three Arab states broke ties with Bonn. When West Germany's first Ambassador arrived in Tel Aviv in August there were anti-German demonstrations. A week later the Auschwitz trial ended in Frankfurt with six former SS officers sentenced to life imprisonment, and eleven others to lesser terms. How could ordinary Germans develop a sense of national pride with such events taking place?

There was, in fact, a dearth of issues that could divert the majority of the West Germans from the pleasures of their summer vacations. In August Brandt tried to enliven the campaign by declaring that, if elected, he would make a bid for negotiations with the Soviet Union on a German settlement. But there was no notable response. Nor could he bring himself to make a very strong pitch. It was not in him. Instead, he favored that curiously distant manner he had already cultivated in his "as told to" autobiography, speaking

of himself in the third person. "He who speaks to you here," he would begin
("*Der der hier spricht*"). It was not electrifying.

Nor were the polls very promising. Some showed him to be less popular
than the SPD itself, and others indicated that young voters, in whom Brandt
was placing so much confidence, were not overly enthusiastic about him. As
election day drew nearer, opinion surveys showed him neck and neck with
Erhard. But the CDU was not deceived, and in early August Erhard felt
confident enough to declare that he would not even consider a coalition with
Brandt. The Mayor was getting a bad press even where he might have
expected to gain some support. *Der Spiegel* sent its feature writer, Hermann
Schreiber, around to put together a Brandt portrait. He wrote in what had
already become the classic *Spiegel* style of patronizing sweet-sour nihilism,
portraying Brandt as a political *Doppelgänger* who was "cop and robber at the
same time." A hatchet job with a toy hatchet, *Der Spiegel's* hallmark.[33] Yet
Brandt faced September 19 with confidence, perhaps believing his own hopes
that the Germans were growing and changing their habits.

They *were* changing. But not as fast as he thought. The federal election
brought what he regarded as a crushing defeat. Erhard won 47.6 percent of the
32 million votes cast, Brandt 39.3 percent. The "People's Chancellor," as
Erhard had begun to call himself, outstripped Adenauer's 1961 showing by
more than 1 million votes. Brandt had gained an equal surplus. But he was not
to be consoled. "The people voted against me, and not against the party," he
told Helmut Schmidt a week later. Nor did it interest him much that the SPD
had made surprising inroads in geographic regions and social groupings
where it had been anathema. There were gains in the traditionally
Conservative areas of Rhineland-Palatinate, Bavaria, and the Saar, gains
among Catholics and Protestants, women and the elderly—a promising trend
for the party future.

Brandt was not to be moved. "I am going to remain in Berlin," he told his
SPD comrades, "and I am not going to be a candidate for the office of Federal
Chancellor in the 1969 election. Do your own dirty work."[34] He wouldn't
listen to Wehner, who asked him to come to Bonn and take over the SPD
Bundestag whip post from Fritz Erler. "Wehner wanted Brandt to stay here
and Erler to go to Berlin," Helmut Schmidt recalled. "Erler didn't want to
switch either—he felt he had worked hard enough. I told Brandt, 'Do what you
like. Keep the party chairmanship. Follow your own inclination.' He wanted
to go back to Berlin. He was hurt, not by the campaign, but by defeat."[35] Klaus
Schütz was there, too, and he remembered: "Brandt didn't expect a majority.
But when the CDU got more than he counted on, it disappointed him deeply.
However, Willy Brandt is a man who often says he's 'had a noseful,' that it
makes him want to puke. I don't want to belittle his resignation in '65. But it

wasn't that, really. He didn't resign. He never thought to give up the party chairmanship. He didn't hang that up on the hook."[36] But he felt really low for a long time, and not much was heard of him until the following year.

It wasn't that bad a life. He still had his chairman's office in Bonn, renovated after Ollenhauer's death with metal, teak, and plastic. In Berlin there was his six-bedroom house in the Grunewald beside a spacious garden and a swimming pool shared with the senate's guesthouse. There were *Gartenzwerge* (lawn decorations) made to look like Adenauer, de Gaulle, and Khrushchev. There were pets, a poodle and a cat. Inside there were books— Brandt was always reading biographies—and a large television set. There was Rut, who led her own life but was available when he needed her. There were Peter, Lars, and Matthias, and he could talk politics with the oldest, who was just turning seventeen. Now and then Ninja came down from Oslo. He had begun to turn from cigarettes to cigarillos and from liquor to wine and beer. November, the season of his annual depressions, was near, and he was in surroundings where his moods were tolerated. Associates believed that in the quiet hours, he had talked to Rut about packing it all in and going back to Norway.[37]

In the spring of 1966 he began a therapeutic research into his own past. The inspiration came largely from his experiences in "the dirty campaign" of the previous summer, when cars with loudspeakers had driven about the Ruhr towns broadcasting the slogan, "We don't elect traitors!" and biplanes towed banners reading: "Where was Brandt in 1948?—in Safety!" and the familiar smear literature made its rounds. His speech-writing aide, Günter Struve, a boyish blond half Brandt's age, had the idea of putting together a selection of Brandt's writings from émigré days. Out came the old sea chest in which Brandt kept some of his personal effects and memorabilia. Over the next six months the two of them combed through the newspaper clippings, mimeographed SAP resolutions, yellowed letters, protocols of exile meetings, handwritten notes—the record of twelve years of work and life outside Germany. He found to his pleasure that the writings spoke for themselves, that "I do not need to justify my actions to anyone," as he wrote in the foreword to the English edition of the exile writings.

He also found that his émigré works showed: "I was not against Germany, but against her despoilers. I didn't break with Germany, rather I was moved by concern for our nation. I didn't choose the easy way, rather I risked my neck more than once. . . ." The election defeat moved him to reflection, he wrote in the postscript:

I often asked myself: Don't you have to try to comprehend those who plainly have such a hard time understanding you, even though they have not exactly handled me with kid gloves? Perhaps it is easier for me since September 1965, which I regard as a sort of watershed.[38]

Finally, there was the attraction for Brandt, the journalist, of making use again of some earlier work—a temptation few journalists resist.

Out of this came *Draussen (Outside)*, a 383-page collection from exile days, published in August 1966. It was organized thematically under chapter headings like: "What Comes After the War?" "Opposition in Conflict," "For and Against the 'Other Germany,'" and "Spain." As a result there was confusion for anyone seeking chronological order. But there were ample footnotes relating some of the wilder accusations against Brandt over the previous twenty-eight years to the factual evidence supplied by his writings.

He was buoyed, too, by a surprising turn of German politics. Ludwig Erhard had taken his resounding election victory as a mandate to proclaim a new policy, which he termed the goal of a *formierte Gesellschaft*—a structured society—whatever that meant. Some Leftists saw in it the seeds of Fascism. But Erhard was in office only two months when blows fell on him from the ranks of his own CDU. First, President Heinrich Lübke stepped out of line from his supposedly nonpartisan office in the Villa Hammerschmidt and declared himself in favor of a "big coalition" between the SPD and the CDU— a most unusual act for a Conservative.

Then old Konrad Adenauer declared that while he was stepping down from what he had treated as the largely ceremonial post of chairman of the CDU, he didn't think Erhard should succeed him. The hunt was on. Rainer Barzel, only forty-one years old, but filled with ambition, declared his candidacy for the chairmanship. A fight ensued, which Erhard won in March at the cost of having to take on Barzel as deputy CDU chairman. From his Bavarian exile Franz Josef Strauss was also pulling strings in Bonn to help topple Erhard. Hardly a week passed without a new foe appearing on Erhard's horizon. In April it was General de Gaulle, who had withdrawn French forces from the NATO command two months before. Now de Gaulle was insisting that the Germans choose, in effect, between their allies in Washington and their friends in Paris. Erhard and Foreign Minister Gerhard Schröder were sworn *Atlantiker,* and said so. This annoyed not only the General, but also Franz Josef Strauss and his sometime CSU colleague, Baron von Guttenberg, who favored the "European" orientation of the French. When de Gaulle came to Bonn in July for talks within the framework of the friendship treaty sealed between him and Adenauer two years before, he and Erhard did not hit it off at all.

Brandt and Wehner noticed the shifting winds, too, and decided to tack to them. Not that their sails billowed out immediately. Wehner was under fire from an anonymous SPD journalist who accused him of turning the SPD into "a Bolshevist party."[39] He was indignant—as in 1957 when various European newspapers charged that he had been a wartime "Comintern agent" in Sweden—and bitter because he felt nobody came to his aid. "I was completely without protection," he murmured to a friend. "No one helped me. I was down, dragged through the gutters and alleys, and Brandt was up on the crest of the wave again."[40] But in Berlin Brandt was having his own difficulties over the fourth round of negotiations on passes for visits to East Berlin. There had been more than 800,000 West Berlin visits in the Soviet sector at Christmas. Now, however, the Communists were demanding more acknowledgment of their thesis that West Berlin was an "entity" separate from West Germany. The last passes agreement was completed in March, and at Easter about 500,000 visitors crossed into East Berlin.

Something else was afoot. On February 7 Walter Ulbricht addressed a letter to the Social Democratic Party leadership proposing a discussion of the situation in Germany. It was the fourteenth such letter sent by the SED to the SPD since 1951. The previous thirteen "open letters" had gone unanswered, and it seems Ulbricht did not expect a response. But this time Wehner and Brandt took it upon themselves to reply, and in March they voiced willingness to join in a dialogue with Ulbricht. Two more letters were exchanged between late March and mid-April. Erhard and Mende were disturbed by what they rightly saw as a flanking maneuver that was bound to undercut if not discredit their government. Late in May SPD-SED agreement was reached. There would be a "speaker exchange" with Brandt, Wehner, and Erler traveling to Karl-Marx-Stadt (Chemnitz) to talk in public on July 14 and a group of yet unnamed SED officials coming to Hannover a week later on the return round. The prospect thrilled Germans on both sides of the national dividing line. It also unnerved Ulbricht, and it caused Wehner to wonder whether his former comrades might seize the opportunity to take him prisoner inside East Germany.

This was the setting as Willy Brandt went before the SPD national convention in Dortmund at the beginning of June. His speech on the first day was something new, a crystalization of his self-therapy. It was entitled "The State of the Nation," and it, too, articulated a way of looking at things that had not occurred to the Germans before.

> No people can endure without losing its inner equilibrium, without stumbling in the moments of internal and external challenges, if it does not say *ja* to the fatherland. We Germans are not allowed to

forget history. But we cannot constantly run around with confessions of guilt—the younger generation even less than the older.

The last Social Democrat to talk about "Fatherland" in a positive sense had been Ernst Reuter, a fortnight before he died in 1953:

Why in heaven's don't we say for the hundredth time that we are struggling for the reunification of our fatherland with peaceful means—at the risk that we actually use the word "fatherland," which wouldn't be so bad for Social Democrats.

Reuter was speaking, however, in private to a group of SPD politicians.[41]

The SPD-SED speakers exchange was the dominant theme at the convention. It seemed to inspire Brandt, who exuded self-assurance as he spoke about the inflation-recession trend afflicting German workers for the first time in years. He sounded confident, too, as he spoke about the 1965 election and the possibility of coalition with the CDU. Wehner also spoke with an assurance scarcely matched in his previous appearances. There was a refreshing amount of laughter at the convention. On June 4, the fourth day at Dortmund, Willy Brandt was reelected chairman with 324 of 329 votes. The delegates gave him a long, standing ovation. Wehner and Erler were also reaffirmed by huge majorities. For the first time in more than a decade it seemed the SPD had a sense of purpose, a feeling of unity, and a determined leadership. The atmosphere of hope against hope had evaporated at last.[42] Two weeks later the speakers exchange collapsed. The pretext? The East Germans found unacceptable the Erhard government's stipulation that their speakers would have to be accorded a specially decreed "free passage" to West Germany, guaranteeing them against prosecution as Communists—a nasty variant of the Hallstein Doctrine, the Ulbricht leadership maintained. But it seems the Russians had also become nervous about the exercise, and Pyotr A. Abrasimov, the Soviet Ambassador to East Germany, said as much to Mayor Brandt when they met at a reception in the Swedish mission in West Berlin.[43]

On July 14, the day Brandt, Wehner, and Erler were supposed to have appeared in Karl-Marx-Stadt, the three made their speeches anyway on radio and television from Bonn. Brandt told the national audience their intention had been to "talk about Germany and what is possible today if people on both sides exert a minimum of goodwill."

Wehner amplified the theme:

Each party will be judged by history whether it had done everything humanly possible, or failed to find forms for living side

by side in divided Germany which are beneficial for the people.
. . . We say plainly that we do not want to become Communist. But
we also say what we are ready and able to do, so that the people in
Germany find their peace, without our demanding that the
Communists must cease being Communists beforehand. That is an
element of peace policy in and around Germany, as Willy Brandt
explained.[44]

Ulbricht and company looked rather foolish on this day, having started the
idea of an exchange and then broken off at the decisive moment. For the first
time since 1933 it seemed the Social Democrats held the initiative in the
eternal contest with the Communists. It was in line with Brandt's convictions.
He had listened to Ernst Reuter speaking of the potential of West Berlin in
the blockade days, when the danger seemed greatest, as "an arrow in the flesh"
of East Germany and later as "the handle with which the door to the East can
be opened." Reuter, too, thought of West German-West Berlin politics as a
way of *influencing* the political developments of East Germany. In a sense he
was right. Germany never was totally divided and is not so today. Whatever
happened of significance in the West had its mirror image in the East, usually
after some delay and usually with some distortion. The same was true in the
East to West direction. Was there repression of writers in the East? You could
expect something like it in the West. Were there youth riots in the West,
youth unrest would follow in the East. Conservatism here meant
Conservatism there. It was a rule of thumb.

The Social Democrats deliberately chose Dortmund in the heart of North
Rhine-Westphalia, for the 1966 convention. There were fully 200,000 SPD
members in the state, and in a month there would be a critical election in this
most populous and most heavily industrialized state of West Germany. The
party hoped to profit from the "creeping inflation" that had sent prices up by
close to 5 percent, put 100,000 workers out of jobs, and piled up huge heaps of
unsold coal, the lifeblood of the Ruhr. When Chancellor Erhard came
campaigning to Gelsenkirchen on the eve of the election he was shouted down
so lustily by angry coal workers who feared pit closings that he had to depart
without speaking.

On July 10 the North Rhine-Westphalia voters dealt the CDU a stunning
blow, cutting the Erhard party's share from 46.4 percent ot 42.7 percent and
raising the Social Democrats to 49.5 percent. Brandt's party came within a
hairbreadth of ruling the state. It was a deathknell for Erhard, the "rubber
lion," as his detractors had begun to call him. Only after excruciating delays
was the CDU able to muster a state government coalition with the FDP,
parallel to that in Bonn.

If that were not enough, looming on Erhard's coalition horizon was a dispute over the new federal budget, which was based on heavy deficit spending. The administration was also under attack from Bundeswehr generals and admirals because of plans to let soldiers become members of the Public Service Workers Trade Union.

Willy Brandt was also having some trouble with the military traditions of Germany. Günter Grass, the novelist, had invited Brandt's sons, Peter and Lars, to play small parts in the filming of his novel, *Cat and Mouse*. Peter already considered himself something of a Left radical, much as his father had been in 1932 at the same age, and it pleased him to perform in a role that mocked militarism. The part called for him and Lars to play with a *Ritterkreuz*—one of the highest German military decorations. German Army officers and the Conservative press had a field day, accusing Brandt of indulging a denigration of German bravery.

"The kids wanted to perform in the movie, and I didn't want to say no," Brandt told SPD comrades who had raised doubts about the film. A party man who attended an executive session where these questions were raised recalled: "Women in the executive said, 'Your sons are a burden for the party—if you can't handle them, send them to private school, as others do, to Switzerland.' Others said, '*Ja, Ja.*' Willy replied, 'You can decide that, if you want. But then you will have a new party chairman if you put the choice to me between being father and being party chairman. Then the choice is easy.' It strengthened his authority and he could only do that because he wasn't trying to be Chancellor."[45]

In August the Social Democrats called on Erhard to resign. Brandt repeated the demand several times, but on August 27 he also declared that the SPD would not join in a coalition with the CDU. Meanwhile, three senior generals had resigned in the dispute over trade union membership for soldiers, and the Defense Minister was in trouble also, because the German version of the *Starfighter* was falling out of the sky almost as often as it flew: thirty-six pilot deaths in sixty-three crashes.

By mid-September there was a full government crisis. One of the Chancellor's political advisers resigned on September 19, a week before Erhard set off for Washington for talks with President Johnson. Rainer Barzel, the young challenger in the CDU, declared: "A boat that has sprung a leak needs people to row and bail and an energetic captain." But Erhard was not energetic. He was merely decent, and that was not enough. President Lyndon Johnson, who was feeling the bite of Vietnam War expenditures, gave Erhard no respite either. He demanded that West Germany increase arms purchases to help offset the cost of stationing American troops in Germany. The Chancellor explained that he had his own financial problems at home and could not meet the demand. Though he was supported on this stand to some extent by the Social Democrats, the last of his pillars abroad collapsed.

On October 2 Konrad Adenauer openly backed Eugen Gerstenmaier, the president of the Bonn Bundestag, as a replacement for the Chancellor. Axel Springer's papers joined in the hue and cry against Erhard. There was a Social Democratic censure motion against him on October 5.

Willy Brandt was keeping a weather eye on Bonn. But he was also busy in Berlin. He had made the acquaintance of Pyotr Abrasimov, the Soviet Ambassador to the DDR in June at a reception organized by Sven Backlund, the Swedish Consul General, who was a born Social Democrat and a born diplomat. Backlund had arranged for them to meet again in late September, and now a third meeting was set up. Brandt crossed into East Berlin for dinner with Abrasimov on October 12—the first time he had gone to the Soviet sector in an official capacity since 1960. They talked for five hours. A few days later Erhard flew to West Berlin to chide Brandt for being too chummy with the Russians and undercutting his own attempts to begin a dialogue with the Soviet Government.

Overworked and fatigued Brandt had a severe coughing spell October 23 (cigarettes?) followed by a sensation of suffocation, and pains in the region of his heart. It was diagnosed at a Berlin clinic as the Roemheld syndrome, a gastrocardial condition created when gaseous inflation of the stomach pushes the diaphragm against the heart, and a fairly common affliction of German males.[46] "I saw death eye to eye," Brandt said later. Along with the experience of the election defeat of 1965 and the sense of satisfaction he acquired from looking through his émigré writings, it contributed to what a young admirer called "his inner serenity."[47] So it was that he remained in Berlin as the hour of reckoning came for the Erhard government.

It is difficult to know just what moved Erich Mende in the last week of October 1966. He was Vice Chancellor under Erhard. He had an ambitious wife; he had girlfriends. He had powerful supporters in the business world. He had friends among the "young Turks" of the Free Democratic Party who thought Liberals could say more than just "Amen" to the policies of the CDU. He had a *Ritterkreuz* from the war for "bravery in the face of the enemy." Yet Mende, the "handsome Erich" with his coiffeured silver sideburns below his curly dark locks, had become a waverer, and he was tempted by the blandishments of the CDU's equally opportunistic Rainer Barzel and pushed to a decision by his FDP colleague Walter Scheel.[48]

When Chancellor Erhard presented his budget, with a projected deficit of over 5 billion marks ($1.3 billion) and substantial tax increases, the Free

Democrats refused to go along. On October 27 the four Free Democrat Cabinet ministers quit the coalition, and the tent collapsed on Erhard. For the time being the Chancellor headed a minority government, while Mende and Barzel plotted a succession. But it was not to be so simple. The CDU was sharply divided between anti-Gaullist pro-Americans, and those who favored the European policies of the French President. Neither faction had any abiding affection for the conniving Barzel, who had begun as a "Left" CDU man and then had swung sharply to the Right. Besides, it was Barzel, everyone knew, who organized the effort to unseat Erhard. There were enough CDU men loyal to the Chancellor to block Barzel from succeeding the man he sought to topple.

A kind of free-for-all began that paralyzed the Erhard caretaker government for four weeks. The CDU fielded four alternative Chancellor candidates. The SPD and FDP leadership were each weighing the viability of going for or against the CDU. A new factor was injected when the neo-Nazi National Democratic Party headed by Adolf (Bubi) von Thadden won nearly 8 percent of the vote in the Hesse election and, with that, representation in th state's *Landtag*. (Most commentators, however, interpreted the sudden, united success of the far Right as a protest against the dallying in Bonn.)

On November 10, in voting in the CDU, Kurt Georg Kiesinger, the dark horse, came from behind to beat out Rainer Barzel, Foreign Minister Gerhard Schröder, and Adenauer's trusty aide, Walter Hallstein, with 137 of the 254 votes. Kiesinger had left Bonn eleven years before at the request of Adenauer to become *Minister-Präsident* of his home state of Baden-Württemburg, leaving behind him a reputation as an orator on foreign policy issues. As governor of that state he built up a new reputation as a *Landesvater,* a patriarch cast in the mild mold of his Swabian countrymen. He was sixty-two years old.

It was his very absence from the cut-and-thrust of Bonn politics that recommended him to the CDU, and Kiesinger, relatively fluent in both French and English, was identified neither with Gaullist nor the Anglo-Saxon factions of his party. There was one blemish. Despite his Catholic upbringing and his affection for the more romantic and metaphysical of the German poets—Lenau, Mörike, and Hölderlin—Kurt Georg Kiesinger had been a Nazi. He joined the NSDAP in 1933 and stayed in it through the war, serving as an official of the Reich Foreign Ministry of Joachim von Ribbentrop. Exoneration came in the form of a "soap ticket" (*Persilschein*) from American denazification authorities indicating that he had been denounced at the end of the war by two Foreign Ministry colleagues as "anti-Nazi," a fact unearthed from American archives by a busy journalist, Conrad Ahlers of *Der Spiegel*.[49] As irony would have it, however, it was Franz Josef Strauss who proved to be Kiesinger's principal backer in the November 10 vote in which Swabian emerged as the choice to succeed Erhard. In exchange for the Bavarian votes he controlled, Strauss demanded that Kiesinger take a Gaullist line, which he did, immediately. Then the haggling began in earnest.

Erich Mende, swinging like a pendulum, spoke of coalition with Willy Brandt on one side and with Kiesinger on the other. A CDU-FDP coalition at this stage would still hold a commanding 294-vote majority in the 496-member Bundestag. A SPD-FDP coalition would have a skimpy majority of three votes. "In fact I would have regarded an alliance with the Free Democrats as a good thing then—if it had been possible," Brandt wrote almost eight years later.

> That it was not possible resulted, for me, not merely from information concerning the attitude one might expect from a couple of FDP deputies at that time in a (parliamentary) vote for the Chancellor, but mainly from the discussion about economic and social policy issues.[50]

Erhard reeled between humiliations and betrayals. Herbert Wehner demanded that the Bundestag require the Chancellor to face a confidence vote, which Erhard surely would have lost. His tongue was like a whip, flicking a balky draft horse:

> The truth is, ladies and gentlemen, that we are dealing with the liquidation of a policy that has failed. That is painful for those who had placed great hopes in this policy. . . . If you wanted to paste together a government that would merely muck its way through as you have done in the last few weeks, the next crisis would already be in sight. You are provoking the permanent crisis, ladies and gentlemen, and you don't help yourselves. I have no advice to give you there—as a party in that way. That's your business. But think about the Federal Republic of Germany, that it doesn't lie on an island . . . We in divided Germany must prove ourselves in democracy. It's getting serious now. Up to today it was just a ceremony in these matters.[51]

The vote on November 8 to compel Erhard to move was 255 to 246—some CDU deputies went along with the SPD and FDP—but Erhard refused to buckle, yet.

Brandt was spending most of his time in Berlin, leaving Wehner to manage the delicate coalition negotiations, but he was not entirely passive. Noting that West Berlin had fifteen Social Democratic deputies and one Free

Democrat, he revived Ernst Reuter's old idea of obtaining full voting rights for the Berliners in the Bonn Bundestag. It had been opposed originally by Adenauer, who knew his parliamentary arithmetic in 1949. But in 1966 it was the Western Allies who fought the proposal, on the ground it would undermine what remained of the fragile four-power authority and their right to be in Berlin at all. On November 14 a disappointed Brandt accused the United States Embassy of "meddling" in German domestic affairs—by denying the Berliners the right to participate in the coming vote for a new Chancellor.[52]

Next day Kiesinger began talking officially with Wehner about a "big coalition" in Bonn. Mende and his Free Democrats concluded a three-hour meeting with the decision to renew their bid to the SPD for a "small" coalition. It was more than just a feint. Mende was frantic, recognizing that he had unleashed forces that could cut him off from power completely. It was a situation of which his wife would say later, "Erich and I wrestled all night in bed." But he had maneuvered himself into a position where he was barred from working with the CDU because it wanted to raise taxes and barred from coalition with the SPD because he couldn't deliver enough votes.

Brandt stayed on in Berlin. He received Ambassador Abrasimov on November 22 at the official West Berlin guesthouse next door to his villa to talk about the future of the city and East-West relations, including the need for a new intracity passes agreement.

Finally between November 24 and 25 the crisis in Bonn reached its climax. Mende pulled out of the negotiations with Kiesinger and declared that the Social Democrats would have to decide whether they wanted a coalition in which Brandt would be Chancellor—with the FDP— or merely be "carried along" as the junior partner of the CDU. But he did not reckon with Wehner, who called him a "male madam," who had viewed the FDP with deepest suspicion for more than a year, and who had in mind the longer-term aim of proving at last that the Social Democrats were *regierungsfähig,* capable of governing, after so many years in the political deserts of Germany.

The bargain was struck without Willy Brandt, who spent the evening of November 24 in Berlin because the airplanes were grounded by fog. Wehner continued negotiating without him, and Brandt arrived after seven hours of driving from Berlin. "All right," he growled about the pending final round with the CDU to seal the pact, "go ahead and do it, but without me." Wehner admonished him: "It is 2:30 a.m. At 9:30 you have to wash, shave, and go to Kiesinger."

"Suddenly, he decided," Wehner continued. "But I had to try it on a completely different basis. I had proceeded from the idea that he would take part in the government, but not in a too consuming position like Foreign

Minister, so that he would not be swallowed up. I thought, Science Minister, Science, Education, and Research, and he agreed. Then all at once, he changed his mind, and he said he would only take part as Foreign Minister. That was something very different, something not so good for his real role as the party leader."[53] Helmut Schmidt remembered it in 1973 this way: "He didn't lead the party, and he doesn't do so today. He didn't want the big coalition. He didn't have the connection to Guttenberg or Strauss, just a little bit to Schröder. He was dragged into the whole affair."[54] Another participant recalled: "He took the big coalition as a gift."[55] In the end, however, the party supported him in his request to enter the coalition as Foreign Minister.[56]

Before the final collapse, some of Mende's colleagues decided to rescue what they could for the FDP. Chief among them were Walter Scheel, who had already been a Cabinet minister in the coalitions of Adenauer and Erhard, and Willi Weyer, the hefty FDP man who was minister of interior in the curious little coalition with the CDU that had existed in North Rhine-Westphalia since the previous summer. Rather than have the big coalition repeat itself in that one state, where the elimination of the FDP would mean the end of the Liberals, Scheel and Weyer chose to save what could be saved. Remembering that the SPD had won 49.5 percent of the vote there in July, and the FDP a still presentable 7.4 percent, they offered to make a "little" coalition in Düsseldorf with the local SPD leader, Heinz Kühn. The deal was completed at 3 a.m., November 26, after the conspirators had drunk their usual rounds in several taverns between federal and state capitals.

Later that Saturday Brandt and Kiesinger announced their agreement to form a big coalition in Bonn, with Brandt as Vice Chancellor. They met in Schaumburg Palace, the building occupied by the Federal Chancellery, and shook hands in front of the photographers—Brandt with tousled hair and tight lips, looking as though he was making a necessary truce with a Fascist in the year 1939, Kiesinger with an almost feline smile, as though he couldn't believe his own luck. They stood Brandt on a suitcase to make him the same height as the 6-foot-3-inch Kiesinger. Both wore dark suits and gray ties— Brandt's plain and Kiesinger's striped. As formal as foes could be, they toasted each other with *Sekt,* the sparkling wine that serves as the German ersatz for champagne. Brandt's demand to be Foreign Minister was still not public knowledge. But he declared firmly that the new coalition was "a partnership for a limited time," meaning until the next national elections in 1969. It was more than a threat.

IX:
Foreign Minister

As a genre the Foreign Ministers of Germany had been a rather poor lot over the previous hundred years—with few exceptions. There had been Walter Rathenau in 1922, who was brilliant, but he was shot and killed by a proto-Nazi posse. There had been the Europe-minded Gustav Stresemann, who died of exhaustion in 1929. But the rest, by and large, were aristocrats, bureaucrats, toadies, and opportunists. Many had fine-sounding names—von Bülow, von Bismarck-Schönhausen, von Richtofen, von Tschirshky, von Kiderlin-Wächter, von Kühlmann—but they were little more than rubber stamps for more powerful men. Others, von Neurath, and von Ribbentrop, ended up war criminals.

It had been the habit of Chancellor Otto von Bismarck to act as his own Foreign Minister in the days of the German Reich, and it was a custom Chancellor Adenauer reverted to until 1955 in form and, afterward, in substance until his retirement in 1963. His deputies, Heinrich von Brentano and Gerhard Schröder made no mark as long as he was Chancellor. Only under Erhard was Schröder able to make a few modest moves for himself in the direction of East Europe, with offers of "renunciation of force" agreements and the opening of some trade missions.

Kurt Georg Kiesinger had made a career of foreign affairs. He would have liked to resume the Bismarck practice, and he tried as best he could. But in Willy Brandt, his coalition partner, Vice Chancellor, and Foreign Minister, he had a rival of incomparable strength. Unlike Kiesinger, who had spent his *Auswärtiges Amt* (Foreign Office) years in grim obscurity, Brandt had been moving in international policy circles for almost three decades—at first in the limited circles of the émigré Left, to be sure, but later in the salons and offices of the mighty. From both milieus he had an inestimable number of acquaintances, comrades, and admirers: the bulk of the Scandinavian Social Democratic leaders who were now serving as Prime Ministers and Cabinet members; Belgium's Paul Henri Spaak; Britain's Wilson; France's de Gaulle;

America's Johnson and Rusk; not to mention Yugoslavs, Italians, Israelis, and even Indians and Japanese. Brandt also had the benefit of being the elected head of a strong and growing party, while Kiesinger was the desperation choice of a party racked by factionalism and gone soft at the head.

Not that it was so simple for Brandt, nor did he expect it to be, despite the obvious advantages he brought to the post. "He who has a sense of history will not lightly overlook the fact that a man of my origin and my convictions has become the German Minister of Foreign Affairs," he said.[1]

Across Germany there were demonstrations against Social Democratic participation in the new coalition—one of them in West Berlin, featuring Peter Brandt, who had been deliberately wearing ragged clothes for several years and now actively identified with the militant Left. Günter Grass also declared his opposition in an angry diatribe. Even within the party some dissension surfaced. There had been a tempestuous 10-hour session of the SPD executive the evening of November 26, before the majority approved coalition with the CDU. When Kiesinger faced election in the Bundestag on December 1, after Erhard's resignation, more than fifty Social Democratic deputies voted against his Chancellorship. But for the SPD leaders, scarred with the knowledge that their party had not shared power in a German Government since 1930, it was an emotional hour. Upon being named Minister of All-German Affairs, Wehner embraced his second wife, who was also an ex-Communist and ex-émigré. "Lotte . . . Lotte," he said in a choked voice. In all the SPD took over nine of the twenty Cabinet posts.

Although it was a dream job for him, Brandt had some misgivings, principally about moving to tight, little Bonn, where he was still something of a stranger, from big, wide Berlin, where he felt at home. Once flying back to the former Reich capital and gazing at the vast gleaming lake of metropolitan lights at dusk, he murmured: "Can anyone tell me why I was crazy enough to leave here?" On being sworn in he told the assembled officials of the Foreign Ministry: "One of the difficulties of this office is that there are a lot of people who think they understand something about foreign policy and there are unfortunately few who understand the nature of this office—I belong to the former many, without being able to count myself among the latter few." For the moment he made his home in West Berlin's Federal Representation Building on a Bonn side street. From there he and Rut moved into the roomy official residence of the Foreign Minister on the Venusberg. There was little time for family matters. But on his fifty-third birthday Wehner ceremoniously presented him a gift from the party—the gold pocket watch that had once belonged to August Bebel, patron saint of the SPD. "It will be well taken care of with you," Wehner said.[2]

Brandt turned over the West Berlin City Hall to his deputy, former pastor

Heinrich Albertz. He took Klaus Schütz and Egon Bahr with him to the Foreign Ministry, where they formed the nucleus of what soon became known as Bonn's "Berlin Mafia." Otherwise there was little he could do under Germany's rigid civil service regulations to make the Foreign Ministry over in his own image. Here and there he could find an SPD member or sympathizer among the professional Foreign Service officers. But they were as rare as albinos in an African tribe. After twenty years of CDU rule and patronage Bonn's diplomats were "virtually all bound to the CDU," observed a foreign affairs specialist. "We could only place one or two SPD people. We would have needed eight or ten years to turn it inside out."[3] Wehner observed later: "He was a significant Foreign Minister. But it meant he had to leave the *Auswärtiges Amt* as it was."[4] For the time being that mattered less than Kiesinger's desire to be his own Foreign Minister and the Chancellor's insistence on running part of Germany's foreign affairs in secret with the aid of Karl Carstens, soon to be his State Secretary.

It was all right for Brandt to call on de Gaulle in mid-December as part of the Kiesinger-Strauss strategy for reviving the axis between Bonn and Paris. But in the first days of 1967 Kiesinger and the CDU cabal in the Foreign Ministry ruthlessly undercut Brandt's first modest attempts to open a new *Ostpolitik*.* Brandt was leery of doing anything that might needlessly offend the Soviet leadership, which had already voiced sharp suspicions of the new Bonn Government. So he authorized simultaneous soundings with Rumania, which was on the outs with the Russians, and Hungary, a loyal Soviet ally. Both countries had evinced interest in talking with West Germany. Almost immediately, however, it emerged that there was a "Rumania first" conspiracy in the Foreign Ministry and the Chancellery—engineered by CDU men who wanted to press ahead for full diplomatic relations with the Bucharest Government.[5] In East Berlin Walter Ulbricht sniffed the wind and smelled rats in the Communist camp. On January 25 his Foreign Ministry issued a sizzling demand that the East European countries reject Bonn's overtures. The Hungarians scuttled back into their Danube lairs. Another Western government might have stepped back. But not Kiesinger. Six days later he received maverick Rumania's Foreign Minister Manescu, and the two countries inaugurated diplomatic ties. Then the Chancellor used this as a pretext to articulate Bonn's claim to be the sole representative of German legitimacy—the Hallstein Doctrine again—in a formal speech to the Bundestag. The Soviet Government responded to the swoop of the German eagle on Rumania with understandable ire, accusing Kiesinger of wanting to

---

*"Eastern policy," as a specific concept in German affairs, had its origin in the Bismarck era.

"swallow up the DDR" and, for good measure, of nurturing neo-Nazis in the
Federal Republic. At Ulbricht's request a meeting of Soviet Bloc Foreign
Ministers was convened in Warsaw early in February to deal with the West
German thrust. Poland and East Germany agreed for their own reasons that
the Bonn initiative had to be blocked. The Czechs and Hungarians were less
concerned. They were also tired of being hectored by Ulbricht, who was
usurping a Hallstein-like right to dictate the policy of others toward his
precious DDR. Nevertheless, it was clear almost immediately that the master
tactician from East Berlin would prevail in the councils that counted in
Moscow.

Brandt was angry, but he was also relatively helpless. The die of *Ostpolitik*
had been cast, and they had come up with a combination that would lose for
three more years.

Curiously, Kiesinger—the supposed expert on foreign policy—was
botching things in almost every direction. He had zipped off to Paris in mid-
January to revive Franco-German friendship and came back boasting that he
and de Gaulle had agreed to conduct policy together "in the grand style and for
a long time." In reality, de Gaulle only wanted to use Kiesinger as an
instrument to pry the Americans out of Europe. For a month or so the
Chancellor played the French game—to the point of complaining on February
27 that the United States and the Soviet Union were welding an "atomic
confederacy" in the form of a nuclear nonproliferation treaty. That infuriated
Lyndon Johnson so much that Kiesinger was forced to apologize. Within a
month the Chancellor had succeeded in annoying the Russians, the
Americans, and the French. It was not an easy situation for Brandt, who was
traveling the foreign circuit in the midst of these controversies. He had gone
to Washington in early February to confer with President Johnson on the
atomic treaty issue and other questions, only to have Kiesinger stir up a new
controversy with the United States a fortnight later. For the moment Brandt
was able to swallow his anger, and he said nice things about Kiesinger in
public: "I have the feeling that Kiesinger is trying to have sincere cooperation
with me and that he informs me about everything."[6] Kiesinger returned a few
favors, letting Brandt join him in laying a wreath at the Arc de Triomphe and
signing the guest book in Elysée Palace.

The two were locked in an uncomfortable embrace. But in the early months
of the big coalition their respective party colleagues at the other levels were
getting on quite well. Finance Minister Strauss and Economics Minister
Schiller were so chummy as they worked together to pull West Germany out
of recession unemployment—over 600,000 out of work—that they were soon
being called "Plisch und Plum," after twin puppies from a Wilhelm Busch
verse. Helmut Schmidt had taken over the SPD Bundestag group after Fritz

Erler died of leukemia in February, and he was working smoothly with his CDU counterpart, Rainer Barzel. When the going got rough between Brandt and Kiesinger, there was always the substitute relationship of Kiesinger and Wehner. In critical situations, when the communications lines snapped, there was Conrad Ahlers, the journalist and former paratrooper who loved to leap into a mess. He was on intimate terms with both Wehner and Kiesinger at this stage.

The big coalition had launched an ambitious *Ostpolitik* program. The trouble was that it had no underlying concept, no real support from Bonn's Western allies. Worse, it was based on a false premise that West Germany could simply go ahead and strike bargains with some of Moscow's allies before dealing with Moscow itself—as if their tail wagged the Soviet dog.

Not that Bonn wasn't trying to start a dialogue with East Berlin. Herbert Wehner had seen to that directly after taking office as Minister of All-German Affairs. He started by saying that West Germany would have to stop referring to East Germany as "the zone," or, more unpleasantly, "the Soviet occupation zone." Even Brandt had referred to the DDR as "the zone" as recently as 1966. It was an expression that grated on East German ears. Kiesinger's usage, "the other part of Germany," was no more acceptable to them, nor did they like it when he later referred to the DDR as "the phenomenon" or "the formation." Wehner was successful in persuading Kiesinger to open a dialogue with the East German leadership. But this effort was ill-coordinated with the other soundings in East Europe and burdened by the deepening mistrust with which Ulbricht viewed the new Bonn leadership.

Willy Brandt attempted to blunt the edge of the still-applicable Hallstein Doctrine in a Berlin speech in March, stating that its presumption of "sole representation" of the Germans characterized merely a "political-moral obligation to be active in German affairs in the world." Kiesinger, too, took a softer line. On April 12 he declared: "We want to get rid of the cramps, rather than harden up, to overcome the gap rather than deepen it." But it was too late to turn Ulbricht from his new course. Five days later the East German leader retorted that his DDR could not accept anything less than "formal recognition and normal relations from state to state." As in the previous year, when it seemed Brandt and Wehner might appear in Karl-Marx-Stadt to speak for the SPD, he jacked up the price to an impossible height. For theatrical effect he proposed a meeting between Kiesinger and his own Premier, Willi Stoph. Ulbricht's true intention lay elsewhere, as he demonstrated later that month at the Carlsbad meeting of Warsaw Pact leaders. The message of the Bloc from the Bohemian spa was stronger "unity of action of the Socialist camp"—meaning no more one-to-one deals with West Germany. To make sure, Ulbricht began pressing for a series of new "mutual assistance pacts" between the DDR and its Communist allies—as if the Warsaw Pact itself did not suffice. It was the diplomatic complement to the Berlin wall.

Nevertheless, on May 10 when Premier Stoph invited Chancellor Kiesinger to East Berlin to discuss "the taking up of normal relations between both states," Kiesinger did not reject the note out of hand. He replied one month later, proposing, with Wehner's coaching, that the two sides authorize emissaries to meet without political conditions. This put the ball in the East German court, and it wasn't until September 18 that Stoph responded with a treaty draft for "normalizing" relations. The Kiesinger-Wehner reply ten days later stuck to the June proposal for a meeting only. Ulbricht dropped the matter. He hadn't wanted a dialogue anyway.

The big coalition numbed the regular political life of West Germany. Debate in the Bundestag—with only forty-nine Free Democrats representing the opposition—soon became perfunctory, reducing the Parliament to "a mere function of notarizing," as Hans Apel, a young SPD deputy, put it.[7] The Barzel-Schmidt combination worked with merciless efficiency in drafting and ramming through legislation conceived in the coalition Cabinet. Critics mockingly called them "the brothers." On the economic front Schiller and Strauss were operating in parallel harmony to pull the Federal Republic off "the valley floor" of recession. Their recipe—a natural outgrowth of Schiller's Nazi-era education in state planning and his addiction to John Maynard Keynes, though alien to Strauss—prescribed a considerable amount of government intervention. Their mottos were: "Enlightened market economy" and "As much competition as possible and as much planning as necessary." As "Plisch und Plum" they put together "medium-term finance planning" that set government guidelines for the next five years. Soon Schiller was holding the first of his quarterly "concerted actions"—private meetings of seventy or more labor and management leaders—whose aim was to keep the unions from asking higher wages and the managers from seeking higher profits. It worked almost too well. Within a year the Federal Republic was out of its economic valley and climbing the mountains again. But the closed-door decisions had a deadening effect; indeed, the *konzertierte Aktion* was the labor-management equivalent of the politics of the big coaltion.

Kiesinger soon institutionalized the camarilla form of government by initiating the "Kressbronn Circle," named for the tiny village in Swabia where he first convened his chief coalition partners to thrash out domestic and foreign problems with sweet privacy and mild wines. He started the Kressbronn practice in August 1967 with Brandt, Wehner, and Bruno Heck, a Kiesinger man who was to become secretary general of the CDU, in attendance. Often Kressbronn meetings consisted merely of monologues by Kiesinger, who was enjoying his press reputation of the moment as "King Silver Tongue." Later Franz Josef Strauss would sit there ostensibly listening, with a big pile of Finance Ministry papers in front of him, working his way through them, making notes, and signing on the dotted lines where he had to. Brandt ground his teeth in disgust and emerged once from a session with Kiesinger muttering: *"Ein Quatschkopf!"* (A dunderhead). Wehner ventured no opinions. In his longer-range view it was no matter whether the CDU coalition Chancellor talked nonsense. That was not the point, especially not at the end of the year when Kiesinger admitted: "If there are conflicts in the big coalition then they are genuine conflicts, by which we either reach a compromise or rule out a solution." Wehner made no bones about his strategy. At the outset he had stated: "We always struggled for the whole power; we didn't get it. Now we have for the first time the chance to acquire half the power and we'll take it."[8] His strategy was to prove that the Social Democrats could govern, and he had some flashy figures in Brandt and Schiller to accomplish this purpose. It was a strategy of embracing the enemy and kissing him to death. A contemporary observer called it "the strategy of going arm in arm" (*Unterfassung*).[9]

In terms of Germany's political past the big coalition had some disquieting elements. It was so all-embracing, so comprehensive, so uniform—or so it seemed—that critics were reminded in their milder moments of Kaiser Wilhelm's exclamation at the outset of World War I: "I know no parties anymore—I know only Germans!" In their nastier moments they were reminded of the Nazis allying themselves with the big businessmen while cultivating the "Socialist" aspirations of the German workers. In the big coalition there were strains of the Pied Piper of Hamelin, a role Kurt Georg Kiesinger would have willingly played for much longer than his agreed term of three years. One of the CDU ministers soon complained: "Kiesinger is governing only with his *Sozis*. Soon we will have nothing more to say."[10] But the SPD was having its aches and pains, too. In May Brandt warned his party comrades "not to become the doormat" of the Kiesinger party, adding, "We are not swallowing any mess of political potage in Bonn."[11]

In this sterile situation the extremists of the Right and Left grew restive. The big coalition had that as a birth defect. It came into being between the state elections of Hesse, where the neo-Nazi National Democratic Party (NPD) won 7.9 percent of the vote, and Bavaria, where the NPD won 7.4 percent. Adolf von Thadden's party won representation in two more state parliaments on April 23 with 6.7 percent in Rhineland-Palatinate and 5.8 percent in Schleswig-Holstein. The NPD had only 30,000 members at its pinnacle. But it was getting millions of protest votes against "the system" in

Bonn, and Bubi von Thadden was drawing huge crowds and enormous attention from most of the foreign press. Not a Nazi himself, von Thadden was nevertheless a spellbinding speaker in the German context—an orator in the mold of an American Huey Long, with sweat and galluses. (His misfortune was to be surrounded by diehard National Socialists, who were also incredibly clumsy and incompetent. "Bonn Is Not Weimar," as a journalist observed, and the Federal Republic was not comparable to the pre-1933 republic.)

What was sauce for the right-wing gander was sauce for the left-wing goose. A group of young people—students, trade unionists, and SPD members—formed what came to be known as the "APO" (an acronym for the "extraparliamentary opposition"). It had antecedents in a university reform movement that had begun in 1965, aiming at a change in the nineteenth-century authoritarian structure of German higher education, and its locus was West Berlin, at the Free University that Ernst Reuter and Otto Suhr had helped to found. To some it was a great irony that the student radical movement should have its birth in Reuter's "outpost of freedom," the city governed for the previous nine years by Brandt. The irony was compounded by the active participation of Brandt's oldest son in the fledgling rebellion and of the sympathetic attitude cultivated toward the New Left by some of the Berlin intellectuals who professed to support Brandt. As Mayor, however, Brandt had done virtually nothing to cope with the rising discontent of the Free University students, though he sat on the board of governors.

That the student rebellion began in Berlin was no accident. It was almost predetermined by the political nature of the founding of the Free University as an anti-Communist institution. That was in keeping with the times and the peculiar situation of Berlin during the Cold War, and its tradition found expression into the early 1960s when its students organized and operated large-scale escapes from East Berlin, including tunnels under the wall. But it was a free university in name only, for its structure had been altered early on to conform with the hierarchical concepts of West German universities—where the professors were supreme and where archconservative dueling fraternities strutted as if Germany had won two world wars. Finally, there was that bad, if revered, German habit of allowing students to spend eight, sometimes even ten years working toward a degree, so that the university as often as not became a kind of substitute home for many. Because they felt repressed—and to some extent they were repressed—a fairly sizable minority of Free University students began forming Leftist action groups. They found models not in neighboring East Germany, but in Mao's China, Ho Chi Minh's North Vietnam, and on the U.S. campus of Berkeley. The Indochina war was nearing a brutal apex, and young radicals were sufficiently outraged to begin demonstrations against American installations in West Berlin. But their primary target remained the university hierarchy as the symbol of a reactionary system. Then as later, the West German educational system proved immune to reform. The West Berlin police cracked down hard from the beginning, clubbing the protesters even when Brandt was still Mayor. Escalation of the dissension was inevitable. By spring 1967 the fronts had formed: small communes preaching Red Guard militance on the one side and West Berlin's anti-Communist police and anti-Communist Springer press on the other. To its shame and discomfort Brandt's SPD found itself on the side of law and order, principally in the person of Brandt's sucessor, Mayor Albertz. It was part of the price paid by the Social Democrats in entering the big coalition with the Christian Democratic Union.

An omen of just how grave the coming confrontation would be occurred on the eve of the visit of Vice President Hubert Humphrey, Brandt's old friend from prewall days, to West Berlin. On April 5 the West Berlin police announced that eleven persons, mostly students, had been arrested on suspicion of planning to assassinate Humphrey; they had been found in possession of "homemade bombs." When Humphrey arrived, it turned out that some communards had mixed a pudding, which they had poured into plastic bags to throw in the direction of the Vice President as a protest against the Vietnam war. But nobody laughed at the truth. Within five years some of the radicals would graduate from pudding to real bombs and bullets.

The situation worsened on June 2 with a tragic sequence of events surrounding the Shah of Iran's official visit to West Berlin. Rezi Pahlevi had been all too familiar to millions of Germans for more than a decade. His troubled love life had spawned a genre of West German journalism called "Soraya sheets," because of their preoccupation with his unlucky ex-wife. He was also notorious among the German Leftists as an incarnation of feudal despotism and murderous anti-Communism. In his unbridled conceit the Shah made sure his Berlin reception would be friendly by bringing along a large claque, made up mostly of toughs from his own secret police. They cheered as ordered when he appeared at the Schöneberg Rathaus and, when some student radicals booed, they waded in with sticks and clubs they had concealed under their coats.

By the time the Shah and his party reached the new Berlin Opera House that evening, a crowd of several thousand had assembled, including a group of several hundred Free University students. Those still indignant over the beatings earlier in the day began chanting: "Murderer, Murderer," and "Shah, Shah, Charlatan." Some eggs, tomatoes, and plastic bags filled with paint flew—landing far from the royal Mercedes. No one expected violence except Police Chief Erich Duensing, who had drawn up what he later called a "battle plan" for crushing the demonstrators. At 8:09 p.m., thirteen minutes after the Shah entered the Opera, German riot police unstrapped their billy clubs, leaped across provisional barriers, and attacked the demonstrators, hitting heads indiscriminately. As Duensing later explained, the tactic was to eliminate "a liverwurst with a stinking left end—you press it in the middle to squeeze it out at the ends." He also employed "grabbers" to seize suspected ringleaders. In the ensuing scramble Detective Karl-Heinz Kurras found himself close to a student who was already being beaten by policemen. Kurras' pistol was drawn. He pressed the trigger, and Benno Ohnesorg, a twenty-six-year-old student of German literature, fell—mortally wounded. Within twenty-four hours West Germany and West Berlin faced a full-fledged student rebellion, galvanized by the martyr death of one of their own.[12] Mainly Socialist in character, the rebellion was as much against the SPD as it was against the CDU establishment. Chief Duensing was handed his hat a week later; Mayor Albertz quit in the autumn.

Brandt had paid scant attention to the Free University problem as Mayor; he was convinced early on that the new generation growing up in West Germany would sooner or later become his supporters, and he had told John Kennedy so in 1961. The idea, as he saw it, was not to win young German hearts and minds by worming one's way into their favor, much less mouthing their slogans. Rather, he seems to have felt that the way to gain the backing of the young was to stand as an alternative to the dominant Conservative attitude in Germany. Now he moved cautiously. Two weeks after Benno Ohnesorg's death he and the other SPD leaders spent more than six hours conferring with a large group of student representatives from all over West Germany and Berlin. The meeting was "tense," according to one of the student leaders. But the Association of German Students said later it was at least "the beginning of a sound discussion."[13]

For the time being, however, Brandt and the SPD did not represent a real alternative on the German political landscape. They were doing their best to fit in as a governing party for the first time. Yes, German society was changing, consciously or unconsciously, but the shocks administered by the extremists meant that it did not automatically move in favor of the SPD. From March to June the party lost small percentages in the state elections in Berlin, Rhineland-Palatinate, Lower Saxony, nearly 9 percent in the Bremen communal elections in October. The CDU gained everywhere—as did the NPD. Kurt George Kiesinger seemed to be riding high. With Adenauer dead—he finally succumbed to the complications attending a bad cold on April 19 at age ninety-one—Kiesinger seems to have thought he could duplicate the old man's "Chancellor Democracy" popularity and authority. He won a strong mandate from the battered CDU at the party's May convention in Brunswick, and his rating in the polls was good. But even then it was becoming plain that he lacked the stamina for a protracted struggle.

Meanwhile, Brandt was off gathering garlands where he could. He went to Scandinavia in late June on a four-country swing and was hailed almost like the hometown boy who made good. Rut accompanied him and shed a tear when they arrived in Oslo's Fornebu Airport. Hundreds of Norwegians had gathered to applaud the pair. In Stockholm Swedes shouted, "Willy, Willy!" when he passed by. The trip was more than a pleasure tour, however. There was work to do. Brandt was seeking support for Bonn's *Ostpolitik,* and the Scandinavians were expressing interest in the Soviet proposals for an all-Europe East-West conference on security questions—a project that was to be six years in the making. In Norway he also got together with Ninja Frahm, now a twenty-six-year-old teacher, and her teacher boyfriend.[14]

In August Brandt flew to Rumania to return the visit of Foreign Minister Manescu. He spent more than five hours conversing with Nicolae Ceausescu, the tough little Rumanian Communist chief, and came back saying that they regarded each other as "representatives of independent governments who know their international duties are not only to build bridges to each other but also to build them in such a way as to make them passable for others."[15]

But his primary attention was on Washington and Moscow, London and Paris. There were three distinct issues: First, the United States was pressing West Germany to accede to the nuclear nonproliferation treaty it had drafted together with the Soviet Union. The Kiesinger-Brandt government was wary of a commitment that might permit nuclear technology to be developed by the atom powers, but bar development by the atomic have-nots. Brandt insisted that the nonproliferation treaty include some provision calling for disarmament steps by the great powers.

Second, West Germany was at last trying to engage the Soviet Union in a dialogue on improving relations—either on practical aspects of trade and cultural relations or on the more ethereal question of a mutual agreement on renunciation of force and "respect for existing borders" in Europe. But for the moment the Soviet leadership wasn't interested, preferring to continue its campaign of vituperation against an allegedly swelling Nazi menace in the Federal Republic.

Finally, West German foreign policy was caught in an increasingly disagreeable web being spun by President de Gaulle. The general was suggesting that West Germany reduce dependence on the United States and NATO in exchange for greater reliance on France and "Europe" as expressed by the French-dominated European Economic Community. This, said de Gaulle on a visit to Bonn in July, would make it easier for the Soviet Union to consider West Germany's *Ostpolitik* overtures. At the same time, France was blocking Britain's new bid to join the Common Market. While Kiesinger and Brandt both valued the friendship of France, they strongly opposed loosening West Germany's American and NATO ties, and they also strongly affirmed the need to have Britain join the EEC. Brandt became Britain's most powerful advocate on the Continent in speeches he made throughout 1967. But de Gaulle was in a beastly mood, and he became so disenchanted with the West Germans that he even raised doubts about France's treaty commitment to help defend the Federal Republic. It was a test for diplomatic talents, and in December Brandt put the problem politely but firmly before the Bundestag:

> Our own interests, which it is our duty to represent, and that which we understand to be the European interest, force us to speak clearly and to recommend precisely at this moment to our French friends not to make things difficult for themselves and others. We think it is not in France's interest to prevent—and that France has no right to prevent—a firm and final opinion in negotiations with Britain. . . . A negative decision would mean stagnation.[16]

It was a busy year: Two visits to the United States for arm-twisting by Lyndon Johnson, Brussels, Luxembourg, Paris, London, Zurich, Scandinavia, Rumania. Yet Brandt was less in the news than he had been in previous years. When 1967 was half over he told an interviewer inquiring about who did what in the coalition:

> First you have to accomplish something before you can sensibly argue over who had the decisive part in it. The people across the country are interested in the first place whether anxiety about their jobs is ceasing and whether we are getting a little more ground under our feet in foreign affairs. That interests them more at the moment than the argument about which party did what. When the Government has more to show for itself the people will show more interest about which party contributed to it.[17]

In November, on the first anniversary of the big coalition, he observed that there had been no celebrations because the coalition was "neither a shotgun wedding nor a love match." But there had been some achievements: unemployment cut from 600,000 to 200,000, prices on an even keel, the budget deficit reduced, industrial output rising again. On November 30 the Federal Press and Information Office took an ad in several leading newspaper showing Kiesinger and Brandt with the modest caption: "Two Men/One Task/The Direction Is Correct."

What was missing in the SPD-CDU alliance, Brandt responded to a question, was humor: "There are too few jokes about it." He loved jokes—to hear them, to tell them, and sometimes to make them. People who sought his favor knew that a quick way to gain his attention was to bring him a new anecdote or *bon mot*. Brandt used them to break the ice of reserve in others and, often as not, to hide his own profound reserve. Jokes served him as a relief; he would laugh so hard that his face would redden, his breath grow short, his eyes crinkle out of sight, as he slapped his knee in sheer pleasure. Until his death in 1961 Joachim Lipschitz had been a valued assistant in Berlin, a man Brandt liked to have around because he was a master of Yiddish dialect stories. Mayor Albertz of Berlin, too, was a good purveyor of jokes. His forced retirement was doubly painful, because Brandt had to send his other wisecracker, Klaus Schütz, to Berlin to replace him. That left Conrad Ahlers, a fast man with a quip.

As sticky as the first year in Bonn had been, 1967 ended on a positive note for Brandt's vision of "a European peace policy." Early in November Yugoslavia indicated that she was interested in resuming relations with West Germany. One month later Brandt got authorization to negotiate the end of the break that had begun ten years before as the first example of the Hallstein Doctrine. In Kiesinger's CDU there had been keen opposition to the change, which marked the end of the last shreds of that ill-conceived policy of Conservatism. At the same time Brandt proposed yet another gesture of conciliation toward East Europe by saying he was "very much for" lifting the ban on the Communist Party of Germany (KPD), which had been imposed on grounds of unconstitutionality in 1956. He and Wehner had something more than East-West relations in mind. Readmitting the Communists to West German political life would counteract the increasing radicalization of the Left by providing a clear alternative to the Social Democrats.[18]

Besides, it hardly seemed justifiable to maintain a ban on the Communists, when old Nazis and their latter-day imitators were free to organize and operate as a legal party. Throughout 1968 the coalition government wrestled with the idea of banning the right-wing NPD, a move Mayor Schütz was pleading for in Berlin as a means of eliminating at least that flank in the struggle with the radical Left. Kiesinger hesitated and, in the end, decided it was better to defeat the NPD in open elections. There was one other CDU reason for keeping the NPD alive: It would have some twenty-two votes in the next Federal Assembly, that quinquennial body of state and federal parliamentary deputies that would gather in 1969 to elect a new German President. The CDU did allow the Communists to reform in the autumn as a legal party with a new set of initials—DKP for "German Communist Party."

In midterm Kiesinger's main desire was election law reform. He wanted to hasten the trend toward a two-party system for several underlying motives. Most obvious: CDU-CSU Conservatives still held the upper hand in West German politics and would plainly be the winner in any standoff with the SPD for years to come. But there was also Kiesinger's personal animosity toward the Free Democrats, who had betrayed the Conservatives so often. The envisaged reform would have created a pure majority system in which the victor of each election district automatically went to the Bundestag—winner-take-all—erasing the "lists" whereby a sufficient number of votes in a given state would allow a party to gain representation in the federal Parliament. Kiesinger offered this proposal also as "an institutional compulsion toward ending the big coalition."

It was an attractive idea, hypothetically, for the Social Democrats, too. But it would have condemned the SPD to opposition for years and, for this reason, Brandt and Wehner told Kiesinger to forget it. Moreover, it had not gone unnoticed in the SPD that the small Free Democratic Party was undergoing a transformation. Erich Mende quit the chairmanship to take over the German representation of Bernie Cornfeld's boldly conceived Investors Overseas Service. At a lively January convention in Freiburg Mende was succeeded by Walter Scheel, and more reform Liberals were elected to the FDP executive. The auspices for eventual cooperation with SPD improved. It would have been folly for the SPD to work for the extinction of a future ally.

It was a peculiar time in the politics of Germany, of Europe, of the world. Old structures were collapsing. Britain pulled her forces back from "East of Suez"; China was in the throes of "cultural revolution." Czechoslovakia, after two decades of turgid Communist orthodoxy, was moving into a missonary Hussite phase of "democratic Socialism," watched with increasing apprehension by East Germany and the Soviet Union. De Gaulle's France lurched to the edge of revolutionary anarchy in a frenzy of student riots. There was a mass march on Washington combining the frustrations of blacks, Vietnam war protesters, and rebellious students. Wherever one turned there was restiveness, discontent.

Brandt got a taste of the ugly mood in early February when he spoke to a group of Social Democrats in Ravensburg. He touched on the French-German relationship, which he hoped was "so strong that even unreasonable governments will not be in a position to weaken it." In a dispatch by DPA, the West German press agency, the remark came out garbled as "rigid un-European thoughts of a head of government obsessed by power." Meaning de Gaulle. The French President elected to make a *cause célèbre* out of the incident, and no amount of tape-playing or apologies could undo it. He sliced two German Cabinet ministers off the invitation list for a state reception honoring President Heinrich Lübke.

President Lübke himself was the subject of a disgraceful slander campaign at this time, alleging that he had helped built Nazi concentration camps in 1944. The documentation for the charges was the work of Soviet and Czechoslovak intelligence services,[19] amplified by East Germany and eagerly gobbled by West German publications, including the widely read *Stern* magazine. It was an immensely successful forgery, which forced Lübke to consider resignation.

Soviet tactics also included a series of secret talks by Ambassador Semyon K. Tsarapkin with Foreign Minister Brandt on the subject of future Soviet-German accommodations. In the course of five meetings early in 1968, Tsarapkin made clear that the Soviet Union wanted the Federal Republic to reduce its "presence" in West Berlin as the quid pro quo for an understanding,[20] a foretaste of the Soviet position in the 1971 negotiations on a four-power Berlin agreement.

It was half-time for Brandt in the big coalition, and he was up for examination again by the SPD. There was a convention in Nürnberg, where he had gone first as a correspondent in 1945. A generation later he and Herbert Wehner were pushed around by the rowdies of the Left. Long-haired youths chanted: "Who betrayed us? Social Democrats!" They threw stones, burned a SPD banner, and ripped down posters. One of the five hundred tore at Brandt's overcoat. Another hit him with an umbrella, to which Brandt said, afterward, it didn't hurt much, "because the man struck out of principle." A faint breath of 1932-33 hung over the Meistersingerhalle. Only this time he was on the inside looking out, and a new generation was chanting the slogans he had once shouted. How full the circle.

He was not dismayed. On the contrary, it was something as familiar as a brand on his skin, and he could say, calmly, alluding also to his radical son Peter:

> Well, youth is not a merit. Age is not a merit. In my experience youth is a credit that grows smaller with each new day. The self-glorification of the young is just as silly as the know-better attitude of the elders. One should say this every day as a father. One hopes the sons say it sometimes to themselves, too.

There was laughter and a lusty cheer.[21] But Brandt also acknowledged that the youth rebellion signified a "sort of crisis" and that Social Democrats should be mindful they were among the targets of criticism in the "still intangible and immeasurable" revolt. He was thinking about the 1969 election and where West Germany's young voters would be by then.

In recognition of the "intangible" transformation of attitudes in Germany he also promised that the convention would take a stand on the Vietnam conflict, which was such an agitant for young people—in Germany as in the United States—waving Viet Cong flags and shouting, "Ho-Ho-Ho Chi Minh!" But it was in *Ostpolitik* where he elected to break new ground. In his March 18 address he took up the controversy over the Oder-Neisse line, behind which lay nearly 40,000 square miles of territory formerly belonging to the German Reich and now held by Poland. Brandt pointed out that 40 percent of the Poles living in the Oder-Neisse regions had been born there after World War II and that nobody dreamed "of a new expulsion" comparable to what had been done with 9 million Germans following the war. He went on:

> It is a further reality that the German people want and need reconciliation with Poland—want it and need it without knowing when they will find their unity as a state in a peace treaty. What emerges from this? From it emerges recognition of—that is respecting—the Oder-Neisse line until a peace treaty settlement.

So speaking, Brandt broke a nineteen-year-old taboo of West German politics, and he also put himself in contradiction to Kiesinger, who had declared only a week before that Bonn could not recognize the boundary "until a peace treaty." Brandt's Oder-Neisse declaration was the first trumpet call of a new and more consequential *Ostpolitik*, a departure from the fruitless formulas of the past, a signal for the election campaign still more than a year away. Although the official Communist party organs of East Europe pooh-poohed it, their correspondents at Nürnberg were buzzing with anticipation.

The Nürnberg convention broke ground elsewhere. It was the first time in three decades that the SPD had Cabinet ministers to present at a party assembly. Yet many of the delegates plainly had nagging ideological pangs about the big coalition. When it came to a vote on whether to approve participation in the national alliance with the CDU, 129 delegates voted no, and 173 voted yes. This meant the rebirth of a Left wing in the SPD. Its power and presence was demonstrated again in debate on a Vietnam resolution—the convention unanimously resolved that the American bombing raids should cease—and in the executive elections. Blaming Herbert Wehner, rightly, for the erection of the big coalition, the Left mustered 57 votes against him. Brandt got 325 of 330 delegate votes. Helmut Schmidt was also elected to the executive.

In spite of the rumbles of dissension, the overall impression of Nürnberg was of a SPD revitalized and self-confident. So much so that the party put out a special booklet collecting comments, reports, and cartoons from the domestic and foreign correspondents who attended. That had not been done before.[22] Not that the SPD was free of fetters, far from it. The party took a drubbing in the state election of Baden-Württemberg in April, dropping back 8 percentage points to well under one third of the total. It was all the more troubling because the SPD was in coalition with the CDU in Baden-Württemberg, just as in Bonn. Taking this as an ominous sign of who would finally succumb in the lethal coalition embrace on the federal level, Brandt briefly considered pulling out of the government. He was persuaded to stay only by the combined voices of Wehner, Schmidt, and Schiller. Wehner spoke of "the gravest crisis the party ever faced.[23]

Since the 1920s the SPD had advertised itself as a "reform party," and here it was involved in government responsibility again—at last—but stymied by the nervous Conservatives of the CDU. The plain fact of it was that the big coalition could not by its very nature, be a reform government. There were too many divergent forces in it. The coalition could legislate improvements for the coal industry, the railroads, and the highway network. But it could do nothing for such neglected areas of West German society as education or health. In the end its only true reform accomplishments were to be found on paper: a set of laws for dealing with a national emergency and a law strengthening federal powers in regulating the country's finances.

As harmonious as the political life of Bonn seemed in those months, and as diligent as the government and the Bundestag may have been, the coalition was doing little more than running in place. This, too, was an "intangible" but essential cause of the frustration that expressed itself in extremism and protest voting across the country. The NPD got close to 10 percent of the ballots in the Baden-Württemberg election. On the other end of the spectrum the young Left had been fulminating in the big cities since February, about the Vietnam war and also about the pending Bonn emergency legislation. They had a brilliant young tribune in Rudi Dutschke, who marched like Napoleon and exhorted like Lenin; his was a convoluted doctrine—a mixture of Marx, Mao, and the late-blooming Herbert Marcuse. Dutschke reveled in his role as a leader of the APO, and he was, in the words of Marcuse, "a sweet demagogue." But in his appeal for "a long march through the institutions" of the Federal Republic he also helped create a curious new polarization.

On the one side was the long-haired Left. On the other was the newspaper chain of the exquisitely combed Axel C. Springer, who controlled 40 percent of the major dailies. Under big headlines the Springer papers were inveighing almost every day against "Left terror." The first stones were thrown against

Springer outlets in Berlin. Then, on April 11, Dutschke was critically wounded on a Berlin street by the bullets of a troubled twenty-three-year-old housepainter who professed to admire Hitler. Overnight the militant Left, numbering no more than 11,000, mobilized five times that number for demonstrations across the country. The chief target was the Springer concern, and for days the young people blocked deliveries and burned what they could of Springer papers. A photographer and a student died of injuries sustained in a melee in Munich. Springer, who had earlier tolerated broad-minded liberal journalists in his stable, turned farther to the Right, embracing the reactionary slogans of Franz Josef Strauss. This shift was to have consequences for Willy Brandt.

The Leftist demonstrations reached high tide in a final campaign against the Bonn emergency laws, which, they charged, were a throwback to Hitler's Enabling Act of 1933. In early May 30,000 demonstrators converged on Bonn bearing banners proclaiming "Emergency Laws Equal Hitler" and "Nazism Began This Way." But there was no violence, and many of the demonstrators fell asleep on the grass of the university's *Hofgarten* during the torrid speeches. One young girl carrying a Vietcong flag was asked if she were a Marxist. "No, I am a Trotskyite," she replied. When told that Trotsky also believed himself to be a Marxist she smiled winsomely and said, "Did he really?"[24]

On May 30, the day the emergency legislation was adopted by the Bundestag, Brandt soberly endorsed the law in a speech that began:

> Our Federal Republic is grown up enough to take the regulation of its domestic affairs into its own hands without limitations. That is, to arrange the precautions on our own responsibility for emergencies which, hopefully, will not happen.

It wasn't long before the Leftist agitation fizzled out. But Peter Brandt had drawn a six-week suspended jail term on conviction of participating in an anti-Springer demonstration in April.

Brandt was on the international circuit again—to Austria in early June for talks with his friend and fellow-émigré, Bruno Kreisky, who had become Foreign Minister for a time, too; later to Yugoslavia for long and harmonious conversations with President Tito. He was making *Ostpolitik*, and in Yugoslavia he was making new friends. Tito had known Herbert Wehner at the Hotel Lux in Moscow, and in the atmosphere of restored relations with West Germany he invited Wehner, too. But the rest of Eastern Europe was quivering at the impulses of "Socialism with a human face" emanating from

Alexander Dubček's Czechoslovakia, becoming ever more nervous over reports of anti-Soviet demonstrations in Prague and Soviet military maneuvers east and north of the Bohemian citadel.

As if in retaliation for Brandt's visit in Yugoslavia, Ulbricht imposed new pass and visa requirements for travelers between West Berlin and West Germany, raising the cost of that traffic by over $10 million a year. From Yugoslavia Brandt went to East Berlin to meet for eight hours with Ambassador Abrasimov—without obtaining any assurance that Moscow was in a mood to go easier on West Germany. The Czechoslovak crisis deepened by the day, and West Germany had become a convenient propaganda scapegoat in orthodox Communist eyes for that, too. Some goat! Ulbricht's agitprop functionaries were claiming with one breath that the Prague leadership was succumbing to West German "imperialism" and with the next to West German "Social Democracy."

Almost as if the Prague events were a dream, the regular business of East-West diplomacy went on, while the Czechoslovak reformers danced toward their doom. There was a serious reason for this: A fairly substantial faction in Communist Europe—including Hungary's Janos Kadar, Yugoslavia's Tito, and even a scattering of Communists in East Germany, Poland, and the Soviet Union—viewed the developments on the banks of the Vltava as relatively positive. They were not yet outvoted by power politicians who wanted and were planning to intervene, if necessary by military force, in the homeland of Jan Hus and Alexander Dubček.

In this setting Brandt traveled to Iceland to the NATO Ministerial Council meeting, where he persuaded the alliance to issue "the signal of Reykjavik"—a bid to the Soviet Bloc to sit down and begin talking about mutual and balanced reduction of troops stationed in Central Europe. The signal was heard but not answered in Moscow, where another kind of troop planning, involving the Warsaw Pact, was already well under way. In mid-July the Soviet leadership seriously considered invading Czechoslovakia to put down the Dubček reform threat, only to have the decision deflected by Brezhnev himself.[25] To distract attention from the Czechoslovak issue Moscow delivered a slap at the West German Government by publishing some of its diplomatic correspondence with Bonn that claimed a "victor power" right to intervene in West German affairs in a moment of crisis.

Brandt got the message, the more easily because Ambassador Tsarapkin conveyed official allegations that the Bonn Government was "interfering in Czechoslovakia." Unintimidated, Brandt told a press conference July 31, "The best that we can do now for Prague is to do nothing," and added, "We are witnesses and observers and nothing else." Then he went off to Norway for his annual vacation.

The August 20-21 invasion of Czechoslovakia by five Warsaw Pact countries shocked neighboring West Germany. The more so because both the Soviet Union and East Germany's Ulbricht had made conciliatory overtures to Bonn only a few days before—probably reflecting the wavering consensus in the Soviet leadership before the hardliners finally won out.

The various efforts on both sides to advance a policy of East-West detente had suffered a sharp setback. Soon, however, it became apparent that by finally approving the occupation of Czechoslovakia, Leonid Brezhnev succeeded in consolidating his power in the Kremlin. He showed the hardliners that he, too could be tough in times of peril—real or imagined. This permitted him gradually to develop a new Western policy in the direction of accommodation and ultimately a degree of conciliation. Along this line Ambassador Tsarapkin was instructed to call on Chancellor Kiesinger less than two weeks after the invasion to say: "It would be nice if we had good relations."

That was Brandt's feeling as well, and, on the following day, September 3, he avoided directly mentioning the Czechoslovakian crisis or the Soviet intervention in an address to representatives of a host of nonnuclear powers in Geneva. Instead, he spoke allusively of "a heavy blow" dealt to the efforts of West Germany and others toward creating "a zone of detente in Europe," and added, "Even so, we remain ready to work for a European zone of peaceful neighborliness." "Willy Brandt's foreign policy views had been astoundingly unchanged since 1948," a historian wrote in 1968.[26] Nor were they much changed from his views of 1939-40. The theses of his newest book, *Peace Policy in Europe,* which he had completed in March,[27] fell into the same line. When the French edition was published at the beginning of 1969, Brandt wrote a new foreword in which he said that despite the "earthquake" effect of the Czechoslovakian invasion, "the extreme hardening of the blocs is not taking place."[28] His calm assurance at the Geneva conference helped persuade fifty-two of the attending delegations to support a German resolution proposing a network of international commitments on renunciation of the use and threat of pressure and force. Only five opposed the resolution. It was no mean accomplishment for a German Foreign Minister.[29]

The Czechoslovakian crisis compelled a pause in Bonn's efforts to formalize a dialogue with the Soviet Bloc. But it did not stop the contacts. Foreign Minister Gromyko was at the United Nations accusing West Germany on October 3 of wanting to "recarve the map of Europe." But on October 8 he was conferring with Brandt at the Soviet U.N. Mission—the first meeting between Bonn and Moscow Foreign Ministers in four years—on the possibility of a renunciation of force agreement. From New York Brandt flew to Chile to conduct a conference of German envoys in Latin America and then went on to Argentina, Uruguay, and Brazil.

The unique parallelism of developments in West and East Germany showed up again in this phase of the nation's history. In the East the DDR's Ulbricht emerged from the Czechoslovakian crisis as the arbiter of Communist policy in Central Europe, functioning in the field of foreign affairs as virtually the equal and sometimes the schoolmaster of the Russians. It eventually contributed to his downfall and disgrace. For the moment, however, he was very powerful.

In the West the Bonn Government suddenly found itself in the unaccustomed position of being an arbiter of capitalist policy with regard to monetary affairs. This was as much a result of West Germany's reestablished economic health—the work of Karl Schiller—as it was debilitation of the economies of France and Britain. For four years Bonn had been mocked as "an economic giant but a political dwarf," a felicitous phrase of a newspaper commentator. Now its refound economic power provided it with political clout as well. How else could one explain de Gaulle's viciousness in rejecting Bonn's repeated pleas to open the gates for British entry into the European Common Market, which he coupled with "a touch of Germanophobia" during a meeting with Kiesinger.[30] Thanks to Schiller's "stability program," the West German gross national product was up 6 percent to $130 billion, and exports had risen by 11 percent. Back in July a council of economic experts had recommended an upward valuation of the *Deutschmark* to cope with the inflationary pressures developing in other Western industrial countries. The Federal Bank followed with an identical recommendation. But that did not square with what Kiesinger was hearing from his industrialist-banking friends. As with so many other critical decisions he hesitated.

By early November speculative money was flowing into West Germany, draining reserves in France and Britain—first by the million and then by the billion. The coalition government stepped in to stanch the flood when it reached the $4 billion mark with what it called an ersatz revaluation. On November 19 a 4 percent tax on exports was imposed, and, at the same time, the federal government declared it "will not revalue the DM." The pressure continued. The British and the French were shouting at the Germans in ugly midnight scenes to revalue their currency and take the pressure off their own sagging monetary systems. Instead, Economics Minister Schiller invited them to Bonn as members of the monetary Club of Ten industrial powers that had grown out of the Bretton Woods currency conference. Bonn refused the pressing demands of the others for three nights and days, during which the Finance Ministers lived on sandwiches and coffee at the sprawling Economics Ministry. On November 22 the battle was over. The *Deutschmark* kept its parity, and the French got a $2 billion credit to support the battered *franc*. The French and British went home growling, and the newspapers of Paris and

London were filled with invidious commentaries about "the Germans." Springer's tabloid *Bild* boasted: "Germany is Number 1 in Europe Again!" The unexpected emergence of West Germany as a potential force to be reckoned with also prompted a New York editor to cable his Bonn correspondent demanding a "takeout" on how Germany was "running loose on the Continent again as a big power. . . ."[31]

It took Brandt weeks to smooth the ruffled feathers of his French and British colleagues. "We are all in one boat, economically and politically," he told a radio interviewer a few days later. The prosperity of our neighbors decides our own well-being to no small degree." Again, on November 28, he observed: "It is devious and harmful to suggest that the Germans strive with economic means for a position of hegemony in Europe." The following day he spoke in the Bundestag with "regret" of the "atavistic instincts of mistrust awakening again in Europe," and reiterated that Germany's aim was "a common policy" toward "European cooperation and eventual unification of our continent."[32]

The turbulent year drew to an end with omens of new confrontations and new opportunities. Controversy fermented over the SPD selection of Gustav Heinemann as its candidate for the Federal Presidency and over the choice of West Berlin as the site for convening the Federal Assembly.

Brandt got a foretaste of election year nastiness when the *Bayern-Kurier,* the weekly organ of Franz jose Strauss' CSU, attacked his aide Egon Bahr, suggesting that he had carried on clandestine talks with officials of East Germany's Communist Party over several years. Brandt acknowledged that Bahr had met East Germans on various occasons "which I knew of and approved of" for the purpose of "gathering opinions." But he was infuriated by the implication that Bahr was somehow betraying West Germany. Red-faced and hoarse, Brandt demanded before a press conference that Strauss and' the *Bayern-Kurier* "produce their material or cease their imputations." In the same vein, Brandt defended Heinemann against a similar accusation by Richard Jaeger, a Bundestag sidekick of Strauss, saying: "I ask myself whether someone could apologize—that should be possible among civilized human beings."[33] But it wasn't. What Strauss and Jaeger had done was to pay out some of the line they had gathered from the information leakers in the *Bundesnachrichtendienst* (BND), Reinhard Gehlen's intelligence agency. The Kiesinger-Brandt government had retired Gehlen the previous May, when he turned sixty-six, and he was still smarting over it. His revenge was to surface data that could compromise the politicians he deemed enemies—chief among them Brandt. The information had been collected by the BND, sometimes in the course of legitimate inquiries but just as often through illegal domestic spying on SPD politicians authorized by Gehlen himself.

Germany is a land where "events" are scheduled long ahead of time—even those that end up with unpredictable consequences. It suits the orderly mind of the nation. Even the unperceptive observer could reckon with certain clashes and contradictions attending the selection of a new Federal President and of a new Federal Chancellor. The events were measurable to a degree, like the action in a familiar play or a family quarrel. What remained immeasurable were those intangibles of quirky behavior by some of the principals, and the undercurrents and riptides that characterized the dynamics of postwar German society. So it was in the great election year of 1969. How would the youth vote when some radicals were shouting for Mayor Schütz's ribs to be broken, and anothers was slapping Chancellor Kiesinger in the face, as a young woman did in anti-Nazi ecstasy in November 1968? What about the businessmen—did they prefer the Conservatism of Kiesinger's advisers or the boldness of Professor Schiller? Most important, what of the FDP, which was again in a position to tip the balances?

The predictable part of the presidential election was that it invited trouble with East Germany and the Soviet Union because the site chosen for it by the presiding officer of the Bundestag was West Berlin. Already in late December the Soviet Foreign Ministry had issued a sharp warning to all concerned that West Berlin was not the place for a West German election, that reprisals would occur if West Germany persisted. Richard M. Nixon's designated national security adviser, Henry A. Kissinger, also warned against the Berlin venue, thinking that it would disrupt the planned visit of the newly inaugurated American President to Europe.

Herbert Wehner, too, was against an election in Berlin and argued heatedly with Brandt about it. But Brandt was adamant, not only because of his nine years as Mayor, but also because he had advocated the Bonn-West Berlin connection as far back as 1949. "It's got to be Berlin," he told Wehner.[34]

As if there were not enough tinder, the choice of presidential candidates had become a source of controversy, along with the fact the NPD would be represented in the electoral college. The CDU had winnowed through Walter Hallstein, Eugen Gerstenmaier, and Rainer Barzel until they finally settled like a swarm of insects on the hapless Gerhard Schröder, who had confided a year before: "I don't want to be Federal President, I want to construct the next—at the latest the next-by-one—Cabinet."[35] But in November the CDU picked him anyway to oppose the SPD's Heinemann. A restrained, well-groomed man who had served already as a Minister of Interior, Foreign Affairs, and Defense, Schröder was anathema to the Left—and a joy to cabaret mimes because of his choppy umm-ahh speech habits. Heinemann was something else. A Lutheran churchman with a voice as dry as the pages of a psalmbook, he had entered politics the better to preach morality. As Justice Minister he had won considerable public respect at the height of the 1968 youth rebellion by declaring on television:

> He who points with the index finger of general accusations at this or that purported agitator or wire puller should keep in mind that the other three fingers point back at himself. I mean to say by this that we all have to ask ourselves what we ourselves did in the past such that anti-Communism could be heightened to a murder attempt.

The arithmetic of the presidential election was not simple. The Federal Assembly consisted of 1036 deputies from the state and federal parliaments. Schröder could reckon on the CDU's 479 and the NPD's 22. That meant he still needed 39 FDP votes out of the Free Democrats' total of 83. But what was the FDP doing? Its jolly new chairman, Walter Scheel, whom many, including Adenauer, had dismissed as a lightweight, was busily rounding up Liberals for Heinemann.[36] It was a high-risk venture, yet Scheel evidently calculated that unless the FDP moved with the changing times it was doomed to an early death. He already had in mind a brand-new alliance with the party of Willy Brandt. A huge drama unfolded.

The first act was almost farcical. Eugen Gerstenmaier the belligerent little Bundestag president who had made a postwar career out of his fleeting membership in the Kreisau Circle's plot against Hitler, was exposed as something of a grafter. He had drawn over $60,000 in federal reparations payments on the spurious ground that the Nazis had prevented him from becoming a professor. When the facts were out, he had to step down on January 31, causing the CDU untold embarrassment.

The next scene was staged by the Russians, who were now genuinely interested in improving relations with West Germany. Ambassador Tsarapkin came to see Foreign Minister Brandt again, to talk about the Berlin assembly, but also about the possibilities for opening air service between West Germany and the Soviet Union. It soon became evident that Brezhnev was serious enough about conciliation to make some concessions. For openers the Russian offered to twist Walter Ulbricht's arm enough to obtain Easter visiting privileges for West Berliners in East Berlin—for the first time since 1966—if the assembly venue was moved.

The United States came on stage soon after with similar pleas for a change of venue. But Kiesinger and Brandt had their backs up. In the middle of all this tugging, Richard Nixon flew to West Berlin, intent on *his* first effort at detente. In a speech on February 27 he declared that the troubled past of

Berlin, with its perennial crisis, made it a natural place to begin a process of East-West detente. Brezhnev listened and understood. First, however, the game of Berlin poker involving the Federal Assembly had to be played out. Nixon was scarcely gone from town when the first delegates to the assembly began arriving, and the Soviet Bloc prepared its countermoves. Brandt said he wasn't worried. He said it in Rome on February 15, in New York on the twenty-fourth, and in Berlin on the twenty-seventh. Wehner wasn't all that worried, but he did call the situation "a soggy mess."

On March 1 East German border guards shut down the highways to West Berlin for two hours, with the excuse that Warsaw Pact maneuvers had just begun in the region. It was cold and snowy. The next day there was another two-hour closure of the *Autobahn* and a slight escalation—the Soviet Air Force warned the United States Air Force in West Berlin that it "could not guarantee the safety" of civilian airline flights. Marshal Ivan Yakubovsky, glaring under bushy eyebrows, was not far away directing his frozen maneuvers; Marshal Andrei Grechko was on his way to India. Nobody, Russian, German, or American was yet prepared to call the Berlin game a "crisis." There would be no further reason to do so. Just at this moment, on March 2, large formations of Chinese People's Army soldiers attacked Soviet units on the Ussuri River frontier, 4600 miles east of Berlin. Next day the conviction drained out of the East German-Soviet harassments on the access routes.

On March 4, the eve of the presidential election, Walter Scheel gathered his eighty-three electors in the roof restaurant of Berlin's Europäischer Hof, a respectable hotel opposite the fairgrounds building where the voting was to take place. He asked for a show of hands on Heinemann and got only sixty— too few to elect the SPD candidate but enough to defeat Schröder. Scheel: "Some friends don't seem to grasp the situation. If we want to go to the election this way tomorrow we might as well jump out of the window here. Then the party is *kaputt*.[37] About 11 p.m., after a hearty meal, he had gained a sufficient number of pledges—seventy-eight deputies. On March 5, after two agonizing rounds in which neither candidate had enough votes, the FDP put Heinemann over the top—512 to 506. The SPD had its first President since Friedrich Ebert forty-four years earlier. The result dazzled the Germans: "A Piece of Power-Change" was the *Stuttgarter Zeitung* headline. Wehner spoke of "the changing of an era," and Brandt warmly hailed Scheel: "The suspicion is finished—that was an impressive performance." There was new tingling in the West German air, and hardly anyone paid much attention to Communists blocking the access routes—an action that continued for two more days.

Were the West Germans rescued from a sharper contest with the Soviet Bloc by the Chinese? Probably. On March 11 Ambassador Tsarapkin called on

Kiesinger to inform him about the Ussuri clashes, and that same day, Ulbricht's *Neues Deutschland* carried an editorial blaming the Chinese for aiding "the Bonn revanchists" in going through with the Berlin assembly.[38] One week later the Warsaw Pact countries followed up with an appeal issued by their Foreign Ministers in Budapest calling for an East-West European security conference beginning with renunciation of force declarations. The tides at last began to favor Bonn, and Brandt. He was in Washington in April for a NATO meeting and called on the alliance to reply favorably to the Budapest appeal. Back in Bonn he appeared in a relaxed and good-humored mood at the campaign congress of the SPD, joking first about soccer and August Bebel and then declaring: "My party has asked me if I intend to determine the guidelines of the next federal government: My answer is *ja*." He tossed some bouquets around to the men he counted on to carry him into office and be on his team—naming Karl Schiller seven times and then mentioning Georg Leber, Alex Möller, and some others. He also praised Wehner extravagantly, although he was annoyed with him. Wehner was complaining that Brandt had neglected his party duties. "We had something going in '67 and early '68," he said, "courses for factory foremen, the backbone of the party. But then it all sank into oblivion. He could allow himself to do it, because he was being cheered as a symbolic figure. But the party rank and file need to eat meat and they weren't getting it."[39]

Brandt was high on Schiller, the maestro of the "concerted action" of industry and labor that had helped revive the economy, the defender of the *Deutschmark*. But Schiller's popularity confronted Brandt with a dilemma. By May hot money was again heading toward West Germany, the bankers feared, and there was not a moment to lose for a true revaluation of the *Deutschmark*.

Finance Minister Strauss was for it, which made a considerable difference. Schiller, too, told Kiesinger on May 8 he wanted to up the value against the dollar by 7 percent. That day Willy Brandt received a telephone call from a high U.S. Treasury Department official urging him to support a revaluation decision. But when Schiller went before the SPD leadership in the barracks to talk about the issue, Brandt never mentioned the call from Washington. In the next day's decisive Cabinet meeting with Kiesinger—who had taken an oath not to revalue before Herman J. Abs, an old Cologne banker—Brandt again was silent about the Washington call. It might well have turned the tables if he had mentioned it. Instead, in the critical hour, as millions of dollars were pouring into German banks, the CDU Cabinet majority followed Kiesinger's lead and postponed revaluation. When Schiller learned from his own acquaintances in the Treasury of the call to Brandt, he asked his party chairman why he had kept silent and left him in the lurch. Brandt did not reply.[40]

Opinion polls in mid-March had given Kiesinger 23 points and Schiller 22.

Brandt trailed with 13, well behind Franz Josef Strauss.[41] Brandt didn't want Schiller to gain the added popularity that would accrue from a revaluation victory and endanger his own hold on the SPD. Nor did he want Kiesinger to benefit in the coming campaign from a decision that could only have been to his credit.

It was a crucial error on Kiesinger's part, for it soon became evident that a still harder *Mark* would have won him votes. On May 11 he made another critical mistake. Swayed by advisers and doubtless by pressure from Strauss, he elected to pursue what was defined inside the CDU as "a nationalist Conservative policy." It reflected the same urge, articulated in the winter by Strauss, to the effect that "Nobody will overtake us on the Right." Kiesinger apparently felt that the largest reservoir of fresh votes for him lay to the right of the CDU in the ranks of Adolf von Thadden's NPD. The stand on the *Deutschmark* was one example, but there were others. Kiesinger adopted a harsher stance toward East Europe, especially the DDR. He supported eased penalties for minor Nazi criminals. He withheld West Germany's signature on the nuclear nonproliferation treaty.[42] He drove Brandt to the brink of resignation by insisting on cutting ties with Cambodia, when that country recognized East Germany.

But all of this was mistaken, for the currents were running ever stronger the other way. Poland's Wladyslaw Gomulka took up Brandt's year-old pledge of Oder-Neisse recognition on May 17, and Brandt replied that West Germany was "ready to talk." The Poland possibility was popular among the West Germans, despite the cries of the right-wing press; a group of Roman Catholic reformers had endorsed the renunciation of the Oder-Neisse lands just before Brandt addressed the issue in Nürnberg in 1968.

In July Brandt called on President Georges Pompidou in Paris and learned that France now felt the time was near when the European Community could be "strengthened" by the addition of Britain and other candidates.

There was more, much more, going for him at home. Kiesinger was playing too close and Conservative with the slogan: "It Depends on the Chancellor." The Germans had grown tired of voting solely on the merits of one man. Even though Kiesinger led Brandt two to one in the popularity polls, the SPD was closer to the mood with its slogan: "We Have the Right Men."

You could see the wave of change rippling across Germany before your eyes. In June 73 of the 115 German dueling fraternities voted at Landau to eliminate the duel as a test of courage—after 150 years of determined slashing. In Mengeringhausen a whole battalion of Bundeswehr reservists got drunk, simply because the maneuver they were supposed to make was code-named "Blue Juniper," the designation of a popular *Schnapps*. At Bergheim some civil servants—a class noted for strait-laced obedience—organized a saucy "stomp in the swamp" mainly to make fun of themselves. *Unerhört!*—unheard of—their civil servant uncles, cousins and fathers would have snapped. Germans, noted for and proud of their xenophobia in the past, were traveling by the tens of millions around Europe and the world on their vacations—and being reasonably hospitable to 1.4 million foreign workers at home. There were Chinese and Yugoslav restaurants in cities like Braunschweig—a 180-degree turn from the time thirty years before when Joseph Goebbels had adjured the nation to "eat German fruit" in one of his nationalist paroxysms. No longer did the majority of Germans believe with Frederick II that "to harm foreigners is to serve your own nation." Rather, there was a sense of harmony, security and comfort such as the Germans had not known since the beginning of the century. The change was also evident in the ability to come to grips with the national past. A poll in 1951 had showed only 32 percent of the population blamed Hitler for World War II. An identical poll taken in 1967 showed 62 percent blamed Hitler.

The stirring was also sparked by the students who had questioned the hitherto unassailable authority of their professors, by the breaking of domestic and external taboos in the policy decisions of Brandt and Scheel, by the coal, steel, and public service workers who launched wildcat strikes to achieve 11 to 15 percent wage increases on the eve of the elections, by thousands upon thousands of Germans who were moving from the formal *Sie* to the informal *Du* in conversation.

Günter Grass, the popular novelist who fancied himself a stormy petrel, or at least a gamecock, sought to capitalize on the new mood by organizing a countrywide independent voter movement on behalf of what he cutely called the "Es-Pe-De." His symbol was a crowing rooster, which he had drawn himself. Soon he mobilized 3000 helpers, including some fairly distinguished professors, writers, musicians, and artists. Grass himself toured 100 of the republic's 248 voting districts, talking, joking, answering questions. The Germans had never seen anything like it. Over and over again his listeners stood up to *bekennen*—to declare themselves for the SPD, much as Christians in the tent of an evangelist. Grass cut sharply into the political tradition of the *Kundgebung*—the rally where the candidate stands on a podium and exhorts the multitudes. It was also a sign of the change.

Finally, there was Brandt, serene and sure. "The sensible boy he always was," his mother remarked shortly before she died in Lübeck on August 4 at the age of seventy-five. He had chosen to campaign in the image that suited him best: the prudent statesman. It was a low-key approach, sometimes to the point of being hard to hear. But it seemed to work. Golo Mann, the historian son of Thomas, lauded him as "the best Foreign Minister Germany has ever had." Brandt himself had made a point of speaking or writing on the anniversaries of the few predecessors whom history had found little wanting: Bismarck, Rathenau, Stresemann. But he interpreted them for his own political purposes. Of Bismarck he wrote: "The word 'dogma' was alien to his policy; his vocabulary had no 'doctrine' in it. . . . The great Chancellor succeeded in external unity, but not in domestic unity."[43] Of Rathenau: "To be patriotic with pride, but without arrogance."[44] Of Stresemann: "A two-sided policy, not a policy of duplicity, as the geographic position of Germany demanded then and still demands."[45]

He had chosen the high road again, and it pleased him. "This is the real me," he told his handlers. He made set speeches with few variations, up and down the country, speaking in a calm, deliberate tone. The fight talk he left to Schiller, who was drawing huge audiences and applause on his repeated accusation that Kiesinger's failure to revalue was bringing inflationary price rises of close to 4 percent. Not that Brandt didn't think he was fighting, too. Inside he was boiling with determination. On a campaign train one night he was drinking a variation of "Captain-Lieutenants"—a concoction of Cognac and Benedictine—with journalists in the dining car at 2 a.m., when he burst out about the big coalition: "I've got to get rid of it. I'll make a new government if I have only a one-vote majority to get rid of those slick monkeys who gave me grades and let me stand around like a dumb schoolboy."[46]

Outwardly he kept cool, and this, in the mounting tension of the campaign exerted a peculiar fascination for voters who had watched him run and lose twice before. Wehner observed: "People need somebody like him. They see a man pulling himself up by his bootstraps, literally. It is more than partiality, it is admiration."[47]

Kiesinger, the man who had expressed such respect for Richard Nixon, had it all upside down. At the very time Nixon was developing a detente policy, his self-styled German understudy was preaching anti-Communism, conjuring a vision of "750 million Chinese armed with nuclear rockets" and pulling all the oratorical stops. He wasn't playing Nixon, but Barry Goldwater.

To emphasize his calm, Brandt interrupted his campaign a few days before the election and flew to New York. At the United Nations he lined up appointments with eight Foreign Ministers in one day, including William Rogers and Andrei Gromyko. Then he zipped back to Bonn and appeared, bright-eyed, in front of the press corps in the rosewood paneled conference room at the Tulpenfeld Plaza. He looked like a man who expected to win an election, and he made so bold as to answer a few questions on how he might run the Chancellery. That was September 23. He also felt confident enough to commit himself on a new kind of coalition, saying that Walter Scheel would cut a good figure as the new Foreign Minister. Scheel, at the same time, said of

Brandt "I admire him as a decent and diligent man. He is the best Foreign Minister we have ever had in Bonn."

Two nights later they appeared with Kiesinger on a television panel program, and Scheel declared: "I am of the opinion that the CDU as the leading party in the Federal Republic in twenty years of rule is showing signs of running down, and that it would be good if the CDU would have the strength to go into opposition by itself." Kiesinger turned the "running down" description around and plastered it on the FDP. But Scheel persisted, saying, "the public ought to know the direction of the thrust." He had already dictated a last-minute campaign ad proclaiming: "Partnership for Progress," meaning the thrust was toward a coalition of SPD-FDP.

Election night September 28 was a three-hour horserace in which a loser became a winner, and a winner turned out to be the loser. Computer projections at 8:15 p.m. led Rainer Barzel to declare: "It is plain that the claim to leadership remains with the CDU-CSU." Sixty minute later the projections reported on the television station showed the CDU neck and neck with the SPD-plus-FDP. Starting about 9:30 p.m. the SDP-FDP combination began to pull away, with a lead of four seats at 10 p.m., six seats a half-hour later, eight seats just after 11 p.m. At this time there were CDU supporters carrying victory torches around Schaumburg Palace, and some CDU enthusiasts were beginning to pour sparkling wine. President Nixon called up Kiesinger to congratulate him on his "triumph." But the Chancellor wasn't feeling triumphant and, in his only appearance before the televison cameras, he spoke not of victory but of his belief that a coalition of SPD and FDP "is not really politically possible."

Walter Scheel sat downhearted in his Venusberg home, having declared: "I am the loser of this election." The FDP had sunk from 9.5 to 5.8 percent. Three hundred feet lower in the Rhine Valley, Herbert Wehner paced around the SPD barracks muttering darkly at comrades who were trying to whip up enthusiasm for the coalition with the FDP: "That's the old commuter party." When Hans Roderich Schneider, the FDP spokesman, heard that on television he telephoned Wehner and warned: "One more crack like that and it's curtains for the coalition."[48]

About 11:30 p.m. Brandt telephoned Scheel, whose party had plunged from 3.1 million to 1.9 million votes, and told the FDP leader he intended nevertheless to bid for a "small coalition." Could he count on a positive response from the FDP? Scheel said, "Ja," and the conversation ended.

Fifteen minutes later Brandt went before the television cameras and microphones. It was already clear that the SPD had won 42.7 percent of the vote: "This is the best result we've ever had . . . the SPD is the largest party; it's won over 1 million additional votes." He went on to point out that the

CDU-CSU had dropped back from its 1965 result. "The SPD and the FDP have more than the CDU and CSU. That is the result." In fact the SPD-FDP had barely 48.5 percent altogether—meaning a tiny majority in the Bundestag. But Brandt was cocksure: "Negotiations are necessary—not with the feeling of being the second runner, but as the only party whose election result expresses an increase of confidence." He felt he had won the national election, and that was enough to make him act accordingly. He would be Chancellor.

X:

The Peace Chancellor

For thirty-six of his fifty-five years friend and foe had relegated Willy Brandt to the eddies of German life, rather than to its mainstream. He had been a representative of "the other Germany" to Germans who opposed Hitler, to the rest, an "émigré." No one lacked a label for him: "Norwegian," "Red," "Traitor," "One of Ours," "Gestapo Agent," "Communist Agent," "Berliner." For a time in the early 1960s when he was wont to drink a lot of *Schnapps* or whiskey they called him "Willy *Weinbrand*"—"Brandy Willy." No doubt about it, he stirred controversy and sometimes passions. By the time he ran for the Chancellorship, Brandt had accumulated an entire wall shelf full of libel and slander files from a multitude of court cases.

Against this backdrop Brandt's bid for the Chancellorship seemed a powerful stroke to pull himself into that German mainstream that he had eluded, that had eluded him for so long. It was not all that Herculean. A thin majority of Germans had assembled who gradually shifted the mainstream in the direction of Brandt and the SPD: toward progressive reform and away from secure Conservatism. After two decades of playing it safe, there was a German consensus for change. In the same fashion Brandt had moved steadily away from the radicalism of his youth and found himself already quite close to the center in German politics. His participation in the big coalition was proof enough. The SPD's Brandt and the German polity converged and finally met in the 1969 national election. Not a total reconciliation, but a meeting. For the moment that was enough.

"I think we are growing out of the old notions," he remarked,

> and have already grown out of a large portion of them. That some-
> one like me says: I know my path was not the same as most of my
> countrymen" is respected much more than earlier—but perhaps just
> because of that I can accomplish something that is useful for our

253

country and our people. Thus we can conclude that our behavior patterns are also changing in other areas. The less-authoritarian is included in that that is, a different way of adapting oneself to power in the old sense of the word.

He had bid for power before, but not with such conviction. This time he said: "Some things ripen even when you don't incline to premature decisions. And when they are ripe, they are ripe. Otherwise they rot—decisions just like fruits." [1]

Remarkably, the spread of votes in the 1969 election was practically identical to that of 1965 and 1961. That is, the SPD and the FDP could hypothetically have formed a coalition twice previously on the joint advantage of one to two percentage points. The difference was qualitative, as became evident almost immediately. Erich Mende's FDP, swollen by discontented businessmen, had been linked with heavy chains of post-Kaiser wealth and post-Nazi Conservatism to the Christian Union parties. Walter Scheel's FDP, pitifully emaciated by his reform course, was free at last to choose another partner. As Horst Ehmke put it on election night: "If they (the Liberals) want to commit suicide then they must throw themselves at the mercy of the CDU, because the people who still voted for them voted for them on account of the SPD coalition."

In the forty-eight hours after the election Scheel and his FDP reformers worked practically without sleep to shore up their fragile bridge to the SPD—first by winning the approval of the state party organization in North Rhine-Westphalia, then in Saarland and the other states. The only major dissenter was Mende, the war hero, of whom a Scheel man said "One Mende doesn't make a Kiesinger," and another, noting Mende had walked out of a critical session pleading "business obligations," that he should be "awarded a medal for vanity in the face of the enemy."

Mende stole off to plot with Conservative friends, including CDU leaders who were well versed in the coalition business and the haggling required to bring it off. Scheel and Brandt knew the time factor was critical, that protracted power-broking could crumble the tiny pillars at the FDP end of the coalition bridge.

Brandt went to President Heinemann September 29 to declare: "On the basis of the results of the federal election I will seek majority approval by the Bundestag for election as Chancellor." What he had to offer was a majority of 254 seats in the 496-member Bundestag—224 Social Democrats and 30 Free Democrats. Nominally, it was a 12-vote majority. But he was aware that with Mende's defection he would get far less. He, Scheel, and their negotiating teams met for the first time on the evening of September 30 in Brandt's

Venusberg home. By midnight they reached "overwhelming agreement" on most foreign and domestic policy issues.[2] Scheel had already scorned a generous bid from Kiesinger—six Cabinet ministries for the FDP and a couple of valuable posts in state parliaments as well. He would get only three ministries in the Brandt Cabinet. The next day Scheel told newsmen, *Die Sache ist schon gelaufen*—"It's in the bag." His press spokesman hammered it home by describing Kiesinger's coalition offer as "rather remarkable," considering that the CDU had wanted "to kill us off as late as last week" with a new version of an electoral reform law. By October 2 Brandt could claim that it was all settled except "a few details," and early in the morning of October 3 the future partners announced agreement on formation of the next government and "far-reaching unanimity" on all policy issues. At the close of the eight-hour debate that preceded this decision in the FDP, Mende and two other Liberals abstained. The SPD Bundestag group required only ninety minutes to approve the alliance.

When Kurt Georg Kiesinger heard about the success of the new coalition, he ranted, "Distortion of the will of the voters," and threatened that the CDU would "catapult the FDP out of the state parliaments!" The old habits died hard. As late as September 30 Rainer Barzel had been counseling that a Brandt government was practically impossible. Now it slowly dawned on the CDU, so accustomed to its dominant role in West German politics, that it had "won the election, but lost power," as a sober observer described it.[3]

On the evening of October 3 Brandt and Scheel called on Heinemann to announce that they were ready to form the new government. It was Friday. When the weekend was over Brandt told Kiesinger he was taking off until the Chancellor election in the Bundestag a fortnight later. He didn't want to sit next to Kiesinger anymore. The speed of the change was as blinding as the change itself. It had taken thirty-six days to form a CDU-FDP coalition in 1965; sixty-five days in 1961. This time it had been done in five. The CDU sat numbed, scratched, and bleeding as if in a traffic accident, and they hadn't even seen the other car coming.

Brandt spent most of the following golden autumn days at the palatial country home of the von Schnitzler family, minor Rhenish nobility. (The black sheep, Karl Eduard von Schnitzler, had turned Communist sometime during the war and emerged as East Germany's leading television propagandist in the 1950s.) It was on a hill above Münstereifel, an hour's drive west of Bonn. Brandt slept late, sipped gin or Scotch or wine, smoked cigarillos, hiked, met now with some businessmen, later with some labor leaders or journalists. He wore heavy brown corduroy trousers, as a Norwegian farmer might have, a jacket without lapels, an open shirt that had seen newer days. He was working on his maiden speech as Chancellor, which he wanted to be a timeless document. Conny Ahlers was there helping him polish a phrase or two; so were Egon Bahr and Horst Ehmke, "our Horst for everything," as Brandt had described the man who stepped into the Justice Ministry after Heinemann became President and now would serve as Brandt's Cabinet troubleshooter.

On the Sunday before he was elected, Brandt had called a group of American correspondents to his Venusberg villa and told them: "We will be a loyal ally but not a comfortable government. I will not be the Chancellor of a conquered Germany, but of a liberated Germany." That was "on background," he said. He also told a Münstereifel visitor on October 9 that he intended to become "a Chancellor of domestic reforms." He quoted a CDU politician who had said, "Democracy is good for the state but bad for society," and commented: "Our position is to overcome the distinction between *Untertanen*—subjects—and *Obrigkeit*—authority, to create co-responsibility in society. We have a potent economy, but we still have terrible discrepancies. There is not enough free flow from one profession to another. People must become less biased." He also spoke of a program of "one hundred days," echoing Roosevelt and Kennedy. He and Scheel were in a hurry, trying hard to catch up on reform after so much dawdling and neglect and in a rush because, deep down, they were running scared. Scared their tiny parliamentary majority might dribble away, scared a perplexed electorate might abandon them, scared that the Russians, Americans, French, and British who had been so content with a bunch of obedient and tractable Germans might turn on them as so often happened in the past.

What he said to visitors in Münstereifel is what he wrote down in his first government declaration: bold proposals for improving relations with East Europe and liquidation of the old policy of confrontation; expansion of the European Common Market to include Britain; profit-sharing and parity with management on boards of directors for the blue-collar workers; reduction of the voting age from twenty-one to eighteen.

> "As for Germany's position in the world, we must connect all we do with a full affirmation of the Federal Republic—less a foreign policy than a German policy. After all, the national existence of the Federal Republic is not provisory. This means caring about what comes in the future in the national sense—that is, moving toward the other part of Germany and not away from it."

He spoke several times of *Augenmass*—"a sense of proportion"—as if to echo Herbert Wehner's definition of 1967, that: "Germany has a critical size—too big to play no role in the balance of power and too small to keep the powers around it balanced." Kiesinger had borrowed this felicitous aphorism for one of his early coalition speeches. Wehner was only too glad to give up author's rights, if it meant getting the CDU to endorse it.[4]

Brandt continued: "The Poles, the Soviets, the Hungarians have their own interests in differentiating their policies toward us. I do not think the DDR can escape this. But we will avoid anything that seems like Social Democratic infiltration of the East. Why break our heads over their problems? We have to do what we think is right and see what comes of it." His eye wandered, and he gazed from his wicker chair on the sunny terrace into the deep blue sky: "What's that bird circling up there?" he inquired. A pair of binoculars was brought, and he focused on a speck in the heavens. Silence. Brandt didn't know a condor from a thrush. Finally Werner von Schnitzler, his host, murmured politely after conning the bird with the naked eye, "It is indubitably a buzzard." Brandt huffed with satisfaction: "That is one problem solved." It was lunchtime, and the menu included his favorite potato pancakes.[5]

Even before Brandt's assumption of office was assured, the Soviet Bloc was astir. The Poles had already hailed the election result. With the German Democratic Republic marking the twentieth year of its founding on October 7, Leonid Brezhnev came to East Berlin, apparently with the secondary purpose of saying a few friendly words about what had happened at Bonn. Ulbricht had been surprised by the sudden turn in West Germany, which contradicted his own conservative view of the national destiny. When he addressed an anniversary audience in East Berlin's Werner-Seelenbinder hall, he mentioned, but did not comment on, the West German election. Instead, he leafed through his new catalog of demands: bar nuclear weapons, prepare to disarm, give up the claim to be the only legitimate German state, recognize all European frontiers, dissolve the NPD, oust "Nazis" from office, build democracy, overcome militarism, and sign a treaty with the DDR. It went on for ninety minutes. Brezhnev spoke for half that time:

> We are for relaxing tensions, for creating truly neighborly relations with all European states including the West German Federal Republic. Naturally, we would welcome a changeover to realism in the policy of the West German Federal Republic and would be ready to respond accordingly.

Ulbricht's speech promptly ran in full on the ticker of the official East German press agency. Brezhnev's remarks were reduced to a 500-word paraphrase that began running at 8:20 p.m. A deliberate snub. On careful reading, it emerged that Ulbricht had retreated from his earlier insistence that Bonn give "full diplomatic recognition of the German Democratic Republic." His new milder note of a treaty "valid in international law"[6] was evidence that Big Brother was peeking. Ulbricht's retreat from a maximum demand indicated that Brandt had acquired some leverage in the German question fully three weeks before he was elected Chancellor in the Bundestag.

On the Giersberg above Münstereifel, Brandt was shuffling scraps of paper scribbled full of notes in his flowing, low-profile script with his favored black felt-tip pen: the names of the people he wanted in his government, some ideas and formulas for his administrative program. There in the clearer air, 1378 feet above sea level, he sorted them out. Schiller would be Economics Minister, of course, and Georg Leber would keep the Transport Ministry. Käte Strobel had done a creditable job as Health Minister and Lauritz Lauritzen as Construction Minister. They, too, could stay. He had promised the Foreign Ministry to Scheel and was content to have FDP men take over two other important Cabinet posts—Hans-Dietrich Genscher for Interior, and Josef (Sepp) Ertl for Agriculture. His other choices were a mixed bag of talent, trouble, and trial. Helmut Schmidt was a natural for the Defense Ministry, and he would do it well, as he did almost everything else. Walter Arendt, from the Miners Trade Union, became a brilliant Labor Minister. Alex Möller, the big insurance man from Karlsruhe, was all right in the Finance Ministry—until he got fed up and quit. The same was true of Hans Leussink, the designated Science Minister, who also pulled out. But he would have difficulty with the stiff Gerhard Jahn as Justice Minister and with Erhard Eppler, a Swabian pietist, as Development Aid Minister. The bumptious Horst Ehmke was predestined to cause collisions as his Cabinet Minister, and the same was true of Conrad Ahlers as his official spokesman. He would hardly hear from Egon Franke as Minister of Inner German Affairs. Finally, Egon Bahr, his loyal disciple, though an unreconstructed nationalist, was bound to draw fire. Bahr would be his special ambassador and his man for West Berlin. Wehner, one of the great parliamentarians of the century, would return to the Bundestag to run interference for the light, quick coalition backfield.

It was not a bad group, compared to some of the cabinets fielded by the CDU, and, with fifteen ministers instead of nineteen, it was handier. But it had some shortcomings, familiar to those who were familiar with Brandt, and these showed up especially in his choice of personal aides. "He was not always lucky in choosing advisers," Schmidt remarked. "He often has little sensitivity in his choice of colleagues," Eugen Selbmann echoed. "In my opinion his weakness was in his choice of assistants—a weakness for intellectuals," said

Kurt Mattick. Ehmke, too, observed: "He makes mistakes in picking people." These comments were made in the spring of 1973, when it seemed that Brandt's fortunes were at their peak.[7]

He was so certain he would win on that election Sunday he had written a pile of cards thanking his helpers for contributing to his victory. It was a hairbreadth win, just the same. On October 21 the Bundestag deputies assembled to choose the fourth Chancellor of the Federal Republic, and when the counting was done Brandt scraped through with 251 votes—a majority of 3, as Brandt had predicted. Four votes had been made invalid by comments like: "No thanks," "Poor Germany," and "Not Frahm." A foretaste of the venom of the coming years, Mende's revenge had already begun.

When the result was announced at 11:20 a.m., Wehner sprang out of his chair and put his left arm around Brandt for a long embrace. Tears came to the eyes of the new Chancellor. Wehner wept, too. It was ninety-one years to the day since Otto von Bismarck had rammed through a "law against the endeavors of the Social Democrats dangerous to the public weal," thirty-nine years since the SPD's last Chancellor, Hermann Müller, had resigned. Rainer Barzel was the first of the CDU to cross from the opposition benches to congratulate the victor. Kiesinger followed. Strauss left the hall, saying he would write. Rut came down from the north balcony to present him a bouquet of roses. Then Brandt went over to Villa Hammerschmidt to receive his presidential letter of appointment. Heinemann broke protocol by embracing Brandt. "Willy," he said. Brandt's eyes moistened again. Before television cameras he said: "I am satisfied, grateful, and a little proud that I am enabled to exercise this high office." He was sworn in at the Bundestag below the huge black and silver eagle of Germany. Outside of the hall Klaus Schütz grinned broadly: "That is the way real revolutions take place."[8]

The outcasts were in at long last, and the emotions were hard to sort out. For younger Social Democrats it was probably less complicated. They had won the election; it was like winning in a soccer game or the national lottery, or being promoted by the boss. For Brandt and Wehner it was a homecoming, a reconciliation, an absolution. Neither man wore the mantle of the German past lightly, and events such as this charged the air with a sense of history, terrible and wonderful. Their tears had begun to form in 1933.

Brandt presented his Cabinet the next day. Its first act, on October 24, was to revalue the *Deutschmark,* which Kiesinger had set afloat before leaving office, by 9.3 percent. For the moment this settled Brandt's bill with Karl Schiller.

He had campaigned for the Chancellorship with the single dominating theme of "building peace," and it had caught on with an electorate that yawned when he struck the peace chord four and eight years before. How could you have peace when you didn't feel safe? the majority of Germans seem to have thought, and the CDU had won again and again by stressing *Sicherheit*—security. Now they sensed a degree of security—the experiment with Brandt was evidence—and they could try something more.

His one hundred days began October 28 with the first government declaration to the Bundestag, and it was filled with reminders that while the Germans may have been at peace with themselves they still had a way to go with some neighbors:

> *Herr Präsident.* Ladies and gentlemen. We are determined to protect the security of the Federal Republic of Germany and the cohesion of the German nation, to keep the peace and to work together for a European peace settlement. . . . The Germans are bound together by their language and history—with all its splendor and misery; we are all at home in Germany. We still have common tasks and common responsibility: for peace among ourselves and in Europe. Twenty years after the founding of the Federal Republic of Germany and the DDR we must prevent a further estrangement of the German nation, that is to come from a regulated next-to-each-other to a with-each-other. This is not only a German interest but also has its significance for peace in Europe and for the East-West relationship . . . The Federal Government . . . offers anew the Ministerial Council of the DDR negotiations without discrimination on either side at the level of governments which should lead to cooperation agreed on by treaty. An internationally legal recognition of the DDR by the Federal Government cannot be considered. Even though two states exist in Germany they are still not foreign to each other; their relations to each other can only be of a special nature.

Later on he said, "Our national interest does not allow standing between East and West—our country needs cooperation and harmonization with the West and understanding with the East." Asking for "peace in the fullest sense of the word with the peoples of the Soviet Union and all people of the European East," he offered treaties of "mutual renunciation of application or threat of force." Specifically, he said Bonn would propose treaty negotiations with the Soviet Union and Poland and would also accede to the nuclear nonproliferation treaty that had been taboo to the CDU.

This was the fundament of Brandt's *Ostpolitik,* which Scheel had fully endorsed. It was complemented by a vow to intensify the *Westpolitik* of expanding the European community and, of course, to be a good member of NATO. But it was *Ostpolitik* that made everyone perk up their ears, especially Kiesinger, who had warned him in his last breath as Chancellor not to "recognize the DDR."

He didn't say it explicitly, but the foreign policy announcements were a kind of declaration of independence for West Germany: a bid to do some things in a German way, for German interests. It was the beginning of the end of blackmail by Russians with fearsome propaganda, by Israel with guilt, by the United States with defense costs, by France with Europe-yes, Europe-no pronouncements.

"The end of blackmail started in 1969 when Brandt said Germany was governed by Germans who had been liberated, not conquered and that he didn't need any lessons in anti-Nazism," Ehmke observed.[9]

The new opposition hissed and booed when Brandt turned with a rhetorical flourish to domestic affairs: "We want to dare more democracy. We will open up our way of working and satisfy the critical demand for information." Then, just as he had promised to be "a Chancellor of domestic reforms," he opened his warehouse catalog of promises: a lower voting age, higher pensions for the old and deductible income for workers, university reform, tax reform, a hard look at the federal armed forces, better care for the sick, more subsidies for sports. It was as Brandt would admit much later, "a bit too much." [10] But he closed with more thoughts on democracy, and it was classic Brandt:

> In a democracy, a government can only work successfully if it is supported by a democratic commitment of its citizens. We are as little in need of blind approval as of pomp and high and mighty aloofness. We do not seek admirers. We need critical people to think with us, to decide with us, to take responsibility with us. The self-awareness of this Government will show itself in tolerance. Therefore it will know how to treasure that solidarity which expresses itself in criticism. We are not the chosen; we are the elected. That is why we seek dialogue with all who exert themselves for this democracy. In recent years some in this country feared the second German democracy would go the way of the first. I never believed this. I believe it less today than ever. No. We are not at the end of our democracy. We are just beginning. We want to be a nation of good neighbors, inwardly and outwardly.[11]

In their initial reactions, the Conservatives of Germany—capitalist and Communist—behaved predictably. East Germany's official press agency accused Brandt of continuing the policies of his predecessor. In the following days the new opposition in the Bundestag had the opportunity to transform their hisses into words: "Where is this trip taking us?" asked Rainer Barzel, the CDU whip, as he accused Brandt of flouting the constitution. Kiesinger spoke of "the avalanche we have tried to hold back for twenty years" with regard to East Germany. Herbert Wehner, back in his old parliamentary form after a three-year hiatus, snapped back at the Conservatives: "I can remember when you spat on your hands as though you were going to work. You spat and you missed a couple of times." Brandt, who tangled with Strauss in one of these sessions, remarked: "The Bundestag has become livelier." Indeed. Overnight, it had become the forum of the nation as never before, and it held television viewers riveted to their sets.

The Soviet Bloc leaders were still perplexed about what was going on in West Germany. They simply had not reckoned with a dynamic and forthcoming government in Bonn, or expected to be taken at their own word on offers and suggestions that had been rejected on the Rhine for two decades. It was coming too thick and too fast for East Germany. When Brandt flew to Berlin on October 31 to say hello to his old constituents, Ulbricht's Foreign Ministry protested that he had no right to do so because of "the status of West Berlin as a separate political entity." Ulbricht accused him of "endangering peace and security."

On November 13 Brandt declared he was prepared to sign the Soviet-American nonproliferation treaty, which was done two weeks later when appropriate assurances arrived from Washington and Moscow. On November 15 the West German Ambassador in Moscow handed over Brandt's note asking for negotiations on renunciation of force. On November 21 a similar note was handed over in Warsaw. It wasn't that the Communists had had no warning. Brandt had dispatched Eugen Selbmann to Warsaw in the previous summer as his SPD confidant to sound out Poles in the Politbüro and the Foreign Ministry on the prospects for reconciliation.[12] Bahr had talked with the East Germans and Russians in an identical fashion. It was the reality that was so unsettling.

Kurt Georg Kiesinger went to Mainz to face the CDU Party congress where he had intended to appear as the election victor. Instead, he was there as a penitent, saying it had been wrong to campaign on the slogan, "It depends on the Chancellor." Not only did he have to listen to scorn from the youth wing of the CDU, but he also had to hear Bruno Heck, his onetime henchman, saying that the Conservatives had lost the young voters, intellectuals, and the press and lacked "a long-range concept." "It is time the party stood on its feet instead of its head," Heck exclaimed, and he recommended that the CDU find a Herbert Wehner, "who showed us how to reckon in decades." Kiesinger's humiliation hardened with the knowledge that his strategy of absorbing the NPD vote had all but failed. True, the neo-Nazis got only 4.3 percent, which was too low for them to be admitted to the Federal Parliament. For that Kiesinger deserved some credit. But most of those 1.4 million votes could have gone the CDU way and kept the Conservatives in power. "I am not in a bad mood, just disappointed," he told a questioner on the second day at Mainz. Although he was reelected party chairman with 82 percent of the delegate votes, the larger majorities for Rainer Barzel and others doomed him. He was already sixty-five years old.[13]

Although his eye was on the East, Brandt's first substantive move was in the West. Following intensive preparations he traveled to The Hague on December 1, where he met a querulous President Pompidou at a summit conference of Common Market countries. The Frenchman opened the meetings with complaints about the perennial British request for entry: "Are we prepared to open the community to Britain and other candidate countries at the cost of weakening and fragmenting it?" A day later he acceded to the friendly peruasion and proposals of Brandt—probably of the British, too— and agreed to go along with Britain's acceptance. London had indicated that if the French were really worried about resurgent German power it wouldn't be so bad to have Britain as a countervailing addition. The Hague summit was an early triumph for Brandt the Chancellor, and nobody caviled when he reported on it to the Bundestag. It also helped to balance his oncoming negotiations with the East Europeans at a time when there were doubts about that in Western quarters. The Nixon Administration, for example, had complained late in November that it was not adequately consulted about the Brandt note to Moscow, although it hastily denied complaining.[14]

The impact of Brandt's *Ostpolitik* was so great in East Europe that Leonid Brezhnev felt obliged to convene a summit meeting of the Warsaw Pact's seven members. Coordination was needed, and Walter Ulbricht had to be soothed. The East German had intervened in late November with the Soviet leadership to prevent Premier Aleksei Kosygin from giving an interview to some West German journalists. Now the great tactician was in Moscow trying to block talks with Bonn and, when that didn't work, voicing his misgivings to the other Bloc leaders about moving too swiftly to accommodate West Germany. The Warsaw Pact meeting concluded with a December 5 communiqué paying heed to Ulbricht's neuroses but also opening the gates for comprehensive negotiations with Bonn. The sop thrown to Ulbricht was

the unanimous view that the unceasing dangerous manifestations of revanchism and the activating of neo-Nazi forces in the Federal Republic of Germany must be kept constantly in mind and sober vigilance must be constantly maintained with respect to them.

The green light for talks was phrased:

> If the new West German Government draws lessons of history, rids
> itself of the ballast of the past and, acting in accordance with the spirit
> of the times, displays a realistic approach to problems causing
> tension in relations between European states, this will be welcomed
> both by Socialist countries and by all peace-loving countries.[15]

There were no conditions.

One day later the Foreign Ministers of NATO issued a statement at the annual winter meeting in Brussels endorsing Brandt's eastern initiatives and also calling on the Soviet Union to begin talks on "improving the Berlin situation and free access." The *Ostpolitik* train was picking up speed.

Foreign Minister Gromyko began formal talks on renunciation of force with Ambassador Helmut Allardt on December 8 in Moscow. The three Western powers formally asked the Soviet Union for Berlin talks four days later. Ulbricht weighed in with a letter delivered to President Heinemann on December 18, proposing top-level government-to-government talks on negotiating "equal relations" between Bonn and East Berlin. For good measure he threw in a draft treaty with nine articles, some of them conveying impossible demands on West Germany: an exchange of ambassadors with East Germany, amendment of "discriminatory laws," and cutting West Berlin loose from the Federal Republic. It was Willy Brandt's fifty-sixth birthday, and Brandt chose to ignore the draft treaty. It was not important; the main thing was to start talking, and a reply to this effect went to Ulbricht on December 20. Two days later a Polish emissary notified the Bonn Government that Warsaw was also ready to open talks. Czechoslovakia, too, had asked for the blessing of *Ostpolitik,* but it was all West Germany could handle to conduct simultaneous negotiations with the Soviet Union, Poland, and East Germany; Brandt asked the Prague leaders to be patient. It was a little breathtaking, less than two months after beginning work as Chancellor.

Even so, the pace of the talks begun in Moscow and Warsaw was too slow for Brandt. He determined that the Foreign Ministry bureaucracy was too cumbersome and too leaky for the delicate nature of the subject—which was a portion of the German national patrimony. Besides, in Ambassador Allardt he had a decided opponent of *Ostpolitik.* In January Brandt persuaded Scheel to let him send Egon Bahr as a special envoy to negotiate the outline of a "normalization" treaty with Gromyko. State Secretary Georg Ferdinand Duckwitz was sent on an identical mission to Warsaw.

In addition to the chill he was feeling from East Berlin, there was the heat at home. Brandt had reported on "the state of the nation" in the Bundestag on January 14, and while he stressed the importance of "the unity of the German nation, he did not once mention the idea of national "reunification"—that old

Cold War cause. This brought out the Conservatives in full panoply. Werner Marx, a CDU deputy who hated to be outdone in Cold War polemics, announced suggestively that Moscow was "asking more of us than the German public knows." Gerhard Löwenthal, a right-wing TV commentator, claimed during his weekly polit-thriller show that the Soviet Union had demanded that Bonn explicitly renounce reunification. Springer's *Welt* said Herbert Wehner's heart still belonged to Moscow. Franz Josef Strauss accused Brandt of a "humble, whining attitude" toward the East and added: "I am not of the opinion that to become everybody's darling you have to be everybody's Arschloch."[16] The new Conservative front swiftly crystalized. Springer, in fact, made reunifiction of Germany one of the core elements of his publishing ideology, and his editorial staff was required to conform or quit. It go so rugged by early February that Connie Ahlers decided to counterattack, with the approval of Brandt, who had said of Springer: "If he wants to play rough then he will get it back rough." In a radio interview arranged with the Bremen station, Ahlers accused the Springer papers of printing "falsified news" about Brandt's *Ostpolitik*. He went further, saying their "disgusting policies" were coming close to violating the Constitution, adding the Leftist student demonstrations against Springer papers in 1968 were "justified today by the behavior of the Springer concern." A howl went up throughout the German press, which rallied against Ahlers. "I don't take anything back," he declared at a press conference on February 5, and added some calming remarks about the Springer newsmen in the room. But Springer himself felt the blow, the more so because he had been instrumental in launching Brandt's national political career in the late 1950s. ("He could never have pulled it off without Springer," Helmut Schmidt remarked "Springer and all his papers transformed Brandt into a national figure."[17] In mid-February Springer sent an emissary to Brandt seeking a truce, and later Brandt received the messianic publisher at his home on the Venusberg—to no avail.

His first hundred days were over, and, despite the drumfire from the Right, he was getting a good press. *Der Spiegel,* which had made fun of Brandt for years, suddenly bid for his favor by hiring Günter Gaus, a Brandt disciple,[18] as its new managing editor. Soon *Spiegel* writers who had belittled Brandt in the past were composing awestruck laudatios. Feature writer Hermann Schreiber hurriedly gathered all the new nice things he had to say about Brandt and put them together with some of his earlier critiques for a picture-essay designed to show that it was Brandt, not he, Schreiber, who had "changed." The book, speciously subtitled "Anatomy of a Transformation," had photographs supplied by Axel Springer, Jr. "Changed?" snorted Klaus Schütz. "I say it's the same Willy as in 1961, as in 1965. It was his critics who changed. Out of it came 'the new Brandt' to explain why they didn't love him before."[19]

Brandt was also faring rather well with the imperious *Frankfurter Allgemeine Zeitung,* mainly because of the liberal-minded commentator, Jürgen Tern, who had characterized the coalition thus: "It presents itself as Left, but doesn't suppress the center." Rolf Zundel, a younger man of the same independent stripe, quoted in the weekly *Die Zeit,* what he had heard around Bonn: "For the first time since Adenauer the Federal Republic has a Chancellor again." To be sure, there wasn't anything to show in the way of major domestic reforms. Friedrich Nowottny, a preeminent television commentator, observed: "They started out bigmouthed about reform and then had to take back their promise for awhile." Two other journalists, Oskar Fehrenback and Dirk Koch, approached the hundred days from the idea of what would have been if Kiesinger were still Chancellor. Their conclusion: student riots, mounting propaganda attacks from the East, and greater economic tensions.

Brandt was preparing to travel to Erfurt to meet Willi Stoph.[20] He went beforehand to Paris, where he got full support for his *Ostpolitik* from President Pompidou; to Copenhagen, where he encouraged the Danes to enter the Common Market; and to London, where he spent ten hours talking to Prime Minister Wilson. A correspondent noted: "A degree of suspicion toward West Germany that has remained a part of British political life since World War II has abated noticeably since the Brandt coalition took power last fall. British-West German relations are in a warm period."[21]

After Erfurt he flew to the United States for his first talks with President Nixon as head of government. They had gotten off on a bad footing when Nixon made that unfortunate phone call to Kiesinger on election night, although Brandt later observed: "To err is human, the more so at that distance."[22] Even now, however, they did not take to each other. The coolness had something to do with Nixon's role in the McCarthy era, which Brandt remembered well, and the German's natural preference for American politicians like Hubert H. Humphrey, who had roots in the American Social Democratic tradition. In the Nixon entourage Henry Kissinger and his squire, Helmut Sonnenfeldt—both refugees from Nazi Germany—had developed a profound suspicion and dislike of Brandt and Egon Bahr long before. An aide reported both men saying they regarded Brandt and Bahr as "pernicious," because they dared to move on their own and "embodied instability in Germany."[23]

In Washington Brandt had three points to make: He was concerned about future relations of the European community and the United States, he wanted to convince Nixon that he was pursuing *Ostpolitik* "free of illusions," and he wanted to emphasize the need for continuing a strong United States military presence in Germany. He also argued that West Germany was not trying to get ahead of others in its approach to the East but "to catch up with our Western partners" who had already established working relationships with the Soviet Bloc.[24]

At this stage Brandt was acting as his own Foreign Minister, following the example of other contemporaries—and other Germans. It caused him some friction in April, when, without consulting Scheel, he dispatched a personal note to Poland's Wladyslaw Gomulka about the ongoing treaty talks. "It shouldn't happen again," said Scheel, when he learned about it, and it took Brandt some time to remove the mistrust he had created. The incident was grist for the opposition, but it also afforded Scheel a welcome pretext to demand—and get—a more central role in the East-West treaty negotiations.

When the controversy over the Gomulka letter broke, Brandt was in Oslo, speaking in the Storting at the invitation of the deputies of the Norwegian Parliament. What other German would get such an invitation? He returned the compliment: "The impressions I received as a young man among you—in good and bad times—are always with me. They make it easier for me in my efforts as a German politician to think at the same time as European and to make my contribution toward securing the peace." His main purpose was to urge the Norwegians to enter the Common Market.[25]

In mid-May Brandt was at Saarbrücken to conduct the SPD convention, where he was confronted with a new problem: the ideological dreams of the young Left. In the previous winter the *Jungsozialisten,* buoyed by the SPD prospects on the federal level, had issued a manifesto calling on the Brandt government to orient "all its actions to the requirements of the coming Socialist society." With a three-vote parliamentary majority, and not a very solid one, that was all Brandt needed! Instead of rapping knuckles, he chose to indulge the young radicals. He said:

> Their advice is valuable to us . . . Open and down-to-earth discussion doesn't weaken us, it makes us stronger. However, I wouldn't think much of dividing up into Left or Right hosts . . . there are political convictions that are to be taken seriously and still do not have a place in the SPD. For you can't be in two parties at the same time.[26]

Helmut Schmidt commented on this as "the unfortunate role of Willy Brandt playing the father figure toward the young" and added: "It was the one big difference of opinion between him and me after 1969. The memory of the 'thirties played a part in it for him, and his own sons. But for me it was just too much tolerance."[27] It was a view shared by Herbert Wehner.

The party had chosen the Saarland for the convention in the hope of exerting a bit of influence on the upcoming state election—and it worked. The SPD picked up 6 percent in the Saar vote a month later, 3 percent in the simultaneous election in Lower Saxony. The party slipped in North Rhine-Westphalia by 3 percent but held onto the coalition with the FDP. Altogether, the elections produced a slight SPD gain. But they were not so heartening for the FDP, which succeeded in surmounting the 5 percent minimum for representation in the state parliament only in North Rhine-Westphalia. Ominously, the state elections were fought partly as a plebiscite on *Ostpolitik* although that was really a question for federal politics. It was becoming clear that the Conservative opposition would use every opportunity to stir up emotions on this issue. In Remscheid, for example, two young housepainters told a visiting reporter they didn't even know who the local candidates were, nor did they care. "I'm voting for the Christian Democrats," said the one, adding, "Brandt and the Social Democrats want to sell us out." The other said: "I am voting for the Social Democrats because I believe we should talk to the East."[28] Polarization had reached the provinces.

On his way to Kassel to meet Willi Stoph and continue the dialogue started at Erfurt, Brandt could look back upon an extraordinary diplomatic endeavor. Egon Bahr had spent more than thirty hours negotiating a treaty draft with Andrei Gromyko in Moscow. State Secretary Duckwitz had met for three rounds with the Polish Foreign Minister, and things were looking good in Warsaw, too. At the end of April East Germany agreed to double the number of telephone lines with West Germany to a total of seventy-four and, additionally, to open telegraph and teleprinter lines between the two halves of Berlin. Overarching all these efforts were the negotiations on a new Berlin agreement begun on March 26 by ambassadors of the United States, Soviet Union, Britain, and France.

The Ides of March boded well for Brandt in Erfurt. But the Ides of May proved more favorable for Stoph in Kassel. East Germany picked up diplomatic recognition from Algeria—the twenty-third state to do so—on May 20. The next morning some 8000 radicals—half of them Communists, the other half supporters of the NPD, all of them taking advantage of new laws allowing greater freedom for political demonstrators—assembled in the North Hessian city where the German-German meeting was scheduled. There were 1000 policemen between them, and that was not enough. Shortly after Stoph got off the train from East Germany, three of the Rightist demonstrators cut down the DDR flag in front of the hotel where the summit meeting was to take place and tore it to shreds. This put Stoph one up, and he spent the first eight minutes with Brandt protesting the desecration of East Germany's black, red, and gold flag with the Communist compass-and-wheatsheaf symbol. Taking the offensive right away he charged that West Germany's laws represented "juridical aggression against the DDR"—*i.e.,* that many of those laws presumed to regulate "citizens of the DDR." He went on to accuse Schmidt, Scheel, Barzel, and Strauss, by name, of "agitation" against East Germany. In an afternoon session Brandt formally apologized for the "incidents," including one that delayed Stoph's appointment to place a wreath at a memorial for victims of Nazism. But he persevered in presenting a twenty-point agenda for future talks between East Germany and West Germany.

It had been a nervous day, filled with nasty remarks inside and outside the conference room. Toward the end the atmosphere calmed down, as in one of the pleasanter fairy tales of the Grimm brothers, who had spent part of their lives in Kassel. Brandt presented Stoph with a facsimile of the *Hildebrandlied,* the oldest known written text in the German language, which belonged to the Grimm Museum collection. Stoph took that and the twenty-point agenda home with him to East Berlin.[29]

Brandt remained hopeful. In Bonn he found that Egon Bahr had brought back a fairly sound basis for negotiation from thirty-six hours of preliminary talks in Moscow—permitting West Germany to reiterate a reunification formula and to be certain that the Soviet Union had renounced its "right to intervene" in West Germany as a victor power. Bahr's success, though limited, stirred the Rightists to new furies. At a May 30 rally the League of Expellees—purporting to represent Germans driven from homelands east of the Oder—denounced Brandt as a "traitor" and "appeaser," and demonstrators shouted slogans like: "Send Brandt to Poland," "Hang him!" Franz Josef Strauss was on hand to speak, but he failed to rouse the 10,000 demonstrators to a volume exceeding that of the loudspeakers. The opposition turned next to the Bundestag, and there the epithets flew again. Wehner was moved to accuse the Conservatives of "stirring the murder-lust of right-wing extremists," and two hundred CDU deputies marched out of the Parliament.[30]

In tactics engineered behind the scenes by Strauss and his supporters, the opposition arranged for the Springer papers to get a version of the secret "Bahr paper" brought back from Moscow a few weeks earlier. The tabloid *Bild* published excerpts from the document June 12, on the eve of the tristate elections. Asked at a news conference whether the leak had damaged the prospects for further talks with the Russians, Foreign Minister Scheel replied, "Yes." It also had the desired impact on the voting. Rainer Barzel, who was emerging as a serious competitor in the *Ostpolitik* tournament, took advantage of the Conservative momentum to raise the idea of a no-confidence vote to topple Brandt. It was only a bluff then, but it was already on Barzel's mind as a serious venture. Brandt was dismayed. The four-power Berlin talks were moving along and, after a visit by Josef Winiewicz, it seemed treaty negotiations with Poland could soon move into a decisive phase.

On June 17, the seventeenth anniversary of the East Berlin uprising, the Conservative forces organized yet another skirmish in the Bundestag. "Turn back before it is too late," admonished Barzel. "It is five minutes to high noon," Kiesinger declaimed. Meanwhile, several thousand ultra-Rightists were rioting against Brandt in Nürnberg and Obersuhl, leaving a dozen injured.[31]

A week later the coalition could take comfort in a strong reendorsement of Scheel at his FDP party convention, which also censured Erich Mende's "evil mania for sniping" and "slander"—in that and in a friendly gesture by Rumania's Premier Ion Gheorghe Maurer, who was visiting Bonn and asked Brandt, Scheel, and Heinemann to Bucharest.

The opposition campaign heated up again in July, when Walter Scheel invited the Christian Democrats to send a Bundestag deputy along with him to Moscow for the final stage of negotiations on a normalization treaty. He and Brandt had decided to send parliamentary deputies from the SPD and the FDP to ensure a "national" consensus on the treaties. The CDU coldly turned down the offer in a letter on July 20, breaking a bipartisan tradition begun by Adenauer in 1955 when he went to Moscow. Three days later Springer's *Die Welt* published another set of Bahr-Gromyko documents purporting to be the entire text of their ten-point protocol, claiming that these proved Brandt had "capitulated" to the Russians. A search for the leakers proved fruitless.

Scheel flew to Moscow July 26 with the blessings of Brandt, U.S. Secretary of State Rogers, and Britain's Foreign Secretary Lord Home. He was accompanied by Bahr, the SPD's Karl Wienand, and the FDP's Ernst Achenbach. No CDU member joined them. Once in Moscow, Scheel found the Russians were back to hard bargaining on the question of reunification, to the point of total rejection of the German proposals. After two sessions with Gromyko he called for a "thinking pause" and repaired to the German Embassy to consult with his companions on the impasse.

Ambassador Allardt was on hand, vexed because he, the son of a Prussian officer, had been shunted aside. His wife, from the minor nobility, was even more vexed; she had left town, and as a result there was neither food nor drink ready for the Scheel delegation when they went into the bug-free inner sanctum of the embassy. It was stifling, and there was scarcely room in that tiny chamber, just thirteen feet by six feet, for the men from Bonn. After a lot of palaver, Ernst Achenbach, who had been a Nazi official in Paris during the war, piped up: "Why don't we offer them a peace treaty?"

"Scheel's eyes lit up, and Bahr nodded," according to a man who sat in that tiny room. Achenbach, Scheel, and Bahr appeared to be ready to throw over the traces of twenty-five years of alliance with the West and make a separate peace deal with the Russians, like their forefathers at Rapallo in 1922, and in a fashion undreamed of even by the opposition in Bonn. "Those were the German nationalists," the participant recalled, "led on by that old Nazi, Achenbach." Karl Wienand, a protégé of Herbert Wehner, objected vehemently: "If you do that I will take the next plane to Bonn and tell the world. As a German parliamentarian I have no vote. But I tell you, you cannot do that." The others gazed at Wienand in perplexity, the participant reported, and then agreed to drop the Achenbach proposal.[32] The ghost of Rapallo vanished from the cement chamber, leaving an unpleasant odor of the German past behind. The group went on meeting until 2:30 a.m., fortified by some coffee provided at last by a reluctant Allardt. Later during Scheel's eleven-day stay the Russians filled him so full of vodka that he became quite drunk and was out of action for a night and a day.

In the end Scheel acted as the sinewy defender of German rights and interests. When Gromyko finally appeared at the German delegation's quarters in the Lenin Hills with a treaty text that had been approved by the Politburo, Scheel pulled out an additional scrap of paper. It was an instruction agreed on by the coalition Cabinet with regard to the Berlin problem. On his return from the Moscow preliminaries, Egon Bahr had warned that the Soviets were allergic to the mere mention of Berlin by West Germany because it suggested a connection of issues they wished to keep quite separate. Sitting opposite Gromyko, Scheel now read aloud from a typewritten sheet:

"The treaty will not be laid before the Bundestag for ratification until a satisfactory outcome of the Berlin negotiations has been reached; the Federal Government has thereby discharged its responsibility for Berlin."

Gromyko pretended not to hear; Scheel read it a second time. Again Gromyko pretended not to hear. Scheel read it a third time and then shoved the sheet of paper across the table. It lay there like a dishrag, while the Germans and Russians talked on. Valentin Falin, the Soviet expert on Germany and later Ambassador to Bonn, furtively pushed the Berlin paper centimeter by centimeter back toward Scheel. When the round was finished, Scheel looked down and found the paper in front of him again. As they stood up to go, Scheel grasped Gromyko's arm and handed the document to him saying, "Herr Minister, you forgot the paper." Gromyko gave up and stuffed it in his pocket, promising to convey it to his superiors. Later, he advised Scheel there could be no enactment of a Berlin agreement without ratification of the Moscow treaty.[33] In this fashion an unbreakable link was forged between the destiny of Moscow's relations with Bonn and the future sanctity of West Berlin. It surely would have come about without Scheel's stratagem. But Brandt was grateful and, after Scheel's party returned August 7 with an initialed treaty text, warmly praised his coalition partner for his work.

A keystone is no larger nor more precious than the stones it holds in place—it is the location that counts. So it was with the Moscow treaty. Rereading the text well after the event it seems almost innocent of deeper purpose or design. A preamble says West Germany and the Soviet Union want to contribute to peace and security in Europe, conform with the principles of the United Nations, and strengthen mutual relations. Article 1 says the two sides "proceed from the actual situation existing in this region" of Europe in seeking detente and "normalization." Article 2 avows conformity with the United Nations Charter and affirms the intent to "settle their disputes exclusively by peaceful means." Article 3 acknowledges the "territorial integrity of all states in Europe within their present frontiers," renounces future territorial claims, and regards all European frontiers as "inviolable"—including the Oder-Neisse line and the boundary between East and West Germany. Article 4 says the treaty has no effect on other treaties to which the two parties adhere. Article 5 deals with ratification procedures. The Germans were also permitted to deposit a "letter on German unity" with Gromyko, stating that the treaty "does not conflict with the political objective of the Federal Republic of Germany to work for a state of peace in Europe in which the German nation will recover its unity in free self-determination." Neat and simple. It did not sacrifice anything that West Germany physically possessed, nor did it grant anything of substance that the Soviet Union did not already have. Yet it became a keystone for a whole structure of East-West accommodations: a four-power agreement on Berlin, a German-Polish treaty, a pact between the two Germanys, negotiations on European security and troop reductions, and more.

For the Germans and the Russians, however, the Moscow treaty had a far deeper impact—something to do with the texture of their national souls, after the shedding of so much heart's blood between them. This was why, from the day it was initialed, practically everyone on both sides spoke of the "historic" nature of the treaty.

Ever since Peter the Great the Russians had sought acceptance as Europeans in Europe. But only sporadically had they been acknowledged by the Germans: in 1759 when 80,000 Russian troops nearly defeated Frederick II's Prussians at Kunersdorf, in 1815 when Russian military power won the Tsar representation at the Congress of Vienna; in 1905 when Tsar Nicholas and Kaiser Wilhelm had a brief cousinly flirt; in 1939 when Stalin and Hitler joined to spite the Western powers and carve up Poland.

Adenauer's 1955 pact with Khrushchev had exchanged German war prisoners for diplomatic recognition, but it left bilateral relations in as desolate a state as they had been before. The Moscow treaty acknowledged the *presence* of the Soviets in Central Europe and, more, a partnership with them in the organization of peaceful relations for the foreseeable future. It cemented the territorial status quo on Soviet terms.

For the Germans of the Federal Republic it meant putting aside dreams, however diminished by time, of recovering lost territory in the East and even of achieving the unity of the shrunken nation. The gain was in being able to shuck off the role of the bogeyman of Europe, in which the Communists had cast them, and to begin relationships as normal neighbors. In place of vituperation—"Soviet dictatorship" as an official Bonn premise and "neo-Nazi peril" as an official Moscow premise—the treaty offered a basis for mutual trust. That was something the Russians and the Germans had hardly ever freely given each other before.

The Soviets badly wanted Brandt to seal the treaty in Moscow with his signature. He agreed, breaking off his vacation in Norway to accept the invitation of Premier Kosygin. There were last-minute twists. One day before Brandt's departure on August 11 from Bonn, Kiesinger and Barzel sent him a letter begging for delay until a Berlin agreement and negotiations with East Germany were further along. In East Berlin Ulbricht disclosed notes to eight Western countries asking for diplomatic recognition of the DDR. Even as Brandt's Moscow-bound jet carrying 132 officials and journalists reached the head of the Bonn airport runway, someone called in a bomb threat; the flight was delayed two hours for a search. Finally, Springer's *Bild* and *Die Welt* carried the entire text of the still-secret treaty later that morning.

Brandt in Moscow: No German trod the pavement of the great city without feeling the leaden past weighing down his feet. Hitler's Panzers, in the name of a "New Order," had reached the outskirts in 1941; the tomb of Lenin had been there to remind them hauntingly of the Communists' new order. Twenty-five years before the Red Army had flung hundreds of German flags into the dust in front of the Lenin mausoleum during its victory ceremony. Now German flags were waving from masts in Red Square. "We have come late, but we have come," Brandt told Kosygin on arrival. Moscow, he found, was "altogether much more European than I had imagined"—an observation that must have gladdened Kremlin hearts accustomed to Adenauer's view that Russia "belonged to Asia."

Brandt took up the European theme in a statement he taped for television for the folks at home:

> Europe ends neither at the Elbe nor at the eastern frontier of Poland. Russia is inextricably involved in the history of Europe, not only as an opponent and a peril, but also as a partner, historically, politically,

in culture and economics . . . My fellow citizens: Nothing is lost with
this treaty that was not gambled away long ago. We have the courage
to turn over a new page of history. . . .

The signing took place in the white-and-gold Hall of Catherine the Great in
the Kremlin Palace with Leonid Brezhnev looking on. Afterward, he drew
Brandt aside for a talk that stretched on for four hours. "It was just a
beginning," Brandt said later. The Soviet leader wanted to get a personal
impression of this unusual German. Later he would observe: "A serious man,
a down-to-earth man and an understanding partner, a man with whom you
can deal constructively."[34] Brandt took the opportunity to raise the subject of
Berlin, saying: "You must understand that I am personally very much engaged
in this question. I can't simply erase a part of my political life that I conducted
as Governing Mayor . . . If we want detente then West Berlin may not remain
a spot of Cold War." He also touched on Berlin in his television statement for
West Germany:

> Tomorrow it will be nine years since the wall was built. Today we
> have—I confidently hope—made a start in counteracting that
> division, so that people will no longer have to die on the barbed
> wire, until the day comes when, so we hope, the division of our people
> may be overcome.

He was tensed up for the talk with Brezhnev, sweating through his shirt. The
Russian made it easier for him by cracking small jokes, and he indicated that
the Soviet Union might be a bit more forthcoming on Berlin in the talks with
the Western Allies.

The next day's program called for the laying of a wreath at the tomb of the
unknown soldier, where unseen loudspeakers broadcast Rachmaninov's
Second Piano Concerto. Kosygin, the economics specialist of the Politburo,
made it clear in a second round of talks that the Russians considered the treaty
a basis for greatly expanded economic cooperation with West Germany. After
five hours of that there was a press conference where Brandt stressed the aim
he had pursued before and after the Berlin wall was built on that August 13
exactly nine years before: "What we are doing is at least to try to reach the
level of our allies as far as relations with the Soviet Union are concerned."
Then he flew home, drained.

In Bonn he told a news conference that he was "certain" that in the
endeavor begun in Moscow, "we have the backing of the great majority of our
people." The polls supported him—one in Munich showed over 80 percent in
favor of the Moscow treaty; in another 79 percent agreed *Ostpolitik* was an

opportunity not to be missed.[35] Then he returned to Norway to finish his vacation.

In East Berlin Walter Ulbricht was having difficulty swallowing the Moscow event. True, *Neues Deutschland* dutifully hailed it as "good news." But then his Council of Ministers issued a declaration of interpreting the treaty as a call for diplomatic recognition of East Berlin by Bonn. That was not what Brezhnev had in mind, and he ordered Tass and *Pravda* to correct Ulbricht. Brezhnev summoned the seventy-seven-year-old German Communist to Moscow and obliged him to sign a joint Warsaw Pact communiqué on August 20 approving the Moscow treaty and proclaiming that West Berlin should "cease being a point of tension and become a site of detente." The old Bolshevik was losing his touch. In July he had turned a political somersault in Rostock, declaring the time had come to recognize "a new situation" in relations with West Germany. But he hadn't consulted anyone in his own Politburo about the policy shift, and Erich Honecker was prompted to try to topple Ulbricht then and there.[36] The Russians didn't back Honecker then, probably feeling that at that time a switch in East Berlin would disrupt plans for the Moscow treaty. Still, it was clear that Ulbricht was more than just obstinate—he was becoming the obstacle to rapproachment between Bonn and Moscow.

Shortly before the seventh round of quadripartite Berlin negotiations began in September, Ambassador Abrasimov asked U.S. Ambassador Kenneth Rush to East Berlin for a long private talk over lunch. "Tell us what you want, and we will reply very quickly," the Russian advised the American. It was obvious then and later that what the Western Allies wanted was a Soviet guarantee of unimpeded access to West Berlin. Rush declined to give a detailed response, but he noted that for the first time in five months the Soviets were evincing interest in the four-power settlement.[37]

Poland, too, determined it was time to proceed into the final phase of negotiations with West Germany, and on September 9 the Brandt government was able to announce that it expected conclusion of a Polish-German treaty by the end of the year.

Each step closer toward reconciliation with East Europe was a step closer toward confrontation at home. Erich Mende had formed a loose "national-liberal" wing within the FDP during the spring. He drew heavy fire from the rest of the Liberals, but he persisted until the FDP executive moved to throw him out, along with two other like-minded Conservatives, members of the Bundestag. Mende and the others beat the leadership to the mark by quitting October 8. They had already taken up relations with Franz Josef Strauss, and they remained in the Bundestag to vote with the Christian Democratic Union.

In a stroke they had cut the nominal Brandt-Scheel majority in the Federal Parliament from twelve to six votes. Some liberals blamed Brandt and Scheel long after for this switch arguing that they could have bought off the defectors by giving them ambassadorships or other administration posts.[38] Now it was too late. "The government majority is crumbling," Barzel crowed. In the state elections of Hesse and Bavaria in November, however, the defections caused a small liberal backlash. Contrary to many predictions the FDP held its own in Hesse with 10 percent of the vote and kept its toehold in the Bavarian parliament, too. The SPD vote was slightly diminished in both states. The Liberals claimed they got a bit of a boost from Andrei Gromyko, who stopped in Hesse to see Scheel for six hours on October 29, a week before the election, though Gromyko's purpose was to talk about larger German questions. The Soviet Government had just instructed Ulbricht to offer negotiations with West Germany; it was a snare. The Soviets knew that if they could also get East and West Germany talking about Berlin access, it would sharply undercut the quadripartite negotiations on that subject. The Brandt government knew that too and refused the bait, waiting until the Western Allies instructed it to begin meetings with Ulbricht's representatives.[39] When Egon Bahr did begin conferring with East Berlin's Michael Kohl on November 27, he was under strict instructions not to discuss anything relating to Berlin. It was like discussing sex without mentioning intercourse, but Bahr and Kohl persisted.

The Brandt-Scheel alliance had its first birthday at the end of October, and they marked it with a press conference in which they vowed to hold together until the end of the legislative term. Earlier, Brandt had denied that his majority was thin, remarking, as he had before, that "Konrad Adenauer became Chancellor with his own vote, after all." Did he have a premonition that he would himself be reduced to a one-vote majority in eighteen months? It seems unlikely. "This federal government is fully capable of action," he told the press October 23. "It is determined to realize the tasks it has set itself. Cooperation between the coalition partners is good. The majority of the government parties is narrow, but sufficient. Narrow majorities are no handicap for effective politics." With reference to the opposition, he said: "We need neither alarmists in foreign policy nor panic makers in economic policy." As if to remind them of the smallness of their base that day the upper house of the Parliament rejected the administration's bill to liberalize laws regulating pornography—forcing it back before an interparliamentary mediation committee.

It was still a fairly happy crew, the Brandt-Scheel team, after twelve months of proximity, if a bit "loud" and "ostentatious," as Gerhard Schröder had observed, not about Brandt, but about other members of the inner circle. The daily routine had settled into place. Brandt started his day about 9 a.m. with a situation report lasting about thirty minutes from Ahlers, the Foreign Ministry's Duckwitz, and, occasionally, Gerhard Wessel from the BND. For a time Wehner was kept informed by breakfasting with Ehmke. Now and then Brandt went over to the barracks to do SPD things.

For Brandt, team spirit was the alpha and omega of his administration, even when it got in the way of hard, clear decisions. "He doesn't like to be voted down," Schütz remembered. "He avoids conflict if he can. It is not necessarily democracy, but it is a style of leadership to use the strength of the leader as seldom as possible so as not to use it up. But he does have an inclination to talk and discuss longer than others."[40] Unfortunately, Brandt's hopes for teamwork were soon dashed—first by rivalry between Karl Schiller and Alex Möller over finances, and then by others.[41]

There was a shirtsleeve informality about a lot of it. The Schaumburg Palace had probably not experienced so much profanity since the last time the housepainters were there. At the annual summer garden party Brandt served beer instead of *Sekt*. Ehmke, whom everyone called "Horst," although he could insist on "Professor Doktor," was a leading exponent of the familiar form of address. Even Scheel had flown to Moscow wearing a sport jacket and a striped shirt. "In comparison to Adenauer's, this government has a weaker authority and, by the same token, less authoritarianism, which has its positive side in the sense of more democracy," Conrad Ahlers observed. "There is no question that we are less elegant, even clumsy. But that is a matter of nature rather than a lack of professional ability."

The *Ostpolitik* negotiations with Poland were quite as intense and protracted as the dealings with Moscow. More than a score of delegations flew back and forth between Warsaw and Bonn in preparation of a treaty, and by November Scheel could step in and complete the negotiations. There was some hard bargaining about the Oder-Neisse line, with the Poles claiming that it had been cemented by the Potsdam treaty and the Germans asserting that it was not yet juridically fixed. There was also a problem of getting the Poles to acknowledge that there were still a lot of *Volksdeutsche*—several hundred thousand of them—remaining in the new Poland. After nine days of talks, however, the German side was content. Scheel initialed the treaty text on November 18.

It was, above all, a pro-Polish treaty, the first on the contested ground in the 1000 years of German-Polish history. The preamble noted that Poland had been "the first victim" of World War II, but also that "a new generation has meanwhile grown up," muting the pain caused by the deaths of 6 million Poles and the forced expulsion of 9 million Germans from the disputed territory. Article 1 affirmed the inviolability of the Oder-Neisse line as the "Western state frontier" of Poland and stated that neither party had territorial claims against the other. Article 2 repeated the renunciation of force formulas of the Moscow treaty. Article 3 proclaimed the intention to further "normalization and comprehensive development of their mutual relations." Articles 4 and 5 were of a procedural nature. In addition, Poland acknowledged the humanitarian problem of the ethnic Germans and vowed to give consideration to repatriation wishes.

Brandt was invited to sign the treaty by Premier Josef Cyrankiewicz, and the date was set for December 7. Before he went, there were some distractions. Herbert Czaja, president of the League of Expellees, accused Brandt of "throwing away 40,000 square miles of German territory." Barzel, a native of East Prussia, called the treaty "painful" and claimed that the expellees had not been consulted. NPD supporters staged rallies against the signing. The CDU arranged to have a meeting of parliamentary deputies in Berlin in early December, and this caused Ulbricht to order traffic stopped on the access routes, sometimes lasting seventeen hours. That was too much distraction. Though the four-power Berlin talks were going badly, this time Ulbricht had carried obstinacy too far. At a Warsaw Pact meeting in Berlin Brezhnev rammed home a formula for a communiqué calling for conclusion of the four-power Berlin talks. Everyone except Ulbricht accepted it, and so the usual "unanimity" was not expressed on that point. It was a rebuff on Ulbricht's own ground.[42]

Brandt went to Warsaw with stronger emotions than he had felt in Moscow. He had with him Günter Grass, from Danzig-Gdansk, and another popular author, Siegfried Lenz from Lyck-Elk in East Prussia. Klaus von Bismarck, a great-grandchild of the Chancellor who had looked on Poles as inferiors, also went along.

Before the signing in the Radziwill Palace, Brandt laid a wreath at the tomb of the unknown soldier and then went with another wreath to the Warsaw ghetto memorial. There, at the edge of the wasteland created by Himmler's SS in 1942, the last domicile of 500,000 Polish Jews, he fell to his knees on the cold, wet stones. It was a reflex, so uncontrolled that he had to wrench himself to his feet a minute later. Brandt had never made any pretense of being religious. But here he was kneeling in front of 30 million Poles, for 77 million Germans—all of them. That evening in a toast at the Wilanow Castle, where he was quartered, he said of his countrymen:

> Many feel as if it is only now that the loss they suffered twenty-five years ago is making itself felt. To a certain extent pipedreams were cherished. But I ask myself whether here in Poland, too, wrongful

ideas—that it was impossible ever to trust us in the Federal Republic of Germany—were not harbored. Time will still be required on both sides.

Although he dismissed his action as "just an attempt to help a lot of people," it was the kneeling that stayed in the mind. On the way home, as German journalists natives of Silesia, pointed out their former homes to Brandt from an altitude of 29,000 feet, the pilot spoke over the intercom: "Herr Bundeskanzler, we have just flown over the Polish western frontier." Brandt was reminded of the wartime anecdote about a father pointing out Germany on a world map to his son and saying: "You see this little spot, my boy—that is Germany." The boy replies: "Does Hitler know that?" Brandt added: "The current Federal Chancellor knows the true place Germany has in the world."[43]

At home Brandt encountered rebuffs in new quarters. Despite the fact that he and Wehner made a special journey to Bremen to attend a convention of Young Socialists, the *Jusos* chose Karsten Voigt, a Leftist, as their chairman. With Voigt's announcement that the *Jusos* were promoting an "anti-capitalist strategy for realizing a Socialist society," Brandt and Wehner came to fear that the group, however small its numbers, could be used by the opposition to frighten off middle-of-the-road voters.[44]

Brandt was hardly back in Bonn when food and wage riots broke out in Gdansk, spreading soon to Western Poland and ending with the ouster of Gomulka, the man with whom he had been discussing reconciliation only a few days before. So much for Poland for awhile.

On top of that he was being buffeted by high-powered critics in the United States who charged that he was going too far, too fast with *Ostpolitik:* Henry Kissinger, Helmut Sonnenfeldt, Defense Secretary Melvin Laird, and the Assistant Secretary of State for Central European Affairs Martin J. Hillenbrand were among the administration officials identified in this category by the Brandt government. Dean Acheson, the former Secretary of State; George Ball, the former Under Secretary; and the two former High Commissioners, Lucius Clay and John J. McCloy, were also listed as suspicious of Brandt's policies. "Nothing will divert me," Brandt said of the spoken and unspoken criticism. But Conrad Ahlers and others were speaking of a "crisis of confidence."[45]

There were some consolations. Berlin's senate, after a lot of wrangling, made him an honorary citizen—at the same age as Bismarck—and he declared with discernible pride: "I remain a citizen of this city." Lübeck was still working on an honorary citizenship for him. It had taken the Lübeck senate thirty-five sessions to agree on a similar honor for its other son, Thomas

Mann, and even then a CDU senator would stay away from the ceremony in 1955 complaining about Mann's wartime broadcasts against Hitler—"when bombs were falling on Lübeck and any shithouse could be smashed." But the Lübeckers were "well known as bad mouthers," Mann noted, "almost like Renaissance Florentines." In time the Lübeck award would come to Brandt, too.

With relief he headed south to Kenya for a winter holiday.

The Moscow and Warsaw treaties were on ice and would stay in that state of artificial preservation until the Berlin agreements were complete. When would the time come to remove them from the refrigerator and serve them up to the Bundestag for ratification? As the year ended Brandt was confident that the four powers would finish the Berlin negotiations "in two or three months." After the new year he was more skeptical. As he told the Bundestag in his report on the State of the Nation in January:

> No one can know whether there will be setbacks again . . . We
> influence events around us, but they affect us still more strongly. . . .
> What concerns us is making things easier, better, for people in both
> German states in relation to one another, and beyond that, a joint
> responsibility of the Germans for peace in Europe and the world.
> That is no exclamation with a warning finger raised, but an honest,
> necessary reference to the topic of national responsibility.

The report was augmented with "materials" worked out by a team of academics and government officials making a factual comparison of East and West Germany for the first time. The study showed that by virtually all measurements the standard of living was about 33 percent higher in the Federal Republic. But it also showed that East Germany was better off in such categories as factory accident prevention and lower infant mortality.

Brandt's skeptical view was borne out in the last week of January when Ulbricht clamped down on the Berlin access routes once more for five days running. The pretext was to counter "provocative demonstrations" of West German presence in West Berlin by Bonn politicians, including Brandt. Trucks carrying food and raw materials to the city were held up as long as thirty hours. It seemed as if the signals from East Berlin and Moscow were changing almost every day. Premier Kosygin wrote to Brandt that the Soviet Union remained interested in improving relations with West Germany.[46] About the same time, however, Walter Ulbricht was telling his Central Committee that the DDR was insisting anew on "normal diplomatic relations" with West Germany, dredging up what seemed to be a discarded formula.[47] A few days later *Pravda* carried an editorial prodding Brandt to ratify the Moscow and Warsaw treaties and cease making unacceptable demands about West Berlin. In retrospect, all of this appeared to be ample evidence that a last-ditch struggle on what to do when vis-à-vis West Germany was being fought in the Communist councils. There were parallel ups and downs in the quadripartite negotiations. Kenneth Rush recalled that Ambassador Abrasimov had been quite chilly in a December session and subsequently surprised the three Western envoys February 5 by treating their first draft proposal as a positive step. Then the Russian turned cold again for almost two months. There were two overriding issues then and later: how to reconcile the Western wish to uphold connections between West Berlin and West Germany with the Soviet demand that the West German presence be "reduced," and how to reconcile Western insistence on unimpeded access to Berlin with the Communist position that East Germany had sovereignty over the access routes.[48]

There was another factor at work, of which the Western Allies had hardly an inkling—the battle over Walter Ulbricht's ouster. The crafty East German had convened that Central Committee plenum in January to prepare the Seventh Congress of the SED, with himself cast as the star performer, as usual. Brezhnev had other ideas. By the time Ulbricht returned from a lengthy stay in Moscow March 14, the plans for his replacement by Honecker were complete. He and Honecker attended the Twenty-fourth Congress of the U.S.S.R. Communist Party in Moscow a fortnight later, but it was Honecker who was given the honor of making the customary speech for the "brother party." Ulbricht did not go quietly; he fought to the end, even after Honecker formally replaced him as First Secretary of the SED May 3. A terrible irony for the old man who had made a lifetime precept of loyalty to the Soviet Union— to end his career accused of contradicting Soviet policy.[49] Even in his demise he succeeded in holding up the Berlin settlement, which he had opposed from the outset.

Soon after Honecker took over, Ambassador Abrasimov called Ambassador Rush over to East Berlin to tell him at a secret luncheon that now—twenty-three years after the Berlin blockade—the Soviet Union was ready to assume responsibility for guaranteeing free access to Berlin. Ulbricht, in this respect, was a victim of Willy Brandt's *Ostpolitik*, though his successor remained a vigorous proponent of *Abgrenzung*—"fencing off"—toward West Germany. Despite the rather gloomy pause created by the Ulbricht succession struggle, there had been some small progress. East Berlin opened ten telephone lines to West Berlin in January, permitting direct conversations across the sector border for the first time since 1952. In February Premier Stoph authorized talks between the East Berlin and West Berlin governments to supplement the quadripartite negotiations and the Bahr-Kohl meetings. The orchestration of a comprehensive settlement between the two parts of Germany plus Berlin was complete. The Brandt government hailed the move as "a sign of goodwill."

The rule of thumb in West German politics was that the opposition party generally won the state elections or made the major gains. This was not disproved in the Brandt-Scheel years, although there were some variations. On March 14 the SPD suffered losses in the West Berlin election, dropping back 6.5 percentage points to about half the vote. The CDU picked up most of the difference. One week later the CDU got 50 percent of the vote in Rhineland-Palatinate, also a gain. But the SPD's 40 percent was a larger gain. The pattern was roughly the same in Schleswig-Holstein in April. As in those held during 1970, these contests were fought almost entirely on federal issues: *Ostpolitik* and national economic conditions. While Brandt declared he was "satisfied" with the election results, he faced difficulties in other quarters. The Leftists' "long march through the institutions" had begun, and they forced a confrontation with the captious Munich Mayor Hans Jochen Vogel, a Brandt favorite. In support of Vogel Brandt accepted a ruling drafted by his old friend, Professor Richard Löwenthal, stating that Social Democrats would never allow differences between their philosophy and that of the Communists to be "blurred." But Brandt temporized about throwing Leftists out of the SPD; the problem would come back to haunt him.

He was also having trouble in his Cabinet, brought on in part by inflationary price rises but also by sharpening personal rivalries. The breaking point came at the beginning of May. West German living costs had risen nearly 5 percent in one year. Yet the government was spending 18 percent more than in 1970, and some of the SPD ministers were demanding additional budget outlays totaling $17 billion. Deficit spending was one thing; this seemed too much. Just at this moment, semiofficial hints of a new revaluation seeped out in Bonn, drawing $12 billion in speculative investments into the West German currency market and forcing Bonn to let the *Deutschmark* float. Faced with all this uncertainty and the heightened demands of his colleagues, Finance Minister Möller decided to quit. He was sixty-eight years old, and he had been through enough stress. Brandt accepted his resignation May 13 and immediately named Karl Schiller to take over the post, making him a kind of "Superminister" for Economics and Finance. At this stage Schiller was a political asset for the SPD in the Rightist camp. Springer papers continued to praise him, while damning practically everything else the Brandt government was doing.[50]

The Möller resignation was perhaps inevitable. For a time it also turned

Brandt's attention to domestic affairs and the condition of his Cabinet. "The Chancellor has swum himself free," declared Rüdiger von Wechmar, his deputy press spokesman, who pointed out how Brandt was ticking off colleagues whose excesses he had tolerated earlier. "Why am I getting this draft now and not earlier," he demanded of his Chancellery aides, and he showed more mettle in arguments with Cabinet ministers, too.[51] Now and then he pounded on the table, to the surprise of men who had known only his "stupefying tolerance," as Wechmar described it.

As before Brandt sought approval abroad and received more there than he ever did at home. He was the other German the world had been looking for and now welcomed, while reminding itself daily of the kind of German it didn't like by running Hitler films and television series about Nazis—even "comic" Nazis. This was most readily evident in the United States and Britain, which, of course, had never felt the jackboots of Nazi occupation. "I have to go to the United States to see Nazis," Brandt drily remarked, "on television." *Time* magazine had made him its Man of the Year for 1970, and in June the man was on his way to the United States again. Yale University awarded him an honorary doctorate with a laudatio that said he had proven the democratic principle of changing leadership in the Federal Republic and provided "hope" with his policy of reconciliation between East and West.

It was important for him to see Nixon again. The basis for a Berlin agreement had been created, and there was movement in other areas of East-West relations: The Strategic Arms Limitation Talks were progressing, and Brezhnev had just signaled interest in NATO's 1969 bid for discussing mutual troop reductions in Central Europe. There was a flurry of concern in the Brandt government in May that arms-troop talks might distract attention from completion of the Berlin agreement, but Brandt had received assurances from Defense Secretary Melvin Laird.[52] For his part, Brandt felt that future relations between the expanding European Community and the United States continued to hold high priority; he was aware of protectionist tendencies on both sides of the Atlantic. He also wanted to inform Nixon about difficulties with East Germany, once the Berlin agreement was done. To underline his point he took along a document prepared for Communist cadres in East Germany that denounced his policies as "a danger" to the Soviet Bloc. For his part Nixon told his German guest about the beginning of his China policy, which, the Chancellor noted in a friendly toast, was another sign of the growing intensity of East-West communication.

In Bonn once again, Brandt decided the time was ripe to resume formal discussions with East Germany on "regulating relations between both states" and end the year-long pause that had followed the Kassel summit. His idea was to raise the desultory Bahr-Kohl talks to a higher plane. "The political weight of the Federal Republic of Germany has not suffered damage but has grown," he said June 25. "However, this is no ground for worries or fears on the part of others. We know our place. I think I know what is possible and what is not. We must always find the correct measure, which was often too difficult in our history." That night he and Rut held the annual garden party at the Chancellery for 1200 guests, including their second son. "I am Lars Brandt," the youth said at the gate. "Anybody can say that," replied the security guard. "Show me your identity papers." The twenty-year-old produced a driver's license and was admitted. There was a populist air about the festivities, for the Brandts had invited foreign laborers from Yugoslavia, Turkey, and Italy, soldiers, nurses, off-duty policemen, and some of the ethnic Germans recently allowed to move from Poland. There was a great hunt for autographs despite the lack of notables. "Let me have your autograph, Count," a man said to an American correspondent. "But I am not a count," the American retorted. "You look like a count to me," said the man.

After sixteen months of pregnancy the Berlin negotiations had at last come to full term. By August 1, 1971, the ambassadors of the four victor powers had met twenty-five times, and now it was clear that the birth of an agreement was being induced. The Soviet leadership understood there could be no ratification of the Moscow treaty and no progress on SALT or their own projected Conference on European Security and Cooperation until a Berlin agreement was concluded. The Russians—virtuosi of diplomatic patience in the past—were growing more impatient with each passing day. To exploit their agitation Ambassador Rush recommended intensified talks, and Nixon, who had stepped in to help things along before, authorized him to proceed.[53] The diplomatic midwives convened for fifty hours over a ten-day period, and on August 23 the document was born.

It was a remarkable achievement in every respect, including the technical, for each tiny step had to be cleared not only with the home offices in Washington, Moscow, London, and Paris, but also with the governments in Bonn and East Berlin. The birth was not without pain. Late in July there was another refugee killing at the Berlin wall—the sixty-fifth shooting by East German guards along the 28-mile barrier in ten years. Understandably, this drew more attention than the four-power negotiations, to which the West Berliners were either apathetic or cynical.[54] Undoubtedly, the shoot-to-kill order was designed to prevent East Germans from being tempted by detente, especially at a time when the Berlin talks were drawing to a close. There were reactionaries on the Western side, too. In the last week of July the Springer papers and Gerhard Löwenthal came out with new leaks, including some of the four-power position papers of February and March and a diplomatic cablegram describing talks between Egon Bahr and Henry Kissinger. *Quick,* an illustrated magazine previously devoted primarily to nudes and love stories, joined the leak contest with some documents purloined by Gehlen people and published under the heading "Bonn wants to give away Berlin." The achievement of the accord overrode these concerns, the accord that ended Berlin's role as a perennial trouble spot. It provided for unimpeded access, with a Soviet guarantee, from West Germany to West Berlin, and it authorized West Berliners to visit East Berlin and East Germany. Beyond this, it permitted West Berlin to retain its connections with West Germany, including a number of federal institutions. It also permitted the Russians to establish a consulate in West Berlin and assured them that the Bonn Government would refrain from constitutional acts in West Berlin. The baptismal initialing of the agreement was delayed until September 3, because the East and West Germans quarreled over translation of the official English, Russian, and French texts. It was not a perfect agreement in anybody's eyes—given all the conflicting interests it could not be perfect. But it was a better deal than expected, and it gave West Berlin years of security. Still, there were strong misgivings both in East Berlin and Bonn. An East German official told an American: "Our state sovereignty is our most precious cause. We lost more than we gained from the four ambassadors." In Bonn the CDU issued a statement saying the agreement "causes us special doubts," and "cannot satisfy us." Franz Josef Strauss went further, denouncing it as "a rubber treaty."[55] Mindful of the extreme skepticism of most Germans toward a pact in which they had no say, Brandt went to Berlin to do some public relations. "As someone who has every right to think of himself as a Berliner I can understand the reservation with which many people in this city still judge the result," he told a group of trade unionists September 6. "'Na *und'* (big deal) they say, and add that they want to wait and see what comes out of it." He went on to defend the agreement as "the most significant development for peace in Europe since the end of the war."

That same day Egon Bahr and East Germany's Michael Kohl met in Bonn to begin the sticky task of filling in the details of the agreement on the German side. They came into conflict almost immediately over what Bonn was authorized to negotiate with East Germany and what was the responsibility of the West Berlin senate in talks with East Berlin. The translation argument played a role in this.

Despite these difficulties Brandt remained confident. He had received an invitation to visit Brezhnev on the Crimea, and he accepted before telling Nixon or anyone else about it. He flew to the Black Sea on September 16, taking Bahr along with him, and spent sixteen hours of the next two days talking, drinking, walking, and speedboating with Brezhnev around the resort town of Oreanda. Brandt later maintained that he had held his vodka better than the Russian. The meeting was altogether extraordinary—unprecedented in terms of hospitality for Western leaders. Brandt came home aglow with impressions of "the first man of the Soviet Union." He spoke repeatedly of a new and positive "realism" on the part of Brezhnev. But he was sober in evaluating his own position with regard to the Russians, comparing it to the German-Russian equation of former days: "The difference is in changed power relationships. In earlier times Russia and Germany were each one of Europe's great powers. Formerly our bilateralism was unlimited. But now we have limited bilateralism." To illustrate this he pointed out that Germany spoke to the Soviet Union as a partner of the United States, NATO, and the Common Market. West Germany, he said, had become "a partner in a businesslike contract" with the Soviet Union. Nevertheless, he and Brezhnev agreed to consult in the future on "political" matters.[56]

Back amid the realities of West Germany Brandt was slapped in the face a week later by a young NPD member named Viktor R. Gislo, who rushed at him during an inspection of the site of the 1972 Olympic Games in Munich. Brandt struck back, as Gislo shouted: "That is for your policy in the East." Then Gislo was seized by the Munich police chief. "Let him alone," Brandt called, as they dragged away the twenty-two-year-old. He was given another sharp taste of opposition in the Bundestag, where Rainer Barzel—referring to the Berlin agreement and the Crimean talks—accused him of being more concerned with "the opportunity of power than with human rights" in Germany. Wehner sprang to Brandt's defense: "You don't want information, you want a demonstration, a confrontation. Why don't you come right out and say you are against NATO?" The Conservative's quick tongue could be infuriating; he was never at a loss for words, prompting Wehner to observe, "I think Barzel changes his oil after every 2000 words."

Barzel was chosen to succeed Kiesinger as chairman of the CDU and, in effect, as the Conservative Chancellor candidate at a convention in Saarbrücken October 4. At forty-seven he had already operated on the far Left and the far Right of the CDU; now he was trying to stay in the middle. Alexander Mitscherlich, the Frankfurt psychoanalyst, described him as "a man of the coming employee culture—he doesn't want to create opposition, he wants to be promoted." More than anyone else, however, he had the ability to infuriate Willy Brandt, who often went livid at the mere sound of his voice. Asked how he regarded the prospect of running against Barzel, Brandt replied: "I will try to rein in my joy." A consolation of sorts came the following week when the SPD's Hans Koschnik won 55 percent of the vote in the Bremen state election—a gain of 10 percentage points and the first solid election victory for the party since Brandt had come to power two years before.

Brandt was sitting in the Bundestag building on a Wednesday afternoon, editing the preface he had written for a collection of Helmut Schmidt's speeches, when word was brought to him from Oslo that he had been awarded the 1971 Nobel Peace Prize. "So, so," he murmured and went on editing. When an SPD man walked in to ask him about some party propaganda against Barzel, Brandt replied with a touch of irony: "I don't have anything to do with that now. I am only responsible for big things, for peace and the like." He had known of the proposals for his candidature as early as the previous spring. Hildegard Hamm-Brücher, the FDP's dedicated State Secretary for Education, had nominated him, as some Frenchmen, Danes, and Americans had also done. He himself recommended that Jean Monnet, the aged patriot of Europe, get the prize. But he was profoundly moved—as a German and as a Norwegian—when it came to him. "The circle closes" he murmured, speaking of his own career and of "one's own relationship to one's countrymen and the other way around." There was a budget debate under way in the Bundestag that October 20, and at 5 p.m. Kai-Uwe von Hassel interrupted the debate on congratulate Brandt. The coalition deputies, a handful of CDU deputies, too, rose to their feet to applaud. Strauss sent a friendly telegram but stayed outside—having declared the previous Sunday that Germany faced the danger of "becoming Socialist within and dependent on the Soviet Union without." Barzel hastily rewrote his Bundestag speech. How could you conduct opposition against a Peace Prize winner?

That night young people carried torches to the Venusberg to celebrate at Brandt's villa. He invited them inside. From the opposition came only Herman Höcherl, a jester of a politician from Strauss' Bavarian wing, who liked Brandt and said so. Talking to members of the Printers' Union that weekend Brandt commented: "If I had attained nothing else I would still be proud of the interim result, that our earnest will to participate in the reduction of tensions is acknowledged, that instead of Germany and war, Germany and peace is the topic that appears in the international press."

Before he could enjoy the sweet fruits of peace policy in Oslo he was obliged to sip the gall of his own party. It was convention time again in the SPD, brought on by the demands of the left wing for a special party debate on economic policy, brought on, too by his own acquiescence at the previous convention in 1970. It was what Herbert Wehner had grown accustomed to calling "a soggy mess." The Leftists were feeling strong, and to a degree they were. They rejected the coalition tax reform program as too weak and then proceeded to raise demands for soak-the-rich revenues—to 60 percent on corporate taxes and upper incomes, instead of the 56 percent recommended by the Brandt leadership. "Leave the cow in the pasture," Brandt pleaded. But they didn't listen to him, or to Karl Schiller. "Actually there are two conventions going on here," said Ehmke. "One with Social Democrats who realize we are in power and running the government, and another with Social Democrats who don't realize that yet, or don't want to admit it." The convention shift was mainly the work of Erhard Eppler, who had stirred the Leftist fires at the district level in the naive expectation that they would burn out faster that way. There were more than 1500 resolutions before the convention, which had to be interrupted after three days of yammering until mid-December, when, after two more theatrical days, the Leftists finally spent themselves.

Brandt took Rut, the "girl from Hamar," with him to Oslo on December 10 for the Nobel award ceremonies, Lars too, and Egon Bahr. Ninja was there in the university auditorium, sharing in the approval of the man the majority of Norwegians were hailing as *"vaar egen* Willy" ("our own Willy)." There were reservations: *Aftenposten,* the big Oslo daily, observed dryly that it was "too early" to honor *Ostpolitik,* and a few Norwegians said they just didn't care much for Germans, including Willy Brandt. Aase Lionaes, the Nobel committee chairman, who had known him as a young man in Oslo, commended him for the "attempt to bury hatred" and then handed him the gold medal and a check for the equivalent of $87,000. Brandt recalled in German that he had been on the losing side for a long and painful time, that he did not count himself among Alfred Nobel's "dreamers":

> The young man who in his time was persecuted, driven into exile in Norway and deprived of his rights as a citizen speaks here today not only in general for the cause of peace in Europe, but also most particularly for those from whom the past has exacted a harsh toll . . . I can hardly afford political dreams now and I have no wish yet to give up my own work.

When Brandt was done he thanked everyone in "perfect *Riksmaal*"—high Norwegian. A torchlight parade, songs, and a big banquet that night capped the trip.

There was one more piece of peace to celebrate. The testy deliberations between East and West Germany and East and West Berlin were complete at last, wrapping up the Berlin package. Bahr flew directly from Oslo to East Berlin in a Luftwaffe jet for the signings. The accords represented a series of compromises, like the umbrella agreement reached by the four powers. But they afforded West Berliners a total of thirty days a year of visits in East Germany and lifted almost all of the restrictions on their transit to and from West Germany. To speed movement of access traffic and eliminate individual transit fees West Germany agreed to pay a $72 million lump sum annually. It took ten minutes to initial the seventy-page documents. In the following week Brandt presented the Moscow and Warsaw treaties to Parliament for ratification, asking the upper house to complete its initial reading in the customary six weeks. When the CDU demanded two extra weeks to compensate for the Christmas holidays, it was plain the Conservatives would use even procedural questions to delay enactment of *Ostpolitik*.

Brandt flew to Florida December 27 to confer with President Nixon again. Their two days of talks at Key Biscayne ranged from questions of troop levels and proposed reductions to Nixon's forthcoming China trip and his scheduled meeting with Brezhnev the following spring. Brandt received assurances that the United States would maintain its military strength in Europe. He, in turn, was pleased to brief Nixon a little about Brezhnev, just as he had been pleased to brief Brezhnev a little about Nixon three months before. That done, he went to Sarasota with Rut, Ninja, and Matthias for a two-week vacation. They were touched by the "helpfulness and friendliness" of their Florida neighbors, and on his return to Germany he spoke of the "inner strength" he had detected at the grass-roots level in America.[57]

Home again, he faced something closer to inner weakness. Hans Leussink resigned from his post as Minister of Education, indicating that he felt the job was hopeless in the face of $136 million budget cut; Hildegard Hamm-Brücher quit her state secretaryship for the same reason. Although reform of the education system had been the top domestic priority when the coalition began, nothing had come of it, partly because the CDU-dominated state governments retained sovereignty over schools and fought the federal incursions. However, Brandt himself could be faulted for failing to put his prestige behind a reform drive. When he spoke on the state of the nation before the Bundestag in February, he did not even mention domestic affairs— dwelling instead on *Ostpolitik*.

The success of the Eastern initiatives showed in other directions, as the Bonn Government grew more confident. It sounded out China and got a favorable response. Brandt accepted an invitation to visit Israel and simultaneously opened talks on resumption of relations with Arab states, which had broken off ties during the Erhard Administration because of secret German weapons sales to Israel. Lebanon and then Egypt took up diplomatic ties with Bonn. In March Brandt spent four days in Iran, putting aside a personal aversion to the Shah in the interest of oil supplies. Even France at long last declared herself ready to accept new candidate countries into the Common Market, a result, in part, of the work of Brandt.

Nevertheless, the ground in Bonn was crumbling under his feet as the coalition pushed relentlessly toward ratification votes on the Moscow and Warsaw treaties. On February 29 Herbert Hupka, an SPD deputy from Silesia who had consistently opposed *Ostpolitik,* quit the party. This reduced the effective coalition to 250 votes in the Bundestag—only two more than needed for a majority. The Hupka defection worked like black magic on the Conservative opposition, which sniffed an infernal opportunity to defeat the Eastern treaties and topple Brandt at the same time. "We would vote against the Sermon on the Mount to get rid of him," a CDU man said. The infection spread in the coalition ranks, too.

From February 23 to 25 discussion of the treaties had been largely confined to the Parliament and the press. Now, with three days of parliamentary debate televised live across the country, it was as if the average West German citizen realized all at once that some essential aspects of the national substance were at stake: the division of the country into two states, the loss through wartime defeat of large territories to the east, the question of how or even whether to deal with the East German Communist Government. Then, in mid-March, Barzel raised the possibility of attempting a no-confidence vote in the Bundestag. For a time some of Brandt's strategists considered turning the tables on the opposition by seeking a confidence vote on the treaties. If the coalition were defeated, the Constitution would require new elections, which the strategists were sure Brandt could win. He vetoed this, partly in deference to the FDP, which was not prepared to handle an election campaign at that time.[58]

The government and the opposition were on a collision course. The switches had been set automatically by the requirement to follow the legislative schedule with a ratification vote on the treaties in early May. Hupka's defection acted as a catalyst. Finally, Hans Filbinger, the governor of Baden-Württemberg, came out against Brandt in the state election of April 23, compelling the SPD to quit the coalition in Stuttgart. The Filbinger decision also suggested the Baden-Württemberg election might be a kind of rump plebiscite on *Ostpolitik.* Roughly one-seventh of the national electorate resided in that state. Huge quantities of campaign money were soon pouring into Stuttgart party headquarters, and Bonn politicians were flying, driving, and walking all over the state. The Springer papers joined the fray with more ammunition stolen from the depots of the Bonn Government, including more fragments of secret protocols of Egon Bahr's Moscow negotiations two years before. Scheel denounced this as "a criminal act," not that the secrets seemed to have much effect on the voters. When Barzel denounced the "rotten secrets" of the Brandt government to a group of broad-hatted Swabian farmers in the town of Münsingen, they gaped uncomprehendingly.[59] Moscow and East Berlin got involved in the campaign, too—the Soviets with an offer to be more forthcoming on acknowledging West German wishes for reunification and the East Germans by granting Easter visiting privileges and easier transit to West Berlin. More than 450,000 West Berliners crossed into East Germany during the holiday week, and 620,000 West Germans took advantage of the Berlin access benefits.

Brandt concluded that the plebiscite effect was rather limited and that it would be awkward if he participated directly in the campaign in a state where the SPD had never gotten more than 37 percent of the vote. He chose instead to make soothing remarks, acknowledging merely that there was "a somewhat confusing and confused looking political landscape." On the eve of the election he flew to London for meetings with Prime Minister Heath and with Queen Elizabeth, who put him up at Windsor Castle. Brandt was borne out in his reserve to the degree that the April election results showed predictable gains for all three major parties. The SPD got 37.5 percent, its best since the war, and the FDP gained almost 9 percent. But the CDU showing of over 53 percent had a dramatizing impact, especially for the timorous on the coalition ship who had begun to wonder whether they were about to sink. Behind the scenes the manipulators went to work. The first to jump was Wilhelm Helms, an obscure forty-eight-year-old FDP deputy from Lower Saxony who had gone into debt on his 118-acre family farm. He had been refused credit assistance by Josef Ertl, the Free Democratic Agriculture Minister, and that Sunday night Helms turned to the CDU for financial support. That reduced the Brandt-Scheel majority in the Bundestag to one vote.

Between Sunday night and Monday evening the Conservatives bought, bullied, and bribed five coalition deputies to join them in dumping Brandt. It was a monumental gamble for Barzel, not only because the no-confidence vote process had never been tested, but also because he had enemies lurking in his own ranks. He thirsted for power, yet he was nervous about seizing it, the more so because he was being pushed by rivals: Strauss and Governor Helmut Kohl of Rhineland-Palatinate. Barzel could have waited another eighteen months for the regular federal elections, which he probably would have won on the issue of growing inflation. The Eastern treaties didn't matter all that much to him; he would have tried a bit of cosmetic negotiation with the Russians and Poles and then put them before the Bundestag himself. He decided to press the issue.

On Monday evening he went to President Heinemann and declared that he had the votes to oust Brandt. "He said he had 251, but in fact he had 252," recalled Karl Wienand, the SPD deputy whip who had himself begun canvassing. "He'd gotten five, but I got one back." Brandt sat as if numbed the while. Barzel too, was numb, knowing that his rivals were "shoving (him) against a rusty knife,"[60] as one of his aides described it, knowing, too, that the CDU wasn't alone in the whispered horse-trading under way behind locked doors all over the federal capital.

As SPD troubleshooter Wienand was invaluable. The son of a construction worker, at the age of six he had watched Nazi toughs trample his father to the edge of death and then beat his mother and sister bloody. Drafted into a penal battalion as a teenager, he was sent into Russian minefields armed with a spade and a dagger—a member of a suicide squad. He had a leg blown off and then served time in a Russian prison camp. "I saw it all," he said years later in the grim monotone that Germans muster for such recollections. Soon after the war he became something of a *Wunderkind* in the SPD—its youngest town Mayor, and then one of its youngest parliamentary deputies. Eventually, Wienand came under the protection of Wehner, who recognized three invaluable qualities in the younger man: an ability to keep his mouth shut, an enormous capacity for hard and even dirty work, and total loyalty to the cause of the SPD.

Now, totaling the support for the SPD in this crucial no-confidence vote, Wienand proved better at arithmetic than Barzel. Between Monday and Wednesday the SPD picked up four CDU votes. Nobody would ever say how or who they were. They did it not just to keep Brandt but to get the treaties through the Bundestag. "Imagine what kind of situation we would have been in if the Moscow and Warsaw treaties were squashed," recalled Wienand. "We would have been isolated in the world and nobody would think we were worth anything as negotiating partners."[61] Truly, the Federal Republic was up to its ears in commitments. Nixon was due in Moscow to substantiate *his* Eastern policy; the Berlin agreement was due for signature and conclusion.

Brandt didn't know with Biblical surety that he would survive. But he had been told by Wienand and Wehner that the coalition had the decisive edge—at least for the no-confidence vote—whether he believed it or not.

On Wednesday, April 26, a mood of grimness spread across Germany. There were "warning strikes" in dozens of factories on behalf of Brandt and *Ostpolitik,* and more than 20,000 West Germans took to the streets in protest demonstrations—in Hamburg, Berlin, Frankfurt, and Offenbach. "Stop Barzel and Strauss now!" was the slogan on many a banner. "I feel sick to my stomach about this vote," said Udo Giulini, a wealthy CDU deputy. "There is an air of adventurism about it." Hans Roderich Schneider, the FDP journalist, noted that Strauss had shouted for "silence in this hall!" when Barzel's bid was announced in the Bundestag: "It reminded me of what we were taught in the Hitler Youth about the Führer, when Hitler pulled out a pistol in the Bürgerbräukeller in 1923 and fired a shot into the ceiling to 'make himself heard.'"[62] The capital was somber as well. Josef Ertl told the Bundestag at the beginning of the debate on the federal budget that he had received several anonymous murder threats on the telephone. Brandt and Barzel both appealed for calm. "A crisis in the heads of the opposition is not a crisis of the state by a long shot," Brandt said. Meanwhile SPD district headquarters up and down the country reported thousands of citizens had called in to apply for party membership.

The drama reached its climax April 27. Kiesinger spoke first, introducing Barzel's bid a few minutes after 10 a.m. Then came Wehner, declaring that the SPD would remain seated as bloc, rather than help Barzel do "his chin-up." Scheel spoke eloquently and almost "elegiacally," as many remarked, of "this small, courageous, abused and beaten, oft pronounced dead and always resurrected Free Democratic Party." Close to noon Brandt had a last word in which he solemnly recounted what his government had accomplished and what it intended still to accomplish. "I am convinced," he said, "we will continue to govern after the vote today . . . And now, ladies and gentlemen, in the usage of Kant, there is nothing else to be done but our damned duty and obligation." The balloting began with the CDU deputies and a handful of FDP men walking to the small Bundestag booths shaped like Paris *pissoirs*. The Free Democrats voted so as to obliterate the secret ballot of those Christian Union deputies who intended to oppose Barzel or abstain. Tumult broke out at 1:12 p.m., when the result was prematurely disclosed: Barzel had lost. Coalition deputies rushed to Brandt and tried to heave him on their shoulders. Amid the shouts and embraces Barzel slumped in his chair, shaking his head in dejection, his cheeks drained of color. Ten minutes later Kai-Uwe von Hassel announced that Barzel had gotten 247 votes—two short of the majority needed to turn out the Brandt-Scheel administration—with 10 nays and 3 abstentions. Wienand's wooing had paid off. Across the country Germans who had been following the Bundestag scene by radio and television cheered and stamped—honking horns, kissing strangers, dancing in the streets. "I ascertain that Dr. Barzel, proposed by the CDU-CSU *Fraktion*, has not attained the votes of the majority of members of the Bundestag," von Hassel declared. More cheering, as Barzel now walked across to congratulate Brandt and Scheel. "Therewith the bill of the CDU-CSU *Fraktion* on document IV/3380 is rejected," von Hassel concluded. Brandt said simply: "The work goes on."

Strauss, striding swiftly to his office, grinned enigmatically, and his eyes twinkled with mischief as he answered an American reporter's questions. The night before he mocked the reporter on television for having written that he had plotted to ruin Barzel. Now he told the same reporter: "You were not in error as often as I said last night. You, you think the world is coming to an end if your Willy Brandt collapses. But you will find out differently."[63] Then he closed the door of his office.

Two years later Brandt pasted together his own memory of the no-confidence crisis with these words:

> At the time I awaited the vote count not at all with sureness of success, but in greater calm than many suspected—for other reasons than did those who later became the objects of a confusing and malicious campaign—I did not rule out that a couple of prominent deputies of the Union would leave their candidate in the lurch.[64]

Among those "objects," of course, was Karl Wienand, the SPD troubleshooter who had volunteered for the dangerous covert operation behind enemy lines. A year later he was charged with having "bought" at least one CDU deputy, Julius Steiner. The accusation could not be proven; Steiner subsequently admitted being in the pay of the East German Ministry for State Security. But Wienand was dragged through the dirt for so long that in the autumn of 1974 he felt obliged to give up his Bundestag seat. Brandt later noted:

> To my surprise several days after the failure of the no-confidence vote a prominent personality of the Union visited me to hear my opinion about a strange arrangement. I should be elected Federal President with the votes of the Union while Barzel would take over the Chancellery with the votes of the SPD.[65]

What followed the vote could only be an anticlimax—a whole series of anticlimaxes. The Bundestag resumed its session later that afternoon, the SPD filibustering to prevent another vote. It was one thing to stop Barzel with a secret ballot, quite another to go on supporting Brandt in an open vote. There was, as Brandt and other speakers had remarked, a sharp "political polarization" in the Federal Republic and in the Bundestag, brought on by the attempted no-confidence vote. It was manifest in such scenes as Strauss' suggesting the Left was tending toward "a Popular Front" and Karl Schiller's responding that the Right was marching toward the Harzburger Front." (See Chapter II.) That exchange prompted Lother Haase, the diminutive CDU deputy from Kassel, to scream at Schiller: "This Nazi! Stormtrooper! Nazi Professor!" As shout followed shout, Wehner cried: "Mr. President! Can't you repel the CDU gnome? The *Gartenzwerg* is running wild!"

The polarity continued on Friday, April 27, when the Bundestag resumed debate on the budget—specifically that for the Chancellery. Brandt preempted Barzel's arguments against ratification, which had begun with *"So nicht"* (not this way) and progressed to *"Noch nicht"* (not yet). The government had its obligations, he said, and would proceed in the face of "a very narrow majority." Barzel wanted revenge, and he got it that afternoon in a budget vote, which was done with a regular roll call. Gerhard Kienbaum, an FDP deputy close to Erich Mende, absented himself. That left 495 deputies. Wilhelm Helms, the renegade, voted with the opposition. A third FDP defector, Baron Knut von Kühlmann-Stumm, abstained. Result: a tie of 246 to 246. The Bundestag was frozen. In total confusion the Parliament stumbled on through three pauses, until a joint council of elders agreed to seek a compromise the following week. The stalemate revealed the political landscape in all its starkness: Brandt wanting his treaties though not fearing interim elections; Scheel, with only twenty-four deputies, fearing elections but wanting the treaties; Barzel, not wanting either the treaties or elections at this point.

That night Brandt and Barzel met for more than four hours. Strauss was there and Gerhard Schröder, too. Out of this parley came the hint of a compromise: Brandt would delay the treaty ratification process a few days and augment the treaties with a bipartisan declaration on German reunification to be "acknowledged" by the Soviet Union. In exchange, Barzel would free a sufficient number of CDU deputies from *Fraktion* discipline to allow the treaties to pass the Bundestag. Strauss seemed to go along. Schröder objected. Brandt, however, was optimistic. In a speech the next day before 50,000 West Berliners he declared: "We have stood the test."

The deadlock was also the moment for egotists and opportunists, however, and over the next seventeen days an incredible poker game developed. At one point Baron Kühlmann-Stumm offered his own personal *Ostpolitik* draft, saying that if it were not accepted he would oppose everyone. At another point the opposition called in Valentin Falin, the new Soviet Ambassador, to join bipartisan negotiation sessions on a "joint declaration," and there he was, sitting in the living room of Brandt's villa with the German parliamentarians. The Russians also tried to influence the proceedings by allowing a new group of ethnic Germans to emigrate to the Federal Republic, and East Germany's Michael Kohl signed a transportation treaty with Egon Bahr as a prelude to better agreements. In the end Barzel was unable to swing his riven mob into line. When ratification of *Ostpolitik* finally came to a vote on May 17 there were 9 no votes and 238 abstentions from the opposition on the Moscow treaty, 17 nos and 230 abstentions on the Warsaw treaty. The coalition scraped through with its 248 remaining affirmative votes. Still, it was "the new beginning" Brandt and Scheel had asked for. They had risked their majority for the policy they conceived and believed in, and they had lost it. The only majority displayed was the 491 votes assembled for the "joint declaration" that held that the German question remained "open," even after the treaty ratification—as if it needed a legislative act to confirm that.

From then on the issue confronting Brandt and the others was new elections, and how and when to bring them off.

In the midst of this turmoil Brandt had flown north to spend some time campaigning for an enlarged Common Market in Denmark, where a national referendum was pending. He arrived in an armored car at 100 miles an hour, wearing a kind of flak jacket under his suit—"a little heavier than normally," as his host and friend, Premier Jens Otto Krag noticed. Brandt spoke extemporaneously in the market square of Abenra, just north of the German border, and in the evening after a press conference, spent two hours with Krag in a Social Democratic meeting on Common Market questions. "Willy Brandt has a great ability to deliver the right answer in fluent Norwegian, and with a lot of charm to it," Krag remembered. That evening they sang songs, too—Brandt in the *Plattdeutsch* of North Germany and the Danes in their tongue. At midnight they ordered a beer at his hotel. Krag: "Very soon his tired head quietly dropped toward his chest—so without finishing the beer I thanked him heartily for his deed and left . . . the renewed experience of our old friendship was essential. Our humor swings alike. We laugh heartily on occasions when others do not know why."[66] Bent Skou, an aide of Krag, said later: "It was fantastic. It was almost an irony of history that a German could be one of the main forces for Denmark to join the European Community. Trust in Brandt was so great that it carried the referendum. He calmed the nerves of the average Dane. Had it been any other Chancellor advocating the same it would probably have been a reverse effect."[67] The October referendum authorized Danish entry.

Four months after Abenra he was in Oslo to make a similar appeal to the Norwegians, who were also holding a referendum on joining the European Community. He spoke in perfect *Riksmaal* as usual, but it was not the Norwegians of the capital who needed persuasion. The farmers and fisherman of the north were fearful of the cloying ties and "inhuman" bureaucracy of Brussels. Ten days after Brandt's visit the Norwegian plebiscite defeated the government's bid for Common Market membership.

Brandt, it seemed, would never let pass an opportunity or an obligation to appear in a foreign country. He was in Vienna for two days at the end of May to attend a Socialist International meeting. In June he flew to Boston to address a Harvard convocation marking the twenty-fifth anniversary of the Marshall Plan, with the announcement of a 150 million mark German Government gift endowing a new foundation dedicated to bringing Europeans and Americans closer together.

In the meantime, on June 3, the Foreign Ministers of the four powers sealed the final Berlin agreement with handshakes, embraces, and kisses—enacting the first and most prodigious work of East-West detente—and the by-product of Brandt's *Ostpolitik*. Nixon had completed his successful visit to Moscow with an initial SALT agreement, and the gate was opened for one European conference on security and another on troop reductions. Brandt entertained both Andrei Gromyko and Poland's Deputy Foreign Minister Josef Czyrek in Bonn that afternoon, and he spoke to Gromyko of "viewing the future with confidence: for the relationship between our states, for the relationship between both states in Germany and the relationship between the states in Europe."

There were other anticlimaxes. Bubbling up from the ferment of the radical Left was a bunch that called themselves the Red Army Faction—a small group mixing utopian socialism, bank robberies, militant anarchism, explosives, slogans, and bullets. Their guerrilla ventures had left four dead and thirty-one wounded in the space of a few weeks. Now the police succeeded in trapping the hard core: Andreas Baader in a Frankfurt shootout and Ulrike Meinhof a little later without a shot. It was almost a comic book illustration of the problem of "domestic security" raised by the Conservative opposition then and later as a cudgel with which to club the governing coalition—as if there would be less radicalism under a CDU administration. It was a terrifying comic book, not a laughing matter, with utterly grotesque accusations from the Right and the naming of Brandt and the SPD as the principal enemies of the radicals—aside from Springer publications. There was a terrible reprise in September when eight Arab terrorists succeeded in taking eleven Israeli athletes hostage at the Olympic Games in Munich, ultimately killing all of them in a gory, suicidal sequence that left seventeen dead, including a German policeman. The blame stuck to the coalition, and there was no more talk of "the merry games" in which the Federal Republic had invested so much money and effort.

The inclination to suicide was a German tradition, especially in politics, as Tacitus recorded. Brandt had to contend with it in July, when Karl Schiller, the number two man in his government, brought a do-or-die showdown on currency policy. With the British pound afloat, speculative money was again flowing toward the Frankfurt exchange. Schiller wanted to keep the money markets open; others, led by Helmut Schmidt, demanded controls. It is me or the market, said Schiller. Economics Minister for more than five years and Finance Minister for one, he thought he had the clout. Brandt was so depressed by this confrontation that he thought for a day or so—not for the first time and not for the last—of resigning. It was a mood that overcame him more and more frequently as the burdens of office weighed him down. Hadn't he walked mutely out of a Bundestag debate in February 1971 when a young CDU zealot accused him of not knowing the difference between democracy and dictatorship? Hadn't he toyed with the Presidency in April?" "Every now and then he had temptations to separate himself from the party," Schmidt recalled, "and we became very anxious. We couldn't reach him for two or three days while he secluded himself on the Venusberg. Once in 1968, once early in 1969. With Schiller it was really serious."[68] Schiller had submitted his resignation July 2. After hesitating four days, Brandt picked it up. Then he named Schmidt as the new "Superminister" for Economics and Finance; Leber took over the Defense Ministry, Lauritzen the Transport Ministry from Leber. Schiller quit the SPD in stages, but by autumn he was participating in a propaganda campaign alongside of Ludwig Erhard on behalf of the CDU against Brandt. The Chancellor noted:

> Was the conflict avoidable? It wasn't really a matter of the factual currency policy decision . . . it was much more a matter of the qualities of this gifted man, who had stirred up practically the entire Cabinet against him and also lost the confidence of the *Fraktion*. That is why I couldn't tell him in good conscience that he would belong to the next Government.[69]

A lot of things favored him, despite the anticlimaxes, and despite his own strong doubts: "Nowhere is it written that we—the Social Democrats and Free Democrats—will make it in the elections. We have much against us— objectively (not only the prices) and subjectively (not only disloyalty)." He was reading the opinion polls week by week and found those that gave him a "too favorable" lead. Yet when another poll put the CDU over the top he noted in a kind of diary: "Wait it out, don't let it make you nervous."[70] Elsewhere there were visible signs of positive change. Bahr and Kohl began negotiating a basic treaty on August 14. By early September it was announced that over 1 million West Germans had been able to take advantage of the eased travel restrictions provided by conclusion of the Berlin pact three months earlier. East Germany proclaimed a prisoner amnesty in October. Bonn began negotiating with Peking on opening diplomatic relations in August and, in October Scheel flew to the Chinese capital to complete the agreement. Poland and West Germany exchanged embassies in September.

Normalization with the Warsaw Government had made it possible for Bonn to extricate 40,000 ethnic Germans from Poland in the course of two years. The *Ostpolitik* harvest had begun.

He and Scheel had announced in June they would seek new elections in November. That meant a parliamentary decision in September, for the Constitution prescribed elections sixty days after dissolution of the Bundestag. With the deadlock persisting since April it was not so easy. Just at the time he and Wehner agreed to seek and lose a confidence vote to start the new elections process, the CDU launched a last-minute maneuver to undercut the coalition plan by "purchasing" a deputy from the SPD. The idea was clearly to try once more for a no-confidence vote, which would have lofted Barzel immediately into the Chancellorship. Luckily, the man selected for defection turned down the lucrative offer and reported immediately to Wehner on September 21.[71] Brandt carried off the loss of the confidence vote the next day, following eight hours of often disgraceful debate. Some coalition defectors addressed the Bundestag with Barzel's express approval—among them, Mende, who accused Scheel of creating "a new Leftist party," and Günther Müller, formerly of the Munich SPD, who spoke of "a Socialist peril." Brandt replied: "Personally, I don't think the Parliament and the parliamentary idea are well served by allowing wanderers from your ranks to dump their garbage here." Barzel cried: "You had your chance and you threw away your chance." Brandt: "The only thing you succeeded in doing is crippling the Parliament."[72] Ironically, the opposition allowed ratification of the administration's transportation treaty with East Berlin, which was designed to improve movement of goods and people between two German states. The confidence vote followed at 6:30 p.m., and Brandt and his Cabinet deliberately abstained so as to force the defeat—248 to 233. The election was set for November 19.

It was not by design, but the Brandt-Scheel government had proven to be a unique crucible for testing the Constitution and parliamentary democracy. To begin with, there had been the experiment of the Left-Center coalition, stretching the possibilities of multiparty choice to a new dimension. There was the test of Article 67—the no-confidence vote, to be followed by the interim elections. In time there would be the test provided by resignation of the Chancellor—all accomplished in an atmosphere characterized by polarization and "crisis." In fact, the Federal Republic was proving its mettle as a veritable fortress of democratic practice on a continent and in a land where the past had provided all too few examples or traditions of parliamentary democracy.

Brandt had the successes of *Ostpolitik* and *Westpolitik* to show for his three years in office, but there had also been continued economic stability and adoption of a packet of domestic reforms. The farmers were in a better frame of mind, having received substantial federal benefits. Fifteen million employees had been given a matching fund program stimulating them to accumulate capital. The federal crime-fighting apparatus had been modernized, the armed forces establishment, too. Housing, health, and social welfare legislation had brought about welcome improvements. Even in the neglected field of education there had been a much needed school and college construction program.

The Social Democrats assembled in Dortmund to celebrate these accomplishments and build up confidence for the election campaign. Their convention opened on October 12 under huge banners proclaiming: "Willy Brandt Must Remain Chancellor." Party membership had swelled to 900,000, a gain of close to 100,000 mainly as a result of the *Ostpolitik* struggle, and Brandt's stance was calculated to appeal to the enlarged group with a combination of overt gentleness and subliminal nationalism. He appealed for "compassion," a word brought to him across the Atlantic and probably borrowed from the campaign of George McGovern by his new ghostwriter, Klaus Harpprecht. He also introduced the concept of "quality of life" into the campaign, citing the Kennedys. "Have the courage to show this kind of sympathy," he cried to the Dortmund delegates. "Have the courage to be merciful. Have the courage to attend to your neighbor. Recall these so oft buried values. Find your way back to yourselves!" Some of the women nearly swooned; some of the men snorted: "Saint Willy'" and "Preacher Willy." The SPD bulletins issued at Dortmund were outlined in black, red, and gold, the national colors, instead of the familiar Socialist red, and Brandt also declared: "This republic, dear friends, is *our* state." At a nighttime rally a miner's band played the "Deutschlandlied"—the national anthem that had been a (misunderstood) symbol of Hitlerism to the rest of the world. "Unthinkable for the Social Democrats a few years ago," a German journalist commented. Heinrich Böll was there, a week before his selection as the Nobel literature laureate for 1972, speaking strongly in support of Brandt and against the "violence" of the CDU and Springer:

> A further kind of violence against which you have to carry out your policy is the engrained, almost inborn feeling of many citizens of this state for whom the Social Democrats were all right as the opposition, but for whom it was a kind of coup d'etat or at least a considerable shamelessness that you came to govern.

Böll declared that he was one of thousands who had joined the Social

Democratic Voter Initiative, founded three years before by his colleague Günter Grass, and he named some prominent fellow Catholics who were working with him. Brandt departed from Dortmund still skeptical, surprising Rut with the statement that the outcome was "by no means certain." He was watching the opinion polls.[73]

The campaign was very rough, regardless of the mild stances adopted by the other principals as well: Barzel posed hopefully on a poster, with his mouth slightly open above the legend, "Our Program for Governing—We Build Progress on Stability"; Scheel in a pensive picture, hand on chin, and the slogan "Let Reason Rule." Campaign spending reached a record high on all sides. A reckoning after the election showed the SPD had spent about $3.5 million on campaign advertisements, as opposed to $15.2 million by the CDU on what its propagandists called "the last free election."[74] Conservatives invested a lot of money in smear literature—the familiar pseudo-documents purporting to show Wehner as Communist and Brandt as a traitor. But in November a new variant was produced by August Naujock, a former Lübeck detective, in the form of an "open letter" asserting that Brandt had stabbed a young man to death in his native city during a clash with Stormtroopers on January 31, 1931. A court injunction seemed only to spread this defamation. The Conservatives got their lumps, too. Günter Grass drove around the country denouncing Strauss as "a 24-carat scoundrel." Barzel faced choruses of catcalls, while Brandt was reaping applause, especially when he listed his opponent's "five positions" in a faintly erotic metaphor about Ostpolitik: "First, no, then not yet, then, not this way, then, yes, and finally abstention in the Bundestag!"

For years it had been considered gauche to demonstrate open commitment to a political party in West Germany. Many Germans remembered in their bones what had happened the last time they committed themselves unequivocally. But all at once it became fashionable to wear campaign buttons and paste on bumper stickers. One showed Brandt resting in a brandy glass, another a scowling Strauss and the question: "Do you want to vote for him?"[75] The SPD campaign managers decided to capitalize on this Bekennermut— this "courage of commitment" that had its roots in the Lutheran Reformation. Toward the end of the six-week campaign they bought out a new poster of a serene Willy Brandt with a trace of a smile and the legend: "Germans—We Can Be Proud of Our Country." The nationalism was no longer subliminal. "Brandt is the most nationalist leader since the war," one of his campaign aides concluded. "Adenauer was European. But Brandt can be nationalist without inhibitions." The aide, Reinhart Bartholomäi, started suggesting the "proud" line in the campaign huddles. Brandt resisted, saying he preferred: "Germans—Have Confidence in Yourselves." Then, ten days before the election, the discussion turned to *stolz* (proud), and Brandt said, "Why not?"[76]

Only Herbert Wehner objected to that and to the "hate propaganda" developed by Albrecht Müller, the young SPD campaign director.[77] But it was working, and Brandt, in the course of his 16,000-mile whistlestop campaign felt more and more confident. He was hoarse, but he was happier in this campaign than any other—his "annual November depression" (according to Horst Ehmke) having been, so to speak, reigned out.

At a critical moment, fifteen days before the vote, the tireless Egon Bahr brought in another *Ostpolitik* harvest. He completed negotiations with Michael Kohl on the Basic Treaty between East and West Germany. To crown it East Germany began releasing the first of 30,000 prisoners—many of whom had been detained for years on political charges. The treaty itself provided for both German states to enter the United Nations, to exchange "permanent representatives" functioning like ambassadors, and to open a great variety of exchanges—including border visits. It covered all of the points set out by Brandt in his meeting with Willi Stoph at Kassel thirty months earlier. Bahr and Kohl were authorized to initial the pact November 8.

From then on it was coasting, although Brandt was still pessimistic on November 10, according to his diary notes. Ehmke, too. In a pool bet with some journalist friends Ehmke chose one of the lowest spreads for the coalition; a foreign correspondent who selected the highest spread won the pool.

By 7 p.m. on November 19 it was clear from computer projections that the Brandt-Scheel coalition had a landslide—a total of 54 percent of the vote with a record 91 percent of the 40 million electorate turning out at the polls. The SPD had its best-ever result with 45.9 percent, and the Free Democrats made a comeback to 8.4 percent. It gave them 271 seats in the Bundestag—a safe majority of 23. Barzel conceded at 8 p.m., as the land lay in darkness under a mantle of snow and ice. Brandt went before reporters and television cameras two and a half hours later: "It is not a moment of triumph, but a moving moment of satisfaction and pride." The only man who had done better was Strauss; he carried Bavaria with 55 percent—a victory he employed five months later to push Barzel of the CDU chairmanship. Rut's eyes sparkled. "I am so happy for Willy,"[78] she told friends. Teddy Kennedy was among the well-wishers gathered in the Chancellery bungalow for the victory celebration; he also said he was glad it was Willy.

Inevitably, there was a letdown. He had strained his vocal chords so badly with talk and smoke during the campaign that he had to enter a clinic for treatment. One part of the cure: no tobacco. He also wanted to revamp his Cabinet, discarding some men he no longer valued: He dropped Conrad Ahlers as press spokesman. Ahlers had made himself doubly vulnerable by leaking too many Cabinet secrets and by winning direct election to the Bundestag from District 152 in Rhineland-Palatinate. It was a relatively simple choice, because law required the head of the Press and Information Office to be a civil servant rather than an elected official.

Ehmke had quarreled repeatedly with several Cabinet members on a variety of minor and major issues, principally with Helmut Schmidt. When Brandt elected to retain Schmidt as his "Number One" teammate, and "with all of Schmidt's preconditions," Ehmke voluntarily withdrew from his job as manager of the Chancellery. Brandt held open a newly created Ministry of Technology and Post. It prompted elder and younger members of the Brandt circle to pause and wonder. Later, Ehmke would remember Leo Bauer, a Brandt crony who died September 18 of a liver condition contracted during six years in a Siberian prison camp. "When Leo died, Wehner was at his bed," Ehmke recalled, "not Brandt for whom he did more. Brandt said, 'Everyone dies by himself.' Bauer's last words were: 'Where is Willy?'" As for Ahlers, Ehmke said: "What he did with Conny was not right. He let Conny play crazy. He covered up for Conny in many situations where he didn't have to, and he pulled some wild stunts—more good than bad. He kept him the way a feudal lord stands by his squire. But when the pressure got too big he let him go and suffer."[79] Schmidt said: "He drops people," though he, like Wehner, conceded that leaks had plagued the Cabinet. Both of them wanted to settle some scores with "those betrayers—You couldn't trust them. Every Cabinet meeting was leaked to *Spiegel*—Ehmke, Ahlers, Genscher, Schiller."[80] But Schmidt and Wehner were annoyed because Brandt had decided to reward Scheel with five Cabinet ministries instead of the three previously held by the Free Democrats. When they balked, Brandt threatened twice to resign. "The so-called threat to resign," Wehner branded it and recalled the scene, with contempt honing his voice: "'Look for someone else,' he said, and then waited to see whether I would say anything against him. First I tried to get him to take it back. He played the *beleidigte Leberwurst* (literally, the insulted liver sausage). The second time I told him 'I heard it twice, and I don't want to hear it again.'"[81] Ehmke added: "He sat up there in the hospital and was sour, handing a scribbled note to Wehner, who was asking him why he wanted to wait another ten days to make a decision, and he replied: 'In the first place I am from Lübeck.'"[82] Wehner was supposed to give a copy of the note to Schmidt but neglected to do so until the Cabinet formation was practically complete. Brandt got his way[83] with the Cabinet and everything else—except smoking. The lack of tobacco made him irritable, he admitted.

He was elected Chancellor a second time on December 14 with a comfortable 269 votes to 223. There were some light moments. An early miscount gave him 289 ballots, causing momentary agony in the oppositon ranks. For the inauguration Brandt pulled on a *Frack* (dress) coat that did not match his cutaway trousers, and Scheel kidded him. Brandt replied that he had created a new style, "a *Frackaway.*"

The next day he told the Bundestag he wanted to be *sachlich*—"as down-to-earth as possible"—and he spoke of anti-inflation moves, the desire to conclude the treaty with East Germany, and, finally, completion of his long-delayed Chancellery budget. He had briefly considered flying to Berlin to sign the Basic Treaty and meet Erich Honecker, but that plan was abandoned when Honecker questioned the possibility of "another Erfurt" and insisted on travel restrictions that Brandt did not feel he could accept. Instead the treaty was signed, with some panache, by Bahr and Kohl on December 21 in East Berlin. Asked what the West Germans could learn from the East Germans, Kohl replied: "To construct a Socialist society and to be modest." Bahr's answer to the parallel question was: "the blessings and the negative aspects of capitalism."

The *Sachlichkeit* of December gave way to the metaphysics of January. In his annual State of the Nation speech Brandt again thrummed the "compassion" and "quality of life" themes, and he dwelt at length on the significance of "a new center, a social and liberal center" established by the electorate. "We want the citizen, not the bourgeois," he told the Bundestag. "We have moved closer to the Anglo-Saxon citizen, the French *citoyen.* In this respect the Federal Republic has become more Western in a period that has stood under the sign of so-called *Ostpolitik.*" He went on in this mild vein for ninety minutes, "Never before has a German state lived in such good harmony with the free spirit of its citizenry, with its neighbors, and its international partners." For once Barzel was speechless.

There was another international monetary crisis in February. But with Helmut Schmidt in charge and in touch with the other Western currency czars, the Federal Republic withstood yet another battering by speculators— $6 billion worth. Another revaluation raised the parity of the *Deutschmark* to a little less than three to the dollar. "The first man on my team," Brand had boasted of Schmidt, and he was. Wehner stepped down as deputy chairman of the party in March.

Brandt was his own Foreign Minister again, scheduling visits to the United States, Israel, and Yugoslavia—and inviting Brezhnev to Bonn. Prime Minister Heath came to West Germany in March, when Brandt was insisting that he spent "80 percent of my time on domestic affairs." They were most cordial to each other. "You and I have met often when I was in opposition and you were in government," Brandt said in an unpublished toast. "Now I can say that we are together." Heath joshed him back: "You don't have the disadvantage of having a Socialist opposition." But Brandt wanted to top that: 'Don't you agree that both of us are the real Conservatives?" A CDU deputy who witnessed this exchange, blanched at the idea of Brandt as a Conservative. But Rüdiger von Wechmar, who succeeded Ahlers, reflected: "There was a great kernel of truth in the remark. Basically Brandt is a national Conservative. He sees the whole detente effort as a contribution toward maintaining the national core of the nation."[84]

In April the SPD held its regular convention in Hannover. The new Left, emboldened once more by election victory, made another attempt to overwhelm the party. Brandt declared: "We don't deliver ourselves to the zealots." But when it came to voting for the next party executive, the Leftists took revenge by collecting votes against Helmut Schmidt and others whom they regarded as Rightists, though he was eventually elected. "The worst possible show," Schmidt growled a few weeks later.[85] Wehner was also grim: "The SPD faces hard times. The new style. He comes, a speech, cheers, he goes. The party doesn't have the people—only one or two to do it all." A Brandt party until he quits? he was asked. "I would dispute it. But in practice that is the way it is going."[86]

Brandt, however, was in splendid form on the international scene. In Yugoslavia he swept the Belgrade Government's twenty-eight-year-old demand for war indemnities of $770 million off the table. "If you talk in terms of billions (of marks) you will have to do it with my successor," he told Premier Dzemal Bijedic on April 19.[87] The blackmail days were over. He and Tito got along beautifully the next day at the island retreat of Brijoni, the more so when Brandt promised credits at generous terms amounting to almost half the Yugoslav claim. He was in Washington at Nixon's request two weeks later to listen to the President's proposals for "a year of Europe" in United States foreign policy and his plans for a new nuclear weapons agreement with Brezhnev. Brandt was skeptical about the "Europe" strategy, which was conceived by Henry Kissinger to link Western Europe to the United States and Japan. But it was Wehner who tagged it "the sketch of a monster."

The Brandt government began talks on normalization of relations with Czechoslovakia in April, the last stage of the problematical aspects of *Ostpolitik*. The Basic Treaty with East Germany was ratified by the Bundestag May 11, virtually completing the formal framework for *Ostpolitik*. Leonid Brezhnev came to town May 18, and Brandt welcomed the visit as a step toward overcoming "a history of sorrows." Here was the first Russian peacemaker at the Rhine since 1814, when General Ferdinand von Wintzingerode had led a corps of Cossacks into Düsseldorf, pursuing Napoleon.

In those sunny spring days, it was fun to be in Bonn, for a change. West Germany was aglow with prosperity and seeming contentment. Insterburg & Co., a quartet of young entertainers, was convulsing the nation with songs and patter that drew laughter not from *Schadenfreude* but from spoofing and nonsense. Gentle German humor instead of bitter German wit. Politics and politicians, too, came in for their share of laughter. Völker Kühn and Roland Schneider, a wit and a musician, set the tape-recorded "we want to dare more democracy" passages of Brandt's inaugural speech to the Bundestag in an ingenious choral-orchestral "polit-hit" with the Chancellor's choppy pathos as a recitative. It sounded, well, pathetic, but no worse than the other Bonn politicians given similar treatment[88] and very funny.

With mutual promises of mutual esteem and Soviet-West German agreements for ten years of economic, industrial, and technical cooperation it seemed that little could go wrong—not with *Ostpolitik*, not with *Westpolitik*, not with the SPD, not with Brandt. He felt, as he had said four months before, "in harmony."

XI:

The End

When does the end begin in a man's life? You can take it back a month, a year, a decade, perhaps half a century to some essential childhood turning point. A man's life. Does it all run together, or does it develop on different levels, professional and personal, sometimes intertwined, sometimes separate, joining in the end? I remember seeing Brandt stonefaced in the Bundestag that morning in April 1972 when he faced the vote of no confidence by the Conservative opposition, having been told that he had enough support to withstand the assault, but perhaps still wondering whether he would in fact make it. I remember him that night in November 1972 in the glass-metal-wood-carpet elegance of the modernistic Chancellery bungalow next to the Schaumburg Palace, when he came in to greet his well-wishers after gaining the greatest election victory a Social Democrat had ever won. Rut was on his arm, nestling her head on his left shoulder. He was smiling as if to say, "I've done it"—and there was really nothing more for him to do. I remember him in November 1973 after he had cast off his last mentor, Herbert Wehner. We were drinking red wine in the Chancellery, he remaining silent when I asked if Wehner was not a person you had either to love or hate, nodding on the first verb and shaking his head on the latter, then saying, "You either love him or reject him." I remember him after the resignation in June 1974, tanned, relaxed, and charming as of yore, full of lively recollections and funny stories, but suddenly darkening when the name "Wehner" was mentioned or when the subject of women was raised. Of Wehner he said, wrongly but plainly convinced (self-convinced?), "He wanted me out since 1972 and I, ass . . ." A pause. "I didn't recognize it." Pacing and puffing the forbidden cigarette the while. He was sixty years old then. Chancellor of the Federal Republic of Germany for four years and seven months, winner of the Nobel Peace Prize, part-creator and principal builder of *Ostpolitik*, victor of two hot election contests, chairman still of the Social Democratic Party of Germany, the ruling party, and its nearly 1 million members. He had flown so high. The wax of his wings had melted, but he did not seem a broken man after his fall.

There was something oddly attractive about Willy Brandt, something mysterious and inexplicable in this outwardly gregarious, charming, even charismatic man—something behind and beyond Brandt the fighter, Brandt the humanist, Brandt the raconteur, drinker, brooder. He had felt that his truncated family cast him out when he was fourteen, when his unwed mother, now married, had borne another son, his stepbrother. He had sought surrogate father, mentors, managers, directors—later, cronies. He had craved the company of women. And always, always he had sought *Nestwärme,* the warmth of the nest, as he acknowledged in the course of several hours of interviews two months after his resignation. But *Nestwärme* found had been *Nestwärme* rejected, again and again. He had even found *Nestwärme* next to that extraordinary body, the German electorate, and, in a way, rejected that, too, toward the end of his Chancellorship.

"A shitty life," he murmured a week before he resigned, with the dimensions of the spy affair growing, growing in his mind, and his grip on himself and his job loosening minute by minute. Around him were jolly fisherfolk of Helgoland, swaying rhythmically at a tavern table to singsong sailor chanties. He considered suicide, he told a colleague later. "If I had had a shooting iron with me then I would have made an end to it," he said in the deepest of gloom on May 4.

Leave the psychologists their case studies, the academics their footnotes, Brandt his own official memoirs, the archivists and their private correspondences for later. What follows is the author's personal account of how Willy Brandt finished his Chancellorship—unauthorized, partially undocumented, possibly highly idiosyncratic.[1]

If one assumes that some politicians, or most, are actors playing roles, then it follows that the actor-politicians need playwrights and directors. The playwright for the politician is the polity—for Willy Brandt the German nation. The people as playwright script a drama that has no beginning and no end, but endless plots, low tragedy and high comedy, climaxes and protagonists, changing scenery and costumes, accompanying music of differing strains, children and aged parents as extras. The directors are the sages and strategists who could not make it on their own as actors. But the actor without a director? It killed the Abbey Theater when the actors took over from the directors. This assumption of a double role, of all responsibility, has killed many a politician, too. Thus, the end began, to my mind, when Willy Brandt shed Herbert Wehner, the mentor-manager-director who had provided him with an election platform in 1959, with a crack at the

Chancellorship in 1961, with the party chairmanship in 1963, with decisive participation in government coalition in 1966 and with parliamentary discipline thereafter.

It happened around Christmas 1972, a little more than a month after Brandt's great triumph at the polls. Wehner, plagued by diabetes, choleric for decades, and worried increasingly by the frazzling of the Social Democratic Party, got the idea that a fresh new man should take over party affairs. He himself was too busy running the SPD Bundestag group. Brandt was occupied with the business of being Chancellor and, besides, had never had all that much time for the party. Helmut Schmidt, the other deputy, was tied up with his Finance Ministry and a burgeoning international monetary crisis pinned on the German *Mark*. Who would do the party things that had to be done—the regional conferences, the training courses, the pep talks, and, most important, the act of controlling the jubilant young hotspurs of the left wing and the grumbling establishment figures of the right wing who were already forming factions, cabals, and hate campaigns against their opponents within the party? Wehner was sick of fighting the old sickness of the German Left, the recurrent infection that went far back, back to the days of Marx, Engels, Lassalle, Liebknecht. He had been deputy chairman of the SPD for fifteen years. He wanted out. To take his place he had in mind a younger, fresher type—specifically, Hans Koschnick, the forty-two-year-old Mayor of Bremen.

But when Wehner disclosed he wanted to step aside as deputy chairman, Brandt misunderstood him, as he had so often before and would again. "I'll fix it," the Chancellor told intimates, "so that Uncle Herbert will remain deputy chairman. I'll tell him I have Heinz Kühn in mind as his successor, and he will get so mad that he will stay on."

Kühn, the bullet-headed, always-tanned Governor of West Germany's most populous state, North Rhine-Westphalia, was nominally a popular figure, a man who could prance before the television lights and cameras and make a convincing appearance. But he was also a devious manipulator, a man who could not keep his word, who shifted, gliding snakelike, when it came to the hard, flat decisions of German politics. In times of crisis Kühn was usually to be found south of the Alps catching a bit of sun—the prototype of the ubiquitous German tourist. Wehner detested him. But Wehner also had his peculiar pride and has awful sense of protocol. Intermediates had predicted to Brandt that Wehner would reject the bait cast so carefully before him. He did. When the angler Brandt told him of his plan, Wehner growled: "You are the chairman, you must decide who is to be your deputy. It must be a person in whom you have confidence."

So it came to pass that Brandt lost the man he wanted and needed and got the man he neither wanted nor needed, Heinz Kühn. Both Wehner and Brandt rationalized it later, Wehner saying he no longer wanted to take responsibility for decisions he did not support but that were made in his name, Brandt saying he had done his damndest to keep Wehner as deputy. But the break was there. From then on, Brandt was a big handsome ship without a navigator to turn him away from the shoals of complacency or the reefs of indecision. In this period Brandt was feeling very sure of himself, with his Berlin crony, Horst Grabert, as his new State Secretary in the Chancellery, and with the Swabian aesthete, Klaus Harpprecht, as his new ghostwriter. Each of these men in his own way was totally isolated from the hurly-burly of Bonn politics. Together, they succeeded in isolating Brandt from the party and eventually from the electorate to a degree unthinkable with Ehmke and Ahlers. At the April convention of the SPD in Hannover, he had felt confirmed in his party command when the Young Socialists, the troublesome *Jusos,* fell back in helpless temporary admiration for the Peace Chancellor while old functionaries lost position after position. At that convention Herbert Wehner got more delegate votes in the election to the party executive than anyone else: 419 of the 428 ballots, to Brandt's 404. If this was an omen Brandt didn't seem to see it. Or if he saw it, he chose to ignore it. There had been more, of course, far more to Wehner's withdrawal than the Chancellor's miscast bait. Brandt had won the federal election of 1972 without, he thought, Wehner's help. It had been a *Willy-Wahl*—a "Willy Election," hadn't it? He had ignored Wehner in the campaign—left him to his own devices—and won.

"I was never so humiliated as in this last election, while he was being celebrated," Wehner told a friend in March 1973. And he remembered older slights. When the SPD's right wing attempted to smear him in 1957, Wehner the ex-Communist stood alone. "I was completely unprotected," Wehner murmured, "alone." Yet when smears were mounted against Brandt in 1961, Wehner and others rallied to his support. He went on: "Brandt wants to stand above the everyday scramble. Let others wrestle, but watch out that it doesn't disturb him. Like (Walter) Scheel, he wants to live majestically. Solidarity? He consumes it."

At that stage in 1973 Wehner was mainly concerned with the young Left, the *Jusos,* who were stirring up so much trouble so soon after the great election triumph. "We could finish them off if the party were different or not so comfortable," he continued. "Party Chinese they write. You can't read it. It's the same as the beginning of the '20s—nothing but splinters al over the place. All the underbrush is gone, and they tear each other to pieces. Marx was right. The second time around history repeats itself as farce—it's never exactly the same. But they could destroy the SPD's opportunities."

Wehner said he was worried, but of course he was always "worried." To Brandt, "I tried to indicate that without saying as much. If only he could have sat down and asked me my views. But he didn't. I think he feels sorrier for himself than for what is happening. I will not be responsible anymore for things that I didn't know about but for which I am still held accountable. I will move more freely. I never wanted to be chairman. I never cultivated or treasured the idea—not for a person of my evolution. I was happy to do what I could do. But the last five years it was less what I wanted than what was thought of me, and that was much more oppressive. I had to let go of the deputyship, against my conscience."

Two powerful men, needing each other and detesting the need. Brandt had won the federal election, but Wehner had won the party executive election. Now they were going down separate tracks, the weeds of suspicion and resentment growing between them as if to obscure the very terminal each had set out to reach. The terminals were not the same, but there was no reason they could not both have been gained on the same track. For Brandt the SPD had always been a vehicle with a double purpose but a single final goal—the reintegration of the German people under the banner of democracy and of the German nation into the family of nations. For Wehner the SPD represented something more— a vehicle for his own reintegration into the German people, as well as for democratization of the Germans.

In 1973 I tried out this idea about the essential difference in the two men's relationship to the party, "That's correctly put," Wehner said. "Brandt never could have stayed Norwegian. Myself, I was a homeless person in all respects. I had nothing with which I could show myself. Brandt and the older men from the SAP, they never had to bury anything. I had to bury almost everything. A Communist must break off all, or he is dead. Some, like him, they are always in the right; they never had to be melted down again. But it was more difficult for me, a broken man who doesn't deny it. In this respect the 'vehicle' analogy is correct."

What was heard in the book-lined living room of Wehner's neat row house on a Godesberg hilltop was was more or less reaffirmed in various other remarks in March, April, and May in Brandt's Chancellery reception room resplendent with Gobelin tapestry; in Cabinet Minister Horst Ehmke's ministerial office filled with modern paintings and sculpture; in Finance Minister Helmut Schmidt's austere but comfortable office near the Rhine. Ehmke (whom Brandt affectionately called "crazy Ehmke" and Wehner later termed "infernal") chewed on the theorem and responded: "There is something to it—that Wehner has a much more intimate relationship to the party and knows the value of party discipline. But both have the problem of being emigrants, the feeling of needing to be accepted, to be embraced by the nation, though neither indulges in self-justification toward the Germans who stayed."

Helmut Schmidt, later to be Brandt's successor as Chancellor, remarked: "If ever the party was a vehicle for Brandt you have to mention Berlin. That was also a vehicle for him. The relationship of Brandt and the party was not everything. Brandt has been more than just a party man. He has run his own life apart from the party. He has not totally integrated himself with the party, not as much as Wehner or I have. Every two or three years there were temptations to separate himself from the party, when we became very anxious. He secluded himself and we couldn't reach him for two or three days at a time."

Beneath the merry surface of a city that had just begun to see itself as a capital there were forebodings. The city had adopted a new symbol: On posters and bumper stickers the "o" in Bonn was a lipstick print of a full mouth puckered to kiss. Did anyone guess, or fear, that behind the innocent lips were sharp teeth, ready to bite and tear?

By 1973 Günter Guillaume, the sleeper spy planted in Frankfurt am Main by his East German masters some seventeen years before, was well installed in the Federal Chancellery as Willy Brandt's liaison man for party affairs. His West German promoters apparently regarded him as "a useful idiot"—the kind of man who didn't shirk tiresome tasks, was willing to work late hours, and manifested no challenging ambitions.

Egon Bahr didn't like the sound of him. Three years earlier, after reading a note in the Guillaume dossier dating back to the mid-1950s, suggesting that a publishing house where Guillaume was employed had served him as a cover for espionage activities, Bahr made a handwritten entry recommending that he be passed by as a candidate for work in the Chancellery. That was later in 1969. But Bahr's reservation had been ignored. Horst Ehmke didn't care for Guillaume either, partly because he, the onetime professor of law and prominent lawyer, thought the unstudied Guillaume not properly qualified. Still, Guillaume had come to Bonn with the enthusiastic support of Frankfurt trade union officials. Besides, he had passed all the security tests. Willy Brandt had no affection for Guillaume, either, "since I viewed him as limited," he said when it was too late.

But Guillaume was diligent, he had been around the Chancellery since January 1970, and now he was the party liaison man—a job he had acquired at the end of 1972 with a monthly wage of 4469 *Marks* (then about $1,500). A squat forty-six-year-old of the type Germans call *"pyknic,"* bespectacled, with a widow's peak darting down his bushy pompadour, the perfect dreary commoner. Guillaume was the kind of man people easily underestimate.

Apparently nearly everyone did.

His "cover" was almost perfect, filled with true and nearly true checkable data. He had learned photography . . . in a trade school? In 1974 Hans Frederik, who had made a profession out of publishing half-truth smears of Brandt and Wehner, completed a manuscript claiming that young Günter had been an apprentice of Hitler's personal photographer, Heinrich Hoffmann, as early as 1942. Further, Frederik claimed that through Nazi connections Guillaume's father had obtained membership in the Hitler party for his son in 1944. The father was purportedly an SS man in Silesia who, like so many other Nazis, succeeded in ducking under after World War II, to resurface later as a postal worker. The elder Guillaume committed suicide in 1948. Could it be the East German Communist intelligence chiefs had discovered his SS past and a son's membership in the Nazi Party? Had they pressed Günter into service as they had the notorious Heinz Felfe? In any case Günter Guillaume, now appearing as an innocent photographer specializing in underwater camera work, appears to have entered the service of what was still the Ministry of Interior's Kommissariat 5 (later the Ministry for State Security) perhaps after a prison sojourn in 1949. Hundreds of ex-Nazis were pressed into service then by the Communists in a kind of blackmail-atonement. Western intelligence agencies indulged similar conversions. It was the Cold War wasn't it? In its nihilism *Der Spiegel* would write about another such case: "According to the All-German rule, if you hit my Nazi, I'll hit your Nazi. . . ." Guillaume was carefully prepared for a Western assignment and provided the cover employment in an East Berlin publishing house called Volk und Wissen (Popular Science). It was real enough. But it was also a dependency of the Ministry of Interior of the German Democratic Republic, which was developing one of the biggest, most elaborate espionage organizations in the world—something like 10,000 part-and full-time agents in the West, mostly in West Germany. Guillaume's training continued for almost six years, not entirely unnoticed by Western intelligence. In April 1954, for instance, the so-called Gehlen organization, still under the control of the U.S. Central Intelligence Agency, reported that a certain Günter Guillaume had entered West Germany briefly on a task of "infiltration" of publishing houses—a test assignment? Eighteen months later the "Investigation Committee of Free Jurists" in West Berlin, another CIA-sponsored intelligence group, put together a lengthy report on Guillaume, noting his association with the suspect Volk und Wissen publishing house and his frequent absences for "training courses."

In those days before mass prosperity in West Germany and mass collectivization in East Germany it was relatively easy to move between the two German states and consequently easy to blend. The interzone trains were usually full on weekends, and traffic both ways was heavy. One could drive East with little formality and walk West to the thin barbed-wire barrier and climb across without much discomfort. Guillaume, the commoner, moved and blended, with Christel, his wife of two years, arriving in West Germany May 13, 1956. "Fleeing the republic," had been a DDR crime since 1953, but that had not deterred the 331,000 East Germans who had headed West in that year of the June 17 workers' uprising. A new wave of repression in East Germany in 1956—brought on in part by the fears of the Communist rulers watching the unrest boiling up in Poland and Hungary—mounted a total of 279,189 East Germans, the Guillaumes included, to register as refugees in West Germany that year. Curiously, however, the Guillaumes did not bother to check in at the emergency reception center in Giessen until September 13— fully four months after their "flight." In the rush of refugees nobody seemed to notice. He got a job as a photographer near Frankfurt and, after a year, joined the SPD—his third party membership. A contemporary recalled him as "the classic type of narrowminded Social Democrat." The SPD happily made him party secretary in a subdistrict of Frankfurt in 1964, and he, the Communist agent, posed convincingly as a right-wing Social Democrat in a region where the Left had always been strong. Rudi Arndt, later the Lord Mayor of Frankfurt, remembered Guillaume warning Social Democrats emphatically against demanding recognition by Bonn of the DDR. Good camouflage.

His diligence and reliability won him respect and, in retrospect, it seems he rarely slipped up. The tip about his 1954 venture westward lay slumbering in Reinhard Gehlen's files in Pullach. The Free Jurists Committee tip was filed away with the West Berlin police, as safe as a gold bar in a widow's mattress. In 1965 Guillaume hired Ingeborg Sieberg as a secretary for the press office of the SPD's South Hesse District. Even her unmasking a year later as an East German spy didn't involve Guillaume with the West German counterintelligence, although his name was noted by them in their records of the case. Amazingly, all this time—since 1957—the Bundesamt für Verfassungsschutz (BFV), the equivalent of the FBI, was looking for a mysterious "G" who had infiltrated West Germany to work on the SPD.

In 1968 Guillaume was elected to the Frankfurt city parliament, which led to his becoming manager of the dominant SPD wing in the city council and to acquaintance with Georg Leber, an influential trade unionist who was then winding up his first term as federal Minister of Transport. Guillaume was picked as Leber's campaign manager for the 1969 national election, and he also impressed Leber's adviser in the Construction Trade Union, Herbert Ehrenberg, who was scouting for reliable—conservative—Social Democrats to help man Willy Brandt's Chancellery.

The rest was almost child's play. In early November Guillaume asked Ehrenberg, who was on his way into the Chancellery as an economics official, to get him a job in Bonn, too. Ehrenberg spoke with a personnel official in the Schaumburg Palace: "I have a good man there in Frankfurt." On November 11 Guillaume was invited to an interview with Horst Ehmke. Ehmke was not impressed, but he was busy with bigger matters at the outset of a new administration that was abuzz with activism and the enthusiastic hope that it could duplicate John F. Kennedy's first "one hundred days."

The fumbling and bumbling that ensued—both by Guillaume and the federal security services—was worthy of a Woody Allen spoof. Guillaume was told to fill out a questionnaire on November 13. It took him two weeks to respond, surely an unreasonable delay for a man who had just asked for a job. No matter. On December 4 the Chancellery security assistant looked at the file but failed to notice the discrepancy between Guillaume's arrival in West Germany in May and his registration in Giessen as a refugee in September. He routinely called in the Giessen reception center's Guillaume file. Again there was a discrepancy between the East German's claim in 1956 to have been with Volk und Wissen from 1949 on and his answer on the questionnaire that he had begun in the East Berlin publishing house in 1951. Meanwhile, the Bonn Security Group, similar to the U.S. Secret Service, came up with a rather bland extract from the fourteen-year-old Free Jurists' tip: "suspected of agent activity in Berlin (West) and the Federal Republic of Germany." But Bonn didn't want more. On December 17 the Federal Intelligence Service, successor of the Gehlen organization, came up with the fifteen-year-old item about Guillaume's westward journey in 1954. Was something wrong with Guillaume, the Bonn assistant, Franz Schlichter asked? A message informed him that Gehlen's successors were satisfied. Schlichter remained suspicious and told Horst Ehmke he thought Guillaume should not be employed. Ehmke took the cue. On the next day, December 23, the head of the Pullach agency telegraphed that Guillaume's employment should be postponed pending further investigation and possible interrogation. The Christmas holidays came and went. On December 30 Ehmke showed the swelling Guillaume file to Egon Bahr, who wrote in a margin: "Even if you have a positive impression, a certain security risk remains right here."

Ehmke called in Guillaume a second time on January 7, 1970, questioned him closely, and demanded a precise *curriculum vitae*. The spy submitted it five days later, and afterward the file was sent to the Cologne counterintelligence specialists. Sloppiness again. After a probe lasting two weeks nothing new was turned up, although the ancient search recommendation about the suspicious "G" lay in the files. Meanwhile, Ehmke had sought assurance from Georg Leber, who replied forthwith: "I'd put my hand in the fire for him."

Leber also wrote a personal recommendation praising Guillaume's "tact, experience, and intelligence." On January 28, a day after the Cologne authorities had sent in their placet, he was hired. His assignment: assistant for connections with managerial associations and trade unions.

Once in, it was hard to get him out. A second check was run by the Cologne boys in September 1970, without result. A third, in February 1971, turned up the fact that Guillaume had referred to a nonexistent East Berlin address in his autobiographical sketch. Frivolity. Since June he had been given more responsibility under Ehmke, extending his liaison tasks to contacts with church organizations. Other pinholes in his cover had been pricked in February of 1957, 1958, and 1959, on Guillaume's birthday, when coded shortwave transmissions from East Germany carried anniversary greetings to "G." They were deciphered in Frankfurt in 1960, but nobody there made the connection. Questions were raised again in September 1972, when an East German agent named Wilhelm Gronau was apprehended in West Berlin carrying an address book with Guillaume's name. Guillaume talked his way out.

During the intense election campaign of October-November Guillaume was entrusted with newer, larger authority. On December 1 he officially began his last job as assistant for the party and organizations of the newly reelected Chancellor. Egon Bahr figured it out this way after it was all over: "They (the East Germans) probably sent out fifty agents in 1956—twenty for the SPD, twenty for the CDU, and ten for the FDP. For years he has nothing much to report. One day he transmits the news that he has been promoted and is going to Bonn. Then (Ernst) Mielke (the chief of East Germany's security police) goes to (Erich) Honecker (who was then responsible in the Communist apparatus for security affairs) and says we have 'X-15' in Bonn. He had to tell Honecker. And then he reports that 'X-15' is in the Federal Chancellery. He had to do that, too. It was luck. The man wasn't all that bright."

After the spy affair broke, Bahr said: "Guillaume started in the Chancellery (as party liaison aide) at the time of the 1972 election, when the question was whether Brandt would go to East Berlin to sign the Basic Treaty with the DDR and to meet Honecker (who had become chief of the Communist Party). That is important to know, since it was a question whether Honecker would come back from Moscow and what the Russians thought about the whole thing. That was something Guillaume could report about that was useful— what we were thinking, what we intended. But otherwise after the election *we thought we would take a break for six months.* So there wasn't much for Guillaume to report to East Berlin anyway."

Amazing, that there were men in Brandt's inner circle in Bonn in 1973 who thought it possible to take it easy for half a year in a country as big and dynamic as West Germany. Brandt seems to have liked this prospect, too. He was looking good, with the electorate and with the party. But Brandt, the man who had worked so long into the nights in the '30s, the '40s, the '50s, the '60s, this man believed he could relax now? sipping a glass of 1964 Margaux while the goons and ginks of German politics were scheming?

In the fateful German spring of 1973 Herbert Wehner received an invitation to talk with Erich Honecker in East Berlin. No coward, Wehner was filled with trepidation. Years earlier, the East German Communists had condemned him as a traitor, a renegade. They had threatened his life and attempted to get him before. The West German security police still guarded him. What did he, the ex-Communist, have to say or do with the German Communists in East Berlin when his ancient foe, Ulbricht, was still alive, though mortally ill and almost powerless?

Wehner had been Minister of All-German Affairs for three years, and he had seen his main task as one of easing the lot of the divided nation in the simplest terms of reuniting split families. It was something he could talk about practically and with conviction. He had been in touch with an East German emissary on this matter through a Scandinavian intermediary for several years. Wehner went to Brandt and asked what he thought of the idea of his accepting the invitation to East Berlin. Brandt told him to go, thinking, perhaps, that he himself should have been the one to speak to Honecker.

Honecker was no stranger to Wehner. The West German had met the Communist chief in the election campaign for the Saar in 1934, when he was twenty-eight and Honecker was twenty-two. "He has the chance to become the first honest politician from the Saar," Wehner observed sardonically in 1973. Now Karl Mewis, the German Communist adversary of the terrible wartime days in Sweden—the man who was in part responsible for the 1937 murder of Brandt's friend, Mark Rein in Spain—had just published his memoir: *On Party Orders*. Some of the passages about Wehner were stricken on Honecker's express order.

Wehner flew to East Berlin May 29, taking with him Wolfgang Mischnick, his equivalent as parliamentary whip of the FDP and a fellow native of Dresden. Safety in numbers, perhaps. It was Wehner's first trip to the Eastern sector of the former Reich capital, formerly the seat of the Communist Party of Germany, in almost forty years. He had left that part of Berlin with the Gestapo on his heels at Christmas 1933, an "illegal" whose comrades were being seized left and right, crossing the Saxony-Czechoslovakia border on skis with his first wife. No wonder he had uncomfortable feelings. Yet it was a tremendous vindication, too: the man officially condemned as traitor and renegade in East Berlin and Moscow being received as an equal, even if by the Inquisition.

That same May 29 in Bonn, the other German capital, Willy Brandt was being informed at about 2 p.m. by Interior Minister Hans-Dietrich Genscher that Günter Guillaume was under suspicion of espionage for East Germany. Genscher had been confronted less than four hours before by Günther Nollau, chief of the BFV, with the results of a painstaking cross-check of bits and pieces of information that seemed to involve Guillaume. It had begun coincidentally at the end of February, when Heinrich Schoregge, a senior inspector in the Cologne office's counterespionage department, came across the memorable French name for the third time in seven years: in the Sieberg case in 1966, the Gronau case in the autumn of 1972, and now in a new case involving a Frankfurt photographer named Gersdorff. Schoregge, a rumpled blond with a hatchet face, looked at a colleague, Helmut Bergmann, who had come in for a cup of coffee and said: "I think I've got a *krummen Hund* (a crooked character) here." Bergmann instantly recalled the ancient case of the mysterious "G" dating back to 1957. That spoor lead them to the curious greetings to "G" which turned out to coincide with Guillaume's birthday. Then they turned up the full Free Jurists' report. On May 11 Bergmann handed in a twenty-page summary containing thirty points of suspicion. This was expanded to a fifty-four-page documentation on May 17 by one of Bergmann's superiors. The boss, Government Director Albrecht Rausch, concluded: "Guillaume is an agent." As easy as it was to put together the facts of the case, it proved tortuously difficult to convince the counterintelligence apparatus to act on it. Günther Nollau saw the material on May 23. He didn't decide to inform Minister Genscher until May 28. Perhaps the enormity of a spy in the Chancellery made him shy away from his duty; in any case he ordered surveillance for Guillaume's wife only, and when he finally went to Genscher on May 29 he told the Interior Minister only of two suspicious elements: the "G" birthday greeting and Guillaume's unexplained activity before his "flight." He never showed Genscher the documentation he had brought with him down the *Autobahn* from Cologne, nor did that otherwise inordinately nosy politician ask for written material. Later Genscher and Nollau would quarrel over who told whom about the sensitivity of Guillaume's post as SPD liaison man—a post the spy was to acquire officially only three days hence. One point the two Saxons agreed on was "extreme secrecy," also that Guillaume should be kept in place until further evidence could be developed. Obviously both men were frightened numb by the peculiar case.

So it was, when Genscher took Willy Brandt aside after a regular Tuesday Cabinet lunch, that the Interior Minister told the Chancellor of the Federal

Republic of Germany, more or less in passing, there was "a more than vague suspicion" against Guillaume. He mentioned only the shortwave radio greeting from East Germany as evidence, adding that the decoding method was not foolproof. Finally, Genscher repeated the Cologne office recommendation that Guillaume be kept on for further surveillance—thus making Brandt an accomplice of the counterintelligence operation. Brandt remembered that Guillaume was scheduled to accompany him four weeks later to Vangasaasen, the summer vacation home he and Rut enjoyed so much. Genscher said he would consult Nollau, or so Genscher would have it; Nollau remembered it differently. But what use was memory when the damage was done, and Guillaume had spent a month in Norway at the Chancellor's side? In the meanwhile, the watch on Christel Guillaume—that is, of the Guillaume apartment—began on May 31 with a lone inspector assigned to the street. He didn't even know what the Guillaumes looked like—no photographs had been supplied. Nor were the Cologne office counterspies ever allowed to confer with Brandt's Chancellery aides, Grabert or Wilke. Later the observation team was expanded to sixteen men, less than half the normal quota for a big surveillance operation. Nollau would not authorize the renting of a room near the Guillaume nest for improved surveillance. As a result they lost track of Christel when she went to the Netherlands for three weeks in the summer of 1973, and they gave up the trail on another occasion when she and an unknown woman spent hours in Cologne switching from taxi, to subway, to streetcar until two o'clock in the morning—in an apparent effort to shake off the counterspy tails.

Nollau pleaded for supersecrecy from the beginning, partially, one may assume, to prevent his intelligence rival, the old Gehlen organization, from getting into his act. The BND had already caused him enough personal grief, and Gehlen had blocked his advancement in the intelligence community in the 1950s. But Nollau paid little attention himself to his call for confidentiality. Subsequent parliamentary investigation established he informed Herbert Wehner that Guillaume was an espionage suspect on June 4, 1973, and he had spoken to him twice more—briefly—about the Guillaume investigation on September 11 and February 18. Up to then this was three times more than Nollau had spoken to Brandt himself about the case. What sort of counterspy was this, who did not have the self-respect to face his chief in a time of his peril, the very man who had helped him out in 1950? (See Chapter V.)

Brandt remained happily unaware of the seriousness of the situation. He was generally inclined to think the best of people with whom he worked, and Guillaume was one who treated him with the proper degree of awe. So unsuspicious, unsuspecting, was Brandt that he did not even tell his most intimate aide and colleague of a dozen years, Egon Bahr. The only persons in his inner circle notified of Guillaume's possible implication were State

Secretary Grabert, a forty-five-year-old civil engineer who had replaced Ehmke as the main Chancellery administrator, and Ministerial Director Reinhard Wilke, forty-three, who was Brandt's personal assistant. Neither was politically sophisticated. Neither was schooled in the intricacies of security.

It was a foolish mistake on Brandt's part not to tell Bahr, whom he had entrusted with so many other state secrets. Equally foolish of Wehner not to discuss Guillaume with Brandt. Or, for that matter Ehmke, who had been responsible for the screening of Guillaume. Whatever Brandt's reason for keeping Bahr in the dark, this error in judgment provided Guillaume with the leeway to remain an agent for another eleven months, a time bomb whose fuse had been generously lengthened. One year later Bahr bitterly recounted: "I had written that note in the dossier that Guillaume was not to be trusted. If I had known of Genscher's visit on May 29 (1973), I would have remembered immediately and intervened to say he has got to go."

The error of omission was soon compounded by another, even worse. Willy and Rut set off for Norway and their annual vacation, accompanied by Guillaume and two Federal Intelligence Service code clerks. Ordinarily, Reinhard Wilke would have accompanied the Chancellor. But he wanted to go to a spa. The number two aide, Wolf-Dietrich Schilling, thirty-six, a counselor on loan from the Foreign Office, was delegated to stay in Bonn and mind the office. Wilke failed to advise Schilling that Guillaume was under suspicion. So when Schilling relayed Bonn messages to Brandt in July 1973 they were decoded by the cipher specialists and handed to Guillaume, who then walked the 600-odd yards to Brandt's cabin with the dispatches. At least two highly sensitive messages came in during the five weeks of July and early August: one a report from Defense Minister Georg Leber on a NATO military committee meeting, the other a letter from President Nixon dealing mainly with the "Atlantic dialogue" that he and Secretary of State Henry Kissinger were trying to develop with the European partners of the United States. Could Guillaume read Nixon's English? There seems to have been doubt about that. He kept the telex messages—against regulations—for weeks, nonetheless.

How could he have been there, a man who, even if he did have the cleverness to play a false role so convincingly, did not, in the memory of those who worked with him in Bonn, seem to have been of the caliber one would expect of a man working for Chancellor Brandt—a man going along as principal aide on a vacation. Rut told a bodyguard she thought Guillaume was "nice"—and Mathias Brandt, twelve, had found an occasional playmate in the fifteen-year-old Guillaume boy, Pierre. But it was one of the most frequently heard complaints throughout Brandt's abruptly terminated second administration, that in these days he surrounded himself with second- and third-raters. The names Harpprecht, Grabert, and Wilke cropped up most frequently. There were others, including Guillaume, certainly no shining light. "He had nothing but toadies around him in the end," one of Brandt's longtime associates said, contempt in his voice. "They shielded him with such devotion that he got out of touch with reality." Another Brandt associate of long standing blamed the Chancellor for indulging himself in "cronies" (he used the German word, *Kumpanen*) who were "incompetent and incapable of doing the work Brandt needed done for him."

A link of suspicion was to be forged between Wehner's May 29 in Berlin and Brandt's May 29 in Bonn, though it was sheer coincidence that Brandt was being informed about Guillaume on the same day Wehner journeyed to East Berlin to meet Erich Honecker. A year later, when Guillaume's exposure opened Pandora's box in Bonn, one of the most virulent rumors to be spread was that Wehner had foreknowledge of the spy. After all, he was friend and sponsor of Günther Nollau, his fellow exile from Saxony. If Nollau was informing Brandt about Guillaume, surely he would have told Wehner, too, wouldn't he? Wehner went to Erich Honecker as fast as he could to warn Erich Honecker, didn't he? So went the right-wing rumor in the summer of 1974. It added heavily to the larger stab-in-the-back legend that had its origins in the break between Brandt and Wehner over the SPD deputy chairmanship, that was cultivated by Brandt zealots and Brandt enemies, and encouraged by the silence of Brandt himself.

Wehner's talks with Honecker in East Berlin on May 30 and May 31, 1973, became part of the existing legend well before the Nollau-Guillaume suggestion was raised in 1974. No matter how often Wehner spoke or wrote about it, no matter how exhaustively he expounded what had occurred to Brandt and others, a taint remained. The German ex-Communist, it was rumored, had taken up with the man who remained a German Communist.

Foreseeing such a pitfall, the man whose soul had been burned by the fires of Stalinism reverted to the practice learned in self-defense against the hardest of masters. Again he made copious notes, memoranda of conversations, just as he had in 1946 for that remarkable biographic-historic document, *Notizen,* which served him in later years against heinous accusation by right-wing polemicists as proof of what he had been and done. He made his first written report on the Honecker talks June 1, the day he got home from East Berlin. He covered ten major points of discussion and mentioned the "sincerity" of the exchange and the "fairness shown me under difficult circumstances" by Honecker and the other German Communists. He emphasized that he and Mischnick had not conducted negotiations, but merely exchanged opinions "to make clear the credibility of the policy of our government." He spoke also of "the heavy heart" with which he had taken up the dialogue.

Prompt as it was, for public purposes Wehner's report unfortunately came too late. ADN, the official East German press agency, had already broken the news of the visit of the West German parliamentarians, a visit not announced beforehand in West Germany. People gossiped that there must have been something fishy about entering the enemy's lair so secretively and then sharing coffee and cake with Erich Honecker at his villa, in the heavily guarded *santum sanctorum* of the East German leadership. No amount of reports by Herbert Wehner could erase suspicion in the minds of those prone to doubt anyway. "There must have been something" went the litany of mistrust. Brandt, who with Bahr had never wanted to get into the messy business of buying out uncles and daughters and political prisoners from the DDR in the first place, seems to have shared some of the doubts about Wehner's Eastern contacts, too. In any event Wehner felt compelled by December to supply Brandt with a detailed catalog of his correspondence with Honecker and Honecker's aides—"for the record."

Brandt and Bahr, it appears, were still sunning themselves in the glory of Erfurt and the idea that they had discovered a key to the problem of national division by presenting a popular democratic alternative within the dominion of Communism. They knew West German television and radio were carrying their message and their alternative, the Brandt alternative, into 75 percent or more of East Germany's households, and that 70 percent or more of the East German population "liked" Brandt, according to polls taken by the SED itself. "Brandt and Bahr wanted the nation," Wehner growled. "But they didn't want to pay for the nation by rescuing prisoners and reuniting families. They wanted to undermine the DDR." It was a variation, perhaps, of Brandt's 1969 dictum that: "I will not be the Chancellor of a conquered Germany, but of a liberated Germany." The Federal Republic of Chancellor Brandt was not to be blackmailed—not by the French, not by the Israelis, not by the Yugoslavs or Russians or Americans, and certainly not by the German Democratic Republic.

Another man fell into the widening fissure between Brandt and Wehner: Karl Wienand, the stocky Rhinelander who was Wehner's deputy as floor manager of the SPD in the Bundestag. It was Wienand who had saved the Brandt-Scheel Administration from dreadful embarrassment in the delicate treaty negotiations with the Soviet Union in 1970, Wienand who rallied the waverers in the critical two days before the 1972 no-confidence vote that would have toppled Brandt *and* smashed parliamentary ratification of the normalization treaties with Moscow and Warsaw. For this Wienand had to undergo five months of parliamentary investigation in the summer and autumn of 1973, most of it without a breath of support from his party comrades, except Wehner. He was boycotted at every turn. When he spotted Reinhard Wilke at an Italian lake resort, which Wilke himself had recommended to Wienand, the Chancellor's nimble aide turned away, murmuring almost under his breath that it would not be "fitting" for them to be seen together. Nor did Brandt want to be identified in public with the man who had saved his Chancellorship. When Wienand finally was allowed to make a plea in his own defense before the SPD parliamentary group and did it successfully, Brandt leaned back in his chair, a few seats away, and gave Wienand a thumbs-up sign that only a few could see.

"It could as easily have been a thumbs-down sign," said one who was there. This was solidarity in the party that pretended to have a patent on solidarity. Yet when the Wehner-Brandt split broadened in the autumn of 1973, it was Karl Wienand who served as the intermediary, as he did again in the summer of 1974, after Brandt's fall.

Following his painful excursion to East Berlin, Wehner along with four other Bundestag deputies, was invited to visit the Soviet Union as a guest of the Supreme Soviet. The five Germans spent eight days touring Moscow, Kiev, and Leningrad. The Soviet Communist leadership, personified by Leonid Brezhnev, already had ample opportunity to become acquainted with Willy Brandt—in Moscow at the 1970 treaty signing, in Oreanda on the Crimea when the Chancellor called on the Secretary General in 1971, and in May 1973 when Brezhnev came to Bonn. Now the Russians wanted to reacquaint themselves firsthand with the wise old Wehner. His companions hardly counted.

The Soviet hosts made this evident by urgently insisting that Wehner participate in private talks on the periphery of the official visit—suggesting that the first meeting take place on the evening of the delegation's arrival in Moscow on September 24. Wehner reluctantly accepted and, after informing the head of the delegation, met on September 25 with an official of the Department for Foreign Relations of the CPSU Central Committee. Later they were joined by a reporter from *Izvestia*. Wehner took along an old SPD comrade who had also worked with Willy Brandt in Berlin. These four reconvened on September 30 and October 1, the last time with Boris Ponomarev, alternate member of the CPSU Politburo, and finally with President Nikolai Podgorny himself. The main themes in the talks, according to Wehner, were East-West detente, the four-power Berlin Agreement, and German domestic politics in relation to both. The Russians also asked Wehner whether the SPD would send delegates to their upcoming World

Convention of the Friends of Peace. He said no, explaining that others from West Germany who would attend were opponents of the SPD (that is, Communists).

A strange encounter for Wehner, who was in Moscow for the first time since he had left by night train toward the end of January 1941 on assignment of the German Communist exile leadership to make contact with the anti-Hitler underground inside the Reich. A reporter asked him if he had taken a look at his old quarters in the Lux Hotel, where Comintern functionaries and foreign Communists were housed before and during the war. Wehner had not, but the reporter had. "What is it like?" asked the ex-exile.

"It looks like a third-class hotel," replied Friedrich Nowottny, the peppery correspondent of West German Television.

"The Lux was *always* a third-class hotel," snorted Wehner.

No, he did not revisit his scenes of yore, though they were certainly on his mind, horribly so. He noted afterward in a memorandum of the conversation that the *Izvestia* man had told him in their first talk, "I know that you are not in Moscow for the first time."

But all this was overshadowed by what Wehner said to the clutch of Bonn journalists who stuck to his coattails and wrote down his every word and some he had not even spoken. He had gone to Moscow in a bad mood over the SPD, a mood that was doubtless aggravated by repressed nervousness about returning to a site of discomforting memories. Already on two occasions in Bonn earlier that month he had given vent to his feelings about the SPD— that it lacked cohesive leadership, that it was running the danger of overtaxing its *Ostpolitik* treaties and agreements. Specifically, Wehner was sore at Brandt and Heinz Kühn for drifting with the soft popularity current, instead of tacking against the hard winds of mounting inflation, labor unrest, and the rampages of the young Left. He was equally disturbed by what he regarded as the conceits of Brandt and Bahr, Scheel and Genscher in believing they could now afford to play *Ostpolitik* with stronger, more nationalist chords. Bahr had conceived of the idea of placing a new West German federal agency, an Environmental Protection Office, in West Berlin and Genscher eagerly pushed it. Wehner knew this would cause serious difficulties East Germany and its Soviet protectors, as it did. At the same time Brandt and Scheel were indulging themselves in the idea that they could compel Czechoslovakia, weakened and isolated by its tragic misadventures of 1968, to accept less favorable terms from Bonn for a treaty of normalized relations.

In Moscow and Leningrad Wehner again vented his feelings, growling that in Bonn "the government lacks a head," and warning once more that it would be perilous to stretch, "to overtax" West Germany's Eastern treaties beyond the carrying power of the words of the protocols themselves. In their zeal for hot stories it appears that a correspondent for DPA, the West German news agency, and *Der Spiegel,* the weekly Hamburg news magazine, refashioned Wehner's comments in such a way as to make him look as though he were attacking Willy Brandt while on Soviet territory. The DPA man even made his version into "an interview" with Wehner. His report, and others of less virulent quality, caught Brandt in midflight from Aspen, Colorado, where he had just received one of his many peace medals, to Washington, where he was due to see President Nixon. Brandt didn't bother to get in touch with Wehner. He believed, he wanted to believe, the press versions of Wehner's comments. By the time he got back to Bonn he was boiling with anger, and nothing Wehner could say or do sufficed to calm or quell Brandt's nagging suspicion that his former deputy had not told him absolutely everything about his talks with the East Germans and the Russians.

A week of painful explanations by Wehner followed: His observations had been "crudely mutilated." He was "saddened to be presented as someone who was resentful of the Federal Chancellor." He was attempting "to find means to help" Brandt to deal with growing economic problems. Perhaps not entirely painful? Confronting a group of agitated Berlin deputies who questioned him about the controversy, Wehner disarmed them right off by alluding to John F. Kennedy, saying: "Some would come to you and say '*Ich bin ein Berliner.'* I don't say that, *Ich bin ein Dresdner.*" But as he confided later to a friend, Berlin was on his mind: "I think more about Berlin than many who constantly talk about it."

Karl Wienand arranged an armistice, and Wehner drove up the winding Venusberg hill road, 300 feet above the Rhine, to Brandt's spacious villa to make amends. Brandt sitting stiffly in an upholstered chair, sipping French wine, was flinty. Wehner, who felt obliged to be conciliatory, said: "Let's try it again." Brandt later would reflect with a grin, "The situation was not lacking in a certain comedy," and compared Wehner's offer to that of a husband returned to his wife after an affair. But it was no laughing matter for Wehner, who noted that after escorting him to the front door, Brandt turned on his heel without a word.

A few weeks afterward Wienand arranged a second meeting, and Wehner again made his journey to Canossa on the Venusberg. This time it went better, and they killed three bottles of red wine. But from then on their relationship resembled an armed truce. Wehner was abjectly disappointed that Brandt hadn't really wanted him to to go Moscow, any more than he had wanted him to go to East Berlin. "In both cases I was mistaken concerning the approval of Willy Brandt, which I had viewed as already given," Wehner said later, adding, "I fear this mistake will have lingering aftereffects."

In other circumstances it might have been tempting to dismiss the developing Brandt-Wehner quarrel as merely the conceits of a couple of aging politicians. There was, however, too much at stake. The credibility of the Social Democratic Party was in the balance between the two giants—its position vis-à-vis the coalition Liberals and the opposition Christian Democratic Unionists, its cohesion in the face of crumbling tendencies on the Left and Right of its own ranks, and, not least, its strength toward the German Communists of the SED. The sparks of the feud were visible upon the Venusberg and encouraged opportunists to fan them to flame. Convinced that Wehner wished to be rid of Brandt as Chancellor, Horst Ehmke, who had once functioned as a go-between—breakfasting with Wehner and lunching with Brandt—began spreading the proposal that Wehner could or should be persuaded to retire. So did another one-time go-between, Conrad Ahlers. A conservative young SPD deputy who had been a Brandt protégé for a time, boasted that he went to the Chancellor and offered: "If you want, I can round up enough votes to dump Wehner from his *Fraktion* chairmanship. Just say the word." Brandt evidently begged off, much as he may have liked the idea. But his disciples assembled forty-seven anti-Wehner votes. Others fed the Bonn rumor mills with suggestions that Wehner's chronic diabetes had taken its toll that he was thinking of retiring, that he was forgetful, that he was senile, that his outbreaks of temper were becoming ever more intolerable.

Gradually the factors that led to Brandt's fall were coming together and meshing. *Ostpolitik,* once so shiny and thrilling, had lost its excitement, bogged down in wearying back-and-forths with Prague, Moscow, and East Berlin, running behind schedule because of West Germany's inability to finance bold or generous Eastern credits. The Free Democrats, mighty dwarfs of West German politics, had knocked the teeth out of a basic SPD domestic reform bill on expanded labor participation in business management. The trade unions, led by the Public Service Workers, were demanding wage increases of over 10 percent. When Brandt finally got around to dealing with the matter at Christmas 1973 he put his prestige on the line, saying that he would not allow increases with two digits. Then, in the face of strikes, he backed down and allowed 15 percent rises.

Brandt was in one of his annual glooms, separated from Wehner, surrounded by well-wishing cronies, frustrated, self-pitying, alienated, the actor without a proper play and now without a director. He left himself to speechmakers, Harpprecht for his own speeches and Kühn for the others.

Why? He was probably bored, ineffably, cosmically bored, and perhaps disgusted as well. Here he was, the Nobel Peace Prize winner, the election victor, the treaty-maker, the prodigal son welcomed and finally justified, the tribune, the conciliator, the man who could stop angry Berlin mobs and calm the overelated citizenry of Erfurt, the symbol, the tolerator—and what was he compelled to do? Mediate wage increases with an overweight union chief? And lose out? In West Germany, a land of overgrown villages, in a capital where a passing train still cut off crosstown traffic as it had seventy years before? He, who had conferred with Brezhnev and Nixon, de Gaulle and Pompidou, Wilson and Heath? Addressed the United Nations General Assembly? Received Kennedy? Had an album of sweet letters from admiring German schoolchildren? There was a gaping disparity between the narrow alleys and narrow minds of the federal German capital and those broad boulevards of international politics to which he had grown accustomed.

Brandt had never really felt at home in Bonn; for the seventh year he was still living in the villa meant for the West German Foreign Minister. Walter Scheel remained comfortable in his own private home nearby. And now the atmosphere in Bonn, in all West Germany, had changed drastically. In the year since his second election it had gone from sweet to sour, from the confidence reflected in his State of the Nation address, in which he dared to call upon his countrymen to develop "compassion"—he used the English word—to the day eleven months later when he felt abandoned by his Cabinet and his party and threatened to resign over the wage-hike issue. He was doing his job, wasn't he? He was at his desk, wasn't he? He indulged his contentious colleagues in their endless discussions, practicing his concept of democratic teamwork as best he could, didn't he? Was this the reward? Where he wasn't bored, he was bitterly frustrated, and to intimates he confided in the most scornful expletives his loathing for many, most, perhaps all of the people he was compelled to have around him—the private contempt of the man publicly committed to compassion.

"The things he says about people you think he respects" said Horst Ehmke. "He calls them 'criminals,' 'crooks,' and worse. He said, 'You have to know that man is always half angel or half swine and which side you are dealing with.'" These bouts of bottomless contempt for colleagues were augmented by periods of pity, perhaps edged with contempt for himself.

"I am finished," he told a shocked guest at his sixtieth birthday party in the Venusberg villa. "I have only a few years to live, I know it. I'm washed up." This in the midst of sixty or so selected guests who had been disposed to celebrate. The person he addressed was the handsome young wife of a Cabinet Minister. She hardly knew what to say. He had a throat-grasping, tie-pulling argument with Ehmke, filled with accusations and expletives, "*Du Arschloch*" and the like. "I wish I had your self-pity!" shouted Ehmke before it was over.

Brandt was confronting many challenges and challengers—overt and covert, objective and subjective. Walter Scheel, the feisty Free Democrat, decided in the late autumn of 1973 to run for the Federal Presidency, succeeding the aging and fatigued Gustav Heinemann. That would automatically force substantial shifts in the coalition Cabinet—an operation bound to create new tensions between Free Democrats determined to hold fast to influential ministries and Social Democrats equally determined to oust Liberals whom they deemed to be obstructionists at best and, at worst, saboteurs.

Thanks in large part to Brandt's generosity and trust, Scheel had secured huge spoils in the sharing of the 1972 election victory—five of fifteen ministries for the party that received less than 9 percent of the vote— including the key Cabinet seats of Foreign Affairs, Interior, and Economics. In Foreign Affairs, particularly, Scheel and his wily State Secretary succeeded in eliminating the influence of the Social Democrats. The bulk of the Foreign Office officials, holdovers from Christian Democratic administrations safe in their positions because of impregnable Civil Service regulations, were only too happy to play along. They had never liked Brandt's and Bahr's and Wehner's practice of *Ostpolitik,* anyway, probably because it had showed them up for the stodgy bumblers they were. Now they had Scheel saying that with the completion of the Moscow and Warsaw treaties, *Ostpolitik* was all done and the Federal Republic could easily afford to raise the ante in dealing with Czechoslovakia.

"We said the process of normalization has just begun with the treaties," observed Eugen Selbmann, the SPD foreign policy specialist in the Bundestag and a longtime aide of Brandt and Wehner. "We are diametrically opposed to the FDP on that." Why hadn't Brandt cleaned out the Foreign Office when he was Foreign Minister himself? "The personnel policy was very difficult. He could place one or two, but that was all. He would have needed eight or ten years for a real housecleaning. Besides personnel policy was something Brandt never paid much attention to, and he often lacked a sensitive touch in choosing aides."

That Brandt had been too soft on the FDP was one of Herbert Wehner's principal accusations before and in his Moscow-Leningrad critique. He was outraged by the machinations of Scheel and State Secretary Paul Frank, whom he branded "the bookkeeper," in stalling a conclusion of an *Ostpolitik* treaty with Prague. "They are making everything *kaputt*," he declared. Brandt had shown his displeasure at Wehner's attitude and remarks immediately afterward by ostentatiously leading Scheel to Wehner's regular chair for a Tuesday coalition meeting in the Chancellery bungalow. To Wehner this meant that Brandt preferred solidarity with his coalition partner to solidarity with his own party comrade. He was not surprised to find a group of Brandt disciples trying to organize his ouster in December when he was up for reelection as chairman of the SPD parliamentary group. He suspected then and later that Brandt himself had sponsored the rebellion, although this was not the case.

Where Wehner left off, the cry against Brandt's lax leadership was taken up by Helmut Schmidt, the person Brandt had demonstratively called his "first man" after the 1972 election. Schmidt, too, was appalled by the FDP advance, which seemed to fill in every new vacuum left by the Brandt leadership. "The FDP should never have gotten five ministries," he complained. "Three would have been the maximum." Brandt was letting the SPD "go to pot," he said in late March 1974. His catalog of errors was much the same as Wehner's six months before. But SPD setbacks in communal elections in Schleswig-Holstein, Rhineland-Palatinate, and his own hometown of Hamburg made Schmidt's charges more penetrating. The SPD had dropped from 54 percent of the Hamburg vote in 1972 to 45 percent in the city-state election of 1974. The decrease in Schleswig-Holstein was from 48 to 35 percent and in Rhineland-Palatinate from 45 percent to 35 percent. A forbidding shift in less than sixteen months, and the prospect for the SPD in the state election in Lower Saxony, where the party held sway, was still worse. A CDU victory in Lower Saxony on June 9 would give the Conservatives a twenty-six to fifteen majority in the Bundesrat, enabling them to block legislation coming up from the lower house ever more effectively.

In his exasperation—or was it presentiment that his own hour was finally near—Helmut Schmidt confronted Brandt directly with a list of mistakes, sins of commission and omission, first in a party executive session March 8 and a few days later in a television broadcast. To the party comrades he said the Brandt government had ignored "the classic fundamental functions of the state" by neglecting the need of citizens to feel socially and economically secure and stirring doubts about the will of the SPD to guarantee national security. He accused the SPD of making "a *de facto* retreat from the center" of German politics. "Now we have made practically all possible switch voters uncertain or in doubt about the SPD. And we have made some afraid . . . some are downright afraid." He blamed this largely on the stentorious demands of the *Jusos* at their latest convention in Munich for nationalization of industries and realization of other Socialist dogmas. "I would be afraid, too," said Schmidt and accused Brandt of being too tolerant toward the young radicals.

The rest of the elements of negligence were already on the record: Brandt had come home from his Norwegian vacation the previous summer and promised a tax reduction, only to have Schmidt disavow him the very next day. He stayed on the south coast of France during the Middle East war when not only the West Germans became nervous about the escalating tensions. Defying the speed-loving death wish of German drivers, Brandt the nondriver authorized a 62-mile-an-hour limit on the highways as a gasoline-saving measure in the ensuing oil crisis, only to lift it later. He left the FDP Minister of Economics to gather the laurels as the manager of the German energy crisis. He was allowing the FDP to remove corporation taxes from his party's revenue reform package, to water down SPD plans for widening labor co-determination in industry management and for increasing capital accumulation by employees, and to disembowel the SPD bill for reforming real estate laws. Nor was there any prospect of forward movement on SPD promises to overhaul the higher education system in West Germany.

It wasn't all bad. The second Brandt-Scheel coalition had passed a fairly progressive anticartel law, kept an orderly financial house in the face of mounting inflation, and enacted some forward-looking labor and social welfare laws. But these measures hardly sufficed to persuade an increasingly disaffected electorate that it was getting the kind of dynamic, progressive, reform-minded leadership Brandt had promised at the outset of each of his legislative terms. Cartoonists who had drawn him with angel's wings at the beginning of 1973 now showed him with wings broken or feathers in disarray. Critics in the party ranks spoke of him as "worn out" or "withdrawn."

Brandt's dry response was: "I'm not standing on a pedestal, but I don't need to be excluded expressly from what people are always calling solidarity."

From Schmidt's corner came the biting comment: "For four years Willy played God and now he's playing the Crucified."

In an hour of abject pessimism, Herbert Wehner growled: "This is a Master Race and it wants a master, it wants a Führer." It was the old authority question in a country where authoritarianism still had a very bad odor. Had Brandt really shown his teeth and slapped a few people around, no doubt he would have been wildly cheered by the masses and at least applauded by Wehner and Schmidt. But that wasn't his style. He didn't want that, never had wanted it. Instead he toyed for a moment with the idea of seeking the Federal Presidency. It was early in March after the local election setbacks of the SPD when he told a friend: "I had the foolish thought for a short while of going for the Presidency." A change was coming, anyway. Schmidt was available for the Chancellery. But he dismissed the temptation, even though he might easily have persuaded Scheel to give up his own presidential ambitions. Besides, he remained wary of Schmidt, who was pushing him hard, too hard.

By 1973 a peculiar triangle had emerged at the summit of the SPD leadership with Brandt at the apex and Wehner and Schmidt at the other two points. Outwardly it seemed to be geometry of strength: Brandt the still popular *Landesvater* and vote-getter, Wehner the great long-term planner and parliamentary strategist, Schmidt the all-around activist. But the tensions among the three were leading to weakness, not strength, at the top of the SPD.

Brandt resented "Uncle Herbert" Wehner because he seemed to act more like a testy aunt than an avuncular friend, and he looked down on his rival Schmidt. Brandt would write later of his objections to Schmidt:

There is a deeply rooted subaltern urge to see authority proven by appearing "powerful." That was not my style in the office of Chancellor. . . . Democracy is not capable of living without respect for others; such respect must begin in the leadership. . . . Inability to respect the other almost always results sooner or later in the contempt one reaps.

Wehner detested the airs and allures of "the Lord of Venusberg" while wishing at the same time to be accepted by Brandt. Of Schmidt he said: "I learned solidarity in the trade unions and he learned solidarity in officer's casinos." Schmidt had mixed feelings toward Brandt—described more than once as "erotic" or "love-hate"—and he had doubts about Wehner's ability to carry on at an advanced age. Wehner was then sixty-seven.

Helmut Schmidt had already given a great deal of thought to the succession problem, and, on occasion, he talked out loud about it, even for the record. He noted that he was only five years younger than Brandt and added "given the expectation that there is no reason he would not stay on, the normal thought of replacement of Willy Brandt would come much later than 1976. In 1978 he'll be sixty five and I'll be sixty. I've always felt that a replacement for a cause of age or incapability would have to be chosen from an age bracket considerably younger than me. I never bother to ponder this nice-nasty circumstance. It is just a fact of life. In case of an emergency, if something nasty happens to him now the question of who would succeed is not very difficult to decide. They would have to choose me."

A little later Schmidt said of his relationship with Brandt: "I offered him my friendship. It was 1959 I think. But he didn't want it. I believe he is a very lonely man. I think he's a little bit afraid of being used by people who come too near to him."

Brandt felt threatened by Schmidt's challenge, especially after the party deputy's public criticism on television in the first week of March. In the Chancellor's entourage there was talk of an attempted *Putsch* by Schmidt. SPD solidarity! Brandt's reaction was to have another go at making common cause with Wehner—who continued to accuse him of trying to be "the philosopher king" of "wrapping himself in his protocol cocoon"—against Schmidt. Wehner accepted. The two met for over five hours at Brandt's home following the Schmidt raid. Together they plotted campaign strategy for the coming Lower Saxony contest, for stiffening the back of the party, for straightening out the coalition with the Free Democrats. "Uncle Herbert is running around like a virgin who's been kissed for the first time," Ehmke commented. But the romance was short-lived, even though Brandt seemed to catch a second wind and begin running in better form.

Nearly everyone who was anyone in Bonn blamed a lot of Brandt's troubles on the man who managed his Chancellery, State Secretary Grabert. In mid-March Brandt seriously weighed exchanging Grabert, a loyal crony, for Egon

Bahr, who had become Minister Without Portfolio and without much to do in the government. But this move, which might have spared some grief, was blocked by Wehner, who regarded Bahr as incompetent and "a puffed-up journalist." Despite all the problems, a well-informed friend opined on the trans-Atlantic telephone from Bonn: "Willy is on his feet again." So it seemed. He, Wehner, and Schmidt had made a joint appearance before a Bonn press conference in a jammed hall at the Tulpenfeld and presented a ringing ten-point program for revitalizing and solidifying the party. The *Jusos* got a stiff warning that the SPD would not tolerate membership of Social Democrats who made local arrangements with West German Communists. There was talk—partly from Schmidt—of throwing out some of the Young Socialists to make an example.

But April had begun. April—the cruelest month for Brandt two years before, as it had been cruel in 1940 when he had to flee Norway and cruel in 1933 when he had to flee the Third Reich. On the surface he seemed his confident self. "The party is in step again," he said in a notice sent to SPD members in the middle of April, and he began cultivating a long-neglected practice of inviting party leaders from the provinces to meet with national officers to discuss "the topic of the week" and coordinate propaganda. There was an echo of his Berlin spirit, perhaps even a ghost of his early SAP agitation speeches in the campaign swing he made through Lower Saxony in the second week of April. "Don't let them knock Germany down for you. Put your common sense as citizens and your pride as citizens to work where you can against the fearmongers."

But the West Germans were still in one of those irrational phases that so often befell the nation. With the lowest inflation rate—7 percent annually—of any major Western country, the citizens of the Federal Republic thought they were undergoing terrible hardships. A typical poll showed a German answering the question how he was doing: "I'm getting on all right." But when the same citizen was asked how the rest of his countrymen were doing he replied: "For the others it's bad." The figures recorded by Infratest in Munich were 67 percent satisfied with their own situation and 76 percent thinking everybody else was in difficulty. A parallel poll by the Institute for Demoscopy established that more and more West Germans thought the government too weak, radicals too strong, prices running ahead uncontrolled, and Chancellor Brandt not the man to handle their troubles. For 45 out of 100 Brandt was no longer their choice. It was almost the margin of his party in the 1972 election.

A year before Erhard Eppler, the Swabian scholar who had found a romantic apotheosis in his post as Development Aid Minister, observed: "Existentialism and inwardness have lost their value on the exchange. There has been a move away from the irrational in German society. But I wouldn't stick my hand in the fire to prove that it is definitive." The irrational moods were back.

People were telling mean jokes about Brandt all across the Federal Republic and buying thousands of copies of a new book of bearded jests about him, the bulk being primitive updates of old jokes about Ulbricht and Hitler. Eighteen months before the most daring remark about Brandt had been a cabaret comment in the Munich *Lach und Schiess Gesellschaft:* "Here comes Brandt with his 300-year-old tortoise face and a touch of class struggle in the corners of his eyes." Now they were resurrecting such klinkers as the one about the head of government (Brandt-Ulbricht-Hitler-Frederick the Great): The Boss heads for the country and his driver runs over a chicken. The driver goes to the peasant to apologize and comes back with a black eye. In the next village he runs over a pig and again stops to console the peasant. This time he returns with a present of ham and fruit. How come, asks the Boss. "I told them I was Brandt's driver and that I had killed the pig," the chauffeur replies. Nine out of ten jokes were of this genre, and only one or two seemed in any way new. "Alfred Tetzlaff," the Archie Bunker imitation created by a former Brandt fan, was given the line "Norwegian emigré Chancellor" to describe Brandt, and it got a satisfactory rating on the West German laughometer. Tetzlaff also indulged in remarks about Brandt's birth out of wedlock—the first to do this for gain since Konrad Adenauer.

As before, Brandt turned to women, and not always to Rut, for *Nestwärme,* for distraction from his melancholy, for consolation in his frustration.

In the eighteen months between his election campaign of 1972 and his resignation a number of extraneous women passed through his life. One held his fancy for a time, and it would appear that he dallied with very few others. "Some people seem to overestimate my strength at my age" he would say months later with a self-deprecating smile to accusations that he been breaking sexual records. In 1972 the Brandt campaign train rolled for thousands of miles around the Federal Republic with a renovated salon car as his private quarters, a luxurious dining car for the press and himself, and well-appointed sleeping cars for journalists and aides. Should a pretty young journalist show her face, she stood a good chance of being invited forward for a time with the Peace Chancellor. One full-breasted SPD loyalist who appeared glassy-eyed at 2 a.m. after her hours up front was hailed with cheers by her male colleagues. "Go ahead and write it," said Jochen Schulz, the late SPD press spokesman. "Our Chancellor is fifty-nine and can make five speeches a day and give eight interviews and still get it up, and Rainer Barzel is already sleeping on his own skin!" But nobody wrote it. Another attractive young woman who worked for a news agency followed the invitation forward and, according to her version, declined the attentions of the Chancellor on the grounds that he was "too fat." Instead, she engaged him in a political discussion that ended, after several bottles of Bordeaux, with a "joint communiqué." It read: "We, the undersigned, vow to do more for the working masses in the event of an SPD victory." It was signed by both.

There were other women in the Federal Republic who, like Susanne Sievers in the 1950s, wanted to flaunt their hours with Willy Brandt, that immensely private man, even if the hours were innocent. In the winter and spring of 1974 while campaigning for the communal and state elections of Schleswig-Holstein, Hamburg, and Rhineland-Palatinate, Brandt resumed the practice of inviting women to the salon car on his private train. Nobody wrote about it this time either for the gazettes. But this time Brandt had Guillaume with him, and Guillaume was no monk. His presence was to put Brandt's brief companionships into a category entirely apart from that of his onetime ministers Karl Schiller and Helmut Schmidt, or even his predecessor, Ludwig Erhard. (A guard from the Bonn Security Group told me that Chancellor Erhard had one night mistaken the bedroom of another guard for one of his female secretaries and leaped into bed with the astonished man.)

The campaign train rolled through Lower Saxony, that curious mixture of rolling hills and flat plains, the villages full of sharpshooter clubs and the cities full of Socialists, black and white cows not far from chic boutiques, the highest High German next to the lowest *Plattsdeutsch*. Minden, Braun-schweig, Osnabrück. There was hearty laughter along the way, as almost always when Willy felt at home with his people. But down the aisle and sometimes in the next compartment his obedient nemesis, Günther Guillaume worked for a master 100 miles to the east of Lower Saxony.

Until the Guillaume revelations, Brandt rated as merely one of a host of German politicians, journalists, and businessmen who indulged in occasional flirtations and affairs. They had their masculine code of *Schweigen,* the German equivalent of a gentleman's silence. Each knew the other knew, and, besides, so what? Nobody was hurt.

Whether for innocent diversion or something more serious, it made no difference in the final outcome. The passages in the nights were noted by Brandt's personal bodyguards in the Security Group, foremost among them, the devoted giant from Cologne, Ulrich Bauhaus.

Since mid-May 1973, thanks to the unspeakable carelessness of the West German security organs, Guillaume had been upgraded from a bureaucrat spy with access to significant but not cosmic secrets to one who had a chance to look at NATO nuclear strategy papers. Even as suspicion thickened and the watch on him intensified, he was a spy with access to strategic secrets and at least the hint of sex secrets. The combination was fissionable, and the timer on the bomb was ticking faster and faster.

"Do you have anything more?" Brandt had asked from time to time, since he had been told, albeit tardily, about the suspicious Guillaume. Each time he was told: *"Nein."* How could they have anything more when Guillaume wasn't even being watched while in the Chancellery, nor had he been watched in Norway. Blunder piled upon blunder as the investigation limped along, piling up in a fashion perhaps endemic to a people so obsessed with the virtues of organization, discipline, and *Obrigkeit*. It was the kind of botchery that prompted Rüdiger von Wechmar, the government spokesman, to remark sardonically when his chauffeur, a wartime tank driver, once took him to Dortmund instead his intended goal of Duisburg: "This is how we lost World War II."

On January 30, 1974, Interior Minister Genscher called in Nollau and told him it was time to complete the investigation, "One way or the other." The security chief asked and obtained a *four-week* period of grace. In March Nollau presented such a thin report on the Guillaume inquiry in the presence of Genscher that when Willy Brandt heard it he concluded it had produced "zero point zero." The Nollau report asserted, for example, that Guillaume had two children, and Brandt advised him the aide had only one, a son. A week later the Attorney General's office rejected the report as insufficient for opening a court case against Guillaume. Chastened, Nollau at last allowed a more comprehensive shadowing of Guillaume himself, this time with the participation of the Bonn Security Group.

Spiderlike, Guillaume had spread his webs very wide. When it was feasible he was at the side of his prey morning, noon, and night.

He had reached the main target, not by brilliance or daring, but by those steadier German virtues: hard work, obedience, conformity, conservatism. He had accomplished something few spies in history had managed—admission to the throne room. How his spy master, Markus Wolf, who had been schooled in Russia, must have rejoiced.

Willy Brandt, an enemy of orthodox Communists from the beginning of his political life more than forty years before, never really had been in their web until he became the main enemy of the DDR. Erich Honecker had warned Herbert Wehner eleven months earlier about the "mistake" of Erfurt in 1970, when Brandt had been cheered so enthusiastically, saying, "We can't have that kind of *Volksfest* anymore." Guillaume was the proof of that, and insurance against it. Brandt, the incalculable factor of destabilization for the DDR, was under observation by one of Honecker's own. It was safer that way for a state that was still unsure of its legitimacy. For the East Germans it must have been titillating, frightening to see how the big Russian brothers viewed it, eminently satisfying in the sense of revenge, which is so dear to Central

European hearts. Hadn't General Gehlen's Nazi-rooted. CIA-founded espionage organization planted a spy as a secretary in the office of the DDR's own Premier, Otto Grotewohl, the turncoat Social Democrat from Braunschweig who became such a valuable asset to the Communists in their effort to transform East Germany into a Communist state? The spy was code-named "Daisy" and her diligence—Gehlen ungallantly called it "overeagerness"—caused her capture and her reported death by guillotine. 'Daisy" and Günter—tit for tat twenty years later.

An East German journalist remembered Guillaume's pose in the Chancellery when State Secretary Michael Kohl, the DDR negotiator turned up for one of his forty negotiating sessions with Egon Bahr on the German-German treaty: "He played the Communist-eater to us and snarled, 'What are you doing here?'" The Guillaume cover was thick enough to deceive East Germans who were not cut into the security operations.

There had been some slippage in East Berlin-those curious birthday transmissions by radio from the East addressed to Guillaume. But that was the kind of sentimentality Communists are wont to indulge. There had been the slips in his cover, and the avoidable links to the Sieberg woman, Gronau, and Gersdorff. But otherwise, Guillaume remained virtually clean.

On April 10 Guillaume drove to France for a vacation in a gray Opel-Cadet. He was alone but tailed by something like a hundred operatives of the Bonn Security Group and the Federal Office for Protection of the Constitution and a dozen or so of their French Securité colleagues. As often before, he put up at the Résidence de France in Sainte-Maxime on the Mediterranean. There was a hint that he would make contact with another agent there. On April 16 he headed back to Bonn, driving straight through the 450 miles. He apparently noticed that he was being followed and tried to shake his shadows, to no avail.

Two days after Guillaume returned, Brandt set off on a tour of Arab countries—Algeria and Egypt—where he was welcomed as a German who owed no high-interest mortgage to the Jewish people. It was foreign policy of a most delicate nature, the turf he knew and liked best. Henry Kissinger was still in the Middle East, acting his negotiator role to appreciative audiences, and Brandt picked up a bit of that action in Cairo. He was skeptical of his fellow-German émigré's veracity but admiring of his talents. He was scheduled to travel a few months later to Moscow to see Leonid Brezhnev again, and, as a new high point, to East Berlin to meet with Erich Honecker. But the Arab tour was his last foreign venture as Chancellor.

At 6:32 a.m. on April 24 a group of nine officers of the Bonn Security Group walked up one flight of stairs at 107 Ubierstrasse, a small apartment house in the "Teutonic" quarter of Bad Godesberg, where all the streets had thoroughly Germanic names. The apartment had a little balcony. There were pine shrubs poking up to the level of the sun porch, and there was a cigarette vending machine facing the sidewalk. Guillaume answered the knock on the door and the announcement that he was under arrest, saying: "I am an officer of the National Peoples Army of the DDR and employee of the Ministry for State Security. I ask you to respect my officer's honor." He volunteered no other information. The search party found he was half packed, ready to flee. He had known his time bomb was about to go off. But Willy Brandt hadn't.

Brandt arrived at the Bonn airport about noon. Genscher was waiting for him, and the luckless Grabert. They took him aside and told him of the arrest. Brandt turned to face television cameras and said his trip had been useful for the European-Arab dialogue. He added, despite what must have been a state of severe shock, that the talks with the Arabs complemented West Germany's *Ostpolitik*. He made some remarks about détente and spoke of the role of the Western alliance in the Middle East as "balanced engagement." Then he drove to the Venusberg. In a kind of memoir he later noted:

> Naturally I turned over the arrest of G. in my mind that evening and in the night. The news that he had been uncovered needn't have disturbed me because I had been told a long time before that there were reasons for suspicion—with the added advice not to change his assignment—that reasons for suspicion could develop and therefore they wanted to observe him. For a long time it looked to me then as though it had been an unfounded tip.

One can imagine Brandt in those first hours after the shock, his face stiff as always when confronted with unpleasant surprises. It must have struck him a terrible blow to realize not only that his Chancellorship was in danger—he had gone through that before—but also that he had been betrayed, totally betrayed for the first time, by a man he had taken into his confidence. He was aware of the criticism that he had a weakness for selecting aides who were inadequate, and there had been cases of associates who did things that did not suit him—Ahlers talking too much about Chancellery affairs to the press, Karl Schiller's egotism on financial policy, Ehmke's uncontrolled political athleticism, and the challenges from Wehner and Schmidt. But betrayal? Never. Brandt had always trusted the men around him, however foolish they may have seemed, largely because he assumed they all looked up to him. It was not the only way in which he deceived himself, but it was the one that did him in. On the other hand, it would require an almost monstrously suspicious head of government, a Stalin, to imagine that his enemies would dare to plant a spy at his very doorstep, to walk at his elbow for twelve months, let alone to doubt that his own intelligence services were fully on top of the situation.

In the diary that was to become a memoir of these days he wrote:

> Although I wasn't entirely unprepared, the proof of the suspicion
> unleashed a good deal of anger in me: What sort of people are they
> who honor an honest effort at reducing tensions—especially
> between the two German states—in this manner. Is it likely in the
> current international atmosphere that Brezhnev and Nixon would
> make use of spies in the anterooms? And if so, how would that effect
> East-West relations. Are we to be reminded once again that our
> situation is unique. Surely I have to ask myself if I was too trusting.

Guillaume confronted his interrogators with defiant silence. His wife
Christel, whom the counterintelligence operatives had observed once going to
a secret dead-letter drop in a park, was also in detention, and she, too, refused
to talk. Nor did there seem to be overwhelming material evidence of
espionage in the sweep of the Guillaume dwelling, among the usual trappings
of bourgeois German family life—knick-knacks on the shelves, crocheted
coverlets, and stuffed chairs—some suspicious film cassettes, a scrap of paper
with a crudely coded reminder of his spy chief's telephone number in East
Berlin (559-3519) and a pile of secret papers belonging to the Cologne
counterintelligence office. Guillaume's mother-in-law, Maria Therese Boom,
and the Horst Försters, friends, had also been detained, only to be released for
lack of evidence.

Brandt told his Cabinet colleagues of the arrest of Guillaume on the
afternoon of his return from Egypt and then conferred briefly with party aides
on what the public should be told. Only a small circle of officials knew of the
affair. Yet Valentin Falin, the Soviet Ambassador, had somehow gotten wind
of it and departed "ass over teakettle for Moscow," as a CIA agent described it.
A full twenty-eight hours passed before the federal government revealed
Guillaume's arrest at 10:30 a.m. on April 25. The detonation was shattering. It
inaugurated a political hunting season in which nearly every major politician
in Bonn became fair game. The chief prize was Brandt, but long after he
resigned the season remained open on others.

Brandt had gone off on the morning of the twenty-fifth as previously
scheduled to open the annual Trade Fair in Hannover, where he spoke with
appropriate gravity about "the overwhelming force of price rises" and the
still-flourishing prospects of German businesses. Shortly before noon the
Federal Press Office issued a statement that Guillaume was "not concerned
with work on subjects classified as secret." An hour later the Federal
Prosecutor's Office in Karlsruhe confirmed that a warrant had been issued for
Guillaume's arrest and that other suspects had been detained. Gerold Tandler,
the spokesman for Franz Josef Strauss, claimed that the spy had access to
"secrets of the first order." A shot in the dark. But well-aimed.

The arrest caused dozens of people to remember curious brushes with Guillaume. Klaus Harpprecht recalled that he was "always hanging around the Chancellor's anteroom" on the southwest corner of the Schaumburg Palace, even when he didn't belong there. Wilke and Schilling, the other two personal assistants of Brandt, remembered how Guillaume had insisted on seeing secret papers in June 1973 and that he showed irritation when he was blocked. Gert Börner, the young man who was putting together Brandt's political archives, thought about how Guillaume had demanded access to the roomful of well-ordered papers in Bad Godesberg in September 1973 and had threatened him when Börner refused. Ulrich Bauhaus, the bodyguard, recalled Guillaume's proximity on the campaign trains and suggested he had piloted girls to Brandt's car. All across the stunned capital droplets of suspicion and information were falling and trickling together until they formed a huge dirty flood, threatening to engulf hundreds of men and women—many of them innocents.

The innocents, but also the incompetents. In February 1975 an all-party investigatory commission of the Bundestag issued a report on its seven months of inquiry into the Guillaume affair. After hearing fifty-nine witnesses in twenty-eight sittings—including Brandt, former Chancellor Kiesinger, Bahr, Genscher, Nollau—the commission concluded:

> Neither in the Federal Chancellery, nor in the Federal Interior Ministry, nor in the Federal Office for Protection of the Constitution did the idea occur to anyone to think about protecting the Federal Republic of Germany from damage if the espionage suspicion against Guillaume, disclosed on the 29th of May 1973 to Minister Genscher and Federal Chancellor Brandt, should prove to be true.

The report blamed practically everyone involved. The Federal Intelligence Service was found to be in a state of "organized un- and disorganization," by Gerhard Wessel when he took over from Reinhard Gehlen. Nollau was found to have "grossly violated his duty" and to be "disqualified as director of the BFV by grave errors and negligence." Brandt's Grabert was accused of "complete inactivity." Genscher, who had plainly lied to the commission about what he had told Brandt, was found to have left "questions open" about his role. Brandt was also charged with "total inactivity"—but only in terms of a blanket accusation that "nobody did anything" to nail Guillaume. Wehner was held by the report to have heard more from Nollau about Guillaume than he had made known in testimony before the commission. Did they know where they were living, and when, in an age of agents, these men who had experienced the ways and means of Communists for most of their adult lives?

Testifying September 25, 1975, before the court of Düsseldorf where Guillaume was being tried for "all-German" *treason*—a juridical anomaly left over from the postwar division—Brandt disclosed that he had received reports of espionage suspicions against the aide as early as 1970, presumably from Egon Bahr and Horst Ehmke. With hardly a glance at the prisoner in the box he identified himself to the five-judge panl as "Willy Brandt, sixty-one, chairman of the Social Democratic Party of Germany." Nor did Guillaume look at his former chief, fifteen feet away, until curiosity overcame him. He said he had treated the original suspicions as "improbable" and then recounted Genscher's first warning of May 1973:

> Herr Genscher did not name Guillaume but said there was suspicion against one of my aides who had a French sounding name. I thought this was quite incredible. Similar suspicions had been raised against another official I knew and had just been proven false.

During the course of more than four hours of testimony, the strain of which was manifest in his stonelike demeanor, he also surmised that the damage caused by Guillaume's spying was "potentially considerable" and "of high interest" to a foreign intelligence agency. Finally, he revealed that during a reunion with Leonid Brezhnev in Moscow in the summer of 1975 the Soviet leader had made a kind of apology for the affair: "We discussed the affair without actually naming the defendant, and the Soviet leader expressed regret."

On April 26, 1974, however, Brandt went before the Bundestag and in a somber voice spoke of Guillaume as "an especially clever and cunning agent" whom he had kept on at the "express advice of the security organs." The spy had not seen secret documents, "because this was not part of his work." He warned against a spy hysteria, saying it would not help anyone to rouse "false emotions among the public." The case had been "a deep human disappointment for him and he blamed Erich Honecker's SED for "a hostile attitude toward the SPD chairman."

"There are periods in time when you feel like saying one is spared nothing,'" he concluded. But he still had not perceived all of the trials that would not be spared him in the coming days and weeks.

There was another headline event in the Bundestag that morning—the final vote on a bill legalizing abortions in West Germany for the first time—a topic that had stirred impassioned debate between the nation's practicing Christians, who still constituted a sizable proportion of the electorate, and the growing number of self-reliant German women who wanted to decide their own destinies. Brandt noted in his memoir that he made the final speech in behalf of the change and that the SPD-FDP coalition carried 247 to 233 with 9 abstentions.

His spokesman, von Wechmar, was instructed to spread calm by telling a press conference that while Guillaume had been cleared for "top-secret" papers, the clearance had been reduced to the category of "secret" because of his duties. This was before people began to remember that Guillaume had been with Brandt in Norway in July 1973. That same Friday another chasm yawned open. Hans Wilhelm Fritsch, the director of the Bonn Security Group, called his boss, Horst Herold, chief of the Fderal Criminal Office in Wiesbaden, to ask permission for interrogation of Bauhaus about Guillaume. Permission was immediately granted, and the robust Rhinelander soon began to unburden himself in his thick Cologne accent. Sure, Guillaume had escorted women to Brandt's quarters on the train and in a hotel, and besides the spy had been screwing Egon Bahr's secretary. It was only a foretaste, but it electrified his interrogators.

On Saturday morning, the chief interrogator, Karl Schütz, a hard-faced cop with white hair and cold blue eyes who headed the Department for Protection of the State, drove south to Wiesbaden to tell Herold about the Bauhaus revelations. Together, they drove back and found their superior, Interior Minister Genscher, attending a meeting. They informed him. Genscher ordered them to tell the federal chief prosecutor, Ludwig Martin, and he asked for a written deposition for himself. Meanwhile, a Bauhaus colleague, Gernot Mager, entered the picture. He had complained months earlier about "sloppy" security practices indulged by the big fellow from Cologne and about Guillaume. He talked now to his superiors in Wiesbaden and stirred their zeal to learn more.

On this Saturday the German Communists spoke up for the first time about the Guillaume affair. On instructions from Honecker the chairman of the tiny West German Communist Party declared: "The DDR and the SED are in no way hostile to Willy Brandt." They didn't have to be hostile any more. Up to this point the unpublished public reaction in East Germany to the Guillaume reports emanating from Bonn was "puzzlement, touched with a bit of pride here and there," an SED official later said. "Some of our people noted that (Franz Josef) Strauss had called Guillaume's the 'performance of the century,' and responded, 'Not bad, getting a man into the Federal Chancellery. What a guy.' Then when Brandt quit, it turned completely around and the reaction was terrible embarrassment." An East German journalist who was touring Bavaria in these first days reported that ordinary West Germans had been gripped by spy hysteria. "I got really nervous down there as an East German," he recalled. "They said terrible things."

On Sunday and Monday the interrogation of Bauhaus continued, in part on the thesis that if they couldn't get anything out of Guillaume they would have to apply pressure elsewhere. It dawned on Bauhaus that he was in a dangerous spot, caught between loyalty to Brandt, to whom he was devoted, and to superiors who had become his inquisitors. Schütz and the other investigators expanded the inquiry to include other members of the bodyguard detail. Gernot Mager drafted his own report.

On Monday Herold was able to call Genscher with the first piquant details. New characters were appearing on stage. Marieluise Müller, the slight twenty-seven-year-old brunette, secretary to Bahr and Günter Gaus (Bonn representative in East Berlin) confessed to her relationship with Guillaume. Soon Ellen Kuchenbecker a full-bodied blonde, twenty-three, who was married to one of Helmut Schmidt's assistants, admitted a liaison with Guillaume and, added that in the same phase, she had also gone to bed with another Brandt aide. There was a third, never named, the wife of a Brandt diplomat. The revelations were astounding. "Sometimes he (Guillaume) serviced all three on the same night and then went home to his wife and took care of her," said a man who saw the protocols. "He was phenomenal."

In Karlsruhe, Ernst Träger, a federal prosecutor assigned to the Guillaume case, and a known CDU sympathizer, told newsmen he was only "at the beginning" of *his* investigation.

Back in Bonn von Wechmar was telling the press that Chancellor Brandt wanted "complete clarification" of the affair. He supplemented his statements of the previous week on Guillaume and state secrets, saying he "had no access to any materials of the Federal Intelligence Service or of the Federal Office for Protection of the Constitution." He added: "Guillaume knew of the Chancellor's future engagements but not of Cabinet papers." Although the spy had been in Norway with him, he had had "no means" to know all that was going on, nor did he have access to materials about East Germany or the Soviet Union. It wasn't Wechmar's fault that he didn't know all of what the other branches of government had already learned. He simply wasn't told—a typical feature of the Federal Republic's jumbled bureaucratic operations, partly explainable by geography. The federal prosecutor in Karlsruhe. The federal police headquarters in Wiesbaden. Nollau's "FBI" in Cologne. Gerhard Wessel's Federal Intelligence Service in Munich. But, off the record, Wechmar was able to confide that Guillaume might have seen secret telegrams while in Norway.

Wechmar also announced two measures taken to indicate the government's displeasure with East Germany at having set a spy on the Peace Chancellor. Günter Gaus had canceled a meeting he was to have had on the morrow with DDR negotiator Kurt Nier and the accreditation of Gaus in East Berlin and the DDR representative in Bonn would be postponed a fortnight to the end of May. Brandt continued routine Chancellor activities such as the usual Monday morning *Lage* (world and domestic situation report)—his last—and a meeting with provincial journalists. But the Guillaume affair was taking more and more of his time. Mindful of the security check revelation that Guillaume had access to classified documents in Norway, he noted that in a conversation with Horst Ehmke, "the possibility of resignation does not go unmentioned, but I still don't take it into consideration." At this point Ehmke offered to resign, "if it would help." Brandt said it wouldn't help, and he should stay.

On April 30 Horst Herold's requested letter was handed to Genscher and a copy went to the chief prosecutor, Ludwig Martin, who immediately telephoned Justice Minister Gerhard Jahn at his home in Marburg. Long a devoted Brandt associate, Jahn in turn telephoned the Chancellor to warn him what was up. Brandt had conducted what was to be his last Cabinet session that morning, addressed a rally for the communal elections in Saarbrücken in the afternoon, and flown to Hamburg in the evening to prepare for a major speech to a trade union audience. He was staying at the luxurious Hotel Atlantik overlooking the sparkling Alster. That night the Chancellor noted in what was becoming a daily diary that Nollau's office had admitted passing Guillaume in 1970 after two screenings on January 26 and September 8 of that year.

It was a bad day, with worse to come. Genscher had journeyed to Wiesbaden to learn in person what was cooking on the Bauhaus-Mager-Guillaume burners. He told reporters the spy had been apprehended not by "pure luck" but by "methodical, tenacious, patient investigation." In Bonn Franz Josef Strauss, who had hated Brandt ever since he had discovered that the two of them had been involved in the '50s with Susanne Sievers, made a new assertion: It was not true, as Brandt said, that Guillaume had no access to sensitive secrets—he had seen all there was to see in the previous July in Norway; the documents carried Guillaume's initials. Somebody, maybe Mager, maybe Ernst Träger, was leaking. Axel Springer's press service also had a claim: Gerhard Wessel had objected to the employment of Guillaume back in 1969. Another leak. It was a half-truth but damaging enough.

Genscher called Brandt in Hamburg the next morning, May 1—May Day, the day of the international working class for the whole of the century and a day on which Willy Brandt was accustomed to make a public speech. It became a day not of proud memories but of new despair. The portly Interior Minister told him he had dispatched the Herold letter, with its initial Bauhaus confessions and portions of the Mager deposition by special messenger. The Chancellor went ahead with his speech to the crowd of 30,000 on Karl Legien Square, and later in the day with the side trip to Helgoland. It was windy and a cold drizzle fell. He made another speech and someone in the back of the crowd cried out: "Guillaume!" In his memoir, *Uber den Tag Hinaus—Eine Zwischenbilanz (The Long View—An Interim Report),* published in

September 1974) Brandt does not mention the Herold-Genscher report or the fact that Guillaume had organized the Helgoland excursion. But the name was beginning to haunt his hours. He also talked to a few confidants, including Karl Wienand, who said later: "For the first time it occurred to me on May 1 that he was going to resign and I told that to my wife." That night, when the full force of the Bauhaus admissions struck him, he fell into a profound depression amidst the songs of his hosts, including, "I'll dance with you into heaven." He murmured his feelings to Lauritz Lauritzen, Minister of Housing. That night he thought of suicide.

Back on the mainland Brandt stopped in Wilhelmshaven and spoke in public for the first time about the spy affair: "I'm not going to allow someone to make me shift my policy, which is basically a correct and necessary policy, merely by planting a louse on me." The rather large crowd cheered. But he noted that same day that an opinion poll showed 63 percent of those questioned thought the spy had caused great harm and 47 percent thought those responsible should resign. It was May 2. The Federal Prosecutor's office entered the Bauhaus case, and Ernst Träger confronted the wretched police captain with arrest. Bauhaus protested vehemently and finally buckled, the small tragedy of a tall man. The torrent increased. Karl Carstens, the parliamentary chief of the Conservative opposition, declared that Horst Ehmke should be dismissed because of his "responsibility" for clearing Guillaume in 1970. From Göttingen, where he was on a speaking engagement, the Minister of Technology and Post said he had no intention of resigning.

In Bonn Herbert Wehner convened the Bundestag Committee on Security to hear State Secretary Grabert report on the affair. He told the ex-engineer with the chronic grin that the committee simply had to have information about the spy's activities during the Brandt vacation in Norway to counter Strauss' charges that Guillaume had "seen everything." Grabert stalled, saying he couldn't produce that for another eight days. Wehner stormed. By that time the Bundestag would be in the midst of its annual budget debate, when the opposition could raise any topic it wanted, including Brandt's negligence or culpability in Norway. "In this critical period nobody could get past Grabert to Willy," Wienand recalled.

That day, also, Erich Honecker's party paper, *Neues Deutschland,* came out with a cramped and awkward editorial alluding to the Guillaume affair, saying it was a pretext for "incitement" against East Germany and "poisoning the atmosphere" between the two German governments.

On Friday, May 3, the business of the federal government virtually came to a halt. Brandt, back in Bonn, was telling associates that he had become the victim of federal investigative authorities who were "more interested in probing his private life than in the background of the spy." In the afternoon he called President Heinemann to tell him he was thinking of resignation. Heinemann offered to stand for reelection if it would help Brandt. The Chancellor also told Helmut Schmidt to prepare himself for the possibility of change and noted in his diary that his deputy was "very surprised" when told "he must reckon with becoming Chancellor very suddenly." Brandt had also heard from Bauhaus, who lamented bitterly about Träger's threats to him.

Herbert Wehner was abruptly brought into the final act of the Brandt drama that afternoon, when Nollau called him and urgently requested a meeting. The security chief arrived at Wehner's house at 4:15 p.m. In the course of fifteen minutes he conveyed the essence of the ten-and-a half-page protocol that had just been read to Nollau by Herold. It was a summary of the Bauhaus-Mager inquiry. Wehner listened in silence. Nollau explained that he and Herold had reason to believe most or all of the information in the protocol would be leaked to the public and added that because of this Brandt would have to step down. Finally, he told his fellow Dresdner that he and Herold would deny it if anyone attributed the protocol information to them.

When Nollau had departed, Wehner tracked down the party manager, Holger Börner, who was attending a SPD meeting in Hesse, and insisted that he come to see him immediately. Börner arrive ninety minutes later, about 6 p.m. Wehner told him what he had heard from Nollau, and Börner, who had become a Brandt intimate, said the Chancellor had to hear this himself, especially since there were potential leaks. They agreed to meet Brandt Saturday afternoon in Münstereifel, the pretty town with medieval walls set amongst the green hills west of Bonn, where the SPD had a training center for party officials—where Brandt had drafted his 1969 government program.

In the evening Brandt got together with Bahr, Grabert, Gaus, and Karl Ravens, who was his State Secretary for Parliament. The Chancellor broached the idea of trying to save his government by purge. Ehmke could go, and Nollau, who would take the rap for failing to nail Guillaume earlier. Schmidt would take over the SPD *Fraktion,* replacing Wehner, who would be given a Cabinet post. Grabert would depart, and von Wechmar, too. Gaus would become government spokesman. They talked of other shifts, too. Genscher? somebody asked. The coalition would collapse if Genscher, the designated FDP chief, were to be dropped from the Cabinet. And what about Scheel? Brandt acknowledged the futility of his plan. He was grasping at straws, when the roof had already been torn away by the flood.

On Saturday May 4 Brandt sat down at a previously scheduled meeting with SPD trade union leaders in Münstereifel on the problems of economic stability and inflation. Heinz-Oskar Vetter, the federation chairman was there, Adolf Schmidt from the miners' union, Karl Hauenschild from the chemical workers, Eugen Loderer from the metal-workers. They talked into the afternoon.

The opposition attacks were intensifying. A Strauss crony claimed that Guillaume had been discovered long before the government was admitting. A CDU agitator accused Brandt of "taking part in the cover-up" of the spy affair, and another CDU man blamed Ehmke. The story about Bahr's secretary and Guillaume appeared in the press.

Wehner and Börner reached Münstereifel in the late afternoon and dined with Brandt. About 7:30 p.m. the Chancellor asked Wehner to talk with him alone, and they went to his room. Brandt was jumpy, and he paced up and down.

"I am wrecked," he murmured. "I am thinking about resignation." Then he haltingly mentioned that the justice authorities were investigating his involvement with women. "I'm glad you brought that up," Wehner replied, "because that makes it easier for me." He proceeded to sketch an outline of what Nollau and Herold had told him twenty-seven hours earlier. Brandt continued to pace, and now and then he groaned.

"You must inform yourself," Wehner urged. "You must look at the papers." Groan. "You must be informed before you make a decision." Groan. Brandt mentioned his thoughts of suicide. They parted after half an hour.

Brandt now turned to Börner, his "Sancho Panza" as Wehner called him, and Ravens. They stayed up late—the two "friends," as Brandt was later to describe them, pleading with him to stand and fight. He noted: "In the night hours I say that my decision to resign is almost fixed. Both friends, to whom I say this, attempt to change my mind." They told him he had probably been worn out by unpleasant developments since the beginning of 1974. He replied that he couldn't exclude that. He was still wavering when he turned in to sleep at 3 a.m. the morning of May 5. Wehner was no longer "a friend," in Brandt's book.

Wienand, who was not a party to the Saturday night agony but heard about it, surmised: "Inside he had made up his mind to resign. But he was still playing games with his ego and his image, and how to do it, and listening to everyone saying 'stay!'"

By noon Brandt's physical condition was beginning to reflect his psychic stress. He was tired, drawn, nervous, perhaps, in the back of his mind, missing cigarettes. (Egon Bahr said later, "If he hadn't given up cigarettes in 1972 he'd still be Chancellor.") Brandt said goodbye to the labor leaders. Then after a brunch, he told the men who stayed behind he had made up his mind to quit. Schmidt had arrived. So had Alfred Nau, the party treasurer. Wehner, sat by, puffing one of a score of pipes that had drawn down the left corner of his mouth years before. There was more bad news in the air. Springer's tabloid

Bild had just published a story linking Brandt lasciviously to a woman journalist.

Everyone was tense. Helmut Schmidt stood up and protested loudly that it was "out of proportion" to resign over the affair and the affairs and leave the SPD to reap the consequences. Wehner protested, too. Nau yelped: "We'll stick it through!"

This drew a sharp retort from Wehner: "Not you will stick it through, but I." He then spoke of the upcoming budget debate and the likelihood that all the detritus stirred by the flood of revelations would be exposed there. Wehner paused for an instant. There were three complexities, as he saw it: the women, the matter of the spy's presence with Brandt in Norway, and the ominous potential of the budget debate. Considering all these, he saw three alternatives for Willy Brandt.

The Chancellor could discharge two key aides as responsible for the affair— say, Grabert and Wilke—and stay on to fight. Or he could resign. But if he decided to stay he had to consider the possibility that the pressure could grow to such dimensions that he would be forced to quit anyway. "I'll stand by you whatever you decide," Wehner exclaimed. "I'll take the consequences and let them hack me to pieces. But you have got to be clear in your mind over the alternatives."

Wehner deliberately avoided telling Brandt which alternative he favored, probably thinking that at such a moment he had no right to recommend to the head of the government and the party the alternative he should choose. It was the same thing he had done the year before in the argument over his successor as deputy party chairman. Brandt wouldn't see the point. He was thinking about *Onkel* Herbert, "*Tante* Herbert," to his mind. It stung him that the great strategist and disciplinarian was refusing to tell him what he should do and, instead, was only telling him what he *could* do.

"It was the classic case of their misunderstanding," said Ambassador Sven Backlund, a rare man who knew and liked both Wehner and Brandt. Soon afterward, Brandt would construct the myth that Wehner had let him down hard that day, leading some journalists and politicians to conclude that the old mentor was in reality "a regicide." Brandt never acknowledged the existence of this myth in public—the facts wouldn't allow it—but he allowed it to flourish in such widely read and believed mass circulation magazines as *Stern* and *Der Spiegel.* The almost suicidal aspects of his own actions went unnoted.

Brandt had always taken as much time as he could possibly afford to make a major decision, a reflection of his angler's philosophy that if he waited long enough the decision would let itself be comfortably hooked and landed. But now time was running out swiftly, and he was still wavering. The discussion dragged on, as discussions usually do in German politics. Börner said Brandt should try for Wehner's second alternative—discharging two aides and sticking it out. Schmidt said Brandt couldn't possibly act that very day as he had implied he might, since he had failed to consult the FDP leadership or Heinemann. "In any case," Schmidt continued, "If you do (resign) then you must remain party chairman because I can't hold the party together by myself." Brandt brightened and observed that, "a Chancellor can resign anytime or try new elections, but I was elected party chairman until 1975." A participant noted: "He was almost childishly grateful to Schmidt for this."

Returning to the Venusberg, Brandt sat at his desk and drafted a letter of resignation with a black felt-tip pen. Scheel came over about 9 p.m., and Brandt showed it to him. They talked well into the night. Scheel, whom he spoke of later as his "confidant," advised him "strongly" against resignation. He also told him that he did not want to be "the last person with whom you talk about it." They parted on the agreement to meet in the morning for a full-scale coalition discussion.

At 9 a.m. on May 6 the black Mercedes sedans began passing through the heavy steel sliding gate of the Federal Chancellery. Scheel came, followed by his Free Democrat colleagues, Genscher and Wolfgang Mischnick, the Liberal party whip. Schmidt was there, and Brandt. Wehner arrived in the rust-red Swedish Volvo that his stepdaughter, Greta, drove.

All present supported the proposal that Brandt should weather the tempest, come what may. Scheel was most eloquent, even passionate, vowing to support Brandt "through thick and thin" (it came out "fire and flames" in German). Only Wehner spoke of some necessary precautions. "We have to clear up three things," he observed, "how Guillaume was hired, what he could have heard or learned, and the scandal reports." He told the circle in the small downstairs chamber how State Secretary Horst Grabert had refused to supply him needed explanations for the upcoming budget debate the week before. "I must have this for the debate," Wehner declared. Brandt kept silent. But when the group broke up after two hours it seemed that Willy Brandt had gotten up his courage again and was ready to stay in office and fight. Concerning resignation, Scheel recalled, "he was no longer absolutely convinced of his decision." After learning of what had gone on from Wehner, Wienand called him to report: "I think we're going to make it." Brandt would stay.

Indeed, that afternoon, about 3 p.m., Brandt made a move that strongly indicated he planned to stand and fight. He called Karl Carstens, the parliamentary whip of the Christian Democratic Union opposition, and asked him to come to the Chancellery at 9 p.m. along with Richard Stücklen, the deputy leader of the Bavarian wing of the Conservatives, to discuss the setting up of a bipartisan investigation of the entire West German intelligence community. Ironically this was Brandt's last initiative as Chancellor and, more than six months later, on November 18, the independent investigatory commission he called into life that afternoon reaped the bitter fruit. It blamed Ehmke, Genscher, and the Federal Office for the Protection of the Constitution, charging them with dereliction of duty, structural deficiencies, misbehavior, lack of experience, and "hectically conducted security inquiries."

Bonn, that sieve among sieves of the world's capitals, was already dripping with rumors during the afternoon. Egon Bahr had told Günter Gaus that a "Brandt bomb" was about to go off, and Gaus had confided as much to a clique of journalists. At least one ambassador also had word that a decision was near. But the inner circle was uncoiled for the moment, apparently persuaded that Brandt was persuaded to stay on, and they went about their various Bonn tasks—"some of them stupid," as Wehner remembered it.

At 6 p.m. the Chancellor grasped the nettle he had warded off for three whole days and received the new Chief Federal Prosecutor, in his office. He showed Brandt the protocol and advised him that Guillaume did in fact see the Nixon letter and a NATO nuclear planning document in Norway—at the very least. "Willy's eyes opened for the first time," an intimate said later. "That finally did it: the combination of Guillaume, women stories, and the NATO report." And Wehner. Brandt then talked to Rut, and she, too, confronted him with reports about the women. It was not a happy time for her; the woman who had stuck by him in other bad moments was now being stretched by the stories of his missteps and also by his black despairs, perhaps closer to her breaking point than ever before. For more than three years she and her friend, Ria Alzen, the owner of a popular restaurant in Godesberg, the Maternus, had met regularly in a back room to pitch pennies into a large green glass acid jar—"for our retirement expenses" they explained in a joint joke. Rut and Ria had been pitching a lot of pennies.

At 7 p.m. Börner and Wehner joined Brandt at the Chancellery. Heinz Kühn appeared, having flown in at the last minute freshly tanned from Madagascar, a place where it was hard to imagine how he could serve the cause of Germany, his home state of North Rhine-Westphalia, or the party in which he had been designated vice chairman a year before at Brandt's behest. The supporting actor had now seen fit to return for the beginning of the last act. True to form it was he, not Wehner, who now declared what Wehner had never dreamed of saying, much less thinking: "Everybody is different. Everybody reacts differently. You have to decide it by yourself, Willy." Kühn was thus the only one of the entire group to withhold support for Brandt's staying in office. But still Wehner had not spoken the redeeming words that he should remain.

Now Brandt made up his mind at last. The letter of resignation got its final polish, and then he sat with the men he had known and worked with so long. Scheel appeared at 8 p.m., and then the other coalition partners. They drank Moselle and even joked a bit. The meeting with Carstens and Stücklen was called off. He dispatched Grabert with the handwritten note to Hamburg, where President Heinemann was officially saying goodbye to the city's dignitaries.

It read:

> Dear Mr. Federal President. I assume the political responsibility for acts of negligence in connection with the Guillaume affair and declare my resignation from the office of Federal Chancellor. At the same time I ask that this resignation become effective immediately and that my deputy, Federal Minister Scheel, be charged with looking after the duties of the Federal Chancellor until my successor has been elected. With devoted greetings, Yours, Willy Brandt.

He had also written Heinemann a short personal note:

> It wasn't easy for me to write the letter Horst Grabert carries. But after thorough reflection there remains no other choice for me . . . I am remaining in politics, but I must get rid of this present burden. Don't be angry with me, and try to understand me and transfer the duties of office to Scheel so that Schmidt can be elected Chancellor.

Within minutes a copy of the first letter was shown to a journalist by one of Brandt's aides, even though those present at the wake were sworn to silence about it until the morrow. "The journalist saw it before Grabert left for Hamburg," Wehner recalled with a growl. "Not even the resignation had a genuine ring to it."

Then Brandt left the Chancellery, writing later, "Should I deny that I departed not without emotion on this evening?" Those who stayed behind worried as they had the night before whether he would last the night. But up on the Venusberg he stayed awake long enough to hear a crowd of torch-bearing fans arrive, chanting, "Don't go, Willy!" A desperate reprise of the cheers he had heard four years and two months before in Erfurt.

Heinemann got the message about 11:30 p.m., and four minutes later the Hamburg radio station, tipped off by its top correspondent in Bonn broadcast the following: "Ladies and gentlemen. We interrupt our music broadcast for a brief news bulletin. According to our Bonn studio, Federal Chancellor Brandt has tendered his resignation . . ."

The climax of a personal and a political tragedy, Brandt's fall came 534 days after he was inaugurated Chancellor. It had been precipitated by persons and forces he had opposed all his life. The Social Democrat Brandt believed in openness. His nemesis, a conspirator, had lived all his life keeping secrets, or trying to. In the end it was mooted that Guillaume, the Communist spy, had joined the Nazi Party on April 20, 1944, when he was seventeen, and later disguised the membership. When the concealed information was discovered, it had led to his recruitment by the DDR espionage service, the story went.

Brandt sought the warmth of women; Guillaume consumed it. Brandt trusted. The Communist distrusted. Brandt believed in democracy. The Communists believed in hierarchy. "I am no plaster saint and never claimed to be free of human weaknesses," Brandt would say to his beloved Berliners five days later. "The Germany of decency is on my side." He would also tell a nationwide television audience on May 8 that one of his motives for resignation had been "signs that my private life was going to be dragged into speculation concerning the spy affair."

After the paralysis of indecision and wavering—He was "wrung out like a washcloth in the end—nothing left but the fluff," a participant in the last deliberations observed—the German hunting season again took hold. The right-wing press campaign was just beginning with the old and new women stories; Nollau was soon to be attacked below the belt. Genscher would get some lumps. Wehner, more lumps. Wienand, too. The SPD put out a statement: "One may expect that the agitation campaign with which Willy Brandt had to contend since the beginning of his political career is going to be continued in the nastiest way."

Helmut Schmidt was nominated by the SPD as Chancellor on May 9 and completed formation of his Cabinet five days later. Scheel was elected President on May 15, Schmidt, vowing continuity, was chosen Chancellor the following day, with Genscher as his Vice Chancellor and Foreign Minister. All very neat.

"German efficiency," Brandt would remark with ironic humor a month later.

In those last hours and days before the new government took over, Willy Brandt rose to euphoria and sank to despair frequently. When he had calmed down a bit, he answered the request of a longtime acquaintance to say what he felt he had achieved in his foreshortened administration. He replied softly: "I know that I contributed something to increasing the respectability of this country—the opposite of isolation. I helped start a process of changes. Not only the temper is different but also the substance. Germany is more naturally adjusted to its neighbors. We absorbed the youth problem." He trailed off.

On the morning after resignation Brandt met his party colleagues in the big Bundestag room reserved for the SPD deputies—more than 200 of them. At his desk were forty-three red roses from Herbert Wehner. (Brandt had become a party member in 1931, forty-three years before.) Wehner had last brought roses when Brandt won the no-confidence vote two Aprils before.

Brandt stood and repeated what he had written Heinemann, that it was not easy for him to quit. "I liked carrying the responsibility of the head of government," he continued. "But I constantly felt the pressure that such an office exerts. And in these last few days I had to face the situation in which I landed through the betrayal of a presumably loyal colleague. My resignation occurs out of the experience of the office, out of my own understanding of respect for the unwritten rules of democracy, and to prevent my personal and political integrity from being destroyed. In that order . . . Now is not the time to yammer, but the time to work hard and fight bravely for the good cause of our nation."

Brandt hadn't wanted roses from Wehner. He had wanted him to say, "Stay!" He now sat in the SPD *Fraktion* room, where portraits of Kurt Schumacher, Erich Ollenhauer, and Fritz Erler hung, and where his portrait would hang, too. There was a full four feet of space between his chair and Wehner's. Brandt's fingers rested on the veneer table, and his gaze was distant, his face a tight mask. He would not find it possible to sit next to Wehner again for weeks, he told a friend, and that was why as soon as possible he went off to Norway for awhile. He felt cast out again: the German from Germany, the Chancellor from the Chancellery, the democrat from the democracy, the advocate of solidarity from the solidarity, the bird from the nest. Only the Social Democratic Party of Germany remained a home for him at this hour.

Did he really have to go? To play the outcast? Objectively, it seems he could have stayed. He had the needed backing, and he probably could have survived what would surely have become a brutal fight; he had come through brutal struggles before. Later he told friends that the incredible clumsiness of the security services was enough to warrant his remaining in office. "I could have stayed," he said. Subjectively, however, he had to go because his own image of himself was in grave peril of being destroyed—the image of the German conciliator, integrator, unifier, the German who stood above pettiness, intolerance, hatred, and dirt.

Wehner got to his feet to deliver a peroration on the Brandt era. In it he spoke of the love he and his fellow Social Democrats felt for Willy Brandt. Nearby, Egon Bahr bowed his head at the word "love" until his chin touched his chest. The man who had served Brandt longest and most devotedly began to weep uncontrollably, covering his eyes with both hands until Karl Ravens patted his back and gripped his arm to console him.

Two blocks away, at the Chancellery where Brandt had still governed only fifteen hours before, a new exhibit was being opened. It commemorated the 800-year history of the Free Hanse City of Lübeck. Brandt, who made the Lübeck motto, *Concordia domi, foris pax,* his political credo, had been scheduled weeks before to attend the opening by the man who handled his agenda, Günter Guillaume. In resigning he had also been true to the saying, "Harmony at home, peace abroad." But on the day the flag of the free city was hoisted in front of Schaumburg Palace, Herbert Willy Brandt Frahm of Lübeck could not bring himself to attend the exhibition of his native place.

Afterword

In the months after his resignation, Willy Brandt found himself locked into an equilateral triangle in which he as party chairman, Schmidt as Chancellor, and Wehner as Bundestag majority leader were the points. The three were equally dependent on each other, like it or not. Brandt didn't like it initially, especially the Wehner part, and he spoke of his expectation that by 1976 there would be only two of them—Brandt and Schmidt. But he gradually accustomed himself to the new role and applied himself as seldom before to his party tasks. He was rewarded in the spring of 1975 with a new popular following in the state elections of Saarland, Rhineland-Palatinate, and North Rhine-Westphalia—which gave the SPD a needed lift. The bridge to Wehner was partially restored. The SPD remained very much a "Brandt party" and Schmidt was grateful for the strength he drew from it, knowing that he did not command the allegiance of the rank and file. Not that it was without awkwardness for both men, for Brandt was placed in the position, as a friend described it, "of telling voters that Schmidt was the best Chancellor they ever had." There was that other lurking possibility: Helmut Schmidt was a sick man, combatting a serious thyroid condition that had laid him low more than once. Should Schmidt die the Chancellorship would naturally fall to Brandt—a reversal of their roles in 1973. Did Brandt want to be Chancellor again? In March 1975 he told me, "No," and sounded convincing. But he had never turned down a great challenge before and there· was little reason to doubt that he would reject such a task if it fell to him.

His therapy was in the familiar mold—a long restorative summer in Norway and, once more, some writing. The product was *Über den Tag— Hinaus—Eine Zwischenbilanz (The Long View—An Interim Report)*, a mixture of diary notes about the Guillaume affair and other critical moments of his second term of office, together with essays on domestic reform policies and foreign issues. In the autumn he began a series of foreign journeys—to Portugal to rally support for the embattled Socialists of Mario Soares, to France to talk about the future of united Europe, to Mexico, the United States, and Venezuela to talk with government leaders about relations between industrial and developing nations. He was very warmly received by President Ford and Secretary of State Kissinger and Presidents Echeverria and Perez. Brezhnev invited him to Moscow again and treated him as a friend. Brandt was still a sure performer on the international stage.

His confidence showed in other ways. He rose in the Bundestag in February 1975 for the first time since his resignation to speak eloquently on the issue of terrorism versus the doctrine of law and order. On the campaign trail there were crowds again shouting, "Willy, Willy." His home life deepened with Rut and the younger boys in a new home on the Venusberg, and he relearned household tasks. A measure of tranquility ensued, and he would write—about foreign affairs and, perhaps, even about himself.

Notes

CHAPTER II. WHO IS WILLY BRANDT?

1. Willy Brandt in a talk with the author, June 1974.
2. *Ibid.*
3. *Ibid.*
4. Brandt. *My Road to Berlin.* New York, 1960, p. 34.
5. Albert Krebs. *Tendenzen und Gestalten der NSDAP.* Stuttgart, 1929, p. 209.
6. Friedrich Meinecke. *Die Deutsche Katastrophe.* Wiesbaden, 1946, p. 53.
7. Brandt. Speech after being named honorary citizen of Lübeck, February 29, 1972. Bundespresseamt.
8. Julius Leber. *Ein Mann Geht Seinen Weg.* Berlin, 1952, p. 117.
9. Brandt. *My Road,* p. 36.
10. William H. Maehl. *German Militarism and Socialism.* Lincoln, Neb., 1968, pp. 86-104.
11. *Ibid.,* p. 40.
12. Leber, p. 256.
13. *Ibid.,* p.275.
14. *Ibid.,* pp. 274-75.
15. *Ibid.,* p. 273.
16. Heinrich Jaenecke in *Stern,* No. 10, 1972.
17. Peter Koch in *Stern,* No. 51, 1973.
18. Leber, pp. 70-71.
19. Brandt. *My Road,* p. 42.
20. *Ibid.,* p. 42.
21. Leber, pp. 234-35.
22. *Ibid.,* pp. 236-39.
23. Heinz Höhne. *Der Orden unter dem Totenkopf.* Frankfurt am Main, 1969, pp. 60, 66.
24. Brandt. *My Road,* p. 43.
25. *Ibid.,* p. 44.
26. Hanno Drechsler. *Die Sozialistische Arbeiterpartei Deutschlands,* Meisenheim am Glan, 1965, p. 63.
27. *Ibid.,* p. 18.
28. *Ibid.,* p. 27.
29. *Ibid.,* p. 75.
30. *Ibid.,* p. 81.
31. Brandt. *My Road,* p. 45.
32. *Ibid.,* p. 46.
33. Drechsler, p. 106.
34. *Ibid.,* pp. 108-10.
35. *Ibid.,* p. 159.
36. Herbert Wehner. *Notizen.* Hamburg, 1946, p. 15. (unpublished)
37. Josef Stalin. *Works,* Volume 6. Berlin, 1952, p. 253.
38. Kurt Tucholsky. *Werke,* Band III. Reinbek, 1961, p. 254.
39. *Ibid.,* p. 980.
40. Brandt. *My Road,* p. 48.
41. Koch, p. 49.
42. Jaenecke.
43. Brandt. *My Road,* p. 48.
44. Jaenecke.
45. Brandt in a talk with the author, 1973.
46. Lev Trotsky. *Was Nun? Der einzige Weg.* Berlin, 1932, pp. 61, 67.
47. Drechsler, p. 246.
48. Brandt. *My Road,* p. 52.
49. *Ibid.,* p. 53.
50. *Ibid.,* p. 54.
51. Leber, p. 272.
52. Manfred R. Beer, *Die Welt,* November 1, 1969.
53. Drechsler, p. 328.
54. Wehner, pp. 37. ff.
55. Brandt, *My Road,* p. 56.
56. *Ibid.,* p. 57.
57. Höhne, pp. 86-89, and Wehner, pp. 37-49.
58. Brandt, *My Road,* p. 57.
59. *Ibid.,* pp. 58-59.
60. *Ibid.,* p. 62.

61. *Stern,* No. 10, 1972, p. 132.
62. *Ibid.,* p. 135.

CHAPTER III. OUTSIDE

1. *Stern,* No. 51, 1973.
2. *Stern,* No. 10, 1972.
3. Manfred R. Beer. *Die Welt,* Nov. 1, 1969.
4. Brandt. *My Road,* p. 78.
5. Karl Kraus. *Die Dritte Walpurgisnacht.* Vienna, 1933. Republished in Munich, 1952. p. 9. (Kraus added that fans of his periodical, *Die Fackel,* obviously expected him to damn the Nazis as he had damned all others who debased the German language. He explained, "there is a kind of evil" so mind-boggling that "the very brain finds itself incapable of further thought."
6. *Arbejder Sangbogen.* Copenhagen, 1947.
7. Bent Skou in a talk with the author, 1974.
8. Jan Valtin. *Out of the Night.* New York, 1941, p. 693.
9. Jens Krag in a talk with the author, 1974.
10. Brandt. *My Road,* p. 63.
11. *Ibid.,* p. 63.
12. *Ibid.,* p. 64.
13. *Ibid.,* p. 64.
14. Brandt. *Draussen.* Munich, 1966, p. 75.
15. Brandt in a talk with the author, 1974.
16. *Ibid.*
17. Trygve Bull. *Mot Dag og Erling Falk.* Oslo, 1955, p. 224.
18. Brandt. *My Road,* p. 67.
19. Bull, p. 270.
20. Brandt. *My Road,* p.64
21. Brandt.*Draussen,* p. 224, and Brandt in a talk with the author, 1974.
22. Brandt. *My Road,* p.67.
23. Dreschler, p. 332.
24. Willy Brandt and Richard Löwenthal. *Ernst Reuter, Ein Leben für die Freiheit.* Munich, 1957, pp. 283-86. See also Wehner, p. 27.
25. Dreschler, p.331-39, and *Geschichte der Deutschen Arbeiterbewegung.* Berlin, 1966, Vol. V, pp. 36-37.
26. Wehner, p. 50.
27. Brandt. *Draussen,* p. 379.
28. *Ibid.* p. 225.
29. Harry Eckstein. *Division and Cohesion in Democracy.* Princeton, N.J., 1966, pp. 78-111.
30. Brandt. *My Road,* p. 67.

31. *Ibid.,* pp. 66-67.
32. Brandt in a talk with the author, 1974.
33. Per Monsen in a talk with the author, 1974.
34. Willy Brandt Archive, May 16, 1935.
35. Dreschler, pp. 339-40.
36. Äke Ording in a talk with the author, July 1974.
37. *Ibid.*
38. Brandt. *Draussen,* p. 278. Back in Oslo, Heinz Epe was instrumental in obtaining temporary asylum for Trotsky in Norway through the offices of the Labor Party in the spring of 1935. Epe fled Norway with his Norwegian wife and child after the Nazi invasion in 1940 and vanished after reaching the Soviet Union.
39. Oddvar Aas in a talk with the author, 1974.
40. Brandt. *My Road,* p. 66.
41. Brandt. *Draussen,* p. 65.
42. *Stern,* No. 51, 1973.
43. Brandt in a talk with the author, 1974.
44. *Ibid.*
45. *Ibid.*
46. Brandt. *My Road,* pp. 69, 73-74.
47. Brandt in a talk with the author, 1974.
48. Monsen in a talk with the author, 1974.
49. Valtin, pp. 694-95.
50. Brandt. *My Road,* p. 75.
51. Hans Meyer in a talk with the author, 1974.
52. Valtin, p. 492.
53. *Geschichte der Deutschen Arbeiterbewegung,* p. 87. See also Wehner, *Notizen.*
54. Brandt. *My Road,* pp. 70-71.
55. Carl von Ossietzky. *The Stolen Republic* (selected writings). Berlin, 1971, p. 21.
56. Brandt. *Draussen,* p. 373.
57. Isaac Deutscher. *The Prophet Outcast.* London, 1963, pp. 160-352.
58. William Shirer, for example, subtitled a chapter on the Rhineland coup in his *The Collapse of the Third Republic,* "The Last Chance to Stop Hitler and Avert a Major War."
59. Brandt. *My Road,* p. 76.
60. Wehner, pp. 128-29.
61. Brandt. *My Road,* p. 76.
62. Brandt. *Draussen,* p. 67.
63. Brandt. *My Road,* pp. 76-77.
64. *Ibid.,* pp. 78-79.
65. Brandt. *Draussen,* pp. 76-77.
66. Willy Brandt Archive, 1936.

67. Brandt in a talk with the author, 1974.
68. *Ibid.*
69. Brandt. *My Road,* p. 82.
70. *Ibid.,* pp. 83-84.
71. *Geschichte der Deutschen Arbeiterbewegung,* pp. 489-91.
72. Dreschler, pp. 344-45.
73. *Ibid.,* p. 345.
74. Willy Brandt Archive.
75. Brandt. *Draussen,* pp. 77-78.
76. *Ibid.,* p. 187.
77. Monsen in a talk with the author, 1974.
78. *Ibid.,* and *Stern,* No. 51, 1973.
79. Brandt in a talk with the author, 1974.
80. Hugh Thomas. *The Spanish Civil War.* New York, 1961, pp. 634-37.
81. *Geschichte der Deutschen Arbeiterbewegung,* Vol 5, p. 154.
82. Brandt in a talk with the author, 1973
83. Monsen in talk with author, 1974.
84. Brandt. *My Road,* p. 90.
85. Brandt. *Draussen,* pp. 377-78.
86. Brandt in a talk with the author, 1974.
87. Brandt. *My Road,* p. 89.
88. *Ibid.*
89. Karl Mewis. *Im Auftrag der Partei.* Berlin, 1972, p. 138.
90. Brandt. *Draussen,* p. 191.
91. Brandt in a talk with the author, 1973.
92. Brandt. *Draussen,* pp. 189-90.
93. *Ibid.,* pp. 215-16.
94. *Ibid.,* p.216.
95. Brandt in a talk with the author, 1973.
96. Brandt, *Draussen,* p. 188.
97. *Ibid.,* p. 190.
98. Monsen in a talk with the author, 1974.
99. Dreschler, pp. 347-51.
100. Brandt. *Draussen,* p. 280.
101. Brandt, *My Road,* p. 95.
102. Brandt, *Draussen,* p. 281
103. Günter Markscheffel in a talk with the author, 1974.
104. Richard Löwenthal in a talk with author, 1974.
105. Wehner in a talk with the author, 1973.
106. Brandt in a talk with the author, 1973.
107. Brandt. *Draussen,* p. 375.
108. *Stern,* No. 51, 1973.
109. Brandt. *Draussen,* pp. 91-92.
110. Brandt. *My Road,* p. 74.

CHAPTER IV. DOUBLE EXILE

1. Leland Stowe. *No Other Road to Freedom.* New York, 1941, pp. 87-88.
2. Brandt. *My Road,* p. 100.
3. John Midgaard. *A Brief History of Norway.* Oslo, 1963, pp. 121-23.
4. Stowe, pp. 92-103.
5. Midgaard, p. 123.
6. Brandt. *My Road,* p. 106.
7. *Ibid.,* 107.
8. Brandt in a talk with the author, 1974.
9. Brandt. *My Road,* p. 107.
10. *Stern,* No. 51, 1973; Brandt, *Draussen,* p. 123, 375; Brandt, *My Road,* pp. 110-11.
11. Brandt, *Draussen,* pp. 123-24. See also Brandt, *My Road,* pp. 112-14.
12. Brandt, *My Road,* pp. 112-14.
13. *Ibid.,* pp. 111-112.
14. *Ibid.,* p. 115.
15. Brandt. *Draussen,* pp. 125, 247; also Brandt, *My Road,* p. 116.
16. Brandt in a talk with the author, 1974.
17. Brandt. *My Road,* p. 118.
18. Monsen in a talk with the author, 1974.
19. Eric Loe in a talk with the author, 1974; Brandt, *My Road,* p. 118.
20. Brandt. *Draussen,* p. 66.
21. Olav Riste and Berit Nökleby. *Norway 1940-1945, The Resistance Movement.* Oslo, 1970, pp. 18-28.
22. Brandt in a talk with the author, 1974.
23. Brandt. *My Road,* p. 117.
24. Quoted in Halvdan Koht. *The Voice of Norway.* New York, 1944, p. 133.
25. Brandt. *My Road,* 124.
26. Brandt. *Draussen,* p. 124.
27. Wehner, *Notizen,* p.151-78.
28. *Ibid.,* pp. 190-91.
29. *Ibid.,* p. 156.
30. *Stern,* No. 51, 1973.
31. Brandt, *Draussen,* pp. 285-86; *My Road,* p. 124; and Willy Brandt Archive.
32. Brandt in a talk with the author, 1974.
33. *Ibid.*
34. Monsen in a talk with the author, 1974.
35. Brandt in a talk with the author, 1974.
36. Brandt, *Draussen,* p. 228.
37. Brandt in a talk with the author, 1973.
38. Brandt, *Draussen,* pp. 289-90.
39. *Ibid.,* pp. 288-308.
40. Brandt, *My Road,* p. 130, See also Brandt, *Draussen,* p. 307.
41. Willy Brandt Archive; Brandt, *My Road,* p. 151; Brandt, *Draussen,* pp. 136-37, p. 306, p. 376.
42. Brandt. *Draussen,* 376.
43. Trygve Lie. *Med England i Ildlinjen.* Oslo, 1956, p. 308.
44. Brandt. *Draussen,* pp. 24-26, 139-64.
45. *Ibid.,* pp. 151-57, 249-50.

46. *Ibid.,* pp. 303-04.
47. Aas in a talk with the author, 1974.
48. Willy Brandt Archive.
49. Brandt. *My Road,* p.131.
50. *Stern,* No. 51, 1973.
51. Wehner, pp. 205-16; Mr. and Mrs. Herbert Wehner in talks with the author, 1973.
52. Leber, p.292
53. *Ibid.,* p. 287. See also, Constantine Fitzgibbon, *20 July,* New York, 1956, pp. 143-44.
54. Brandt in a talk with the author, 1974; Brandt, *Draussen,* pp. 121, 374; and *My Road,* pp. 131-40.
55. Brandt, *My Road, 139-40.*
56. Fitzgibbon, p. 145.
57. Brandt. *My Road,* p. 141.
58. Brandt. *Draussen,* p. 310.
59. Mewis, pp. 307, 308.
60. Brandt in a talk with the author, 1974.
61. Brandt, *Draussen,* pp. 271-72.
62. Inge Scheflo in a talk with the author, 1974.
63. Brandt. *My Road,* p. 147.

CHAPTER V. ROADS TO BERLIN
1. Carola Stern. *Ulbricht.* Cologne, 1964, pp. 121-22.
2. Brandt. *Der Zweite Weltkrieg* (brochure). Stockholm, 1945, p. 56.
3. Brandt. *Draussen,* pp. 51-54.
4. *Ibid.,* pp. 52-55.
5. *Ibid.,* pp. 338-39.
6. *Ibid.,* p. 339.
7. *Stern,* No. 51, 1973.
8. Brandt. *My Road,* p. 155.
9. Emanuel Benda. Quoted in Arnold Brecht, *Mit der Kraft des Geistes.* Stuttgart, 1967, p. 462.
10. Brandt. *My Road,* pp. 154-55.
11. *Ibid.,* 155.
12. Albert Speer. *Inside the Third Reich.* New York, 1970, p. 642.
13. Brandt. *Draussen,* pp. 129, 56.
14. Brandt. *My Road,* pp. 155-56.
15. Brandt. *Draussen,* pp. 130-33.
16. *Ibid.,* (Excerpted from *Criminals and Other Germans*), pp. 58-61, 168-74.
17. *Ibid.,* p. 373.
18. Aas in a talk with the author, 1974.
19. Erich W. Gniffke. Cologne, 1966. *Jahre mit Ulbricht.* pp. 52, 74-75.
20. *Ibid.,* p. 117.
21. *Ibid.,* pp. 126-47.
22. Louis Wiesner in a talk with the author, 1974.
23. Gniffke, pp. 159-60; and Ruth Andreas-Friedrich, *Schauplatz Berlin,* Munich, 1962, pp. 224-27.
24. Gniffke, *Jahre* p. 168.
25. *Ibpd.,* p. 184.
26. Clausewitz had written in 1832 in his book *Of War:* "War is nothing but the continuation of political concourse with the admixture of other means."
27. Monsen in a talk with the author, 1974.
28. Annemarie Renger in a talk with the author, 1973.
29. Brandt in a talk with the author, 1973.
30. Brandt, *Draussen,* pp. 328-30.
31. Brandt. *My Road,* p. 163.
32. Monsen in a talk with the author.
33. Brandt. *Draussen,* p. 340.
34. Brandt in a talk with the author, 1974.
35. *Ibid.,* 1973.
36. Brandt, *Draussen,* p. 333; and Brandt, *My Road,* pp. 163-64.
37. Brandt. *Draussen,* p. 56.
38. *Ibid.,* p. 341.
39. Brandt. *My Road,* p. 164.
40. Brandt in a talk with the author, 1973.
41. Brandt. *My Road,* p. 165.
42. Brandt. *Draussen,* pp. 334, 342-43.
43. *Ibid.,* p. 343; and Willy Brandt Archive.
44. *Ibid.,* pp. 344-47.
45. Andreas-Friedrich, pp. 235-38.
46. Brandt. *My Road,* pp. 167-68.
47. Willy Brandt and Richard Löwenthal. *Ernst Reuter.* Munich, 1957, pp. 362 ff.
48. Brandt. *My Road,* p. 174.
49. Wiesner in a talk with the author, 1974.
50. Brandt. *My Road,* pp. 177-78.
51. Aas in a talk with the author, 1974.
52. *Ibid.;* Brandt, *My Road,* p. 178.
53. Brandt. *Draussen,* pp. 347-52.
54. In Brandt's official account he had met Rut "just before the end of the war" in Stockholm. See *My Road,* p. 164.
55. Monsen in a talk with the author, 1974.
56. Willy Brandt Archive.
57. Brandt. *Draussen,* p. 353.
58. *Ibid.,* p. 336.
59. *Ibid.,* p. 356-57.
60. Reinhart Bartholomäi in a talk with the author, 1973.
61. Brandt in a talk with the author, 1973.
62. Renger in a talk with the author, 1973.
63. Brandt in a talk with the author, 1973.
64. Brandt. *Draussen,* pp. 353-56.
65. *Ibid.,* p. 361.

66. Brandt in a talk with the author.
67. Brandt. *Draussen,* pp. 359-64.
68. Brandt. *My Road,* p. 184.
69. Brandt in a talk with the author, 1973.
70. Brandt. *Draussen,* p. 335.
71. Renger in a talk with the author, 1973.
72. Gniffke, pp. 255-64.
73. Andreas-Friedrich, p. 248.
74. Kurt Mattick in a talk with the author, 1973.
75. Willy Brandt Archive.
76. Brandt-Löwenthal. *Reuter,* pp. 399-430. See also Walter Krumholz. *Berlin-ABC.* Berlin, 1968, pp. 408-09.
77. Monsen in a talk with the author, 1974.
78. Günther Nollau in a talk with the author, 1973.
79. *Ibid.*
80. Brandt, *My Road,* p.205.
81. Brandt-Löwenthal. *Reuter,* p. 452.
82. Wehner in a talk with the author, 1973.
83. Brandt in a letter to the author, 1975.
84. Norwegian friends of Brandt who wish to remain anonymous.
85. Brandt. *My Road,* p. 205.
86. Brandt. *My Road,* p. 222.

CHAPTER VI. ISLAND AND MAINLAND

1. Brand-Löwenthal. *Reuter,* p. 437.
2. Brandt in a speech to the SPD Berlin district conference, January 14, 1949.
3. Renger in a talk with the author, 1973.
4. Brand in a note to the author, 1974.
5. Brandt-Löwenthal. *Reuter,* p. 492.
6. *Ibid.,* p. 516.
7. Brandt. *My Road,* p. 211.
8. *Ibid.,* p. 214.
9. Günter Neumann. *Die Insulaner.* Berlin, 1954, p. 9.
10. Alfred Grosser. *Die Bonner Demokratie.* Düsseldorf, 1950, p. 136.
11. Bartholomäi in a talk with the author, 1973.
12. Abraham Ashkenasi. *Reformpartei und Aussenpolitik.* Cologne, 1968, pp. 68-69.
13. Renger in a talk with the author, 1973.
14. Brandt in a talk with the author, 1974.
15. Brandt-Löwenthal. *Reuter,* p. 542.
16. *Ibid.,* p.542
17. *Ibid.,* p. 541.
18. Brandt. *My Road,* p. 215.
19. *Ibid.,* p. 216.
20. *Ibid.,* p. 210.

21. Ashkenasi, p. 73.
22. Wehner in a talk with author, 1973.
23. *Berliner Stadtblatt,* July 18, 1950.
24. Renger in a talk with the author, 1973.
25. Ashkenasi, p.83
26. Brandt in a talk with the author, 1973. (An attempt by the author to solicit Neumann's views met with no response. Neumann died in 1974.)
27. Askenasi, p. 81.
28. Mattick in a talk with the author, 1973.
29. Ashkenasi, p. 81.
30. Brandt in a talk with the author, 1973.
31. Wehner in a talk with the author, 1973.
32. Monsen in a talk with the author, 1974.
33. Wehner in a talk with the author, 1973
34. Claire Mortenson. *Da War ein Mädchen.* Munich, 1961 (unpublished). See also *Der Spiegel,* No. 21, 1974.
35. Letter dated March 1, 1948. Willy Brandt Archive.
36. Brandt. *My Road,* pp. 222-26.
37. *Ibid.,* p. 226-27
38. Loe in a talk with the author, 1974.
39. Brandt. *My Road,* p. 226.
40. Ashkenasi, p. 95.
41. Reinhard Gehlen. *The Service.* New York, 1972, p. 149.
42. Brandt-Löwenthal. *Reuter,* p. 601; Brandt. *My Road,* p. 219.
43. Brandt. *My Road,* p. 227.
44. Heinz Lippmann. *Honecker.* Cologne, 1971, p. 155.
45. Brandt. *My Road,* p. 245.
46. *Ibid.,* p. 246.
47. Ashkenasi, p. 99.
48. SPD Party Convention. *Protokoll.* Berlin, 1954, p. 90.
49. Brandt. *My Road,* p. 247.
50. Löwenthal in a talk with the author, 1974.
51. Brandt. *My Road,* p. 247.
52. Bartholomäi in a talk with the author, 1973.
53. Ashkenasi, p. 133.
54. Mattick in a talk with the author, 1973.
55. Mortensen.
56. Stern, pp. 196-202.
57. *Ibid.,* p. 228.
58. Brandt. *My Road,* pp. 249-51.
59. Klaus Schütz in a talk with the author, 1974.
60. Ashkenasi, p. 137.

61. *Ibid.,* p. 141.
62. Brandt. *My Road,* pp. 251-52.
63. *Ibid.,* p. 252.

CHAPTER VII. THE FRONT-LINE MAYOR

1. Wehner in a talk with the author, 1973.
2. Ashkenasi, pp. 145-46.
3. Brandt in a talk with the author, 1973.
4. Ashkenasi, pp. 148-51.
5. *Ibid.,* p. 150.
6. Eleanor Dulles in a talk with the author, 1974.
7. Brandt. *Begegnungen mit Kennedy.* Munich, 1964, p. 36.
8. The author attended the Bundestag debate of March 20-25, 1958.
9. SPD Party Convention. *Protokoll.* Stuttgart, 1958, pp. 326.
10. Brandt in a letter to the author, 1974: "I doubt very much that (Peter) Blachstein raised *this* suspicion against me at Dortmund."
11. Townsend Hoopes. *The Devil and John Foster Dulles.* Boston, 1973, p. 466.
12. *Dokumente zur Berlin Frage.* Munich, 1962, pp. 301-19.
13. *Ibid.,* p. 336.
14. Axel Springer. *Von Berlin aus Gesehen.* Stuttgart, 1971, p. 45.
15. Ashkenasi, p. 162.
16. Heli Ihlefeld. *Anekdoten um Willy Brandt.* Munich, 1968, p. 35.
17. Wehner in a talk with the author, 1973.
18. Ashkenasi, pp. 165-69.
19. Brandt. *Begegnungen,* p. 37.
20. Brandt. *My Road,* pp. 266.
21. Wehner in a talk with the author, 1973.
22. Ihlefeld, p. 81.
23. Schütz in a talk with author, 1974.
24. Quoted in Heinz Scholl. *Willy Brandt-Mythos und Realität,* Euskirchen, 1973, p. 74.
25. SPD Party convention. *Protokoll.* Godesburg, 1959, p. 53.
26. *Ibid.,* pp. 74-77.
27. Ashkenasi, pp. 176-77.
28. Wehner in a talk with the author, 1973.
29. *Protokoll,* 1959, pp. 99-100.
30. Helmut Schmidt in a talk with the author, 1973.
31. *Stern,* No. 51, 1973.
32. Brandt. *My Road,* p. 268.
33. *Minneapolis Tribune,* December 14, 1959.

34. Wehner. *Wandel und Bewährung.* Frankfurt, 1968, pp. 232-48.
35. Wehner in a talk with the author, 1973.
36. Schütz in a talk with the author, 1974.
37. *The New York Times,* August 25, 1960.
38. SPD Party convention. *Protokoll.* Hannover, 1960, pp. 558-680.
39. Brandt. *Begegnungen,* p. 51.
40. *Ibid.,* p. 41-45.
41. *Ibid.,* p. 47.
42. Lippmann, p. 189.
43. Walter Ulbricht. *Liselotte Thomas et alii.* Berlin, 1968, p. 211.
44. Hermann Zolling and Uwe Bahnsen. *Kalter Winter im August.* Oldenburg, 1967, p. 103.
45. *Ibid.,* p. 78.
46. Otto Frei. *Neue Zürcher Zeitung.* September, 1961—conveyed orally to author as authoritative report from East German official.
47. Zolling-Bahnsen, p. 116.
48. Schütz in a talk with the author, 1973.
49. Zolling-Bahnsen, pp. 11-15.
50. Stephen A. Koczak in a talk with the author, 1961.
51. Zolling-Bahnsen, pp. 15-22, 130-31. Brandt later wrote, "I cannot confirm this quote," in a letter to the author, 1975.
52. Brandt. *Begegnungen,* p. 63.
53. Wehner in a talk with the author, 1973
54. Willy Brandt Archive.
55. Brandt. *Begegungen,* pp. 70-71.
56. Zolling-Bahnsen, pp. 148-49.
57. Willy Brandt Archive.
58. Willy Brandt. *Der Wille zum Frieden.* Hamburg, 1971, p. 67.
59. Zolling-Bahnsen, p. 152.
60. *Ibid.,* p. 159.
61. *The New York Times,* September 13, 1961.
62. Brandt. *Begegnungen,* p. 93.
63. SPD Party Convention. *Protokoll.* Karlsruhe, 1964, p. 25.

CHAPTER VIII. BARRIERS TO BREACH

1. *The New York Times,* October 1, 1961.
2. *Stern,* No. 52, 1974.
3. Brandt. *Begegnungen, p. 100.*
4. *Ibid.*
5. The author witnessed these scenes as a reporter.
6. Brandt. *Begegnungen,* pp. 110-21.
7. Willy Brandt. Second German Televi-

sion Channel, September 25, 1964.
8. *The New York Times,* April 14, 1962.
9. SPD Party Convention. *Protokoll.* Cologne, 1962, pp. 56-86.
10. Brandt. *Begegnungen,* p. 153.
11. *Ibid.,* p. 154.
12. *The New York Times,* September 2, 1962.
13. Brandt. *Begegnungen,* pp. 163-64.
14. *Ibid.,* pp. 160-74.
15. Wehner. *Wandel,* pp. 254-60.
16. *The New York Times,* January 18, 1963.
17. *Ibid.,* April 26, 1963.
18. Brandt. *Begegnungen,* p. 177.
19. Zolling-Bahnsen, p. 233.
20. Brandt. *Begegnungen,* pp. 212-13.
21. *Ibid.,* p. 179.
22. Brandt. *Koexistenz, Zwang zum Wagnis.* Stuttgart, 1963.
23. Zolling-Bahnsen, p. 207.
24. Brandt. *Begegnungen,* pp. 231-42.
25. SPD *Jahrbuch* 1962/63. Hannover, 1964, p. 1.
26. "According to my own understanding to classify me as an atheist is off the mark. Agnostic would come closer, but I belong to the Evangelical Church." Brandt in a letter to the atuhor, 1975.
27. SPD Party Convention, *Protokoll.* Karlsruhe, 1964, pp. 130-52.
28. Zur Person. *Zweites Deutches Fernsehen,* September 25, 1964.
29. *Der Spiegel,* No. 33, 1965.
30. Horst Ehmke in a talk with the author, 1973.
31. Wehner in a talk with the author, 1973.
32. *The New York Times,* April 20, 1965.
33. *Der Spiegel.* No. 33, 1965.
34. Schütz in a talk with the author, 1974.
35. Schmidt in a talk with the author, 1973.
36. Schütz in a talk with the author, 1974.
37. Brandt said that despite the currency of this story, it is inaccurate, in a letter to the author, 1975.
38. Brandt. *Draussen,* pp. 365-66.
39. *Stern,* No. 39, 1974.
40. Wehner in a talk with the author, 1973.
41. Brandt-Löwenthal *Reuter,* p. 701.
42. SPD Party Convention. *Protokoll.* Dortmund, 1966, pp. 15-841.
43. *The New York Times,* June 20, 1966.
44. Wehner. *Wandel,* pp. 371-72.
45. Bartholomäi in a talk with the author, 1973.
46. Ehmke in a talk with the author, 1973.
47. Bartholomäi in a talk with the author, 1973.
48. Hans-Roderich Schneider. *Walter Scheel.* Bonn, 1974, p. 79.
49. Conrad Ahlers in a talk with the author, 1972.
50. Brandt. *Über den Tag Hinaus.* Hamburg, 1974, p. 33.
51. Wehner. *Wandel,* p. 375.
52. *The New York Times,* November 14, 1966.
53. Wehner in a talk with the author, 1973.
54. Schmidt in a talk with the author, 1973.
55. Bartholomäi in a talk with the author, 1973.
56. Brandt in a letter to the author, 1975.

CHAPTER IX. FOREIGN MINISTER

1. Ihlefeld, p. 16.
2. Ihlefeld, pp. 7-57. (The watch had been handed to Brandt three years earlier by Swiss Social Democrats when he delivered a memorial address to the fiftieth anniversary of Bebel's death, in Zurich.)
3. Eugen Selbmann in a talk with the author, 1973.
4. Wehner in a talk with the author, 1973.
5. *The New York Times,* January 2, 1967.
6. *Der Spiegel,* No. 6, 1967.
7. Dirk Bavendamm. *Bonn unter Brandt.* Vienna, 1971, p. 191.
8. *Ibid.,* p. 187.
9. *Ibid.,* p. 183.
10. *Ibid.,* p. 194.
11. *The New York Times,* May 9, 1967.
12. *Ibid.,* June 9, 1967.
13. *Ibid.,* June 16, 1967.
14. *Der Spiegel,* No. 28, 1967.
15. *The New York Times,* August 8, 1967.
16. *Ibid.,* December 16, 1967.
17. *Der Spiegel,* No. 26, 1967.
18. *The New York Times,* November 11, 1967.
19. An American intelligence agent in a talk with the author, 1975.
20. *The New York Times,* February 3, 1968.
21. *Ibid.,* March 19, 1968.
22. *Nürnberg im Spiegel der Presse.* Bonn, 1968.

23. Bavendamm, p. 256.
24. *The New York Times,* May 31, 1968.
25. *Ibid.,* August 9, 1968.
26. Ashkenasi, p. 195.
27. Willy Brandt. *Friedenspolitik in Europe.* Frankfurt, 1968.
28. Willy Brandt. *Reden und Interviews.* Bonn, 1969, pp. 139-40.
29. *The New York Times,* October 8, 1968.
30. Conrad Ahlers in a talk with the author, 1968.
31. Author's archives.
32 Brandt. *Reden,* pp. 91-96.
33. *The New York Times,* December 3, 1968.
34. Wehner in a talk with the author, 1974.
35. Bavendamm, p. 248.
36. Schneider, p. 102.
37. *Ibid.,* pp. 103-04
38. *The New York Times,* March 11, 1969.
39. Wehner in a talk with the author, 1973.
40. Karl Schiller in a talk with the author, 1971. Brandt wrote, "I cannot recall this call from Washington" in a letter to the author, 1975.
41. Bavendamm, p. 274.
42. *The New York Times,* May 12, 1969.
43. Brandt. *Friedenspolitik,* pp. 8-9.
44. Brandt. *Der Wille zum Frieden.* Hamburg, 1971, p. 303.
45. *Ibid.,* p. 313.
46. Karl-Heinz Kirchner in a talk with the author, 1973.
47. Wehner in a talk with the author, 1973.
48. Schneider in a talk with the author, 1969.

CHAPTER X. THE PEACE CHANCELLOR
1. Hermann Schreiber and Sven Simon. *Willy Brandt.* Düsseldorf, 1970, pp. 126-27.
2. *The New York Times,* October 1, 1969.
3. Bavendamm, p. 301.
4. *The New York Times Magazine,* November 30, 1969.
5. *Ibid.*
6. *The New York Times,* October 7, 1969.
7. Talks with the author.
8. *The New York Times,* October 22, 1969.
9. Ehmke in a talk with the author, 1974.
10. Brandt in a talk with the author, 1974.
11. Brandt. *Reden, pp. 13-30.*
12. Selbmann in a talk with the author, 1973.
13. *The New York Times,* November 18-19, 1969.
14. *Ibid.,* December 4 and 6, 1969.
15. *Ibid.,* December 5, 1969.
16. *Der Spiegel,* No. 3, 1970.
17. Schmidt in a talk with the author, 1973.
18. Brandt later said the "disciple" characterization was "both an exaggeration and an understatement" in a letter to the author, 1975.
19. Schütz in a talk with the author, 1974.
20. See Chapter I.
21. *The New York Times,* March 4, 1970.
22. A member of the National Security Council who asked anonymity.
23. *Ibid.*
24. *The New York Times,* April 4, 1970.
25. Brandt. *Reden,* pp. 191-96.
26. *Ibid.,* p. 226.
27. Schmidt in a talk with the author, 1973.
28. *The New York Times,* June 12, 1970.
29. *Ibid.,* May 22, 1970.
30. *Ibid.,* May 31 and June 5, 1970.
31. *Ibid.,* June 18, 1970.
32. Talk with the author. The participant asked for anonymity.
33. Schneider, pp. 112-13.
34. Hermann Otto Bolesch. *Typisch Brandt.* Munich, 1973, p. 79.
35. *The New York Times,* August 15, 1970.
36. *Ibid.,* June 20, 1971.
37. *Ibid.,* September 24, 1971.
38. Schneider in a talk with the author. 1971.
39. *The New York Times,* November 17, 1970.
40. Schütz in a talk with the author, 1974.
41. *The New York Times,* August 13, 1970.
42. *Ibid.,* December 4, 1970.
43. *Ibid.,* December 13, 1970.
44. *Ibid.,* December 14, 1970.
45. *Ibid.,* December 20, 1970.
46. *Ibid.,* February 11, 1971.
47. *Ibid.,* January 30, 1971.
48. Kenneth Rush in a talk with the author, 1971.
49. *The New York Times,* June 20, 1971.
50. *Ibid.,* May 11, 1971.
51. *Der Spiegel,* No. 22, 1971.
52. *The New York Times,* May 27, 1971.
53. Rush in a talk with the author, 1971.

54. *The New York Times,* August 14, 1971.
55. *Ibid.,* September 5, 1971.
56. *Ibid.,* September 20, 1971.
57. *Ibid.,* January 17, 1972.
58. Willy Brandt. *Über den Tag Hinaus,* p. 39.
59. *The New York Times,* April 21, 1972.
60. *Ibid.,* April 26, 1972.
61. Karl Wienand in a talk with the author, 1974.
62. Schneider in a talk with the atuhor, 1972.
63. Franz Josef Strauss in a talk with the author, 1972.
64. Brandt. *Über den Tag Hinaus,* p. 39.
65. *Ibid.*
66. Krag. *Dagbok.* Copenhagen, 1973, pp. 211-12.
67. Skou in a talk with the author, 1974.
68. Schmidt in a talk with the author, 1973.
69. Brandt. *Über den Tag Hinaus,* p. 43.
70. *Ibid.,* pp. 42-22.
71. *The New York Times,* September 26, 1972.
72. *Ibid.,* September 23, 1972.
73. Brandt. *Über den Tag Hinaus,* p. 46.
74. *Dokumentation über die Werbekampagnen.* Bonn, 1973, p. 12.
75. *The New York Times,* October 25, 1972.
76. Bartholomäi and Albrecht Müller in talks with the author, 1973.
77. Wehner in a talk with the author, 1973.
78. *The New York Times,* November 20, 1972.
79. Ehmke in a talk with the author, 1973.
80. Schmidt in a talk with the author, 1973.
81. Wehner in talk with the author, 1974.
82. Ehmke in a talk with the author, 1974.
83. Brandt in a letter to the author, 1975, wrote in comment on this passage: "It's not so."
84. Rüdiger von Wechmar in a talk with the author, 1973.
85. Schmidt in a talk with the author, 1973.
86. Wehner in talk with the author, 1973.
87. *The New York Times,* April 20, 1973.
88. Politparade, Musik aus Studio Bonn. The Netherlands, 1972.

CHAPTER XI. THE END

1. The great bulk of the subsequent account is based on interviews with the principals: Brandt, Wehner, Bahr, Wienand, and others. H. E. Ambassador Sven Backlund of the Kingdom of Sweden was helpful in the preparation. The account draws on the German Bundestag Report of the second Investigatory Commission concerning the Guillaume affair, numbered 7/3246 and dated February 19, 1975, and also on Willy Brandt's essay-memoir, *Uber den Tag Hinaus—Eine Zwischenbilanz (The Long View—An Interim Balance),* published in 1974 in Hamburg by Hoffmann & Campe. In addition I have referred to: press accounts by DPA, the German News Agency; *Die Zeit, Stern* and *Der Spiegel* of Hamburg; the *Süddeutsche Zeitung* of Munich; the *Frankfurter Allgemeine Zeitung* and *Frankfurter Rundschau;* and, *Vorwärts* of Bonn. Willy Brandt has not read this account and cannot be held responsible for it.

Index